Raising
the Torch of
Good News

Raising the Torch of Good News

CATHOLIC AUTHORITY AND
DIALOGUE WITH THE WORLD

EDITED BY

Bernard P. Prusak

THE ANNUAL PUBLICATION OF THE
COLLEGE THEOLOGY SOCIETY

1986

VOLUME 32

UNIVERSITY
PRESS OF
AMERICA

Lanham • New York • London

Annual Publication • 32

CONTENTS

INTRODUCTION:
CREDIBILITY IN A WORLD CHURCH

Bernard P. Prusak
Villanova University

In his opening address to the Second Vatican Council, on October 11, 1962, Pope John XXIII spoke of the Catholic Church "raising the torch of religious truth."[1] He envisioned a Church which desires to be the loving mother of all, benign, patient, full of mercy and goodness toward the brethren who are separated from her. Carrying the theme of light further, Pope John compared the Council, then beginning, to daybreak rising in the Church, a forerunner of most splendid light. As he saw it, "It is now only dawn."

The title of this volume of essays carries forward the imagery of John XXIII. Truth should be like a light which attracts. That is the essential nature of the Good News of Jesus Christ. And so raising a torch is an apt symbol for the Church's ministry of teaching. But as those who teach know so well, what is taught is frequently offered in a context of authority and discipline. The message of Good News is not separable from those prickly issues, nor from that of freedom.

Over the course of four years, Vatican II addressed itself to the themes of unity which were so important to John XXIII: unity within the Catholic Church, but with recognition of the valuable diversity of local churches (*Lumen Gentium*, 13 and 23); unity with those Christians from whom we are separated; and our relationship and unity with those who follow non-Christian religions. In its discussion of unity the Council recognized that an essential component of the modern human experience is a heightened sense of the dignity and freedom of the human person.

Promulgated in the last year of the Council, the first section of *Nostra Aetate*, the Declaration on the Relationship of the Church to Non-Christian Religions, begins by observing that humans of our time "are being drawn closer together and the ties between various peoples are being multiplied."[2] The document then acknowledges that the various religions all seek to answer profound questions about the meaning and purpose of life that arise within universal human experience. Such reflections find their conclusion in the final section of the declaration: "The ground is therefore removed from every theory or practice which leads to a distinction between men or peoples in the matter of human dignity and the rights which flow from it." Any discrimination because of race, color, condition of life, or religion is explicitly rejected.

Later in that same year of 1965, *Dignitatis Humanae*, the Declaration on Religious Freedom, was promulgated. The way it began is again significant: "A sense of the dignity of the human person has been impressing itself more and more deeply on the consciousness of contemporary humans."[3] The words that follow are particularly relevant to the theme of this volume: "the demand is increasingly made that humans should act on their own judgment, enjoying and making use of a responsible freedom, not driven by coercion but motivated by a sense of duty." John Courtney Murray pointed out that the Council only dealt with religious freedom in a narrowly limited technically secular sense, . . . "but the text itself was flung into a pool whose shores are wide as the universal Church. The ripples will run far."[4] That has proven prophetic. Vatican II called for freedom in the world outside the Church. Since the Council the issue of freedom within the Church itself has become more and more prominent.

Truth, especially if it is Good News, cannot be forced upon others by the sheer force of authority. Dialogue and consensus are not alien to the Christian community. Even Vatican I's rejection of the fourth Gallican article of 1682 did not intend to exclude dialogue between Rome and other churches within the universal Church *prior* to infallible statements.[5] To say that the infallible teachings of the Roman Pontiff are irreformable of themselves and not from the consent of the Church does not exclude prior consultation if the Pope truly teaches what the Church believes.

Leaders and informed teachers, such as the pope and bishops, and pastors and theologians, must speak to and for the community of believers called Church. But the mere repetition of authoritative teachings is not enough. Truth must be recognized as a value in order that it be accepted. Participatory dialogue which values the relevant experience of those who are believers is thus an important component in the process which leads educated contemporary persons to the consensus which is the reception of truth.

Writing against the Gnostic heresies of the second century and recognizing the "more powerful preeminence" of the Church of Rome, Irenaeus of Lyons said, "it is necessary for every Church, that is, the faithful everywhere, to agree with the Church of Rome."[6] Vatican I invoked those words to strengthen its teaching on the perpetuity of papal primacy, and infallibility.[7] The pyramidal ecclesiology and the defensive context and mood of that council, held at a time when democratic perspectives were perceived as inimical and threatening to the Church, explains why the next phrase of Irenaeus was omitted: "for in her the apostolic tradition has ever been preserved by the faithful from all parts of the world."

In his speech opening Vatican II, Pope John disagreed with "those prophets of gloom, who are always forecasting disaster, as though the end of the world were at hand."[8] They see nothing but prevarication and ruin in our era. Instead he saw a new order of human relations and believed that everything, even human differences, lead to the greater good of the Church. Vatican II recognized the Church's responsibility to pay attention to the world around us, by scrutinizing "the signs of the times" and interpreting them in the light of the Gospel (Gaudium et Spes, 4). As Robert Gnuse's article in this volume reminds us, contemporary biblical scholarship more and more appreciates that even the Hebrew Scriptures reflect a process of critical dialogue between ancient Israel and her neighbors. What we accept as revelation came through the creative dialogue of a community of believers with various historical contexts.

The task of theological reflection is a process which engages the entire community of faith and not simply professionals, whether ministers or theologians. As Vatican II recognized, "in holding to, practicing, and professing the heritage of the faith, there results on the part of the bishops and faithful a remarkable common effort."[9] In that context the process called theology is related to the element of human experience in its deepest sense. The decision to become a believer within a tradition involves one in a dialogue, since a historical faith community is called to participate in the expression and formulation of faith in a way that responds to the human questions of its own time. In our search for meaning and theological understanding we must always build bridges of interpretation whereby the Christian vision responds to the questions emerging from changing worldviews.

Many theologians of our time see Vatican II marking the beginning of a new era in the Catholic Church. Its reality has caught up with its name, catholic. For the first time it is incarnate within every continent and culture, and no longer bound by a Graeco-Roman Mediterranean, or by the limits of Europe. In its dialogue with the world, the Catholic Church must now practically work out the implications of the "unity in diversity" espoused by Vatican II.

The title of this volume has taken up the symbolism of torch and light used by Pope John. But we in the United States cannot forget another symbolic torch on which we focused our attention during the very year in which these papers were written and presented. That is the torch on the Statue of Liberty, gift from the people of France, "eldest daughter of the Church," to the people of the United States. Standing in the harbor of New York, that statue holds aloft a welcoming torch of light, symbolizing openness, hope, and possibility for a new life. It was etched into the memories of a multitude of immigrants, including my own father who first saw it from the deck of a ship that had sailed from Cherbourg, on his journey from Czechoslovakia. A brightly lit and refurbished torch is a cherished symbol of the responsible and participatory freedom which our country offers and celebrates. That torch should also make us remember those who were once brought here by force, to be slaves. It challenges us to implement a genuinely human freedom and dignity in our time by our economic and political policies. Such concerns are reflected in the recent Pastoral Letters of the bishops in the United States.

Through the contributions of John Courtney Murray, Vatican II's Declaration on Religious Freedom reflects the input of our own country's experience of pluralism as a value. Do we "United Statians" have anything more to contribute? Will we be heard? Do Churches older in the faith value our insights? How does the image that Church leaders in Europe have of our country and culture affect whether they are open to understanding the contributions which our Church and its leadership might make? Have Church leaders in Rome really taken the time to know us in all our complexity or have they embraced a stereotype? Do we have a responsibility to educate those who live in places where the faith has been present longer about its vibrancy in our people, and in our many Catholic colleges and universities?

Do we in turn value the insights of those parts of the Church that are as young, or even younger? Do we listen, both to Rome and to the universal Church, in the ways that we should? Such questions are our agenda for the future in a world Church. They are also the "stuff" or essence (ousia) of the articles in this collection, selected from papers presented at the 1986 convention of the College Theology Society held at Xavier University in Cincinnati on the theme "Authority and Structure in the Churches."

I appreciate the confidence and support of all my colleagues in the College Theology Society. I especially wish to thank Teresa C. Byrne, the editorial assistant of Horizons for her invaluable help with the proofreading of the manuscripts.

NOTES

1. Text in Walter M. Abbott and Joseph Gallagher, eds., *The Documents of Vatican II* (New York: Guild Press, 1966), pp. 710–19, here 716 & 718.
2. *Ibid.*, pp 660–68.
3. *Ibid.*, p. 675.
4. *Ibid.*, p. 674.
5. *Pastor aeternus*, chapter 4. See Henricus Denzinger and Adolfus Schönmetzer, *Enchiridion Symbolorum* (Barcelona: Herder, 1965), no. 3074.
6. *Adversus haereses* III, 3, 2.
7. Denzinger-Schönmetzer, no. 3057.
8. Abbott, p. 712.
9. *Dei Verbum*, 10, in Abbott, p. 117.

Part One

LEARNING FROM THE PAST

SPEAKING OF AUTHORITY AND CHARISM
FROM THE NEW TESTAMENT

Richard J. Dillon
Fordham University

ABSTRACT

A survey of the use of the word "authority" (*exousia*) in the New Testament reveals its kinship with "freedom" rather than constraint and the roots of Christian "authority" in charism rather than law. Paul, struggling to correct a misused "authority" in Corinth (I Cor 8:9), was applying the heritage of Jesus' authority, which had demolished barriers raised by the Law amongst human beings and between humans and their physical environment. Indeed, the *exousia* claimed by and for Jesus in the gospels involved his freedom from the strongest boundaries defended by religious Man: the orthodoxy of a religious elite (Lk 7:1-10); religious law made an end in itself (Mk 2:23-28); the moral verdict that segregates good people from bad (Mk 2:1-12).

Jesus' "teaching with authority," made the concluding caption of the Sermon on the Mount by Matthew (7:29), is derived from prophetic charism rather than extrinsic precept ("not as their scribes"). Rooted thus in the divine gift that has been received, such authority comports greater ethical seriousness rather than less, inasmuch as the Father's unlimited bounty inspires a moral commitment which must be commensurately unlimited and unconditional (Mt 5:43-48). Moreover, since this authoritative teaching is that of the risen One, who continues to address his Church through the gospel discourses (Mt 28:18-20), there can be no "orthodox," legalized, and boundary-drawing "teaching of the Church" that is not under constant critical review over against the words recorded in the gospels.

I can think of no greater contribution that we who teach can make to students' early lives than the thrill of rediscovering the content of ancient religious language. The words are so numbingly familiar, and they are often blocked at the unprecedently low threshold of boredom and distraction among our constituents. Take the word

Father Dillon is Associate Professor and former Chairman of the Theology Department at Fordham University (Bronx, NY 10458). He holds a doctorate in Sacred Scripture from the Pontifical Biblical Institute in Rome, and has been a contributor to New Testament Studies, the Catholic Biblical Quarterly, Worship, and the Jerome Biblical Commentary.

"authority," for example: it makes an unpleasant sound in young ears, comporting, as it does, the cramping strictures put on one's self-determination by overprotective parents, moribund traditions, and unresponsive institutions. But the very heightened anti-institutional temper of our times makes the discussion of authority all the more timely and urgent: what it means and does not mean, why it is indispensable to healthy personalities and stable societies, and what special significance it has in Christian speech.

I. Linguistic Background

A surprising discovery awaits even the casual inquirer into the word's background. The Greek and Latin equivalents had a sense practically synonymous with *freedom*, whereas the two words would sooner strike the modern ear as antonyms![1] The Greek *exousia* denoted the right and possibility to act or decide, hence the room given to one's own "initiative" (Lat. *auctoritas*). Rather than intrinsic ability (*dynamis*), *exousia* expressed the freedom from extrinsic hindrance or constraint that was granted by law, certified by society's sustaining institutions, and secured by the power of the State. The Greek term is, in fact, the participial inflection of the verb *exestin*, which meant "it is free' (in the open, unrestricted), hence "it is permitted." *Exousia* thus connoted right, entitlement, permission and commission; it expressed, in the full spectrum of human relations, the "freedom to act."

In the Bible, we find no real equivalent to *exousia* in the ancient Hebrew, which sooner expressed a relationship of authority by means of a metaphor ("be in the hands of").[2] Later books of the Septuagint and the New Testament show that *exousia* could be predicated of God, exercising his right of dominion over the universe of his making[3]; of Satan, insofar only as God granted his "freedom to act" (so Luke 22:53)[4]; of angels, as sentinels of the Creator's order[5]; finally, of course, of Jesus and his disciples, to whom freedom to act and to judge is granted by God and, in turn, by Jesus himself.[6] A survey of the use of *exousia* in the New Testament consolidates our early impression of the kinship between "authority" and "freedom"; for "freedom" is, in fact, the best definition of what dominical "authority" contains.

II. Authority Exercised and Bequeathed by Jesus

Authority in the Disciple

As exegetes schooled in form-criticism, we begin the investigation on this side of Easter. In correspondence with enthusiastic converts who inflated their Christian freedom to the point of fanaticism, Paul gave a lesson in the root-meaning of *exousia* and, at the same time, established a crucial principle of New Testament "authority": that it is rooted in *charism* rather than law. The letter in question is First Corinthians, where both the verb *exestin* and the noun *exousia* function in a recurrent exhortation against the misuse of the freedom granted by the gospel. Unexpectedly, the two words designate that very misused *freedom* itself, and not some higher power Paul invokes to restrain it! He does not set authority and freedom against each other, but accepts the risks of a church order in which the two are understood as one and the same endowment.

Twice Paul cites the motto of Corinthian enthusiasm, *panta moi exestin*, "all is permitted to me"; but each time he hems it in with a first concern for the good of the community: ". . . but not all is beneficial" (I Cor 6:12), ". . . but not all is constructive" (I Cor 10:23). In the latter case, the slogan was touting the enthusiasts' immunity to the taboo that scrupulous confreres placed on meats marketed after ritual slaughter in pagan temples.[7] Paul endorsed this emancipation, at least in principle ("nothing is profane of itself"—Rom 14:14; see Mark 7:15); but concern for tender consciences among his constituents prompted him to condition the endorsement: "See to it that this *authority* (*exousia*) of yours does not become an obstacle to weaker members" (I Cor 8:9).[8] It is obvious that this potentially divisive "authority" had been instilled by Paul's own preaching (I Cor 8:4-8; Rom 14:13-15:2), hence that the motto, *panta moi exestin*, might nearly have been his own![9] After all, he had interpreted the gospel in terms of salvation apart from works of the Law through faith in the Crucified (Rom 3:21-26; Phil 3:4-11, etc.), and he had greeted the lavish gifts of the Spirit which generated Corinthian enthusiasm as an exhilarating foretaste of the world to come (I Cor 1:7; Rom 8:18-25). For him, Christ was the end of the Law (Rom 10:4) and, with it, of all the rigid barriers it had erected between human beings (Gal 3:23-29) and between humans and their physical surroundings (Rom 14:14). He thus understood the believer's *authority* as a *freedom* from religious man's nervous antagonism to the world of the everyday and the all-too-human, an alienation nurtured for generations by pharisaic Judaism. He did not contend that we are free of taboos and castes by natural endowment, but only by the grace (*charis*) of God received in Christ. Our "authority" over a hitherto bedeviled world is thus rooted in the *charisma* of the redeemed, and also conditioned by the demands of their fraternity.

In his liberating conviction that "nothing is profane of itself," Paul was, of course, remarkably close to the teaching of the historical

Jesus,[10] and so we might take this cue to turn to the instances of *exousia* claimed by and for Jesus in the gospel tradition.

The Authority of Jesus

Let us propose, by way of organizing the data and connecting it to Paul's, that the *exousia* of Jesus in the gospels involved, above all, his *freedom* from some of the most durable boundaries that sinful humanity defends: (a) the stifling orthodoxy of a religious elite; (b) religious laws become ends in themselves; (c) the moral verdicts that segregate good people from bad.

(a) *The Caste of the Religious Elite*: Jesus' collision with the pious Establishment is documented throughout the gospel tradition and from its earliest strata. Our attention is drawn by the miracle story with which the collectors of Jesus' sayings certified the authority of one of the first compilations of them: the cure of the centurion's servant, which comes close upon the end of the "Sermon on the Mount/Plain" in both Matthew (8:5-13) and Luke (7:1-10).[11] Appropriately for the sayings collection (Q), the story quotes the memorable plea of the pagan soldier: "Speak only the word, and my servant shall be healed" (Mt 8:8/Lk 7:7). But what gives this entreaty its particular christological substance is that the soldier is himself "a man set under *authority*," who thus knows "how authority works" (NAB) and can acknowledge the word spoken "with authority" (Mt 7:29).[12] Jesus, in turn, extols the faith which has made this recognition: "I have not found such faith in Israel," a conclusion to which Luke's version gives a powerfully ironic setting by putting Jewish intermediaries between the centurion and the Master (7:3-5). The faith that responds to Jesus' "authority" is thus shown to breach the fortified boundaries of the chosen people. And his "authority" is clearly a *freedom* from the institutionalized orthodoxy which gives some people their exclusive claim to God's favor.

(b) *The Straightjacket of Religious Law*: Declarations of the "authority" of the Son of Man punctuate the series of controversies in Mark 2 (vv. 10, 28). The last of the series, prompted by the disciples' harvesting grain of the sabbath (Mk 2:23-28), interprets Jesus' astonishing "indifference" to cultic and ritual regulations[13] in terms of the eschatological "authority" of the Son of Man (2:28). That interpretation appears to be the first of a series of adjustments undertaken in the synoptic tradition to mollify the radical spirit of Mk 2:27, an *ipsissimum verbum Jesu* if there ever was one: "The sabbath was made for man, not man for the sabbath"![14] Its interpretive partner, v. 28, correctly understands this pronouncement as an assertion of the *exousia* of the eschatological "Man," a measure of the supreme sovereignty with which he acts on earth.[15] And what a measure! The sabbath precept, which bound the angels as well as humans and marked off sacred time for the service of the divinity, is here turned to the service of humanity! "That the Christians who transmitted these words were shocked by them is only too understandable. Only Mark (2:27) offers this radical assertion. . . . Matthew and Luke omit the saying entirely."[16]

(c) *Moral Verdicts Segregating Good from Bad*: At the beginning of Mark's controversy series, the cure of the paralytic gives a picture of dominical "authority" rooted in charism: "that you may experience the authority that the Son of Man has to forgive sins on earth— he said to the paralytic . . ." (Mk 2:10). The old nexus of physical ills and moral guilt apparently inspires this illustration of Jesus' *exousia* through his charism of healing; and Matthew's reworded conclusion to the episode makes explicit the extension of both to the Church: "they glorified God who had given such *exousia* to humans" (Mt 9:8). Now, under the power of the approaching Kingdom and the "authority" of its spokesmen, not only the precepts and barriers of the Law but all basic moral gradations and distinctions among people become immaterial. Such "authority" meant a *freedom* to erase that most cherished and fortified of all boundaries, conventionally seen as the very *raison d'être* of organized religion: the distinction between good people and bad people! The one who wields such authority, and grants such freedom, stands to be recognized as the "Son of Man," the judge of the world.[17]

The discussion gets worrisome at this point. Is not an "authority" so interpreted inimical to the social order, a warrant for anarchy and self-gratification? Just so we reach the crux of the matter: Jesus' *authority* means *freedom* for greater moral seriousness, and not less! We now turn to verify how this is so.

Jesus' Authority and the Greater Responsibility

The first episode of the public life, in Mark 1:22-28, is an episodic snapshot of the victory proclaimed for the Exalted Christ in Phil 2:9-11; and it is framed by proclamations of his *exousia*: "what is this? A new teaching with authority . . ." (1:27, with missionary consequence in 1:28); "he was teaching them as one having authority, and not as their scribes taught" (1:22). Framing the exorcism as they do, these proclamations reveal Jesus' *exousia* to be an authority of *charism*, not of extrinsic precept; it is proper to a prophet rather than a scholarly repetitor, for it is based on the immediacy of the gift imparted with God's Spirit, not the research and retailing of what others have taught. Matthew shows us how this standard of authority, "not as the scribes," furnishes the key to Christian moral responsibility when he seizes the programmatic statement of Mk 1:22, emblazoned as a banner over the Marcan account of Jesus' ministry, as the point for inserting the great "Sermon" on the Mount, concluded with the selfsame words at Mt 7:29: "he was teaching them as one having authority, not as their scribes taught."

Where it stands in Matthew, this assertion can embrace not just *how* Jesus taught, but *what* he taught, since an extensive compilation of his words, nearly all absent from Mark, now comes before the Marcan sentence.[18] Moreover, the sentence now sounds a loud echo of the title-sentence of one of the Sermon's major sections, the so-called "Antitheses" (Mt 5:20-48), whose editorial "headline" reads: "Unless your righteousness *exceeds* that of the scribes and pharisees, you will not enter the Kingdom of Heaven" (5:20). None other than Josef Ratzinger, earlier in his career, taught us so persuasively concerning this "righteousness of *excess*,"[19] that its demand rises to the overflowing measure of the divine gift we have received. Accordingly, each of the six "Antitheses" pushes the point of compliance with God's will forward of the letter of the Law, in effect disqualifying law as the adequate foundation of a Christian conscience.[20] Not law, indeed, but the *gift that has been received* founds the moral conscience of Jesus' followers. Not the alien command which constrains us from without, but the experience of a father's unlimited bounty inspires a Christian morality which is commensurately unlimited and unconditional.[21] The sixth "antithesis," climaxing the series at Mt 5:43-48, makes this crucial correlation explicit: "Love your enemies . . . , that you may be children of your Father in heaven, for *he* makes his sun rise on the evil and the good . . ." (Mt 5:44-45; see Lk 6:35).[22] The *gift* of God's indiscriminate bounty, unconditioned by its recipients' dispositions, grounds the *obligation* to show similarly unconditional goodness to fellow creatures. Here is the "something more" (Mt 5:47), the righteousness of "excess," which is demanded of those who know they were redeemed by the sacrifice of the "righteous one for the unrighteous" (I Pet 3:18; see Rom 5:8), wherein God "did not even spare his own son" (Rom 8:32).

Jesus' "new teaching with authority" thus instilled an unconditional *obligation* rooted in an unconditional *gift*; it was a summons to full moral integrity and authenticity, implied in the comparison, "not as the scribes taught." Here, too, *authority* means *freedom*, a freedom from extrinsic duress of the legal code, which fashions a facade of rectitude while leaving the will and the heart unreconciled. Such freedom requires greater ethical seriousness, not less, since it chooses personal integrity and wholeness in a world which sooner awards its respect to correctness of appearance, gained by hair-splitting legalism and nervous dissimulation!

III. The "New Teaching kat' exousian," and "The Teaching of the Church"

In light of what has been said, how should conscientious people respond to the clarion cries for "the teaching of the Church" ringing all around us these days, so often from throats that seem bent on silencing discordant voices and erasing all diversity in their communions?

First of all, let us take a salutary *caveat* from the grand finale of Matthew's gospel, which gives essential focus and summation to all we could say on "authority" in the New Testament. The Easter proclamation, "all authority in heaven and on earth has been given to me," is applied to the commission to "make disciples," and this, in turn, is articulated in the activities of "baptizing" and "teaching." The Matthean accent rests, of course, on the second activity, inasmuch as the content of the teaching is specified: "all that I have commanded you"—pointedly referring to the words of Jesus uniquely synthesized in Matthew's book (Mt 28:18–20).[23] Moreover, the direct relation of this "making disciples" activity to the final word of the book—"and behold I am with you always . . ."—means that the risen Lord acts directly in the Church where the words he spoke are instilled. No human authority takes his place here below, nor does "church teaching" gain momentum of its own independently of a sustained and critical measurement against his recorded words. The keystone Christian belief that the risen One is alive and speaks directly to the Church, as her teacher and judge, through the study and proclamation of Scripture, ought to hold securely in check the "Catholic" temptation to apotheosize the Church and speak of her as a quasi-independent, self-contained teaching authority, directing us all from outer space somewhere!

And this is just the impression one gets these days from many who speak to us of "the teaching of the Church," as if citing a celestial agency outside and beyond its faltering members. What is more, many seem to cite "the teaching of the Church" in order to reestablish all those things which Jesus' authority demolished! These include the old procrustean "orthodoxy" that quarantines all dissent, the ritual precepts which preempt human concerns and vicissitudes, the comfortable barriers between right people and wrong, and the extrinsic legality which keeps Christian pharisaism alive. Christian "authority," on the other hand, as defined in the New Testament, can never be severed from the liberating *gift* that has been received in Christ; it always proceeds from that *charisma* which embodies the claim of its Giver, always intent on transforming the world through our frail action. Because this is my Creator's gift, it is truly *mine*, and yet it never leaves his hand to become my private possession.[24] This is why such "charismatic" authority cannot license moral laxity, but instead inspires the much greater moral earnestness of people who recognize their own gifts, not somebody else's rules, to be the basis of ethical imperatives. Such was the only answer, but the conclusive answer, that Paul was able to give to the problem of misused "authority" in Corinth.

Of course, all this makes for a much untidier organization than many ecclesiastics can bear. Charisms, after all, as promptings of the uncharted Spirit of God, cannot be kept under control by the institution. And of all the charisms bestowed on the Church's prophets, teachers, even theologians, perhaps the most troublesome, and the most unwelcome at chancery and curia, is that of *critical intelligence*. This is the endowment which forces its recipient, even against his prior dispositions, to pose annoying questions like the following: Does this teaching or discipline really pertain to the core of the gospel? Does this Church structure truly serve the credibility of the Church and the fulfillment of her contemporary mission? Does this or that issue of contemporary life demand public testimony from Church officials as part of their witness to the gospel? And by the same standard, does some other issue deserve all the attention that some churchmen give it?

These are not questions we ask *of* authority, they are questions we ask *with* authority—*kat' exousian*—the authority of God's gift, made to bad and good alike, to mighty and lowly, to the churched and the unchurched. It is, as Paul taught us, the *authority* which is one and the same as "the *freedom* of the sons of God."

NOTES

1. On what follows, see the article by W. Foerster, "*exestin, exousia . . .*," in G. Kittel, ed., *Theological Dictionary of the New Testament* II (trans. G. Bromiley; Grand Rapids: Eerdmans, 1964), 560–75.

2. *Ibid.*, 564f.

3. See Dan 4:17 (= Aramaic *sheḷēt*); Sir 10:4; Apoc 16:9. Several other Apoc passages refer to *exousia* given by God to the forces of nature: 6:8; 9:3,10,19.

4. See also Acts 26:18; Col 1:13; Apoc 13:2ff.

5. See Apoc 14:18; 18:1. This is related to the use of the plural "authorities" (*exousiai*), along with "principalities," "powers," and "dominions," as part of the rich nomenclature of the angelic (or demonic) ruling powers of the cosmos, a usage shared by the NT with its hellenistic environment (see Foerster, *art. cit.*, 571–73).

6. Note the special use of the word in John's mission language, in reference to both Jesus (Jn 5:27; 17:2) and his followers (Jn 1:12; see figuratively Apoc 22:14). Further instances of "authority" granted to Jesus' followers: II Cor 10:8; 18:10; I Cor 9:4–6,12,18; Acts 8:19.

7. See G. Bornkamm, *Early Christian Experience* (New York: Harper and Row, 1969), pp. 123–25; G. Theissen, *The Social Setting of Pauline Christianity: Essays on Corinth* (Philadelphia: Fortress, 1982) pp. 121–43.

8. "Authority" here is usually rendered by other English words which better express the thought, such as "liberty" (RSV, NEB), "freedom" (BJ). See Rom 15:1–2.

9. But see H. Conzelmann, *First Corinthians: A Commentary* (Hermeneia series; Philadelphia: Fortress, 1975) pp. 108–10; J. C. Beker, *Paul the Apostle* (Philadelphia: Fortress, 1980) p. 165.

10. See Mark 7:15, and E. Käsemann, *Essays on New Testament Themes* (Chicago: Allenson, 1964), p. 39f.; H. Braun, *Jesus of Nazareth* (Philadelphia: Fortress, 1979), p. 54.

11. The sequence of a matrix "sermon" (Lk 6:20–49) and the healing story (Lk 7:1–10) had thus already been created in the "Q" collection of Jesus' sayings, independently joined to Mark's sequence by Matthew and Luke. "The position of the story shows that it is meant to strengthen the authority of the preceding sermon. And for the 'Q' transmitters, it is significant that their vision reached out beyond Israel." See A. Polag, *Die Christologie der Logienquelle* (Neukirchen: Neukirchener Verlag, 1977), p. 158.

12. By using Mark 1:22 as the concluding sentence of his "Sermon on the Mount" section, Matthew reinforces the relationship between the Sermon and the healing story by creating the echo of the keyword *exousia* between Mt 7:29 and 8:9.

13. H. Braun, *Jesus of Nazareth*, p. 63.

14. See E. Käsemann, *Essays*, p. 38f., and the analytical demonstration by A. Hultgren, *Jesus and His Adversaries* (Minneapolis: Augsburg, 1979), pp. 111–15.

15. H. E. Tödt, *The Son of Man in the Synoptic Tradition* (Philadelphia: Westminster, 1965), pp. 132f.

16. H. Braun, *Jesus of Nazareth*, p. 61.

17. H. E. Tödt, *The Son of Man*, pp. 129f.

18. This is noted by most commentators. See also E. Schweizer, *Matthäus und seine Gemeinde* (Stuttgart: Katholisches Bibelwerk, 1974) p. 53; A. Sand, *Das Gesetz und die Propheten* (Regensburg: Pustet, 1974), p. 158.

19. *Introduction to Christianity* (New York: Herder/Seabury, 1970) pp. 193–98.

20. G. Bornkamm, in *Jesus of Nazareth* (New York: Harper and Row, 1960) p. 103, suggested summarizing the "Antitheses" under the formula "*not just . . . but even*":

Not just (1) murder, (2) adultery, (3) legally invalid divorce, (4) legally invalid oaths, (5) unwarranted revenge, (6) hatred of one's own kind, *violate the will of God* revealed in the Mosaic Law, *but even* (1) anger and insult, (2) lustful thoughts, (3) any divorce, (4) any oaths, (5) any revenge, (6) hatred of enemies.

21. The appropriateness of the old (OT) relational structure to Matthew's concept of "righteousness" is much in dispute. A good survey, with position taken in favor of this, is found in R. A. Guelich, *The Sermon on the Mount: A Foundation for Understanding* (Waco, TX: Word, 1982), pp. 233–37. It seems possible to defend both the priority of gift over human performance in the order of things and, on the other hand, this gospel's heavier emphasis on the performance aspect of Christian "righteousness." See R. Mohrlang, *Matthew and Paul: A Comparison of Ethical Perspectives* (Cambridge Univ. Press, 1984), p. 80.

22. The agreement of Mt and Lk (= Q) on the sequence of the command and the childhood-promise indicates that it is very likely traceable to Jesus' own speech. See D. Lührmann, " 'Liebet eure Feinde,' " *Zeitschrift für Theologie und Kirche* 69 (1972), 412–38, here 427ff.

23. See G. Bornkamm, "The Risen Christ and the Earthly Jesus," in J. M. Robinson, ed., *The Future of Our Religious Past* (New York: Harper and Row, 1971), pp. 203–29, here 222ff.; G. Barth, in Bornkamm-Barth-Held, *Tradition and Interpretation in Matthew* (Philadelphia: Westminster, 1963), pp. 134–35.

24. Well brought out in the essay, " 'The Righteousness of God' in Paul," in E. Käsemann, *New Testament Questions of Today* (Philadelphia: Fortress, 1969), pp. 168–82.

THE OFFICE OF THE BISHOP IN ORIGEN

Aaron Milavec
The Athenaeum of Ohio

ABSTRACT

The author undertakes to describe the perspective of Origen of Alexandria relative to (1) the nature and scope of episcopal authority
and (2) the limitations of episcopal authority stemming from reflections upon inept bishops. Origen situates the bishop's authority *vis
à vis* the long and arduous task of attaining Christian perfection. As
a rule, those who would securely advance in the ways of wisdom
must have capable spiritual guides. Within the clerical hierarchy of
the church, consequently, the bishop ought to be manifestly most
advanced and, as a consequence, capable of being the enlightened
mentor for all those in his congregation who are at various other
inferior stages on the route toward perfection. When a bishop fails
to exhibit the skills required of his office, Origen regards this as a
serious aberration. In such instances, Origen considers how advanced Christians are to think and to act in the face of a bishop who
approves deeds which Christ would have censured and censures
deeds which Christ would have approved. The author closes his
study by making a few contemporary applications of Origen's thought.

Along with the practice of collegiality, the bishops assembled during Vatican II thought it timely to reintroduce the early patristic
tradition wherein the episcopal office was principally ordained toward the service of studying, of teaching, and of exemplifying the
Gospel of Jesus Christ. Among the Church Fathers, Origen (d. 254),
most especially, would have been pleased with this modern attempt
to renew the episcopal office in the image of what he regarded as
the principal tasks of the episcopal ministry. In his own day, Origen
never found an occasion wherein he was inspired to prepare a systematic analysis of the office of bishop. Nonetheless, this issue is

*Aaron Milavec has been responsible for the formation of future priests and lay min-
isters during the last fifteen years. Currently he is the Associate Professor of Historical
Theology at The Athenaeum of Ohio. His professional training includes an S.T.B.
from the University of Fribourg (Switzerland) and a Th.D. from the Graduate Theological Union (Berkeley). His insightful study of the dynamics of spiritual empowerment within the early church has been published under the title of* To Empower
as Jesus Did *(New York: The Edwin Mellen Press, 1984)*

incidentally addressed throughout his writings. In harmony with the theme chosen for the 1986 Annual Convention of the College Theology Society and in recognition of the ongoing quest by the bishops of our Church better to understand and more faithfully to fulfill their office, I will pursue the scattered clues offered by Origen so as to sketch some aspects of the theory and practice of the office of bishop during the first half of the third century. My reflections upon Origen will be grouped under two headings: I. the nature and source of episcopal authority and II. the limitations of episcopal authority stemming from reflections upon inept bishops.

I. The Nature and Source of Episcopal Authority

Origen's understanding of episcopal authority rests upon the presupposition that every Christian is called to be perfect. Even though it may not be true, as Eusebius asserts, that Origen was the pupil of Clement while he grew up in Alexandria, nonetheless, it is clear that the ideal image of the Christian gnostic found within Clement dominates Origen's thoughts and feelings as well. Origen joins with Clement, consequently, in proposing time and time again that the road to perfection is a long arduous attainment which gradually purifies and redirects the whole person in harmony with the standards and wisdom of God.[1] It is no surprise, therefore, that recent converts begin with only a superficial perception of the literal meaning of Scripture and only after being guided through progressive stages, gain a discernment of the hidden mysteries of God's wisdom and guidance which lie concealed behind these words.[2] In parallel terms, it is no surprise that these same converts begin with only a physical fear of the torments of the damned, and only after they have made a certain progress toward Christian perfection, relish wisdom and the divine standards of excellence for their own sake.[3]

Origen, along with most other Fathers of the Church, takes it for granted that the novice advances securely precisely because he/she has a capable spiritual guide who is further advanced on the route. Just as a student cellist submits to the direction of ever more proficient mentors according to the progress made, so too, the Christian within the congregation expects to find ever more proficient guides among the ordained clergy to stimulate, to guide, and to correct him/her along the way. Within this spiritual hierarchy, Origen specifies the bishop as the one who ought to be manifestly most advanced and, as a consequence, most capable of discharging the office whereby he functions as the enlightened mentor for all those in his congregation who are at various other stages on the route toward perfection.[4]

According to Origen, the Church stands as the roadside inn wherein humankind, which has been grievously wounded by the vices and delusions of this world, finds safety and healing.[5] Those who enter the Church are brought there by Christ, the merciful Samaritan, who, unlike the Torah-priest and the Prophet-Levite, did not pass humankind by, but out of compassion stopped and "went to him and bound up his wounds, pouring oil and wine" (Luke 10:34). Once brought into the inn, Origen assures us that Christ, for an entire day and night, stays by the bedside using his healing art so as to further effect the treatment that he began on the route. Finally, being forced to leave, the master Physician turns his patient over to the innkeeper giving him the solemn charge of conscientiously continuing the healing process that he himself has begun until such a time that the patient is entirely cured. The innkeeper, in Origen's reckoning, is none other than the bishop of the Church. He is the one who has witnessed Christ's healing art during the short time that he was on earth. He is the one now charged to exercise this same ministry until Christ returns again on the Last Day for the purpose of repaying him for all his efforts on behalf of the wounded. On the basis of this metaphor, Origen makes clear that the bishop stands within the Church as one who has been trained in the art of healing and has been charged by Christ to exercise this art for the benefit of all. As such, Origen presupposes that the bishop's authority rests upon his tested skills in apprenticing others into the selfsame perfection of life which he himself embodies.

Someone who would be cured by a physician must, in faith, accept his diagnosis and assiduously follow the program for healing which has been prescribed. So, too, someone who would participate in an art or a science must submit themselves to be trained under the direction of those who competently exercise that particular art or science.[6] Since Christian perfection is an acquired art achieved by virtue of human efforts harmonized with "the ceaseless working of Father, Son, and the Holy Spirit in us,"[7] it follows that faith functions as the necessary disposition whereby the neophyte surrenders to the discipline of the bishop and his assistants for the purpose of acquiring the very skills which distinguish them as masters in the art of Christian living.[8]

In Origen's day, the adult catechumenate testified to the fact that there were no instantaneous and effortless transformations of life.[9] The success of this transformative process required that the candidate entrust him/herself to a teacher, an exorcist, deacons, presbyters, and, finally, the bishop who supervised the final Lenten intensive wherein the catechumens assembled in the "house of God" each morning before going to work. During these early morning hours, the personal instructions of those bishops which have come down to us contain explicit warning not to expect an instantaneous or effortless transformation due to some supposed power of the rite itself.[10] Quite to the contrary, the Church Fathers emphasized that the Holy Spirit does not force her entry into the soul and that immoral tendencies do not instantaneously die in the water immersion to be miraculously supplanted by the dispositions of Christ. On the contrary, purification is presented as a gradual process requiring persistent efforts both before and after baptism. At one point, Origen likens Christian transformation to the gradual process whereby crushed grapes ferment into wine.[11] At another point, Origen interprets the whole of the Christian life as beginning with the passage through the Jordan, a symbol of baptism, but continuing during the forty years under the instruction and discipline of God in the desert wandering prior to the final combat which will win the promised land.[12] At still another point, Origen calls to mind that the Logos had to pass through forty-two stages in gradually "descending into the Egypt of this world."[13] Christians, having been met in the depths of their degradation, are now certain that the route is secure for them to ascend, stage by stage, in order to attain "the place from whence he descended."[14]

A skill which is gradually acquired is only gradually lost. Origen has no room for the medieval notion that, due to a single mortal sin, one's cumulative sanctifying grace can be suddenly lost. Quite to the contrary, when Origen wishes to illustrate how Christians, due to neglect, might lose their graced perfection, he deliberately sets about describing the comparable case of how a master physician or geometrician might lose his acquired art:

Suppose . . . one had become gradually acquainted with the art or science, say of geometry or medicine, until he had reached perfection, having trained himself for a lengthened time in its principles and practice, so as to attain a complete mastery over the art. To such a one it could never happen, should he lay down to sleep in the possession of his skill, that he would awake in a state of ignorance. . . . According to our point of view, then, so long as that geometer or physician continues to exercise himself in the study of his art and the practice of its principles, the knowledge of his profession abides with him [undiminished]. But, if he withdraws from its practice and lays aside his habits of industry, then, by his neglect, a few things at first will gradually escape him, then by and by more, until in the course of time, everything will be forgotten and be completely effaced from memory. It is possible, on the other hand, that when he has first begun to fall away and to yield to the corrupting influence of a small negligence, he may . . . recover that knowledge which hitherto had been only slightly obliterated from his mind.[15]

Origen's illustrative case study makes it clear that Christian perfection can only be gradually lost due to neglect of its practice. The resumption of dedicated efforts, accordingly, can suffice to regain those habits of understanding and judgment which have been effaced due to negligence.[16]

Origen is so consistent in the application of his principle of gradualism as to envision that progress and education will take place, even in the world to come:

> Although an individual may depart from this life less perfectly instructed ... , he will be capable of receiving instruction in that Jerusalem, the city of the saints, i.e., he will be educated and molded, and made a living stone, a stone elect and precious, because he has undergone with firmness and constancy the struggles of life. ... There he will come to a truer and clearer knowledge of that which here has been already predicted, namely, that "man should not live by bread alone, but by every word which proceeds from the mouth of God." And this is to be understood as referring to the princes and rulers who both govern those of lower rank and instruct them and teach them and train them in divine things.[17]

In effect, therefore, Origen envisions a heavenly hierarchy based on the same standards which ought now to prevail among the earthly hierarchy: each one who is endowed with spiritual attainments ought to be appointed to the corresponding position in the Church so that he might render a willing and capable service to those less advanced on the way. Finally, at the time of the consummation of all things, Origen speculates that the Lord Christ, who is King of all, will take his place within the kingdom and personally undertake the training of those who have sufficiently advanced so as to profit from his most exalted wisdom.

In effect, Origen's presentation of Christian perfection as an acquired art now comes into full focus. On earth and in heaven, nothing is attained effortlessly and instantaneously. Relying upon the grace of God, each one progresses securely and gradually under the mentorship of spiritual masters who themselves exhibit more advanced skills in the very art that one is acquiring. The bishop, presbyters, and teachers in this scheme of things, represent the foremost exemplars and insightful mentors who serve those who are less advanced. According to this horizon of understanding, the source of the bishop's authority cannot accordingly be sought within his consecration or his juridical standing within the community. On the contrary, it is precisely because a presbyter is recognized as an accomplished guide and as a worthy spiritual father prior to his consecration that he is consecrated as bishop.[18] As such, the charism of the man crowns the episcopal office with dignity; the office does not confer the charism.

But this is the theoretical best case. What does Origen notice of actual bishops who may not be the most advanced and who, due to imperfections, render improper judgments and offer misguided counsel? To this our attention now turns.

II. The Limitations of Episcopal Authority Stemming from Reflections upon Inept Bishops

Origen himself had suffered under what he rightly regarded as the unappreciative regard of his own bishop, Demetrius, at Alexandria. Having attained a perfection which matched or surpassed that of the existing presbyters within the Alexandrian community, Origen was undoubtedly perplexed that he was not being called by his bishop to be a presbyter. We can speculate that Origen's self-castration on the pretext of preventing scandal to those who accused him of improper conduct with his students was seen as an impediment. In any case, we do know that Origen eventually left Alexandria to travel and, instead of returning to his catechetical school in his home diocese, he settled, at the age of forty-five, within the community of Caesarea where he was quickly ordained presbyter—thus recognizing his true worth.

Demetrius, learning of Origen's ordination, sought to have him deposed on the grounds that the bishop of Caesarea had committed a breach of ecclesiastic discipline by ordaining a member of the Alexandrian Church and, what is more, a eunuch. When this failed, charges of heresy and of keeping close contact with Gnostics were being aired and Origen, with great effort, was forced to justify himself to the bishops of Palestine. Demetrius' charges threatened either to expel Origen from the presbyterate or to have him renounce his deepest insights. The sudden death of Demetrius cut short a major crisis; nonetheless, the two years of living as a presbyter with a black cloud hanging over his head must have left Origen distressed and hurt. In his commentary on John, which he again undertook after the attack upon him had abated, he spoke of his departure from Alexandria in the biblical imagery of a "deliverance from Egypt."[19] The identity of the harassing Pharoah can be easily imagined.

Once Origen began to deliver his homilies on the three-year cycle of readings at Caesarea, he included scattered references to the defective character of those appointed to ecclesiastic offices: (a) bishops fail to devote themselves to probing the Scriptures and have contempt for those who do;[20] (b) some are even tainted with heresy;[21]

(c) others, in their pursuit of wealth or power downgrade the exalted dignity of their episcopal office.[22]

Where a bishop fails to exhibit the spiritual perfection which is required by his office, Origen regards such a situation as an aberration caused either by a failure on the bishop's part or by inadequacy in the discernment process whereby he was initially appointed.[23] An unworthy bishop, in Origen's judgment, stands effectively among the laity while the perfected lay person may be the true bishop in God's eyes.[24] That this should be the case, however, does not lead Origen ever to suggest a forceful replacement of the inferior bishop by the superior layman whose value to the community is being lost. Quite to the contrary, Origen makes use of his reflections upon the holy family to offer a pastoral justification within this irregular situation:

> If Jesus, the son of God, was submissive to Joseph and to Mary, ought not I myself to be submissive to the bishop whom God has assigned me as father? Ought not I to be submissive to the priest preposed for me by the Lord? I think Joseph understood that Jesus was superior to him at the very moments that he was being submissive to him and, recognizing the superiority of his inferior [son], Joseph directed him with fear and restraint. Let everyone reflect on this: it often happens that a person of lesser worth is placed over others who are superior, and it sometimes happens that someone inferior has more value than the one who directs him/her. When the person who is elevated in [ecclesiastic] dignity comes to understand this, this person will not appear proud due to his elevated rank but will recognize that his inferior is perhaps superior just as [in the case of] Jesus [who] was submissive to Joseph.[25]

This judgment of Origen implies that a Christian's advance in perfection need not be effectively limited by an inferior ecclesial guide who, knowingly or unknowingly, endeavors to act the pedagogue and prevent anyone from manifesting skills superior to his own. In such a case, humility and patience are called for, but Christ remains the true norm of perfection and the bishop of such advanced souls (1 Pt 2:25).

But what of the case when, due to his imperfections, a bishop renders defective judgments against a member of his church? Campenhausen summarizes Origen well on this point:

> If a bishop, from personal dislike or selfish motives, or, it may be, simply from error and human weakness, turns an innocent Christian out of the

Church, such a decision is null and void in the eyes of God and can do no harm to the person on whom it is passed. This view is explicitly emphasized in opposition to a radical hierarchical theory. Those who claim episcopal jurisdiction, it is asserted, appeal in their proceedings to the promise of the keys to Peter. . . . This, Origen goes on, is correct only in so far as the bishop himself is like Peter in his life and can in fact pass judgment with the same degree of authority. But if he himself is "entangled in the snares of his own sin," then he binds and looses "to no effect." It would be a risible delusion to assume that anyone could exclude his fellowmen [women] from salvation simply "because he enjoyed the title of bishop."[26]

But even aside from defective excommunications, an imperfect bishop endangers the spiritual welfare of those within his church because he is prone to approve deeds which Christ would have censured and to censure deeds which Christ would have approved. In some cases, the whole pastoral order within a community would be deeply subverted by a bishop who asserts his own defective judgment and imagines that it is equivalent to the judgment of Christ. Furthermore, since those under training cannot be expected to have powers of discernment which exceed their authorized mentors, the whole system of mentoring within a church community would be distorted to serve the standards of an unworthy bishop rather than the standards of Christ. Thus, Origen cautions his readers against resting secure with those bishops who merely pretend to have the skills associated with their office.[27] At one point, Origen even goes so far as to advise those who are intent upon true advancement to deliberately test the spiritual physician to whom they would submit their souls for healing.[28] This advice is satisfactory for someone of the status of Origen, but may have little relevance for the neophyte. The beginner has no clear notion of the nature of his/her sickness nor of the best remedies available for a cure. Except in the case of gross negligence, it remains, in actual practice, for physicians to correct and to dismiss physicians, for bishops to correct and to dismiss bishops.

Conclusion

In conclusion, Origen justifies the episcopal authority entirely on the basis of the bishop's actual spiritual perfection as achieved through the selfsame processes whereby every Christian grows in Christ. No sacramental rite nor grace of office can magically supply what is seriously lacking within the person of the episcopal candidate. In effect, therefore, the very office of the bishop is demystified and the holder of this office, while accredited as the most spiritually advanced, must continually demonstrate himself worthy of his ministry and calling in the eyes and hearts of his people and in the eyes and heart of God, the true and final judge.

During the Middle Ages, when the mystique of office was firmly in place and the sacramental system was imagined to function without any hindrance on the part of the moral or intellectual qualities of the minister, the sober realism of Origen was largely silent. Nonetheless, one can note that certain bold stonemasons, when crafting the scene of the final judgment over the central portal of the rising Gothic cathedrals of Europe, were not prevented from showing that some of those being dragged by horned beasts into the gaping mouth of hell or being boiled alive in pots of oil wore the same exalted miters that paraded on the heads of the bishops of the Church of the day. Perhaps bishops themselves relished such a reminder; perhaps the stonemasons explained that "those bishops presented" did not have any resemblance to any living bishops but referred to those bishops of an evil age in the dark past or the distant future. In any case, when there was little sober realism to be found regarding the episcopal office, the stonemasons left a witness which remains to this day.

As to our own period, I would surmise that the parish priest in a small, rural parish is the nearest functional equivalent of the bishop-pastor of Origen's day. Even so, in an age when so few priests are given over to consuming their days and nights with breaking open the Scriptures and acting as the spiritual guides for their people, I am tempted to say that there is today no functional equivalent to the bishop-mentor of Origen's day. Moreover, to have a ministry of the likes which Origen knew firsthand, first requires an entire community wherein spiritual perfection is the principal task which gives worth to living. Most church communities are largely distracted from such things. This being the case, Origen is a faint echo of a former era which has passed away—an echo which faintly disturbs and challenges the present era. This voice, for those who have time and patience to hear it, is an unsettling and ghostly presence which calls the present ecclesial order into account. According to the tale of Dickens, Scrooge was converted and renewed by a series of such ghostly spectres. Is it not possible that Origen may someday appear as the Ghost of the Church Past which works for the conversion and renewal of our present church?

NOTES

1. Origen repeatedly characterizes Christian perfection as a gradual attainment. See, e.g., *Princ.* 2.11.5–7. For a careful study of the stages of perfection spelled out in various works of Origen, see Karen Jo Torjesen, *Hermeneutical Procedure and Theological Method in Origen's Exegesis* (Berlin: Walter de Gruyter, 1986), pp. 85–109.

2. *Princ.* 2.4.8.; *Hom. in Num.* 27.1; *Commentary on the Song of Songs* 3.

3. Origen thought that texts which suggest the "eternal torments" of the damned, e.g., Matt 18:8 had a certain pastoral efficacy for those who, at the initial stages of conversion, were only motivated by the avoidance of pain (*Cels.* 3.65f & 78f). In point of fact, Origen speculated "that every sinner kindles for him/herself the flame of his/her own fire and is not plunged into some fire which has already been kindled by another" (*Princ.* 2.10.4). This internal flame, Origen identifies as the perturbations caused by the divinely induced awareness of one's shameful, unholy deeds and their attendant disorderly passions. In this fashion, God's justice in the world to come is not viewed as vindictive but as being the healing remedy to burn away one's iniquities. For a more comprehensive study of Origen's thought in this area, consult Jacques LeGoff, *The Birth of Purgatory* (Chicago: University Press, 1984), esp. pp. 53–55.

4. *Comm. in Matt.* 14:22 & *Cels.* 3.48. Joseph Wilson Trigg, in his recent book, *Origen* (Atlanta: John Knox Press, 1983), and in his article, "The Charismatic Intellectual: Origen's Understanding of Religious Leadership," *Church History* 50 (1981) 5–19, seems to suggest at times that the source of the bishop's authority is his "intellectual achievement" while at other times he emphasizes that it is "a radically charismatic" gift entirely outside of human mediation. In my conversations with Trigg, I discovered that he wished to regard charismatic authority as rooted within achieved spiritual insight and holiness of life. In those instances where he denies "human mediation," it is more by way of showing that the ordination rite cannot confer that spiritual insight and holiness of life which are the ground of the bishop's authority.

5. *Hom. in Luc.* 34.

6. Even in the domain of the physical sciences, post-critical philosophers of science acknowledge (a) that positivism, objectivism, and pragmatism present elliptical and misleading notions of science and (b) that every scientific domain functions as a "fiduciary framework" which can only be assimilated through a process of self-donation which enables one to be apprenticed in modes of thought and judgment which are not instinctively one's own. See, for example, Michael Polanyi, *Personal Knowledge* (New York: Harper & Row, 1964), pp. 264–98.

Augustine, in his prologue of *On Christian Doctrine*, considers those Christians who would bypass human teachers by claiming that the Holy Spirit alone is their teacher. To those who make such a claim, Augustine retorts that, to be consistent, such persons should never presume to teach anyone what they have so acquired but to send inquirers directly to the same Holy Spirit which was their source. Augustine then goes on the demonstrate that just as each of us learns to read from teachers, so too it is providential that God provides teachers who offer the skills whereby Christians might learn to read the Word of God in order to arrive securely at discerning the hidden sense without any error.

7. *Princ.* 1.3.8. Origen finds no incompatibility in asserting that the transformation of our lives is, at one and the same time, due to divine initiative and human initiative. Origen, it will be remembered, does not live in a world which distinguishes events which are caused by God from events which are caused by Nature. Every "natural event" is fashioned and interiorly guided by the cosmic Logos. The work of personal

sanctification requires a realignment of human efforts with this selfsame Logos in whose "image and likeness" humans were initially crafted. As a master physician makes interventions, not by way of creating or designing the healing process, but by way of discerning how to enhance processes which are already operative before, during, and after his intervention; so, too, the spiritual physicians within the Church use their art by way of enabling and assisting what God is already directed toward accomplishing within each individual soul.

8. For the uninitiated, faith functions primarily as the disposition of self-surrender which accompanies the spontaneous admiration with which the novice regards the functional skills of his/her self-chosen master. For an analysis of how the function of faith changes and how critical powers are related to faith, see Aaron Milavec, *To Empower as Jesus Did* (New York: The Edwin Mellen Press, 1982), pp. 193–98.

9. Every prophetic historical movement thrives by virtue of having mastered the art of imparting a new consciousness to its participants. Christianity was no exception to this rule. The design and artful implementation of the adult catechumenate during the first five centuries effected such human transformations. As the adult catechumenate disappeared and as infant baptism shortly after birth became the familiar practice, however, the traditional forms of efficacy once manifestly evident within the manifest conduct of the adult catechumens gave way to a spiritualized and hidden efficacy within the soul of the infant. Thomas Aquinas, for instance, spoke of the faith and virtues imparted to the soul of an infant as not being evident since it is as though such effects are asleep (*Summa Theologica* 3.69.6). The door was thus open for imagining that the rite, in and of itself, effected an instantaneous and effortless transformation since intentional effort and willing cooperation could not be imputed to infants.

More appropriately, Paul emphasizes "faith in Christ" which Origen understood as meaning subjection to be influenced by and to reside within the wisdom, righteousness, and person of Christ as the Logos. Faith is never specified as propositions about Christ which warrant intellectual assent.

10. Cyril of Jerusalem (d. 386), e.g., in his instructions to catechumens does not hesitate to cite failures and to incite candidates thereby to renew their efforts for self-transformation. "If you just continue in your evil disposition," he warns, "you cannot expect to receive God's grace for even though the water will receive you the Holy Spirit will not" (*The Catechetical Lectures* 4).

11. *Series Commentary on Matthew* 16 & *Commentary on The Song of Songs* 2.

12. *Hom. in Jos.* , introduction.

13. *Hom in Num.* 27.3.

14. *Ibid.*

15. *Princ.* 1.4.1 English tr. by Alexander Roberts et al., eds., *The Ante-Nicene Fathers*, Vol. IV (New York: Charles Scribner's Sons, 1926). Minor changes in grammar and punctuation have been effected in order to accord with contemporary usage.

16. Origen compares the deliberate attention and practice of someone intent upon accomplishing the superhuman feat of tightrope walking with those efforts deployed by someone intent upon acquiring the virtues required for blessedness. See *Cels.* 3.49.

17. *Princ.* 2.11.3 See also *Princ.* 2.11.6f & 3.6.9.

18. During this period, the consecration or ordination of a bishop was not understood to confer special supernatural powers. In most instances, bishops were selected from among those persons who had completed their catechumenate within the community and had, over a period of years, distinguished themselves in various other ministries. Within this arrangement, there was little room for a mystification of the rite of consecration since ideally the wisdom and grace of the episcopal candidates

were well-recognized both before and after the rite. The rite served to confirm the choice of the community and to transform his functional identity vis à vis the community. The invocation of the Holy Spirit served to emphasize that the new bishop was charged with going beyond the wishes of his electors and his own personal preferences in order to serve as a discerner and spokesman for what God calls his community to believe and to do.

19. *Comm. in Joh.* 6.2.

20. *Cels.* 6.7.

21. *Hom. in Num.* 9.1.

22. *Hom. in Gen.* 16.5. Origen accuses some bishops of refusing to rebuke the evils of society lest they fall out of favor with the people (*Hom. in Josh.* 7.6).

23. At the death of a bishop, in most instances the presbyters within the community would assemble together and usually choose someone from among themselves as candidate for the vacated office. The presbyters' choice would then be brought before the entire congregation for their approval. Under these conditions, it seems apparent that the qualities and performance of existing candidates were very well known to all those involved. When unsatisfactory candidates were raised to the office of bishop in such circumstances, Origen might rightly suspect that the presbyters were poor judges of character or were swayed by secondary considerations in making their choice. Origen makes mention of clerical intrigue and nepotism in his homilies at Caesarea (*Hom. in Num.* 22.4 *Comm. in Matt.* 16.22 & 16.8).

24. *Hom. in Num.* 2.1 & *Series Commentary on Matt.* 12.

25. *Hom. in Luc.* 20.6 English translation by author from the French of Henri Crouzel, *Origène: Homilies sur S. Luc, Source Chrétiennes*, Vol. 87 (Paris: Cerf, 1962).

26. Hans von Campenhausen, *Ecclesiastical Authority and Spiritual Power* (Stanford: University Press, 1969), p. 259.

27. *Series Commentary on Matt.* 24.

28. *Comm. in Ps.* 37.2.

CHRISTIAN COMMUNITY AND CHRISTIAN UNDERSTANDING: DEVELOPMENTS IN AUGUSTINE'S THOUGHT

William J. Collinge
Mount Saint Mary's College

ABSTRACT

In *De moribus ecclesiae catholicae* (388), Augustine uses descriptions of Christian community life in support of the claim that the Catholic Christian faith is true. Beginning with the Donatist controversy, his conception of the Church changes in such a way as to render the moral behavior of Christian communities less employable for apologetic purposes. But Christian community life, structured around sacramental practice, becomes increasingly important to him as a means to understanding and verifying what Christians believe.

I. Introduction

Throughout Augustine's work there is a link between the idea of love and that of the Church: the Church is that community which is made one in the true love of God and neighbor. There is also a link between love and knowledge, involving among other factors a dependence of knowledge upon love. Therefore there is a relation between the life of the Christian community, based on love, and the knowledge of the truth of what Christians believe. While this much is constant, Augustine's thought undergoes significant development on the question of what that relation is. This development is based in turn on a shift in Augustine's thought regarding the relation between the observable life of the Church and the true love of God and

William J. Collinge received a Ph.D. in philosophy from Yale University in 1974. From 1974 to 1980 he was Assistant Professor of Philosophy at Loyola Marymount University. Since 1980 he has been Associate Professor of Theology and Chairman of the Theology Department at Mount Saint Mary's College (Emmitsburg, MD 21727). He has published (or has forthcoming) articles in Augustinian Studies, Contemporary Philosophy, The American Benedictine Review, The Living Light, Horizons, *and* Faith and Philosophy.

neighbor. The occasion for this shift was Augustine's increasing involvement, after he became bishop at Hippo in 395, in conflict with the Donatists. The purpose of this paper is to trace these developments, without losing sight of the continuity in Augustine's ecclesiology.

II. De moribus ecclesiae catholicae

Augustine's earliest sustained treatment of the Church appears in De moribus ecclesiae catholicae (388), which, with De moribus Manichaeorum, forms a diptych aiming to show the superiority and greater coherence of Catholic doctrine and practice compared to that of the Manichaeans.

Most of De moribus ecclesiae catholicae is concerned to establish how reason and scripture, both Old and New Testaments, agree that to live rightly is to love God and neighbor. In the concluding part of the book, Augustine examines the life of the Catholic church at some length in order to show that this love is in fact found there. An apostrophe to the Church as a whole, extolling its charity ("[Y]ou . . . embrace such love and charity for the neighbor that there is found in you a powerful remedy for the many diseases with which souls are afflicted on account of their sins . . ."[1]), is followed by enthusiastic descriptions of the anchorites and coenobites of the desert, the clergy, and, in considerable detail, the lives of urban monastic communities. The emphasis throughout is on charity; thus, in the case of the urban monks, "Charity is safeguarded above all. It rules their eating, their speech, their dress, their countenance. It is charity that brings them together and unites them."[2]

Augustine acknowledges that some Catholics are superstitious or worldly-minded, but their example cannot legitimately be used to undermine his case: "It is not surprising that in such a great multitude of people you should be able to discover some whose lives you can condemn. . . ."[3] Of these, Augustine adds, some will repent, while others will be separated at the final judgment, as weeds from the wheat (Matthew 13:30).

The descriptions of Christian community life in De moribus, and related descriptions emphasizing the power of Christian faith to transform people's lives, in works of the same period,[4] serve to give rational support to belief in the truth of Catholic Christianity. First, they enhance the auctoritas of the Catholic church in matters of religion. Auctoritas is a word for which there is no exact English equivalent, but it means something like "stature," in regard to trustworthiness or credibility: "Authority—auctoritas—for the Roman is a non-coercive force, founded upon tradition and social position, . . . an essentially moral influence. . . ."[5] If a religion can transform people's lives in a way that an audience finds praiseworthy, its truth is not proved but its credibility is enhanced for that audience.[6] Second, they give evidence that a person can, by believing the Christian religion and living in accordance with it, make progress toward a life that is intellectually and existentially coherent and satisfactory. This appears to be the "criterion of verification" that De moribus implicitly puts forward, at least when it is read together with the account of Augustine's transition from Manichaeism to Catholic Christianity given in the Confessions (397–401). It is the criterion by which Manichaeism failed and Catholic Christianity succeeded for Augustine.[7]

This second point is related to what Augustine says about the progression from faith to knowledge. Faith, according to Augustine, must precede understanding, to which it leads by a cleansing or purification of the mind.[8] Augustine's earliest writings treat this point in somewhat Platonic terms: one has faith and one "purifies the mind" by training it through an ascetic life and the liberal disciplines to become accustomed to intellectual rather than corporeal matters. What one can understand depends on what one loves; thus one must divert one's love from the sensible world to God. Augustine comes to see this diverting to be a result of living according to the Christian commandments,[9] which reduce to love. As De moribus ecclesiae catholicae puts it:

> You [Manichaeans] approach the consideration of divine things, which are more sublime than you suppose, with minds dull and sick from a poisonous diet of corporeal images. For this reason, the way to deal with you is not to try to make you understand divine things now, which is impossible, but to make you eventually wish to understand them. Only the pure and sincere love of God which manifests itself especially in one's way of life . . . can bring this about.[10]

The descriptions of Christian life in De moribus could serve to evoke a love for the Catholic community and a desire to share in the love which holds it together, thus purifying the mind of weakness due to sin[11] and enabling progress in religious understanding.

III. The Donatist Conflict and the Holiness of the Church

Upon becoming bishop at Hippo in 395, Augustine of necessity became involved in conflict against the Donatist sect, then well entrenched in north African towns as a rival to the Catholic party.[12]

The Donatists' central emphasis was on the empirical holiness of the Church, which was to be, in a phrase they loved to quote, "without spot or wrinkle" (Ephesians 5:27). They would have agreed whole-heartedly with the ideal of the Church in De moribus ecclesiae catholicae, except that they would reject the claim that this holiness is in fact to be found in the Catholic church (and also they would reject the stratification of the Church implicit and later explicit in Augustine's monastic ideal). In replying to the Donatists, Augustine preserves the basic lines of De moribus' view of what the Church is and ought to be, while making some significant shifts of emphasis that render the empirical life of the Church much less serviceable for apologetic purposes. In these respects, his reply to his later opponents, the Pelagians, who also stressed the empirical holiness of the Church, "without spot or wrinkle," will be continuous with that to the Donatists.

The Donatists regarded themselves as the "pure" Church, the congregation of the saints, the faithful remnant.[13] Petilian's rhetoric, "But there is no fellowship of darkness with light, nor any fellowship of bitterness with the sweet of honey; there is no fellowship of life with death, of innocence with guilt, of water with blood,"[14] is characteristic. This purity was, as Peter Brown explains, an essentially ritual matter and was construed by the Donatists in a very narrow fashion: "For the Donatist Church was 'pure' in an obvious and not particularly exacting sense: it had kept itself pure from a single, unspeakable crime, from traditio, the sacrificing of the Christian 'Law'; that is, from a crime committed by total strangers in a conveniently distant past."[15] Augustine saw no reason why the act of traditio was to be the one and only touchstone of churchly purity. The Donatist idea of purity logically ought to be extended to exclude all manner of other violations of human fidelity to God.[16] This argument enabled Augustine to score some immediate polemical points, urging that the Donatists were inconsistent and not really pure.[17] But of greater importance is his challenge to the very idea of a pure Church in this world and his development of a concept of a "mixed Church" in its place. This idea of the Church, to be discussed below, then serves as the basis for his reply to Pelagian claims about the purity of the Church, "without spot or wrinkle" in a moral rather than a ritual sense.[18]

Augustine, in his response to the Donatists, needs to establish that the holiness of the Church, which is mediated to its members through the sacraments, does not depend on the holiness of the Church's individual members, in particular the ministers of the sacraments. The holiness of the Church, the basis of the efficacy of the sacraments, is that of Christ, Augustine sometimes says, or that of the Holy Spirit, he says in other places. "The two explanations are complementary," Patout Burns points out. "Charity is the gift and presence of the Holy Spirit, with whom Christ alone baptized."[19]

Charity, the gift of the Holy Spirit, is "the divine power resident in the community which makes its sacramental action salvific."[20] The Church is understood as the communion of those bound together by the unity of the Spirit, and the bond of this unity is charity. Augustine often quotes Romans 5:5, "The love of God is shed abroad in our hearts by the Holy Spirit which is given unto us," to argue that charity is the manifestation of the Spirit and the essence of the Church. "For this is that very love which is wanting in all who are cut off from the communion of the Catholic Church."[21] Again with reference to Romans 5:5, Augustine asks, "By what does one get to know that he has received the Holy Spirit?" He answers, "If he love his brother the Spirit of God dwells in him. . . . Let him see whether there be in him the love of peace and unity, the love of the Church that is spread over the whole earth. . . . There cannot be love without the Spirit of God."[22] In a number of passages, Augustine directly identifies this charity with the Holy Spirit.[23] By the love that is the gift of the Holy Spirit, Christians are made to be—in the words that are central to Augustine's view of monasticism—"of one soul and one heart toward God."[24]

As in De moribus, charity is the bond of the Church, but now Augustine sees it as the supernatural gift of the Holy Spirit and thus ultimately invisible. Its primary outward sign is the unity of minds and hearts in the Church. "How shall we not be in darkness? If we love the brethren. How is it proved that we love the brotherhood? By this, that we do not rend unity, that we hold fast charity."[25] Thus, in the case of the Donatists, the simple fact of their schism from the main body of the Church establishes that they do not possess charity. After citing 1 Corinthians 13:1-3, Augustine goes on in De baptismo, "But those are wanting in God's love who do not care for the unity of the Church; and consequently we are right in understanding that the Holy Spirit may be said not to be received except in the Catholic Church."[26]

IV. The Empirical Church and the True Church

Already in De moribus, Augustine had contrasted Christian and Manichaean asceticism in terms of their intention, Christian love versus Manichaean fears of uncleanness.[27] In the anti-Donatist writings, intention plays a greater role, as a determinant both of the morality of actions and of sacramental efficacy. "Not what the man does is the thing to be considered; but with what mind and will he does it."[28] Without the intention of charity, no action is good, not even almsgiving or martyrdom.[29] Therefore, even if the Donatists acted in all respects exactly as did the Church of De moribus, their schism would nullify any salvific value in their actions.[30] Within the Catholic church, however, "Charity covers a multitude of sins" (1 Peter 4:8); it enables the forgiveness of those sins which even the baptized Christian will still commit.

> And how fares it with him concerning his other sins, of which it is said, "If we say that we have no sin, we deceive ourselves, and the truth is not in us" [1 John 1:8]? Let him hear that which will set his mind at rest from another place of Scripture; "Charity covers a multitude of sins."[31]

Thus, Augustine's emphasis on the supernatural gift of charity as the basis of the true Church leads to a decreased importance of the empirical holiness of the Church, whether Donatist or Catholic. In the Pelagian controversy, this becomes more explicit still, though there the discussion is put in terms of the gift of faith rather than of charity; see especially the striking passage in Contra duas epistolas Pelagianorum 3.5.14, where Augustine at some length contrasts a person who exercises perfect sexual continence, has sold all his property and given it to the poor, does not ask for return of what has been taken from him, but is damned for lack of "true and certain faith," with another who has intercourse with his wife for pleasure, becomes angry when injured, contends in court for his property, does not give alms liberally, but is forgiven by God and saved for his faith.[32]

Not only does charity avail to forgive sins, but there are many within the empirical church who do not belong to the true Church, the brotherhood of charity. In De moribus, Augustine acknowledged the existence of such people, who will be separated like weeds from the wheat at the final judgment, but he seemed to regard them as an insignificant minority. In the Donatist controversy, they became more important in his view of the Church. Augustine constantly contrasts the Donatists' unwillingness to tolerate those guilty of traditio, or those who have contracted guilt through baptism or ordination by traditores or association with them in churchly fellowship, with the Catholics' tolerance of sinners within their communion.[33] His repeated response to Cyprian's claims, upheld by the Donatists, that baptism by heretics is invalid, is to parallel baptism by heretics with baptism by wicked Christians.[34] In contrast to De moribus, the "weeds" within the Church are now seen as the majority. Thus,

> Others are said to be in the house [the Church] after such a sort, that they belong not to the substance of the house, nor to the society of fruitful and peaceful justice, but only as the chaff is said to be among the corn. . . . Of this countless multitude are found to be the crowd which within the Church afflicts the hearts of the saints, who are so few in comparison with so vast a host. . . .[35]

Likewise, in De catechizandis rudibus (405), Augustine speaks of the "many drunkards, covetous, defrauders, gamblers, adulterers, fornicators," etc., in the Church, and of "those crowds [which] fill the churches on the feast days of the Christians which likewise fill the theaters on the ritual days of the pagans," and refers to them as a temptation to God's elect.[36]

The true Church, "composed of those that are good and faithful, and of the holy servants of God dispersed throughout the world, and bound together by the unity of the Spirit [spiritali unitate], whether they know each other personally or not,"[37] is thus only a minority within the empirical church, and this minority is ultimately invisible. "Certainly it is clear that, when we speak of within and without in relation to the Church, it is the position of the heart that we must consider, not that of the body."[38] The true Church is, in language Augustine begins to use in De catechizandis rudibus, one of "two cities," whose members are "united to one another by the likeness of their ways and deserts,"[39] the City of God, "created . . . by the love of God carried as far as the contempt of self."[40] The relation of the City of God to the empirical church in Augustine is a difficult question.[41] The City of God is invisible, yet is sometimes seemingly identified by Augustine with the visible church, in which alone, possessing true faith, true baptism, and proper concern for unity, it can be found. For present purposes, though, it is sufficient to recognize that it does not include many, perhaps most, of the members of the empirical church. Thus the way of life of the members of the empirical church cannot be directly used as evidence of the truth of their faith.

It might seem that Augustine could continue at least to use the lives of monastic communities in the Catholic church in this way, as he did in De moribus. For despite his increasingly negative view of the lives of most members of the empirical church, he retains a generally positive view of the life of monks. In 407, he rebuts Donatist criticism of monks by a favorable comparison of their lives with those of the Donatist Circumcellions.[42] A monastic community, Augustine says, quoting St. Paul, should be "a spectacle to the world."[43] In monks' daily lives, "through all the passing needs of men's lives something sublime and permanent will be revealed, namely charity."[44] In this, monks manifest what the true Church is and the empirical church ought to be but often is not, the community of those bound together as one by charity.[45] Despite this, Augustine does not appeal to the lives of monastic communities as evidence of the truth or the divine basis of their faith. To the extent that he uses monastic life for apologetic purposes, it is for a different sort of "apologetics," one motivated "by the desire to hold up to the worldly Christians of his day a supreme ideal of life."[46]

The distance Augustine has travelled from De moribus is perhaps clearest of all in Letter 208, written in 423. It is addressed to Felicia, a virgin and apparently a former Donatist, who is troubled by the scandalous behavior of some Catholic clergy and tempted to revert to Donatism. Even among bishops, Augustine says, there are sheep and goats, good grain and chaff, the latter of which will ultimately be separated out by God. The Donatists arrogate to themselves the task of separation, which belongs to God, but in reality those who are tainted by schism cannot have an untainted flock. We ought instead "to persevere to the end, . . . and by the strong weight of our charity to bear with the lightness of the straw."[47] Good Catholics, though they seek to imitate good clergy, do not place their hope in human ministers, but in the Lord. As for the Donatists, however, "even if an apparently laudable conduct seems to point out some of them as good, the very division makes them bad."[48] Her own virginity would profit her nothing if she "were to go out of this world separated from the unity of Christ's Body."[49]

V. Knowledge of God through Sacramental Practice

Augustine continues to see the Church as the community bound together by true charity. But in the controversy against the Donatists he emphasizes the invisible nature of the supernatural gift of charity. Exemplary moral conduct is no sure sign of it, and hence the exemplary behavior of Catholic Christian communities cannot safely be used as evidence of the truth and divine basis of Catholic Christian faith to outsiders. This very development in Augustine's thought, however, actually enhances the role of community life for Catholic Christians, as a context for and a means to understanding God and God's relationship with his people.

Augustine in his later writings continues to emphasize, indeed gives greater emphasis to, the dependence of knowledge upon love. As he increasingly emphasizes the further point that true love of God and neighbor is found only in the Catholic church, it follows with greater force that there alone is true knowledge of God: "for the only way to truth is by love, and 'the love of God,' says the apostle, 'is shed abroad in our hearts by the Holy Spirit who is given unto us.' "[50] As Augustine identifies this charity with the Holy Spirit, so that by living in charity one is sharing in the divine life, he can more clearly affirm a connection between Christian life and the knowledge of God, which he has all along held to be a participation in the eternal Word of God. Thus, in De Trinitate, growth in love and growth in knowledge of God are mutually reinforcing aspects of Christians' renewal in the trinitarian image of God, which is a participation in the Trinity itself.[51]

Simply to become aware of the fraternal charity which constitutes the Church is therefore to experience God.

> You may say to me, I have not seen God; can you say to me, I have not seen man? Love your brother. For if you love your brother whom you see, at the same time you will see God also, because you will see Charity itself, and within dwells God.[52] Let us purge the eye by which God can be seen. . . . There is something you may imagine, if you would see God; "God is love." What sort of face has love? what form has it? what stature? what feet? what hands has it? no man can say. And yet it has feet, for these carry men to church; it has hands, for these reach forth to the poor; it has eyes, for thereby we consider the needy. . . .[53]

This love is a starting point for growth in all knowledge of God, as in De Trinitate 8.8.12 it is the starting point for Augustine's exploration of the Trinitarian image within human subjectivity. Of course it must be coordinated with study of the Scriptures and Church doctrine, as De Trinitate 8-15 is coordinated with De Trinitate 1-7, but progressing in love is part of the way one comes to understand what the scriptures and doctrines mean.

> For that cannot be loved which is altogether unknown. But when what is known, in however small a measure, is also loved, by the self-same love one is led on to a better and fuller knowledge. If, then, you grow in the love which the Holy Spirit spreads abroad in your hearts, "He will teach you all truth" [John 16:13]. . . . So shall the result be, that not from outward teachers will you learn those things which the Lord at that time declined to utter, but be all taught of God; so that the very things which you have learned and believed by means of lessons and

sermons supplied from without regarding the nature of God . . . your
minds themselves may have the power to perceive.[54]

Participation in the community of that love which is the gift of the
Holy Spirit is, we might conclude, necessary for sound theology.

When Augustine draws on the life of the church as a theological
resource in his later writings, he does not pay especial attention to
the exemplary moral behavior of Christians. Neither does he draw
on the more structured life of charity which characterizes monastic
communities. What really matters as a sign of the presence of true
charity in a Christian community is the preservation of unity with
the Catholic church in sacramental practice. It is that sacramental
practice upon which Augustine primarily draws in relating Christian
life to Christian knowledge.

"There can be no religious society, whether the religion be true or
false, without some sacrament or visible symbol to serve as a bond
of union."[55] If the Church, the community of love in the Holy Spirit,
is in a sense the body of God, as depicted in the passage from *In
epistolam Johannis* 7.10 quoted above,[56] God especially ought to be
able to be seen in the outward acts which constitute Church as a
visible community. Accordingly, the Church's sacramental practices
increasingly become a point from which, rather than to which, Augustine's theological arguments proceed. This is particularly true in
De baptismo, where he has to defend, against the authority of Cyprian, the Church's practice of not rebaptizing those baptized by
heretics and schismatics. Mindful of the reproach, "The Lord says
in the gospel, 'I am the Truth.' He does not say, 'I am custom,' "[57]
Augustine acknowledges that custom must give way to manifest truth.
"But when truth supports custom, nothing should be more strongly
maintained."[58] The custom in question is not decisively refuted by
the arguments of Cyprian and his colleagues, or of the Donatists, and
therefore it is the "safest plan" (*tutissima ratio*)[59] to abide by it. It
is probably of apostolic origin, like many other practices which are
universal in the Church are but not found in Scripture or the proceedings of councils.[60] In an argument reminiscent of his defense of
the *auctoritas* of the Catholic Church against the Manichaeans,[61]
Augustine admits he might have been converted to Cyprian's views,

had I not been induced to consider the matter more carefully by the
vast weight of authority, originating in those whom the Church, distributed throughout the world amid so many nations . . ., has been able
to produce . . ., men whom I could in no wise bring myself to think
had been unwilling without reason to hold this view, . . . because one
must not lightly, without full consideration and investigation of the
matter to the best of his abilities, decide in favor of a single individual,

or even of a few, against the decision of so very many men of the same
religion and communion, all endowed with great talent and abundant
learning.[62]

Augustine is writing *De baptismo* at about the same time as he is
finishing the *Confessions*, and one can see in his account of salutary
consuetudo in *De baptismo* the inverse of his account of sinful *consuetudo* in the *Confessions*. Book 8 of the *Confessions* portrays Augustine struggling to exercise free choice against the weight, or chains,
of *consuetudo*, built up by sin and ultimately the result of Adam's
sin.[63] Though this is expressed primarily in terms of Augustine's
individual will, the *Confessions* already show a collective dimension
to sin, especially in Book 2. It is not a great step to his later view of
the two cities and to seeing the *civitas terrena* as a *massa damnata*
through the force of sinful *consuetudines*, while the City of God is
"bound together by the powerful bond of custom,"[64] the *consuetudines* of sacramental practice.

These customs are an essential part of the outward expression of
the love which is (or is of) the Holy Spirit and which binds the true
Church together. Without them, one does not abide in the love that
leads to true knowledge of God. In turn, they themselves become
charged "with a mysterious and enduring validity."[65] As the outward
expression of God's sharing of his own life with humankind, they
assume a position like that of the Scriptures as a basis for knowing
God and his relationship with his people. In Augustine's own theology, the most obvious example is his reliance on the practice of
infant baptism. In *De baptismo*, Augustine is defending infant baptism as "the firm tradition of the universal Church." It may be difficult to explain what it effects in infants, "yet no Christian will say
that they are baptized to no purpose."[66] In the controversy against
the Pelagians, it becomes clear to him what that purpose is, to free
them from inherited original sin:

> Whosoever denies this, is convicted by truth of the Church's very sac-
> raments, which no heretical novelty in the Church of Christ is permitted
> to destroy or change, so long as the Divine Head rules and helps the
> entire body which he owns. . . .[67]

VI. Conclusion

Thus, as Augustine's thought develops, the theological importance
of Christian community life increases, even as its availability for
apologetics diminishes. In *De moribus ecclesiae catholicae*, Augustine can point to the Church and say to those outside the Church,
"See how love rules the lives of these people," even though he admits

that some do not live in this love. But against the Donatists he comes to the view that only relatively few Catholic Christians really live in charity, and that it may not be outwardly evident who they are, for the gift of the Holy Spirit is invisible. While monastic communities above all others should continue to manifest this love, Augustine is now concerned with the example they set for other Catholic Christians rather than for those outside the Church. The visible sign of the true Church, the community of charity, which comes to be really important for Augustine is no longer the moral behavior of Christians but their unity in the practice of the sacraments. This is in one sense only a negative sign—no one who does not participate in this unity can belong to the true community of love—and thus it is a necessary but not a sufficient condition for a proper understanding of God. But, positively, the sacraments which bind the Church can, for those who partake of them and reflect upon them, become a uniquely privileged source of understanding of God and of themselves in relation to God.

This last point is continuous with the overall argument of De moribus, when read together with the Confessions, that one's commitment to the Catholic faith will be "verified" in one's growth in religious understanding and in a congruous and satisfactory way of life within the Catholic church. But for two reasons this argument is no longer used, and no longer available for use in apologetics. The first is Augustine's insistence on the invisible nature of the true Church. The second is Augustine's unwillingness or inability to defend, on grounds with which his opponents might reasonably be expected to agree, his claim about the true Church: that it is the communion of true salvific faith and charity, and while not coextensive with the visible Catholic church, does not extend beyond those baptized and in union with it.

The connection of Christian practice with Christian truth—that Christian practice can serve as a ground for belief in the truth of, and a means for the understanding of, what Christians believe—is an important, though neglected, element in Augustine's thought. It is one which is congruent with much of contemporary philosophy as well as with such theological movements as liberation theology. Retrieval of this theme in Augustine can make a significant contribution to contemporary theology.[68] But, seen from a contemporary point of view, there are serious weaknesses in both phases of Augustine's thought studied in this paper.

De moribus ecclesiae catholicae rightly keeps before us the point that the life of Christian communities is the strongest factor in Christian apologetics, serving not only to make Christian commitment more attractive but actually to make it more reasonable. As George Lindbeck states, in his own "cultural-linguistic" theory of religion which bears some affinity with Augustine's understanding of religion, "Apologetics becomes primarily a matter of appropriate communal praxis."[69] But Augustine's view of the Church in De moribus is vulnerable to the strictures against "Augustinian perfectionism," with which Archbishop Rembert Weakland recently made headlines.[70] It can lead either to an unrealistic assessment of actual Christian behavior or to a sectarian view, like Lindbeck's, which confines the Church to those actually living exemplary Christian lives, such as monks.

To this the idea of the "mixed church" in the anti-Donatist writings is preferable; it reminds us that, as Archbishop Weakland says, "The church is a broken society . . . we live in a community of broken people . . . we minister as broken people."[71] But Augustine's version of this idea is weakened by a dualism between the "elect" who truly belong to the city of God and the majority of members of the empirical church, who do not ultimately share in the divine life—a dualism stronger than his earlier Manichaean dualism between the "elect" and the "hearers." At least the Manichaean "hearers" could be reincarnated as "elect." A more adequate approach, consistent with other elements of Augustine's thought, and certainly more likely to lead to the kind of community life conducive to an apologetic use, would be to emphasize that Christian community life manifests, or ought to manifest, the divine life of charity despite and even in the human brokenness of the church collectively and its members individually.

Augustine's later view of the Church also seems unduly to narrow the epistemologically significant elements of church life to sacramental practice rather than moral conduct. This undercuts somewhat the case he makes in his early writings for the moral auctoritas of the Catholic church, and limits the range of Christian practice on which he draws for understanding Christian doctrine. But, from Augustine's point of view, this limitation is necessary, because the maintenance of unity in sacramental practice (a compliance with church "authority" in a different sense) is the only guarantee that apparently exemplary moral conduct really is motivated by genuine charity. Perhaps a modern retrieval of Augustine's linkage between Christian communal practice and Christian understanding could diverge from Augustine at this point, and see God's "body" on earth not only in the "feet" that "carry men to church," but also, in the "hands" that "reach forth to the poor" and the "eyes" that "consider the needy" whether inside or outside the Catholic or even baptized Christian community.[72]

NOTES

1. *De moribus ecclesiae catholicae* (*De mor. eccl.*) (388), 30.62 (J.-P. Migne, *Patrologia Latina* [PL] 32, col. 1336), here quoted in English translation by Donald A. and Idella J. Gallagher, *The Catholic and Manichean Ways of Life*, volume 56 of *The Fathers of the Church: A New Translation* [FC] (Washington, D.C.: The Catholic University of America Press, 1966). This paper uses "Catholic" and "Catholic Christian" in Augustine's sense, to refer to Catholic Christians as distinct from Donatists, Manichaeans, etc.

2. *De mor. eccl.* 33.73 (PL 32, col. 1341).

3. *De mor. eccl.* 34.75 (PL 32, col. 1342).

4. *De vera religione* (390), 3.5 (*Corpus Christianorum Series Latina* [CCSL] 32, pp. 191–92); *De utilitate credendi* (391) 17.35 (*Corpus Scriptorum Ecclesiasticorum Latinorum* [CSEL] 25, 1, p. 145).

5. Gerald Bonner, *St. Augustine of Hippo: Life and Controversies* (Philadelphia: Westminster, 1963), p. 231.

6. William Collinge, "The Role of Christian Community Life in Augustine's Apologetics," *Augustinian Studies* 14 (1983): 63–73.

7. In addition to the article cited in note 6, see William Collinge, "Augustine and Theological Falsification," *Augustinian Studies* 13 (1982): 43–54.

8. See, for instance, *De ordine* 2.9. 26–27 (CSEL 63, pp. 165–66), *Soliloquia* 1.6.12 (PL 32, col. 875–76).

9. *De diversis questionibus 83*, 48 (391) (CCSL 44A, p. 75).

10. *De mor. eccl.* 17.30–31 (PL 32, col. 1324).

11. See *De mor. eccl.* 2.3 and 30.62.

12. For an account of Donatism and Augustine's conflict with it, see Bonner, pp. 237–311.

13. Bonner, pp. 284–86; Peter Brown, *Augustine of Hippo* (Berkeley and Los Angeles: University of California Press, 1969), p. 214.

14. Quoted in Augustine, *Contra litteras Petiliani* (*C. litt. Pet.*) 2. 39.92 (CSEL 52, p. 75), English translation by Rev. J. R. King, in volume 4 of *A Select Library of the Nicene and Post-Nicene Fathers of the Christian Church* [NPF], First Series (New York: Charles Scribner's Sons, 1887).

15. Brown, pp. 219–20.

16. This is a recurrent argument in *De baptismo Contra Donatistas* (*De bap.*) (ca. 400); see, for instance 4.4.5 (CSEL 51, p. 226). (4.4.6 in English translation, by Rev. J. R. King, NPF 4).

17. For example, *C. litt. Pet.* 2.23.53 (CSEL 52, pp. 51–52).

18. *De gestis Pelagii* 12.27 (CSEL 42, p. 80). See Brown, p. 348.

19. J. Patout Burns, *The Development of Augustine's Doctrine of Operative Grace* (Paris: Etudes Augustiniennes, 1980), p. 69. This book is a major source for my view of the general development of Augustine's thought.

20. Burns, p. 59.

21. *De bap.* 3.16.21 (CSEL 51, p. 212).

22. *In epistolam Johannis ad Parthos Tractatus* (*In ep. Joh.*) (before 410; 406–7?) 6.10 (PL 35, col. 2025–26), English translation by Rev. H. Browne, revised by Rev. Joseph H. Myers, NPF 7, diction and punctuation here modernized.

23. *In ep. Joh.* 3.12, 6.8, 7.6 (PL 35, cols. 2004, 2024, 2032); *In Johannis evangelium Tractatus* [*In Joh. ev.*] (after 410) 32.8 (CCSL 36, p. 305); *De Trinitate* 15. 18.32, 15. 19.37 (CCSL 50A, pp. 508, 513).

24. Acts 4.32, as cited in *In Joh. ev.* 39.5 (CCSL 36, pp. 347–48). Augustine habitually adds "toward God" (*in Deum*) to the Lucan text. On Augustine's use of this text, see Luc Verheijen, *Saint Augustine's Monasticism in the Light of Acts 4.32–35* (Villanova, PA: Villanova University Press, 1979).

25. *In ep. Joh.* 2.3 (PL 35, col. 1992).

26. *De baptismo* 3.16.21 (CSEL 51, p. 212), verb singular in first clause in Latin text.

27. *De mor. eccl.* 33.72–73 (PL 32, col. 1341).

28. *In ep. Joh.* 7.7 (PL 35, col. 2033) See also *In ep. Joh.* 8.5, 8.9, 10.7 (PL 35, cols. 2038, 2040–41, 2059); *De bap.* 6.25.47 (CSEL 51, pp. 323–24): *De opere monachorum* (400–01) 25.32, 26.34 (CSEL 41, pp. 578–79, 581); Burns, pp. 59–63 and texts cited there.

29. *In ep. Joh.* 6.2 (PL 35, col. 2020), *De bap.* 1.8.10–9.12 (CSEL 51, pp. 155–58)

30. *De bap.* 1.9.12 (CSEL 51, pp. 157–58).

31. *In ep. Joh.* 5.3 (PL 35, col. 2014).

32. *Contra duas epistulas Pelagianorum* 3.5.14 (CSEL 60, pp. 502–03). Part of this passage is quoted in Brown, p. 348.

33. See, for instance, *De bap.* 4.9.12–4.12.18 (CSEL 51, pp. 238–244) (4.9.13–4.12.19 in English translation).

34. For instance, *De bap.* 4.4.5 (CSEL 51, p. 226) (4.4.6 in Eng.).

35. *De bap.* 7.51.99 (CSEL 51, p. 371); see also *De bap.* 5.27.38–28.39 (CSEL 51, pp. 293–97).

36. *De catech. rud.* 25.48 (CCSL 46, pp. 171-2). English translation by Rev. Joseph P. Christopher, *Ancient Christian Writers*, vol. 2

37. *De bap.* 7.51.99 (CSEL 51, p. 371).

38. *De bap.* 5.28.39 (CSEL 51, p. 296).

39. *De catech. rud.* 19.31 (CCSL 46, p. 156).

40. *De civitate Dei* 14.28 (413–26) (CCSL 48, p. 451). English translation by Henry Bettenson (Harmondsworth: Penguin Books, 1972).

41. See Gerhart Ladner, *The Idea of Reform: Its Impact on Christian Thought and Action in the Age of the Fathers* (New York: Harper Torchbooks, 1967 [1959]), pp. 239–83, esp. 259–79.

42. *Enarrationes in Psalmos* [*En. Psalm.*] 132.6 (407) (CCSL 40, p. 1930).

43. 1 Corinthians 4:9, quoted in *Sermo* 356.1 (426) (PL 39, col. 1574).

44. *The Rule of St. Augustine* 5.2 (*Praeceptum*), text in Luc Verheijen, *La Règle de Saint Augustine, I: Tradition Manuscrite* (Paris: Etudes Augustiniennes, 1967), p. 430. Translation by Mary T. Clark in *Augustine of Hippo: Selected Writings* (New York: Paulist, 1984).

45. See *En. Psalm.* 132.1 (CCSL 40, p. 1927); Verheijen, *St. Augustine's Monasticism* (note 24 above), p. 65; Ladner, pp. 361–62.

46. Ladner, p. 275.

47. *Epistula* [*Ep.*] 208, 4 (CSEL 57, p. 344), English translation by Sr. Wilfrid Parsons, S.N.D., FC 32.

48. *Ep.* 208, 6 (CSEL 57, p. 346).

49. *Ep.* 208, 7 (CSEL 57, p. 346).

50. *Contra Faustum Manichaeum* 32.18 (397–8) (CSEL 25, 1, p. 779). English translation by Rev. Richard Stothert, NPF 4.

51. William Collinge, "*De Trinitate* and the Understanding of Religious Language" (1977), accepted for publication by *Augustinian Studies*.

52. *In ep. Joh.* 5.7 (PL 35, col. 2016). See the closely parallel text in *De Trinitate* 8.8.12 (CCSL 50, pp. 286–87).

53. *In ep. Joh.* 7.10 (PL 35, col. 2034).

54. *In Joh. ev.* 96.4 (CCSL 36, p. 571), English translation by Rev. James Innes, NPF 7.

55. *Contra Faustum Manichaeum* 19.11 (CSEL 25, 1, p. 510).

56. Text at note 53.

57. Libosus of Vaga, quoted in *De bap.* 3.6.9, 6.37.71 (CSEL 51, pp. 203, 334).

58. *De bap.* 4.5.7 (CSEL 51, p. 228) (4.5.8 in Engl.).

59. *De bap.* 3.2.3 (CSEL 51, p. 198).

60. *De bap.* 2.7.12 (CSEL 51, p. 187).

61. *Contra epistolam Manichaei quam vocant Fundamenti* 4.5 (397) (CSEL 25, 1, p. 196).

62. *De bap.* 3.4.6 (CSEL 51, 202).

63. *Confessiones* 8.5.10, 8.9.21, 8.10.22 (CCSL 27, pp. 119, 126–27).

64. *De bap.* 2.9.14 (CSEL 51, p. 189).

65. Brown, p. 222.

66. *De bap.* 4.23.30 (CSEL 51, p. 258) (4.23.31 in Engl.).

67. *De nuptiis et concupiscentia* 1.20.22 (419–20) (CSEL 42, p. 235), English translation by Peter Holmes, NPF 5.

68. I argue this point in "The Relation of Religious Community Life to Rationality in Augustine," delivered at the 1985 Annual Meeting of the College Theology Society and accepted for publication in *Faith and Philosophy*. I wrote that paper and this one in close succession and as parts of the same project, and revision for separate publication has increased their overlap. Still, the overlapping themes, which are here treated from a theological and historical point of view, are there dealt with from a philosophical point of view.

69. George Lindbeck, *The Nature of Doctrine* (Philadelphia: Westminster, 1984), p. 12.

70. "Weakland Warns of Neo-Augustinianism in Church," *National Catholic Reporter* 23:4 (November 14, 1986), p. 2. I wish to thank Archbishop Weakland for sending me a copy of the full text of the talk quoted here, delivered before the annual conference of the Call to Action organization, Chicago, November 1, 1986.

71. "Weakland Warns," p. 2.

72. Text at note 53 above.

THE HISTORIAN AND THE REFORMER: GAINING A CRITICAL PERSPECTIVE ON THE ISSUE OF AUTHORITY

Jo Ann Eigelsbach

ABSTRACT

While many recognize the necessity of the recovery of authority as rooted in community and consensus, the vision of the Early Church as a "Golden Age" dissolves into romanticism without analytic tools that can address the complex history of ideas and events which determine the contemporary situation. The historian can bring to light an ongoing history of contexts that shape the assumptions and imaginative framework in which the options of our own time may be understood.

In view of the larger project of historical understanding and critical analysis, this essay presents one late nineteenth century perspective, that of Wilfrid Philip Ward, disciple of Newman and key English Roman Catholic writer and editor during the Modernist Controversy. Bernard Lonergan's description of the dialectic of authority from community to institutional complexity, and Matthew Lamb's discussion of pluralist political dialectics are presented as tools for analysis of the issue of authority at the turn of the century and in the present.

Contemporary conflicts over the understanding and exercise of authority in the Church are the product of a complex history of ideas and events. Awareness of this history is invaluable; to criticize or to attempt to reform what one does not understand is an exercise in futility.

At present, many recognize the necessity of the recovery of authority as rooted in community and consensus, and often their frame of reference is a vision of the New Testament or of the Early Church

Jo Ann Eigelsbach received the M.A. in Historical Theology from Marquette University and the Ph.D. in Religious Studies from The Catholic University of America. She has taught at Catholic University and Loyola College and developed courses for adults and catechists on a variety of topics. She is a member of the AAR Working Group on Roman Catholic Modernism and the Lonergan Workshop. Her publications include, "The Intellectual Dialogue of Friedrich von Hügel and Wilfrid Ward" in The Downside Review for April 1986.

as a "golden age." The insight dissolves into romantic nostalgia if left at that, without the analytic tools that can address the situation in the complexity of its sociological, political, economic, cultural, and philosophical dimensions.

What is chosen and acted upon must first be conceived as possible; what is not envisioned within the range of possibility cannot be chosen. Behind every choice, every movement for change or reform, lies a spectrum of imaginative options. Towards a deeper understanding, the historian can bring to light the assumptions that lay behind concrete historical options and the imaginative frameworks out of which they emerged. The horizons of the past comprise an ongoing history of contexts that shape the assumptions and imaginative framework in which the historical options of our own time may be understood.

The nineteenth century was a critical period for church authority as the Papacy struggled for power and identity in the social upheavals and political realignment of Europe, and new currents of thought challenged the assumptions and conclusions of an ahistorical scholastic philosophy. Two general lines could be taken: religious authority stood or fell with the old political order which therefore must be preserved; or a new understanding of religious authority was required in the new situation. Roman Catholic thinkers responded to the crisis, working out various understandings of authority in the Church. Among these responses was that of Wilfrid Philip Ward, disciple of Newman and key English Roman Catholic writer and editor at the time of the Modernist Controversy.

In view of the larger project of historical understanding and critical analysis, this essay presents and evaluates Ward's views and concrete strategies. Bernard Lonergan's description of the dialectic of authority from community to institutional complexity, and Matthew Lamb's discussion of pluralist political dialectics provide tools for analysis of the issue of authority in Ward's time and in our own.

I. The Intelligibility of Authority

Authority is legitimate power.[1] This power originates in the cooperation and consensus of a community in the present and in history, and functions to meet the needs and promote the interests of the community. A community is a group united by common experience, understanding, judgments and goals. As social organization becomes more complex, authority functions to bring the achievements of the past into the present, to organize and direct the hierarchy of cooperating groups, distribute the fruits of cooperation, and exclude disruptive elements. Commonly understood and accepted patterns of cooperation evolve into institutions within which individuals are designated as authorities: leaders in times of stress; judges in disputes; and other functionaries.

The Dialectic of Authority

The legitimacy of authority depends on the authenticity of the common meanings and values of the tradition and of persons and communities at each level and stage in the process. Authenticity is never a secure once-for-all achievement. The way authority is exercised in a community can promote or restrict responsible human freedom and its self-corrective process.

At any level and stage in the development of the tradition the option of inauthenticity is possible and the inauthentic response can become part of the common heritage of knowledge and policies.[2] The structures of authority established in the community promote the self-corrective process of responsible human freedom when they permit the questions to be raised that would allow the fruits of inattentiveness, misunderstanding, irrationality, and irresponsibility to be revealed and corrected.

When the established structures of authority in the community impose and reinforce systems of thought and action so that the natural self-corrective process of human intelligence is impeded, authority promotes inauthenticity in the tradition and at the same time calls its own legitimacy into question. When this situation becomes extreme, revolutionary change that would dismantle and reorganize the structures of the community may be the recourse of those who seek to recover the authenticity of the tradition, and their response, in turn, would have its own possibilities of authenticity or inauthenticity.

The dialectic of authority is the complex and concrete interaction of authenticity and inauthenticity in the community as a whole, in its designated authorities, and in the individuals who are subject to those authorities. In a global view, it appears in the conflict between an institutional ideal and its imperfect realizations.

Lonergan uses an heuristic construct, Cosmopolis, to describe the possible corrective to the cycle of decline that results when new ideas with the potential to reform and develop the tradition are suppressed by a dominant group in the name of practicality.[3] Cosmopolis represents a possible critical viewpoint that identifies the good neither with the new nor with the old, that challenges the notion that only ideas backed by force can be operative, and that witnesses to the possibility of ideas being operative without such backing.

Lonergan's framework outlines the development of the function of authority from simple to complex, from community to institution, its developments and aberrations. This provides a tool for analysis of the dialectic of authority in particular situations, and establishes a starting point for discussion. It also provides a frame of reference for awareness of the historian's own understanding of authority, which, although bracketed in the attempt to reveal Ward's particular horizon as expressed in his own terms, nevertheless operates as background to the telling of the story. The frame of reference once again comes to the fore when the historian wants to move out of the story to reflect, analyze, make comparisons, draw conclusions, and to invite dialogue and criticism.

II. *Wilfrid Ward*

Wilfrid Philip Ward, a key figure in English Roman Catholicism from 1882 to 1916, was the son of the famous Ultramontane W. G. Ward. He dissociated himself from his father's views and became the disciple of Newman, interpreting Newman's vision of the Church for a troubled time. On the one hand, he saw the necessity of authority and viewed the principle of authority in the Church as the bulwark of social order. He also realized the critical importance of grounding the principle of religious authority in terms intelligible to modern science and philosophy. On the other hand, he recognized the need for reform. From Newman he derived a model that would allow for gradual reform without endangering the necessary principle of authority.

The heart of Ward's life and work was his preoccupation with a two-fold challenge to Catholic faith: from without, the spread of agnosticism and skepticism; and, from within, the necessity of reform. At a time when Catholic writers usually appealed to a small intellectually isolated audience, Ward's essays presented the case for the intellectual credibility of theism and of Roman Catholicism in the public forum of the most prestigious periodicals of his time. His biographies of W. G. Ward, Cardinal Wiseman, and Cardinal Newman are noted for their excellence. As editor of *The Dublin Review*, the leading Catholic periodical in England, he broadened its scope and readership.

Ward believed that inevitable and necessary reform was best introduced in the context of an historical understanding of the fundamental principles of Christianity, which included adaptation to changing philosophical and cultural contexts. In this way, revolutionary changes could be accomplished with a minimum of unsettlement to people's spiritual lives. His popular essays and reviews offered a view of Christianity in an historical, evolutionary framework, that was designed to establish a context for understanding the changes necessary in the contemporary situation.

III. Authority: Ward's Spectrum of Options

Protestant Liberalism

Ward had an ongoing quarrel with the Protestant Liberal position represented by Matthew Arnold and Arnold's niece, novelist Mrs. Humphrey Ward. To Ward, they represented a second and third generation of the attitude of the Oxford Noetics, who accepted no authority and subjected all premises to the questioning of individual reason.[4] The loss of the guiding principle of authority which counterbalanced the skeptical tendencies of individual reason had ultimately led to agnosticism or an unacceptable "Reduced Christianity."[5]

Ahistorical Scholasticism

The manual theology of Wilfrid Ward's seminary days offered little that would achieve credibility with the broader intellectual public that Ward addressed. It defensively over-emphasized the role of authority, and presented it almost as an end in itself, detached from the workings of other elements in the Church. Authority was legitimated by an argument that Jesus, by miracles and the Resurrection, proved his claim to divine authority, which he delegated to the Church, handing over supernatural truths and promising the guidance of the Holy Spirit. Such supernatural legitimations, and their direct connection to the status quo, became problematic in the light of biblical and historical criticism.[6]

Ultramontanism

Wilfrid Ward's father, W. G. Ward, became famous for the jest that he would like to see a Papal Bull each day at breakfast with the Times.[7] In the course of his intellectual journey from the Liberalism of Thomas and Matthew Arnold to the Oxford Movement and eventually to Roman Catholicism, he became convinced that the independent intellect needed restraint and guidance, and that without them, pessimism and skepticism were inevitable. For him, the authority of Rome was the bulwark against intellectual chaos. A large number of infallible utterances was desirable, constituting firm ground in the midst of skepticism and agnosticism. He championed the Ultramontane cause in the debates of the 1860s and '70s.

However, while recognizing the *principle* of authority revered by the Ultramontanes as the bulwark against intellectual and social chaos, his son, Wilfrid Ward, objected to the canonization of its particular historical forms and the exaltation of Papal authority detached from its roots in the dynamics of the tradition.

For Wilfrid Ward, the options of Ultramontanism, Scholasticism, and Protestant Liberalism were unacceptable. He found in Newman the key to an adequate understanding of the proper relationship between authority and individual reason.

Newman

Ward's analysis of the Church, inspired by Newman, grounded the principle of a central authority in the common experience of the need to preserve group identity and continuity. He saw the need for the power of definitive judgment of conflicting interpretations of tradition—in Ward's view, an important advantage of the Roman Church over the Anglican, where no one party could claim to speak for the Church. He located the function of authority in the process of historical development, understood as a dynamic of resistance and assimilation. And he ultimately located the intelligibility of authority and of infallibility in the context of spirituality.[8]

IV. The Necessity and Character of Authority

Authority, in Ward's view, was the *Catholic* principle which stood in contrast to the *Protestant* principle of private judgment. It represented the time-honored wisdom of tradition in contrast to the assertions of individual reason. The excesses of individual reason set loose by the Enlightenment had become a disintegrating force in society, and the corrective of authority was needed. The wisdom of the Christian tradition safeguarded in the Roman Catholic Church by the principle of authority, was, for Newman and for Ward, the only viable opponent to the forces of atheism and secularism.[9] Ward offered his interpretation of a commonplace theory of sets of mutually conditioning orders. The order of society depended on morality, and morality ultimately depended on religious conviction, engendered and supported by the structures of the institutional church. The integrity of the Christian tradition could only be maintained by the authority and discipline that the Roman Catholic Church alone had preserved.

Authority and Reason

Authority was the necessary and natural counterweight to individual reason. Ward, following Newman, understood reason as a secondary operation working from the basis of first principles but not establishing them. When individual reason tried to prove or establish first principles, skepticism was the inevitable result. He pointed out that "free" reason usually uncritically operated out of the reigning secularist and naturalist assumptions of the culture.[10] Authority, as the articulation of the wisdom of tradition, provided first principles and set the terms within which reason could successfully operate.[11]

Ward intended to move beyond positions that placed authority and reason in opposition, exalting one to the deprecation of the other.[12] Authority was the embodiment of "the reason of the race," and there was a mutually corrective relation between the individual reason and authority.

> . . . the reasoning of one generation naturally issues in conclusions which form the 'groundwork' of social life for the individuals in the next. And in this way a very few achievements of the individual Reason come to affect the whole race; and the successful struggle of Reason against Authority in one generation may issue in a change in the 'groundwork' which is due to Reason, although it does not necessarily affect all individuals through the medium of their own reasoning faculties.[13]

The role of the individual reason was to test in a limited way, use, and correct the larger fund of knowledge. The test of authority was a practical one, and practical certainty and trust in authority came from the gain in fruitfulness and coherence that the knowledge in question gave to individual experience.

Authority in the Context of Ward's Apologetics

Ward developed arguments that represented a new approach to apologetics, grounding belief in concrete experience rather than in abstract logic. He shifted the terms of the discussion from proof to practical certainty, and regarded the act of belief as an integrated process of action and reflection rather than the function of a detached reason.

Ward's apologetics for authority had a commonsense, practical basis. His concept of authority always had experiential and historical connotations, and never meant the absolute reign of "officialism."[14] Recognition of the existence and need for authority could be gained from observation of the interaction of communities and individuals in everyday life.[15] Authority represented the cumulative and enduring wisdom that outweighed the narrow range of knowledge available to personal experience. It made sense for the individual to make use of such a resource, and so the acceptance of authority could be a rational choice.

Ward distinguished blind trust from the intelligent use of authority, which he called "rational trust," and noted that such trust is a normal occurrence in everyday social life. Rational trust was based on the idea that individuals could understand a discovery or an expertise and see that it "worked" in practice sufficiently to place trust in the discoverer or expert, without having to repeat the discovery or having the expertise on their own.[16] If individuals found the authority trustworthy on points within the range of their experience, they could reasonably choose to extend that trust to areas beyond.

The individual depended on the expertise of others; in religion, this expertise was embodied in the tradition and authority functioned as the guardian of the tradition. Saints and mystics were the pioneers in religion, their perceptions were fully developed, whereas those of others were primitive. It was possible to place a rational trust in their vision and counsel as embodied in religious traditions.

For Ward, church authority was a specific instance of a general function necessary for the identity and continuity of any organization.

> All civilized communities draw up, as they grow, with increasing precision, the rules which experience shows to be necessary for their preservation. . . . The difficulties in allowing such claims . . . are difficulties not against modern Rome only, but against the action of the Christian Church from the first, in preserving unity of polity and doctrine by the exclusion of heresy.[17]

History demonstrated that the necessity of authority was simply a practical one. In contrast to the ahistorical emphasis on authority in the theology he studied as a seminarian, Ward viewed the function of authority within the evolutionary dynamics of tradition. It did not function alone or arbitrarily, but as one element in relation to others in a larger process.

Authority in an Evolutionary Context

The value of church authority was derived from its function in the process of development of the tradition. Ward's view of the progress of the Church involved an interaction of thinkers, saints, and rulers, representing the interests of truth, devotion, and stable rule. Each of these groups in its own way represented the corporate authority of the Church.[18] Rulers guarded the tradition established by the saints, and thinkers advanced the wisdom of the Church by creative intellect. Ward envisioned a balance of the mystical, intellectual, and governing functions comprising what he termed "the constitution of the Church."[19] Ward described the dynamic of the Church's development as one of *resistance and assimilation*. Resistance was the function of authority and assimilation was the task of individuals who carefully tested new theories. Ward's concern was for peaceful transitions in the process of development; both conservation and experimentation were necessary. Before the Modernist episode, he thought that if the preservation of the unity of faith must take precedence over intellectual advances in certain conflict situations, the assimilative principle would guarantee the eventual restoration of equilibrium. Later, he qualified the latitude he allowed for restraint.

The Uses and Abuses of Authority

In view of the balance of functions, Ward argued for both intellectual freedom and restraint, insisting that the power of restraint must be exercised with prudent judgment and that the role of church authority in intellectual matters necessitated consulting theological experts. In Ward's view, abuses of authority were ultimately self-destructive.

> To reject what is not mere brilliant speculation but is the practically unanimous verdict of the scholars, is unnecessary persecution; it may chasten a few, but many will rebel and feel that they have right on their side. The point comes at which submission of the human intellect amounts to a denial to it even of such powers as make a *rationabile obsequium* to the Church herself possible or reliable. Thus authority in forcing its prerogative may undermine the whole of its own basis.[20]

Ward also made it clear that he saw room for the functional adaptation of authority to differing circumstances, but allowed no compromise on the *principle* of authority. At the time of the discussion in the 1890's of Anglican-Roman Catholic Reunion he wrote:

> There may have to be great changes within the church before the separated bodies can again recognize her. But if no other principle, except that which she has retained, can ultimately withstand the inroads of religious negation, may we not hope that forces on all sides will even-

tually tend towards the desired reunion? The central Authority, as a fact, and not a mere name, is an essential part of the Church thus conceived. But its practical claims and action may vary in the future as they have in the past.[21]

While Ward's theology of the Church allowed authority a latitude with which Protestants and more democratically minded Catholics would be uncomfortable, he also brought the rationale for Church authority down to earth. The grounding of authority as practical necessity, and its interpretation as a function in dynamic relation to other functions, left its concrete form and exercise open in principle to adaptation and change.

V. Ward's Practical Strategies

Ward's essays were usually occasioned by specific events or contemporary articles or books. The 1890s were a time when ecumenical issues were of central interest in the discussion of Anglican Orders and of the attendance of Catholics at the national universities and in the Synthetic Society. Ward found himself in a awkward position as both reformer of, and apologist for Roman Catholicism. To argue for the reasonableness of Rome became difficult after the turn of the century, when the actions of Rome became increasingly defensive. The Joint Pastoral of 1900 and the Encyclical *Pascendi* in 1907 put Ward's views to the test in practical strategies.

The Joint Pastoral of 1900

In 1899, criticism of the actions of the hierarchy in the *Times* by distinguished Catholic scientist St. George Jackson Mivart provoked a controversy that led to his excommunication.[22] Sympathies for Mivart occasioned more outspoken criticisms in the press. Alarmed by this display, Ward hoped a cycle of rebellion and repression could be avoided, and warned "wise liberals" not to provoke authority.[23]

It seemed the cycle was to continue when, on December 31, 1900, the English bishops published a Joint Pastoral letter that outlined a view of the Church divided into two groups, the *ecclesia docens*, the teachers, which included the Pope and the bishops, and the *ecclesia discens*, the taught, which included everyone else, disparaging religious thinkers who would presume to instruct the hierarchy. By 1901 Ward was advising reformers on strategies for a time of repression.[24] The Pastoral insisted on the teaching of Vatican I on authority, but omitted the limitations that the Council had introduced. Such an unqualified assertion of the role of authority and the passivity of the laity left no room for Ward's vision of the Church or for the work that he espoused.

Ward regarded the Pastoral as based on a false analysis of the actual process observable in Church history. His response to the Pastoral was to avoid direct confrontation, yet go to the root of the problem by offering a more accurate analysis of the process and by interpreting the Pastoral in the context of other Church documents that would moderate its authoritarian claims.

Having attempted to neutralize the content of the Pastoral by outlining its proper context and function, Ward introduced the distinction between the roles of pastors and theologians in a commentary on Church history.

> Looking back now at the great Doctores Ecclesiae, with the halo round their brows, we may forget to separate their position from that of the pontiffs and bishops who in the long run have sanctioned the results of their labors. But in their own lifetime they did their work not, for the most part, in virtue of any position as members of the *Ecclesia docens*, but prompted by their loyalty, devotion, and genius, and sometimes in spite of opposition on the part of unworthier holders of official status. . . . A great pastor is therefore not a great Doctor Ecclesiae. . . . It is the select few . . . [theologians who] have been the very life of the Christian Church on the intellectual side, not the crowd of forgotten bishops, many of them excellent rulers, some of them good theologians, but many more of them men of action rather than of thought.[25]

In another article, "Liberalism as a Temper of Mind," Ward reflected on the best strategy for scholars in a time of repression. The opposition of authority could only be disarmed with solid research, and even under restrictions, there were still fields of research and thought where much useful work could be done. Students should follow Cardinal Newman's advice and accumulate facts rather than give vent to feelings. Ward cited St. Thomas: a tyrannical ruler must be proceeded against *non privata presumptione, sed auctoritate publica*.[26] Could not, he suggested, the gradual accumulation of the work of many scholars form a weight of opinion to be designated an *auctoritas publica*?

Ward and Pascendi

The Encyclical *Pascendi* dealt a crippling blow to the efforts of Roman Catholics to address the issues of modernity. Its sweeping condemnation of "Modernism" grouped together in one unholy fraternity everyone outside the scholastic mold—moderate reformer and militant atheist alike. The remedy for heresy was to be rigid scholastic training, strict censorship for seminarians and clerics, and vigilance committees in every diocese.

Although his loyalty was strained to the limit, Ward never took the step of public opposition to Church authorities. With other moderates, he generally took the view that public silence, instead of the support desired by the conservatives and by Rome, was the appropriate way to express dissatisfaction. However, because of his position as editor of a Catholic periodical, Ward was forced to either accept the Encyclical in print or resign.

Ward viewed *Pascendi* as ultimately putting the authorities in a position that would be impossible to maintain. He conceived of his interpretation of the Encyclical as a "golden bridge" that could be used to retreat from indefensible positions, and that the authorities would, if and when they faced the facts, be grateful for such an escape. A golden bridge would be a better strategy than open confrontation.

> In what I shall publish anyone will be able to see that I regret much of the document. Nevertheless I think it also a duty to do what I can to prevent the ultimate effect of the part I regret from being worse than it need be and to help the authorities to recede from the appearance of taking up a position disastrous to Catholic thought.[27]

Ward's essay appeared in the January 1980 issue of the *Dublin Review*.[28] Rather than opening with the customary enthusiasm of the Catholic press for papal utterances, he made a brief statement of his duty as editor. Because authority had spoken, further discussions of the questions involved in the reconciliation of Catholic tradition and modern thought had become inappropriate for the moment, but apart from a full discussion, certain misunderstandings needed to be corrected. These concerned the impression that some doctrines taught by great theologians from Aquinas to Newman were condemned.

Ward's article was cryptic and formal. He managed to satisfy the requirements, but the task was odious to him and had pushed his integrity to the limit. He had written to his friend Willie Williams:

> I told our censor that I must resign unless I could intimate for those who read carefully that while I accept the Encyclical as a pontifical act, I do not in my own mind like it. . . . I think theological minimism a necessity. Yet it is now getting to a point when it runs very close to sheer equivocation. . . . I believe even excessive minimism to be jus-

tifiable *under* the system while it lasts as the only way out of greater evils. Yet one should not in any way approve of the system. . . .[29]

After the article, Ward was unable to get a censor for the review. From 1908 to 1916 only two of his thirty articles concerned the reconciliation of Christianity and modern thought, and both were book reviews. He retained his editorship, but the work he had envisioned was severely curtailed.

VI. *Ward's Later Reflections*

For Ward, Newman provided two ways of avoiding the impossible choice between ecclesial anarchy or dictatorship: understanding the process of development in history; and having a community of Catholic scholars.

In his introduction to the 1915 edition of Cardinal Newman's *On the Scope and Nature of University Education*,[30] Ward reflected on Newman's goal of a recognized body of scholars in the Catholic University that would operate as a subordinate authority or a buffer between Church authorities and individual scholars.

> The guiding principle of the ruler is expediency. Such a university as Newman contemplated, on the other hand, would reach its synthesis or its practical *modus vivendi* between theology and modern research guided solely by scientific interests—theology, of course, being included among the sciences. The results thus reached would place at the disposal of Rome a body of probable conclusions which must command the respect of scholars and thoughtful men.[31]

This community would gradually produce a rational and coherent body of thought that would serve as a center of gravity for both rulers and scholars. The history of modernism, Ward asserted, would have been widely different if Newman's ideal had been realized.

> If such a body were habitually tolerated by Roman authority, men like Loisy and Tyrrell, instead of being goaded to extremes by total lack of sympathy in authoritative quarters, might have conceivably taken their place in the good work, ... Such scholars, living in the society of other learned men who understood them, would not improbably have become genuinely more moderate from the presence of an opposition that was really scientific. . . . The Encyclical 'Pascendi' read by itself is an eloquent witness to just that state of things I have spoken of which Newman desired to remedy, namely that Rome felt herself to be solicited by opposite extreme parties; that she felt the practical alternative to lie

between sanctioning unbridled liberty and taking measures of the ut-
most severity against innovation. This arose from the absence of a recognized body of discriminating thought in these complex questions.[32]

In these reflections on authority, Ward modified some of his earlier
views. Wise rulers and loyal theologians did not as individuals seem
to be likely to produce a *modus vivendi*; there was need for a recognized group of scholars. The tribunals in Rome were too close to
the politics of authority, and the Pontifical Biblical Commission had
been taken over by non-scholarly conservatives. The Catholic University seemed to offer hope for more neutral ground where the
intellectual questions of the day could be aired and the authority of
a consensus of Catholic scholars could be formally established.

Ward also qualified his acceptance of intellectual repression as a
temporary measure necessary to protect faith in certain situations
and to be eventually compensated for in the broad context of history.
While he never retracted his earlier statements, in his later writing
he indicated the disastrous implications of such a policy for the
credibility of the Church in the future.

VII. *Mon-archy, Syn-archy, and the Dialectic of Authority*

Matthew Lamb uses terms mon-archy and syn-archy to describe
contrasting ways of dealing with a situation of pluralism.[33] The fact
of pluralism in itself does not mean a fundamental relativism of
values. The crucial issue is the mediation of a pluralism of values
with its contradictory and complementary differences.[34] Syn-archy
[pluralist cooperative (syn) principles (arche)] attempts to relate pluralism to responsible human freedom by creating, sustaining and
changing social orders through a process in which the interests of
the whole community are represented, and mediating differences in
ways that promote responsibility and freedom. Mon-archy [one (mon)
principle (arche)] reflects an inability to relate pluralism to responsible human freedom and attempts to settle the issue of pluralism
by imposing a particular set of social and cultural meanings and
values through dominative power, creating, sustaining, and changing
social orders through a process in which only the interests of one
controlling group are represented.[35]

The rationale for the impositions of mon-archy is that there would
otherwise be an-archy [no (an) principle (arche)]. Together, the ideas
of mon-archy and an-archy imaginatively exclude the possibility of
syn-archy. This leads to a misunderstanding of the dialectics of pluralism. The real dialectic is between mon-archy/an-archy and syn--

archy, not between mon-archy and an-archy, for mon-archy and an-archy are opposite sides of the assertion that pluralism and order ultimately exclude one another.[36]

Syn-archy affirms that pluralism and order include one another, but that genuine order is not imposed but mediated through the particular self-corrective processes of learning and doing of free and responsible individuals. Syn-archy means the attempt to promote these processes and the conviction that out of this process there will emerge a "bar of enlightened public opinion to which naked power can be driven to submit."[37] It accepts human beings where they are, but does not leave them there insofar as their orientations toward intelligent truth and responsible freedom are repressed or oppressed.[38] It is not the appeal to mass opinion, but to authenticity, to enlightened opinion.

Ecumenical dialogue provides a concrete and contemporary example of the process of syn-archy at work. At its best, it does not call upon participants to renounce deeply held convictions, but emphasizes the dynamics of dialogue with others arising out of those convictions. Such dialogue is not mere talk. Self-communication necessitates self-examination. Self-examination in the context of the dialogue generates self-critical reflection and action. It issues in calls for renewal within the self, community, and the tradition where there have been distortions and contradictions. Such a process promotes reform, growth, change. Out of it may develop affirmations of common convictions, not superimposed, but based on consensus.[39]

Lamb's analysis of the nature and dynamics of authority indicates that the recovery of authority as cooperation and consensus is the antidote to the illusions of mon-archical dominative power, and provides a general perspective for discussion and evaluation of the issue of authority in particular historical contexts.

Ward on Authority: Two Views

Ward's empirical grounding of authority had clear advantages for a more adequate self-understanding of the Church in the context of modern thought, and for dialogue with those who would find "supernatural" legitimations problematic. Ward's recovery of the "rationality" of authority and tradition was valuable, in the context of his apologetics, as an antidote to the excesses of rationalism. However, the analysis of authority as representing the "reason of the race," without further qualification, is incomplete and neglects the complexity of authenticity and inauthenticity that comprises the concrete historical life of a tradition. The idea of a community of scholars who could temper each other's views and produce a consensus of scholarly opinion, and the need for the recognition of the authority of such a group in the modern Church is also a significant, if underdeveloped, insight. Such a group would carry its own potential for authentic and inauthentic responses to the issues.

An objection to Ward's views is that his language of constitution, balance, and duty was an superimposition of categories on a clearly mon-archical structure. Contemporary critics were quick to point this out. What church, they asked, was Ward describing?[40] Further, the unverifiability of the categories was revealed by abuses of authority. There were no concrete checks and balances in Ward's scheme; it really amounted to a "gentlemen's agreement," and when the authorities did not behave in gentlemanly fashion, there was little recourse.

Looking at Ward's views on authority in the total context of his approach to apologetics, another view is possible. Ward's intention was to expand the range of imaginative possibilities beyond the unacceptable monarchy/anarchy options. It was his style to introduce the new in the guise of a commentary on history. For him, the Church retrenched against the Enlightenment was an aberration in view of a broader historical perspective. Reform would be a recovery of the principles of that wider movement. His appeal was to "the essential largeness of the capacities of Catholicism viewed historically," and he called for the abandonment of the "siege mentality" that had dominated the Post-Reformation Church.[41]

Ward was not hopelessly sanguine, eulogizing a nonexistent church; rather, his portrayal of the Church in historical perspective was an attempt to artfully introduce an imaginative option that could become the first step toward actual change.

However one evaluates the success of Ward's particular approach and strategies, it is clear that he wrestled with the central issue. How could the principle of authority be preserved without accepting monarchy, and the concrete reform of abuses be achieved without anarchy? Ward recognized the dilemma of monarchy/anarchy as inadequate and envisioned the institutionalization of a syn-archical process in the Catholic University.

Imaginative Options

Ward's thought in his turn of the century context is a part of the history of wrestling with the complex and critical issue of authority and order. The false dilemma of mon-archy/anarchy seems perennially to reemerge, and the development of syn-archy is ever precarious and fragile. At the root of the issue in whatever concrete historical form, is a spectrum of imaginative options. The recovery and discovery of this spectrum of options is the link between the issue in its turn of the century context and in our own. The examination and analysis of this spectrum in various historical contexts provides understanding of the dynamics and the history of wrestling with the issues of authority and order. This understanding, in turn, can be the basis for a critical perspective on the range of imaginative options in our own time and offer insights for our own efforts to wrestle and to reform.

NOTES

1. The summary above is based on Bernard Lonergan, "Dialectic of Authority," in *A Third Collection: Papers by Bernard J. F. Lonergan, S. J.*, ed. Frederick E. Crowe, S. J. (New York: Paulist Press, 1985), 5–12. Previously published in *Authority*, ed. Frederick J. Adelmann, S. J., Boston College Studies in Philosophy, vol. 3 (Chestnut Hill, MA: Boston College, 1974), 24–30. See also B. Lonergan "Existenz and Aggiornamento," in *Collection: Papers by Bernard J. F. Lonergan, S.J.*, ed. F. E. Crowe, S. J. (New York: Herder and Herder, 1967), pp. 246–47.

2. See Bernard J. F. Lonergan, *Method in Theology*. (New York: Herder and Herder, 1972), pp. 298–99.

3. See Bernard J. F. Lonergan, *Insight: A Study of Human Understanding* (New York: Harper and Row, 1958), pp. 236–42. Cosmopolis stands for the corrective to both the shorter cycle of decline that results when groups representing a narrow range of interests use force to overthrow the previous controlling group and to dominate the community, and the longer cycle of decline in which the practicality of common sense becomes short-sighted, pp. 689–90. In *Method in Theology*, Lonergan deals with similar concerns referring to the *method* of dialectic rather than the *viewpoint* of Cosmopolis.

4. See Wilfrid Ward, *William George Ward and the Oxford Movement* (London: Macmillan, 1893), pp. 383–84, 390–91.

5. See "Reduced Christianity," *Dublin Review* (hereafter *DR*) 151 (October 1912), 417–18, and "The Spirit of Newman's Apologetics," *New York Review* 1 (July 1905), 3–14.

6. Reflecting on the work of Loisy, Baron Friedrich von Hügel commented: "The ... position that our Lord himself held the proximateness of His second coming, involves the loss by churchmen of the prestige of directly divine power, since Church and Sacraments, though still the true fruits and vehicles of his life, death, and spirit, cannot thus be immediately founded by the earthly Jesus himself." See "Alfred Firmin Loisy," *The Encyclopedia Britannica*, 11th ed. (Cambridge: The University Press, 1911), 16:928. Quoted in Lawrence Barmann, "Friedrich von Hügel's Ideas and Activities as Modernism and as More Than Modernism," in *Modernism: Origins, Parameters, Prospects*, eds. Ronald Burke and George Gilmore (Mobile: Spring Hill College Press, 1984), p. 67.

7. On the roots and rationale of W. G. Ward's Ultramontanism, see Wilfrid Ward, *William George Ward and the Catholic Revival* (London: Macmillan, 1893), pp. 130–53.

8. See "R. H. Hutton as a Religious Thinker," *DR* 20 (July 1888), 1–21.

9. See "Cardinal Newman and Constructive Religious Thought" in *Men and Matters* (London: Longmans, 1914), pp. 47–91. First published as "Cardinal Newman and Creative Theology," *DR* 138 (April 1906), 233–70.

10. *Ibid.*, 376.

11. See "The Philosophy of Authority in Religion," *Hibbert Journal* 1 (July 1903), 689.

12. The philosophers of the Enlightenment had taken their stand on individual reason in opposition to authority. In Ward's view, his contemporary, Arthur Balfour, in *Foundations of Belief* went to the other extreme. Ward offered careful corrections in a lengthy review, "The Foundations of Belief," *Quarterly Review* 180 (April 1895), 488–520. Republished in *Problems and Persons* (London: Longmans, 1903), 133–83.

13. *Ibid.*, 163; see also 167–68.

14. "Philosophy of Authority," 678.

15. *Ibid.*, p. 680. See also "The Exclusive Church and the Zeitgeist," the epilogue to *The Life and Times of Cardinal Wiseman* 2 vols. (London: Macmillan, 1897), 2: 537–38.

16. "Authority and Reason," *American Catholic Quarterly Review* 24 (April 1899), 171.

17. "The Exclusive Church," 537–38.

18. "Philosophy of Authority," 685.

19. Ward's source for this conception was Newman's 1877 "Preface" to the Third Edition of *The Via Media*.

20. "For Truth or for Life II," *DR* 140 (April 1907), 276. See also "The Spirit of Newman's Apologetics," 9.

21. "Exclusive Church," 582. Ward cited the deposing power as an instance of this sort of variation.

22. See John D. Root, "The Final Apostasy of St. George Jackson Mivart," *Catholic Historical Review* (January 1985), 1–25.

23. In "Liberalism and Intransigeance," *Nineteenth Century* 47 (June 1900), 960–73, Ward wanted to differentiate the "experts," who would reform the Church, from the "extremists," who would actually prevent progress. Cited as experts were "Firmin" (Loisy), Tyrrell, and Blondel.

24. "Liberalism as a Temper of Mind," *Monthly Register* 1 (August 1902), 177–79, and (September 1902), 217–21.

25. "Doctores Ecclesiae," *Pilot* 3 (22 June 1901), 774–76. Published in slightly shortened form in Maisie Ward, *Insurrection versus Resurrection* (London: Sheed and Ward, 1937), pp. 137–41. Cited from 140.

26. "Liberalism," 220.

27. Ward to Alfred Fawkes, 28 November 1907, Wilfrid Ward papers (hereafter WWP), University Library, St. Andrews, Scotland, VI 12 1(b).

28. "The Encyclical Pascendi," 142: 1–10.

29. Ward to Williams, 14 December 1907, WWP, VII 318a.

30. (London and New York, Everyman's Library Edition, 1915; reprint ed., 1955), vii–xxiv.

31. *Ibid.*, xi.

32. *Ibid.*, xii-xiii.

33. Matthew Lamb, "Christianity Within the Political Dialectics of Community and Empire," *Method: Journal of Lonergan Studies* 1 (Spring 1983), 1–30. Also published in *Cities of Gods: Faith, Politics and Pluralism in Judaism, Christianity and Islam.* ed., Nigel Biggar (New York: Greenwood Press, 1986), pp. 73–100.

34. Lamb, p. 3.

35. Dominative power is the repression of the interests and questions and the actions expressing those interests and questions of those seeking to expand effective human freedom.

36. Lamb, p. 11. Lonergan's comments in *Insight* reinforce this point: "The problem is not met by setting up a benevolent despotism to enforce a correct philosophy, ethics, or human science. . . . The appeal to force is a counsel of despair. So far from solving the problem, it regards the problem as insoluble. . . . If it is to be a solution and not a mere supression of the problem, it has to acknowledge and respect and work through man's intelligence, and reasonableness, and freedom. It may eliminate neither development nor tension, yet it must be able to replace incapacity by capacity for sustained development. Only a still higher integration can meet such requirements.

For only a higher integration leaves underlying manifolds with their autonomy yet succeeds in introducing a higher systematization into their non-systematic coincidences." (See p. 632.)

37. Bernard J. F. Lonergan, "The Role of a Catholic University in the Modern World," in *Collection*, p. 115.

38. Lamb, 11. See also Lonergan, *Insight*, pp. 632–33.

39. Lonergan notes: "While [dialectical method] will not be automatically efficacious, it will provide the open-minded, the serious, the sincere with the occasion to ask themselves some basic questions, first about others but eventually, even about themselves. It will make conversion a topic and thereby promote it. . . . [Dialectical method] takes its stand on discovering what human authenticity is and showing how to appeal to it. It is not an infallible method, for men easily are inauthentic, but it is a powerful method, for man's deepest need and most prized achievement is authenticity." In *Method*, 253–54.

40. See R. E. Dell, "Mr. Wilfrid Ward's Apologetics," *Nineteenth Century* 48 (July 1900), 127–36.

41. "Introduction" to *Problems and Persons*. (London: Longmans, 1903), xix. The siege mentality is described in Ward's "The Rigidity of Rome," *Nineteenth Century* 38 (December 1895), 786–804. Republished in *Problems and Persons*, 66–98.

AUTHORITY AND PERSUASION:
IGNAZ VON DÖLLINGER

William Madges
Xavier University

ABSTRACT

This essay examines the work of Döllinger at the Munich Congress
of Catholic theologians in 1863 in order to describe the broader
historical context within which the current debate about the relationship of the theologian to the official magisterium of the Roman
Church takes place. The essay suggests that Döllinger's speech at
that Congress offers an instructive and interesting model of the theo-
logian-magisterium relationship, in which the theologian recognizes
his/her obligation of fidelity to infallibly defined dogmas of the Church,
but exercises responsible freedom in the domain of non-infallible
doctrine. The value of Döllinger's proposal lies in its insistence that
theology must be both academically rigorous and historically conscious and that theological differences are to be resolved with the
persuasive weapons of *Wissenschaft*; its relevancy lies in its suggestion that the charismatic function of good theology sometimes
requires the theologian to appeal to public opinion within the Church
in order to change the Church.

Introduction

Ignaz von Döllinger (1799–1890) and the Munich Congress of Catholic scholars he convened in 1863 are worthy of consideration on
their own merits. They occupy an important place in the history of
Roman Catholic theology in the nineteenth century. The current
situation of renewed reflection upon the relationship of the theologian to the official magisterium of the Roman Church, however,
makes the recalling of Döllinger's speech at that congress especially
apposite. In that speech, "The Past and the Present of Catholic Theology," Döllinger discussed in a paradigmatic, interesting, and in-

William Madges received his Ph.D. from the University of Chicago. He has also been
a research fellow at Freiburg and Tübingen, West Germany. Presently he is Assistant
Professor at Xavier University (Cincinnati, Ohio 45220). His article "Hermeneutics"
appears in The New Encyclopaedia Britannica.

structive way three important issues involved in the contemporary debate.[1]

Those three, interrelated issues are: 1. The nature and extent of the theologian's freedom of research and of expression with regard to the Church's official teaching. 2. The kind of subjection the theologian owes to propositions or definitions that derive from the *ordinary* magisterium of the Church. 3. The existence or non-existence of the theologian's right to dissent *publicly* from any official teaching of the Church.

Döllinger's views on the latter two issues are significant in themselves and in the reaction they evoked from Rome. On the one hand, Pope Pius IX's letter *Tuas Libenter* (21 December 1863), written in response to the Munich Congress, was the first official papal document to use the term "ordinary magisterium."[2] In this letter, the pope proclaimed a view that has long since become familiar to Roman Catholic theologians, viz., that the obedience of the theologian must extend not only to those things defined as divinely revealed by general councils or the Apostolic See, but also to those matters which "are handed down as divinely revealed by the ordinary teaching power of the whole Church spread throughout the world."[3] On the other hand, Döllinger dealt both theoretically and concretely with the matter of public dissent. In his opening address to the Catholic scholars gathered in Munich, Döllinger proposed the idea that a crucial task of the theologian was the formation of public opinion within the Church. A few years later, he was forced to decide whether this idea of the public nature of the theologian's function included public *dissent*. His affirmative response to this question is attested by the pseudonymously published *Der Papst und das Konzil von Janus* (Leipzig: E. F. Steinacker, 1869) and *Römische Briefe von Konzil von Quirinus* (Munich: R. Oldenbourg, 1870), both of which sought to mobilize public opinion against the imminent definition of papal infallibility at Vatican I.[4]

Thus, in order to reflect upon the broader, historical context within which our current debates fit and in order to appreciate the contribution of an important nineteenth-century Church historian and Catholic theologian, let us now turn to the Munich Congress of 1863, Döllinger's speech, and the reaction they evoked.

I. Döllinger and the Munich Congress of 1863

Döllinger, who was the principal organizer of the Congress, had to struggle to bring the meeting into existence. The situation in Germany during the third quarter of the nineteenth-century, both church-political and socio-political, illumines why this was so. On the one hand, 1863 was an embattled year within the Church. In the very same month (August, 1863), in which Döllinger, Bonifacius Haneberg, and Johannes Alzog sent out their invitations for the Munich meeting, another Catholic congress was held in Belgium, at which Charles Montalembert argued for recognition of the religious and civil liberties which had been disputed since Félicité de Lamennais had begun to campaign for them. Earlier that same year (March, 1863), Jakob Frohschammer was suspended from his priestly duties. In *Über die Freiheit der Wissenschaft* (1861), he had asserted the independence of philosophy and scientific method from the Church's teaching authority. His censure was but the most recent in a series of condemnations directed against German Catholic theologians.[5] The condemnations, however, did not derive solely from pontifical congregations. Even among theologians themselves, controversy raged.[6] Representatives of neoscholastic theology (particularly strong in Mainz) often engaged in literary skirmishes with representatives of "modern" theology (generally operative in Tübingen and Munich).

On the other hand, a contest between the forces of liberalism and the forces of conservatism was also underway in society. The ideas of Enlightenment philosophy, the deeds of the French Revolution, the nationalistic aspirations in Italy and Germany, and the social turmoil of the 1848 uprisings all contributed to the turbulent milieu within which the Church had to define its course. The ultramontane emphasis upon papal authority, the increased centralization of power in the curia, and the identification of the Church's magisterium with the hierarchy can be viewed as reactions designed to counterbalance the revolutionary ideas and events of the nineteenth century that threatened to spread chaos in society.[7] In such an environment, it is not surprising that cries for greater freedom, encomia of modern political and religious philosophy, and critiques of the ancient institutions and privileges were often met with profound suspicion, if not outright opposition.

The stated purpose of Döllinger's proposed conference was not revolutionary—at least not at first glance. Döllinger called the meeting to unite German-speaking Catholic theologians in support of vital, "scientific" scholarship, in defense of responsible academic freedom, and in opposition to the spirit of intolerance, which permeated certain segments of the European church community.[8] But a number of Catholic theologians were chary to add their names to the invitation to the Congress. Some rather progressive theologians, such as Johannes Kuhn (1806–1887) and his Tübingen colleagues, hesitated publicly to support the conference out of fear that it would provoke greater divisions between the Roman and German parties of theology and evoke the displeasure of the papacy.[9] By contrast, other theologians, such as J. B. Heinrich (1816–91), objected to the content of the program, specifically its intent to marshal support for German academic freedom against the voices of intolerance. If the program's reference to those who "lacked the spirit of Christian patience and reconciliation" and who "encroached upon academic freedom" was meant to refer to the bishops, the Congregation of the Index, or the Apostolic See, or if the Congress was designed to give even the slightest hint of support to the complaints against Rome from Frohschammer, Huber, and other "radicals," then Heinrich and his colleagues wanted nothing to do with Döllinger's conference.[10] More importantly, the papal nuncio in Munich, Archbishop Gonella (1811–1870), strongly opposed the conference because he feared that it would undermine the submission of Catholics to official church authority.[11]

In the end, Döllinger succeeded, despite defections and opposition, in gathering together eighty-four scholars in the Abbey of St. Boniface. He had gotten all the German bishops, except the bishop of Paderborn, to permit their theologians to attend, if they so chose.[12] On September 28, the Congress opened with the celebration of Mass by the archbishop of Munich (von Scherr) and the recitation of the profession of faith of the Council of Trent. Immediately thereafter, Döllinger gave his address on the past and present of Catholic theology. In this speech, Döllinger surveyed the development of Christian theology from its origins in the Greek spirit and he described the characteristics necessary for an adequate contemporary theology.

Döllinger commenced his address with a definition of theology as "the scientific consciousness which the Church has of itself, of its past, present, and future, of the content of its teaching, of its order and its norms for living." In other words, Döllinger asserted from the outset that any theology worthy of the name had to be both scientific (or what we might call today "academic") and historically conscious. Theology certainly possessed an "unchangeable divine core," but it could present that core only in "the enveloping skin of fragile investigation and humanly limited knowledge," which was conditioned by its age and culture.[13]

In order to be scientific, theology had to emulate the probing research and critical method of the other academic disciplines. Theology, Döllinger said,

cannot content itself with a smaller measure of critical acuity and conscientious investigation; it also may not neglect any source of knowledge, any scientific means offered by the modern period. The times are past in which one could regard him/herself as a good dogmatic theologian without thorough knowledge of exegesis, church history, patristics, and the history of philosophy.[14]

Döllinger concluded that a country's ability to provide a vital theology to meet the needs of the Church in the modern world was directly proportional to its possession of truly academic institutions of theological study.[15]

Theology had to be academic, but it also had to be historically conscious. According to Döllinger, theology needed to recognize not only in a general way that it bore its treasure in earthen vessels, but also, more concretely, that "the Christian religion is history and can be fully understood and evaluated only as an historical fact in the light of the course of this development" over the millennia. In this regard, when the interests of science were taken as the criterion, the Protestant Reformation brought more good than ill to the Church for it made known the sources of historical knowledge and caused the principles of historical investigation to be put into practice.[16] Unlike the Protestant theologian, however, the Catholic theologian could not be satisfied with an understanding of the New Testament and the history of the Reformation.

Rather, the Catholic theologian can do nothing but conceive of the entire course of the Church in the light of a great process of development, a continual growth from the inside out, not like the growth of a tapeworm but like that of a tree, into which the mustard seed of the apostolic age developed itself. The theologian, accordingly, cannot arbitrarily take out a piece, a section of time, and content him/herself with its study; rather he/she must investigate the Church in the totality of its life-expressions and in its historical continuity from the beginning to the present and must exhibit it to him/herself and to others in the most adequate way possible.[17]

The opposition of this conception of theology to the neo-scholastic view becomes even clearer in Döllinger's articulation of how the tradition of the Church was to be understood and transmitted. The Catholic theologian, said Döllinger, was not to treat tradition the way that a miser treats a treasure he has buried in the ground. Of course, the miser *has* a treasure, one to which nothing is added or taken away, one which can be dug up after centuries and found to be the same. But such a treasure, Döllinger declared, is dead and fruitless. Döllinger's view of the way tradition was to be handled was quite different:

In the Church and for her science, however, tradition and its content is living, progressing; it bears within itself rest and movement, stability and development, uniformity and multiplicity. The teaching that has been handed on cannot have an effect upon spirit and life, without spirit and life having an effect back upon it. Tradition is most effective by bearing in itself a continually, interiorly active seed of life. It can, however, also become small and narrow and crippled in the hands of spiritual crudeness, which passes itself off as conservative theology, so that it shrivels up like an old body and, in its impotence—having been abandoned even by life forces—it is no longer capable of producing both life and light. For dogma, in the form of ecclesial definitions, offers in itself only words which, however rich in substance, however carefully they may be chosen and defined, still always first need spiritual fructification through theology and the teaching office [Lehramt]. These words, while they become brilliant jewels in the hands of a theologian who possesses and gives life, become dead pebbles under the manipulations of a crude mind that acts mechanically.[18]

Germany—not France, Italy, or Spain—had become the bearer and custodian of theological science in the nineteenth century for it promoted scientific acuity and unceasing investigation.[19] German Catholic theology could now claim preeminence because it possessed and carefully nurtured what Döllinger called the "two eyes of theology," viz., history and philosophy.[20] Scholasticism, by contrast, was deemed defective because it possessed only one eye, that of philosophical speculation.[21] And in his speech Döllinger sharply criticized the myopia or poor vision of contemporary Spanish and Italian scholasticism.[22]

Döllinger's emphasis upon the scientific and historically conscious nature of theology, however, did not entail—at least not in 1863 or earlier—a claim that academic theology was independent of the official magisterium of the Church nor did it require a denial of a place in the Church to neo-scholasticism.[23] With regard to the former issue, Döllinger claimed that the Catholic theologian was simultaneously bound and free. Döllinger suggested, in fact, that the theologian felt free precisely because he/she had given "him/herself over, once and for all, by a decisive act of choice . . . to the direction and teaching authority [Lehrautorität] of the Church, which he/she recognized as the divinely willed and divinely illumined caretaker of the truths of salvation and the teacher of the peoples."[24] This submission was liberating insofar as it freed the theologian from the slavery of tormenting uncertainty and nagging doubt about the essentials of Christian faith. Moreover, critical, scientific investigation of the Church's teaching was not incompatible with fidelity to the official magisterium since even the sharpest testing would ultimately result only in "the confirmation of church teaching rightly understood."[25] Döllinger was so convinced of the theoretical harmony of free theological inquiry and obedience to the teaching authority of the Church that he could say to his audience that the theologian's

> entire intellectual life and investigation is only a becoming one with it [i.e., the authority of the Church] in a continually growing fervor so that, if it should ever disappear or become mute for him/her, he/she would nevertheless not believe, understand, or teach differently from it.[26]

With regard to theologians of an opposing or different view, Döllinger advocated respect and restraint in judgment. Döllinger admitted that the current existence of two different theological directions in Germany, the Roman (neo-scholastic) and the German (modern), was more a positive than a negative phenomenon, "only provided that both are truly scientific and that they permit each other *reciprocal* freedom of movement." (Emphasis mine.) Döllinger continued:

> This freedom is as indispensable to science as is air to breathe to the body. And if there are theologians, who want to withdraw this lifebreath from their colleagues under the pretense of danger, then this is a shortsighted and suicidal beginning.[27]

But then, what was a theologian to do about a colleague he/she suspected of theological errors? Combat them "with purely scientific weapons and only with such weapons," Döllinger replied.[28] Convinced that theological truth was attained only by passing through errors, Döllinger concluded his address to the Munich Congress with the following exhortation:

> And so may each one of us, if the temptation seizes him to judge sharply the real or alleged errors of a colleague or even to suspect the orthodoxy of a book and its author, be mindful of the words of the greatest Christian poet [Dante, *Paradise*, 19, 79]:
> Now who are thou, that on the bench would sit
> In judgment at a thousand miles away,
> With the short vision of a single span?[29]

Theology's Tasks

In his speech to the Munich Congress, Döllinger touched upon several tasks of contemporary theology. I would like to summarize three of them, focusing especially upon those aspects of the tasks that illumine the relationship of authority and persuasion.

One important task Döllinger outlined was the formulation of a new model of theology, one, unlike the neo-scholastic model, that would integrate critical history and philosophical speculation in the doing of dogmatic theology.[30] This new model of theology would possess authority to the extent 1) that it was professionally competent, and 2) that it was universal like the Church. By this Döllinger meant that theology acquired authority insofar as it was able to integrate the past, the present, and the future. Döllinger was particularly concerned about the future:

> It [i.e., theology] cares for the future in that it does not—as often happens—bury and artificially conceal the gaps in the system that are still present, but rather confirms their existence and simultaneously rejects every rash, autocratic attempt to clothe the opinions of a school with the authority of ecclesial doctrine and to use them in theological construction as material equivalent to and on a par with the general teaching of the Church.[31]

Döllinger wanted theology to be free, as was appropriate for any *Wissenschaft*; but he also wanted it to be responsible. All theological opinions were not equally valid. Some possessed greater adequacy and, therefore, possessed greater authority. A truly authoritative contemporary theology had to be able critically to assess and to reformulate current deficient formulations of Christian faith. Being "critical" meant not only delving more deeply into and testing more thoroughly the sources of theological reflection, but also refusing to retreat in fear when research led to "unwelcome results that were not compatible with preconceived judgments and favorite opinions."[32] Theology, after all, was to play a prophetic and charismatic function in the life of the Church.

But what if this prophetic function brought one into conflict with the religious authorities? The freedom, even obligation, of academic theology to follow research where it led did not, however, mean that theology should oppose the official magisterium of the Church in solemnly defined matters. At this point, the Munich Congress made a distinction between the response of the theologian to solemnly defined (i.e., infallible) truths and his/her response to other truths, presented by the Church for belief, but not infallibly defined. Although Döllinger was fearful that discussion of the relationship of the theologian to the Church's official magisterium would lead to greater division within the group of scholars, all but four of the Congress participants endorsed the following two theses:[33]

1. The internal adherence to revealed truth, which is taught in the Catholic Church, is an important and necessary condition for the progressive development of true and comprehensive speculation in general and for the overcoming of the errors presently regnant in particular.
2. Whoever occupies the point of view of Catholic faith is bound in conscience to submit, in all his/her scientific investigations, to the dogmatic decrees of the infallible authority of the Church. This subjection to authority in no way contradicts the freedom that is natural and necessary to science.[34]

Non-infallible doctrine, therefore, constituted the domain in which responsible theological freedom was to be exercised. And in this domain, only the weapons of persuasive "science," not the weapons of coercive force, were to be used in combatting inappropriate theological opinions.

Pope Pius IX, however, was not satisfied with the limitation of the Catholic theologian's faith commitment to defined dogmas. *Tuas Libenter*, which was written as a response to the Munich Congress, declared that subjection of conscience was also due the *ordinary* magisterium of the Church, including "the decisions pertaining to doctrine which are issued by the Roman congregations:"

> But, since it is a matter of that subjection by which in conscience all those Catholics are bound who work in the speculative sciences, in order that they may bring new advantages to the Church by their writings, on that account, then, the men of that same convention should recognize that it is not sufficient for learned Catholics to accept and revere the aforesaid dogmas of the Church, but that it is also necessary to subject themselves to the decisions pertaining to doctrine which are issued by the Pontifical Congregations, and also to those forms of doctrine which are held by the common and constant consent of Catholics as theological truths and conclusions, so certain that opinions opposed to these same forms of doctrine, although they cannot be called heretical, nevertheless deserve some theological censure.[35]

This more restrictive view of the freedom of the theologian passed from *Tuas Libenter* into the mainstream of Catholic theology by means of the Dogmatic Constitution of Vatican I, which, in its chapter on faith, declared that

> by divine and Catholic faith all those things must be believed which are contained in the written word of God and in tradition, and those which are proposed by the Church, either in a solemn pronouncement or in her *ordinary and universal teaching power*, to be believed as divinely revealed. (Emphasis mine.)[36]

It is important to note that this view derived from Joseph Kleutgen's (1811–83) *Die Theologie der Vorzeit verteidigt* (1853–60), which
delineated the neo-scholastic conception of theology and identified
the Church primarily with the hierarchy. *Tuas Libenter* took over
the language and line of argument of Kleutgen, who later was a
consultor of Vatican Council I's deputation for the faith when it
inserted the term "ordinary magisterium" into the text of the constitution. It should be further noted that a number of bishops at
Vatican I found the terminology strange, but that the deputation for
faith got it accepted by replying that the term and its meaning were
from *Tuas Libenter*.[37]

Another important task of theology, Döllinger suggested, was the
formation of right and healthy public opinion.[38] In his address to
the Munich Congress, Döllinger declared:

> It is theology which gives existence and power to right and healthy
> public opinion in religious and ecclesial matters, the opinion before
> which all ultimately bow—even the heads of the Church and the bearers
> of power. Similar to the institution of prophecy in the age of the He-
> brews, which stood next to the ordered priesthood, there is also in the
> Church an extraordinary authority [*Gewalt*] in addition to the ordinary
> authorities, and this is public opinion. Through it academic theology
> [*theologische Wissenschaft*] exercises the power [*Macht*] befitting it,
> which, in the long run, nothing can withstand. The theologian namely
> judges and adjusts the phenomena in the Church according to ideas,
> while the unthinking masses operate in the opposite fashion. All gen-
> uinely reforming activity, however, consists finally in making every
> institution or exercise in the Church correspond to its idea.[39]

What Döllinger seems to be suggesting here is a two-fold authority
of theology, analogous to the two-fold authority of the official magisterium. Theology's usual method of operation is *in* the academic
community *for* the Church. Here theology's authority depends upon
its power to persuade professional colleagues and the official heir-
archy of the Church that its formulations are adequate interpretations
of the deposit of faith for the present situation and that its creative
proposals are beneficial for the future life of the Church. This is the
usual or *ordinary* means by which theology obtains recognizable
authority.

Sometimes, however, theology can obtain *extraordinary* power or
authority. This happens when theology applies its art of persuasion
not merely to the academy of professional colleagues and the hierarchy of the Church, but extends its exercise to the masses. Theology
then comes to wield extraordinary power insofar as it has molded,

and perhaps even mobilized, public opinion. Just as the extraordinary authority of the official magisterium is (usually) invoked to combat a situation of crisis in the Church, so too the extraordinary authority of theology is to be invoked only in matters absolutely crucial to the life of the Church.[40] Döllinger thought that the reconciliation and reunification of the separated Christian confessions was such a crucial matter. And it is in this context that he set out his ideas on the right of the theologian to form and to use public opinion.[41] Recognition of what is good and true in the other Christian churches, a thorough evaluation of the deficiencies in one's own, and the honest willingness to work at removing the obstacles towards reunification constituted the third principal task of contemporary theology that Döllinger proposed to his audience.[42]

Concluding Remarks

What, then, are we to say in our assessment of Döllinger? Should he be dismissed as a representative of what Peter Eicher calls the "bourgeois theology" that runs in a straight line from Lammenais to Küng? Or should he be ignored because he refused to accept Vatican I's declaration on papal infallibility and was consequently excommunicated (17 April 1871) by his bishop?[43] I think not. Rather, I suggest that his theological program be called to mind again today as something very worthy of consideration.

I presume that most Christian theologians can affirm at least the following emphases of Döllinger's program as good and necessary in our own day: the emphasis on the scientific character of theology, the necessity of theology's critical fidelity to the tradition and contemporary experience, the demand that persuasion, and not coercion, be the modus operandi in theological discussion, and the need for theologians responsibly to accept and courageously fulfill their prophetic function for the present and future life of the Church.

But even if concurrence may be presumed on these points, Döllinger's speech to the Munich Congress of 1863 still raises a difficult question: Is it part of the function of theology to use public opinion in revitalizing and changing the Church? Max Seckler has found this proposal extremely problematic, for it seems to make theology no longer a "critical partner" of the episcopal cathedra, but rather gives it the calling "to bend the heads of the Church with the help of public opinion." Seckler continues:

> The political intention of theology to influence [Wirkabsicht] is thereby counterfeited into a political method of influencing [Wirkmethode].

Theology operates no longer only as a science and with scientific methods, but as an *agitator* that brings public opinion into play for support of its goals, which it believes it can attain in no other way.[44]

Is such an exercise of authority legitimate for theology? It must be admitted that the appeal of theologians to the popular media, with the intent of shaping public opinion, is fraught with danger. A carefully nuanced theological position may appear in popular journals and newspapers as a crude caricature; a developed theological argument, demonstrating fidelity to the tradition of the Church and adequacy to contemporary experience, may be transformed into a shallow slogan. Nonetheless, situations may sometimes demand risking these dangers. Döllinger, I think, formally described some of the key aspects of such special situations. The formation and use of public opinion within the Church was, he observed, an *extraordinary* task of theology. Its legitimacy was rooted in the theologian's prophetic charism and dependent upon its aim to help cure a serious illness in the Church.[45] And even when he/she adopted an openly critical posture to certain systemic illnesses in the Church, the theologian was not to endeavor to establish his/her theological viewpoint as an independent authority with the Church. In both the ordinary and extraordinary exercise of authority, the theologian was to work with persuasive arguments drawn from the sources of theology and to apply them only in the *service* of the Church.

Of course, Döllinger's comments about the role of theology in the Church received little approbation in Pius IX's church. But in today's Church, conceived—in the words of Vatican II—as the entire people of God, does not Döllinger's advocacy of the public function of theology and of the legitimate authority of the people within the Church (i.e., public opinion) have a greater claim to intelligibility?[46] To consider again Döllinger's speech and the Munich Congress of 1863 is, I submit, not only to see the broader historical context in which our contemporary discussions occur, but also to recapture a living resource from the Church's history for the nurture and revitalization of the people of God.

NOTES

1. Max Seckler observes: "Bei Ignaz von Döllinger treten in der Frage nach dem Verhältnis von Theologie und Lehramt einige neue Aspekte auf, die Interesse verdienen. Im ganzen gesehen, erscheint der Konflikt, den dieser Mann der Wissenschaft mit der Kirche im 19. Jahrhundert geführt hat, wie ein Paradigma für den ganzen Jammer, den Wissenschaft und Wissenschaftler im neuzeitlichen Katholizisimus durchgemacht haben." "Kirchliches Lehramt und theologische Wissenschaft: Geschichtliche Aspekte, Probleme und Lösungselemente," Die Theologie und das Lehramt, ed. Walter Kern (Freiburg: Herder, 1982), p. 45.

2. Francis A. Sullivan, Magisterium: Teaching Authority in the Catholic Church (New York: Paulist Press, 1983) pp. 122–23. For pertinent excerpts from the letter, see Heinrich Denzinger and Adolf Schönmetzer, eds., Enchiridion Symbolorum Definitionum et Declarationum de Rebus Fidei et Morum (Freiburg: Herder, 1965), par. 2875–80.

3. Denzinger and Schönmetzer, par. 2879. Henry Denzinger, The Sources of Catholic Dogma, trans. Roy J. Deferrari (St. Louis: Herder, 1957), par. 1683. See Yves Congar, "Pour une Histoire Sémantique du Terme 'Magisterium,' " Revue des Sciences Philosophiques et Théologiques 60 (1976), 95. Boyle argues that the term "ordinary magisterium" appears to be original with Kleutgen, although Kleutgen thought of himself as defending a very traditional idea. Kleutgen's idea passed into papal teaching (Tuas Libenter) through the influence of Cardinal Reisach. John Boyle, "The 'Ordinary Magisterium': Towards a History of the Concept (2)," Heythrop Journal 21 (1980), 24. The two parts of Boyle's article are henceforth referred to as Boyle 1 and 2. The first part appears in Heythrop Journal 20 (1979), 380–98.

4. Both of Döllinger's works were translated into English: The Pope and the Council, by Janus, authorized trans. from the 2nd German ed. (New York: Scribner, 1869); Letters from Rome on the Council, by Quirinus, authorized trans. (New York: Pott & Amery, 1870). Since the curia did not take the initiative in forming public opinion about the deliberations of Vatican I, Döllinger's Roman Letters were "almost the only source from which any detailed account of the proceedings in Rome was to be had." The condensed reproduction of Döllinger's biased reports in various newspapers, according to Victor Conzemius, determined the view of many in a one-sidedly negative way. "Catholicism: Old and Roman," Journal of Ecumenical Studies 4 (1967), 430–31.

5. Boyle 1, 382–83. See J[ohannes] Friedrich, Ignaz von Döllinger: Sein Leben auf Grund seines schriftlichen Nachlasses, 3 vols. (Munich: C. H. Beck, 1901), 3:272.

6. Friedrich, 3: 271–73.

7. Boyle 2, 23–24. See also Joseph Hoffman, "Théologie, Magistère et Opinion publique: Le discours de Döllinger au Congrès des Savants Catholiques de 1863," Recherches de Science Religieuse 71 (1983), 256. Congar notes, 95–96, that it is only since the beginning of the nineteenth century, especially due to the influence of Gregory XVI, Pius IX, and Vatican I, that "magisterium" has come to refer to the hierarchical leaders of the Church.

8. Pius Gams, ed., Verhandlungen der Versammlung katholischer Gelehrten in München vom 28. September bis 1. Oktober 1863 (Regensburg: Georg Joseph Manz, 1863), pp. 6–8. See also Friedrich, 3:288 and Hoffman, 256.

9. Friedrich, 3:286–88.

10. Heinrich also resisted the view, which perhaps could be read into the invitation to the congress, that beyond the boundaries established by formally declared dogma, there existed unrestricted subjective freedom for the Catholic theologian. Heinrich

also opposed the idea that theology need not be built upon the foundations of ancient philosophy. Friedrich, 3: 288–92.

11. Gonella wrote to the Secretary of State: "They [the theologians] know very well that the diocesan church authority in Germany does not generally show itself very vigilant in such matters, at least in what regards measures to be taken against pernicious books and their authors. So it is that anyone who knows the state of things and the nature of the persons involved will give little weight to the last sentence of the programme in which there is talk of due submission to church authority. The very fact of the meeting that is being announced entirely without the knowledge of the bishops, while also dealing with Catholic theology and other sciences, shows well enough how sincere that statement is. . . . I allow myself to observe, with due submission, how necessary it seems to me that the Holy Father take some opportunity to remind the bishops of Germany to be more vigilant over the tendencies of many professors in these universities, who elevate themselves to the status of judges and custodians of true Catholic doctrine and of the way it is to be propagated, while the bishops, who are the real depositories of doctrine, remain silent and permit the younger clergy to imbibe such principles." Matteo Eustacchio Gonella, "To Cardinal Giacomo Antonelli," 21 August 1863, in Boyle 1, 384–85. Friedrich remarks, 3:307, that the Congress was in danger of collapsing because of Gonella's interference and that Döllinger was thus impelled personally to write to a few bishops for support.

12. Gams, pp. 10–12; Friedrich, 3:307. It is interesting to note that Bishop Martin of Paderborn was chiefly responsible for editing the draft of the constitution on faith presented to the Council of Vatican I and that he appointed Joseph Kleutgen to serve as his theologian. See Gerald A. McCool, Catholic Theology in the Nineteenth Century: The Quest for a Unitary Method (New York: Seabury Press, A Crossroad Book, 1977), pp. 220–21.

13. Ignaz von Döllinger, "Die Vergangenheit und Gegenwart der katholischen Theologie," Kleinere Schriften, gedruckte und ungedruckte, ed. F. H. Reusch (Stuttgart: Cotta, 1890), p. 161. The speech is also printed in Gams, pp. 25–29 and in Johann Finsterhölzl, ed., Ignaz von Döllinger, Wegbereiter heutiger Theologie (Graz: Styria, 1969), pp. 227–63. Subsequent references to the speech refer to the pages in Kleinere Schriften, but page numbers will also be given for Finsterhölzl's version, which is more readily available.

14. Döllinger, "Vergangenheit," 184–85; Finsterhölzl, p. 252.

15. France served as an example. In the Middle Ages, it was preeminent because the University of Paris pursued theology in a scientific manner; it was regarded as one of the three great indispensable institutions of Christendom. In the nineteenth century, however, France had no theologians of the caliber of previous great ages because it had no theological institute of higher learning. Instead, it had only eighty-five "pastoral" seminaries. Döllinger, "Vergangenheit," 167, 179–80; Finsterhölzl, pp. 233, 246–47.

16. Döllinger, "Vergangenheit," 169; Finsterhölzl, p. 236.

17. Döllinger, "Vergangenheit," 186; Finsterhölzl, p. 253.

18. Döllinger, "Vergangenheit," 189–90; Finsterhölzl, pp. 256–57.

19. Döllinger, "Vergangenheit," 180–81; Finsterhölzl, pp. 247–48.

20. Döllinger, "Vergangenheit," 184; Finsterhölzl, p. 251. In an earlier speech to the students of the University of Munich as rector, Döllinger spoke of history and philosophy as the "two eyes of the human race." Irrthum, Zweifel und Wahrheit. Eine Rede an die Studierenden der königl. Ludwig-Maximilians-Universität in München; gehalten am 11. Januar 1845 (Regensburg: Georg Joseph Manz, 1845), p. 31.

21. "Man lebte nur in der Gegenwart, man begriff und kannte nur das Fertige, nicht das Werdende, nicht die auch für das religiöse Gebiet gültigen Gesetze der geschichtlichen Entwicklung. Die Theologie war sozusagen einäugig; sie besass das spekulative, sie entbehrte das historische Auge." Döllinger, "Vergangenheit," 166; Finsterhölzl, p. 233.

22. Döllinger, "Vergangenheit," 171–72, 176–77; Finsterhölzl, pp. 238, 243–45. This critique caused a cry of protest from some. Friedrich, 3:323–25.

23. Concerning the change in Döllinger's attitude towards Rome and the papacy, see Remigius Bäumer, "John Henry Newman and Ignaz von Döllinger: Der ungleiche Gewissenskonflikt zweier führender Theologen anlässlich der Unfehlbarkeits-definition," Newman-Studien 11 (1980), 32–46, especially 32–33.

24. Döllinger, "Vergangenheit," 190; Finsterhölzl, pp. 257–58.

25. "Da wir gläubige Theologen sind, so wissen wir, dass auch die schärfste Prüfung nur immer wieder zur Bestätigung der richtig verstandenen kirchlichen Lehre ausschlagen werde." Döllinger, "Vergangenheit," 187; Finstershözlz, pp. 254–55.

26. Döllinger, "Vergangenheit," 191; Finsterhölzl, p. 258.

27. Döllinger, "Vergangenheit," 195; Finsterhölzl, p. 262.

28. Döllinger distinguished between a dogmatic and a theological error. By the former, he seemed to mean a denial of an official dogma of the Church; by the latter, a view that was questionable, but that nonetheless did not violate any specific dogma. Thus: "Ist es ein dogmatischer Irrtum, ein Verstoss gegen die klare allgemeine Lehre der Kirche, welcher begangen wird, so darf er freilich nicht ungerügt bleiben und muss zürckgenommen werden. Ist es aber ein bloss theologischer, also dem Gebiete der wissenschaftlichen Erörterung angehöriger Irrtum, dann soll er auch mit rein wissenschaftlichen Waffen und nur mit solchen bekämpft werden." Döllinger, "Vergangenheit," 195; Finsterhölzl, p. 262.

29. Döllinger, "Vergangenheit," 196; Finsterhölzl, p. 263.

30. ". . . the old house that was built by scholasticism has become dilapidated and it can no longer be helped by means of repairs; rather, it can only be helped by means of a new construction. . . ." Döllinger, "Vergangenheit," 193; Finsterhölzl, pp. 260–61. For a brief, yet clear exposition of some of the salient differences between the scholastic and modern models of theology, see McCool, pp. 169–75.

31. Döllinger, "Vergangenheit," 194–95; Finsterhölzl, pp. 261–62.

32. "Also tiefer graben, emsiger, rastloser prüfen, und nicht etwa furchtsam zurückweichen, wo die Forschung zu unwillkommenen, mit vorgefassten Urteilen und Lieblings-meinungen nicht vereinbaren Ergebnissen führen möchte, das ist die Signatur des echten Theologen." Döllinger, "Vergangenheit," 187; Finsterhölzl, pp. 254.

33. Friedrich corrects the version offered in the Proceedings, which states that only three did not subscribe to the theses. Friedrich, 3:330. See Gams, p. 119.

34. Gams, pp. 97–98. It should be noted that a third thesis was proposed for acceptance: "3. Die Versammlung misskennt keineswegs die Fortschritte, welche die neure Zeit in allen Zweigen der Wissenschaft darbietet; aber sie glaubt zugleich, dass der speculativen Forschung der Gegenwart Nichts förderlicher sein könne, als ein unbefangenes Studium der grossen Tradition christlicher Philosophie, welche die Resultate des antiken Denkens in sich aufgenommen und weitergeführt hat." This thesis evoked considerable debate, involving, in particular, Strodl and Deutinger from Munich, Werner from St. Pölten, and Mayr from Würzburg. The latter advocated some views similar to Döllinger's, but emphasized more strongly than he the autonomy of academic disciplines. See Gams, pp. 98–118, especially 110–13. Since no counterproposals met with the satisfaction of all, the third thesis was tabled until the next meeting (1864) of Catholic scholars.

35. Denzinger, par. 1684. See Vatican II's *Lumen gentium*, par. 25. Concerning Pius IX's displeasure, see R[oger] Aubert, *Le Pontificat de Pie IX (1846–1878)*, Histoire de L'Église depuis les Origines jusqu'a nos Jours, 21 ([Paris]: Bloud & Gay, n.d.), pp. 208–09.

36. Dogmatic Constitution, "Dei Filius," in Denzinger, par. 1792. Denzinger and Schönmetzer, par. 3011. As Sullivan has observed, p. 123, this statement does not explicitly define the infallibility of the ordinary universal magisterium. But it would not be difficult for some to infer it "as a theological conclusion from the obligation on all the faithful to believe what is taught by this magisterium, in view of the basic principle that the whole Church cannot err in its faith." Without explicitly affirming the infallibility of papal encyclical letters, Pope Pius XII did in fact assert, in *Humani generis* (1950), the restriction of theological discussion concerning controversial matters on which the pope had spoken. Denzinger, par. 2313. See "Teaching Authority of the Church (Magisterium)," *New Catholic Encyclopedia, Supplement*, 1979 ed., for a pre-Vatican II description of the roles of the official magisterium and the theologian: "Absolute and unquestioning obedience to their [i.e., the hierarchy] teaching, whether definitively and infallibly taught or not (few Catholics thought of making any distinction) was looked upon as the hallmark of the Catholic. The primary, if not exclusive, role of the professional theologian was seen as that of defending and explaining the teaching of the official magisterium; theological debate was confined to questions to which the magisterium had not yet addressed itself."

37. Boyle 2, 21 & 25.

38. Friedrich claims that this idea, for which Döllinger was frequently rebuked by the theologian Scheeben, originated with Joseph de Maistre. Friedrich, 3: 316, 694, note #16.

39. Döllinger, "Vergangenheit," 184; Finsterhölzl, p. 251. Note that the context in which Döllinger introduced this idea was his discussion of the desire to reconcile Catholicism and Protestantism. He was not advocating some kind of opposition to the papacy or curia. See *Irrthum*, p. 8.

40. It is important to remember that even in such extraordinary situations, the theologian acted in service of the Church and that his/her work was borne by the Church: "Wir wissen auch, dass unsere Geistesarbeit für jene Kirche und in jener Kirche vollbracht wird, welcher der göttliche Geist sich niemals entzieht. Aus ihr, vermöge der Gliedschaft an ihrem Leibe, empfangen wir die höhere Erleuchtung, jenes Licht der Gnade, ohne welches in göttlichen Dingen das Geistesauge verschlossen bleibt, welches dem Theologen erst die Weine seines Berufes erteilt." Döllinger, "Vergangenheit," 187–88; Finsterhölzl, p. 255. Concerning the possible place of protest of the laity in the Church, see Finsterhölzl, pp. 29, 47, 57.

41. Döllinger claimed that it was the particular task of German theology "to reconcile the separated confessions once again, but in a higher unity." Three conditions had to be met for this reconciliation, but neither the majority of Protestants nor the majority of Roman Catholics willed to make the conditions reality. Döllinger, "Vergangenheit," 182–84; Finsterhölzl, pp. 249–51. Döllinger's criticism of his Catholic colleagues on this point caused protest from his audience. See Friedrich, pp. 3: 325.

42. Finsterhölzl, p. 32, claims that the desire to reunify the churches was one of Döllinger's reasons for opposing papal infallibility.

43. See Döllinger's letter to Archbishop Scherr, 28 March 1871, outlining his reasons for not accepting the Vatican decrees. *Briefe und Erklärungen von I. von Döllinger über die Vatikanischen Dekrete: 1869–1887* (Munich: C. H. Beck, 1890), pp. 90–92.

44. Seckler, p. 49. Cf. Finsterhölzl, pp. 47–48.

45. Compare Döllinger's speech to the Munich Congress with the following statement: "Whenever a state of disease has appeared in the Church, there has been but one method of cure—that of an awakened, renovated, healthy consciousness; and of an enlightened public opinion in the Church. The very best will on the part of ecclesiastical rulers and heads has not been able to effect a cure, unless sustained by the general sense and conviction of the clergy and of the laity. The healing of the great malady of the sixteenth century, the true internal reformation of the Church, only became possible when people ceased to disguise or to deny the evil, and to pass it by in silence and with concealment; and when so powerful and irresistible a public opinion had formed itself in the Church, that its commanding influence could no longer be evaded." Döllinger, The Church and the Churches; or, the Papacy and the Temporal Power, trans. William Bernard MacCabe (London: Hurst and Blackett, 1862), p. 10. In the latter context, Döllinger noted that public opinion need not be viewed as a force opposed to the papacy, but, in fact, that it was a force necessary to and supportive of the reforming work of the popes, including Pius IX.

46. Finsterhölzl, pp. 55–57, points out that, although he did not conceive of the possibilities for the engagement of the laity in the Church in as broad terms as J. B. Hirscher, Döllinger affirmed the foundation of such engagement with his endorsement of the idea of the universal priesthood.

Part Two

SPEAKING TO OUR MOMENT:
AUTHORITY AND FREEDOM IN THE
CHURCH

AUTHORITY AND STRUCTURE IN THE CHURCHES: PERSPECTIVE OF A CATHOLIC THEOLOGIAN

Charles E. Curran
Catholic University of America

ABSTRACT

I was told in the summer of 1979 that my theological writings were under investigation by the Vatican Congregation for the Doctrine of the Faith. In the summer of 1986 Cardinal Ratzinger, the Prefect of the Congregation, informed me that the Congregation decided with the approval of Pope John Paul II that I "will no longer be considered suitable nor eligible to exercize the function of a Professor of Catholic Theology." This paper discusses what I consider to be the five most significant issues involved in the present dispute—the role of the theologian, the possibility of public theological dissent from some noninfallible hierarchical church teachings, the possibility and right of dissent by the Christian faithful, the justice and fairness of the process employed in my case, the academic freedom of Roman Catholic institutions of higher learning and of Catholic theology.

In the fall of 1985 I agreed to accept the kind invitation of our Convention Program Committee to give this plenary session on the topic "Authority and Structure in the Churches: Perspective of a Catholic Theologian." Since that time there has been some water over the dam. The Vatican Congregation for the Doctrine of the Faith has urged me to "reconsider and to retract those positions which violate the conditions for a professor to be called a Catholic theo-

Charles E. Curran earned an S.T.D. degree at the Gregorian University in Rome and an S.T.D. with specialization in moral theology at the Academia Alfonsiana in Rome. He is currently Professor of Moral Theology at The Catholic University of America where he has taught since 1965. Curran is a former President of the Catholic Theological Society of America and of the Society of Christian Ethics. He has authored and edited more than twenty books. The latest books are Faithful Dissent (Sheed and Ward, 1986) and Toward an American Catholic Moral Theology (University of Notre Dame Press, 1987). The Chancellor of Catholic University has initiated the process to withdraw Curran's canonical mission to teach theology in an ecclesiastical faculty. As part of that process a faculty committee is now hearing the case.

logian." According to Cardinal Ratzinger, the Prefect of the Congregation, there is an inherent contradiction if "one who is to teach in the name of the Church in fact denies her teaching."[1]

This paper will attempt to be faithful to the original topic by focusing on the pertinent issues and aspects involved in my present case. From the very beginning I am conscious of my own prejudices and biases. This paper is presented from my own perspective and therefore is bound to serve as an apologetic or defense of my position. However, at the same time I have the broader intention of using this case to raise up the important issues which the theological community, the hierarchical teaching office in the Roman Catholic Church, and the total people of God need to address. The subject of this paper will thus be specifically Roman Catholic, dealing with the role of the theologian in the Roman Catholic Church. However, the questions raised and the issues discussed have not only an indirect interest for other Christian churches and other Christian theologians, but they also deal directly with many of the same realities which arise for all Christian churches and all their theologians. Before pointing out and discussing the more specific issues involved in this case, it is important to recognize the context and the presuppositions for the discussion.

I. Context and Presuppositions

The general context for this paper and for the entire case is that of the Roman Catholic Church and Catholic theology. I have made it very clear that I am a believing Catholic and intend to do Catholic theology. Despite my intentions, I still might be wrong; but I maintain that my positions are totally acceptable for a Catholic theologian and a believing Roman Catholic.

The mission of the entire church is to be faithful to the word and work of Jesus. God's revelation has been handed over and entrusted to the church which faithfully hands this down from generation to generation through the assistance of the Holy Spirit. Roman Catholicism recognizes that revelation was closed at the end of apostolic times, but revelation itself develops and is understood in the light of the different historical and cultural circumstances of the hearers and doers of the word.

Roman Catholic faith and theology have strongly disagreed with the emphasis on the Scripture alone. The Scripture must always be understood in light of the thought patterns of our own time. The Catholic insistence on the Scripture and tradition recognized the need to develop and understand God's revelation in Jesus Christ in the light of the contemporary circumstances. The early Councils of the fourth, fifth, and subsequent centuries illustrate how in matters touching the very heart of faith—the understanding of God and of Jesus Christ—the living church felt the need to go beyond the words of the Scripture, to understand better and more adequately the revelation of God. Thus, the Christian Church taught there are three persons in God and two natures in Jesus. Fidelity to the tradition does not mean merely repeating the very words of the Scripture or of older church teaching. The Christian tradition is a living tradition, and fidelity involves a creative fidelity which seeks to preserve in its own time and place the incarnational principle. Creative fidelity is the task of the church in bearing witness to the word and work of Jesus.

In carrying out its call to creative fidelity to the word and work of Jesus, the church is helped by the papal and episcopal roles in the church. The existence of this pastoral teaching function of pope and bishops in the church must be recognized by all. However, there has been much development in the understanding of the exact nature of that teaching office, how it is exercised, and what is its relationship to the other functions connected with the office of pope and bishops in the church. Much of the following discussion will center on what is often called today the ordinary magisterium of the papal office. This term ordinary magisterium understood in this present sense has only been in use since the nineteenth century.[2] A Catholic must recognize the pastoral office of teaching given to pope and bishops, but also should realize that this teaching function has been exercised in different ways over the years.[3]

These aspects briefly mentioned in this opening section are very important and could be developed at much greater length and depth. However, in this paper they are being recalled as the necessary context and presuppositions for the discussion of the issues raised by the case involving the Congregation for the Doctrine of the Faith and myself. I understand myself to be a Catholic theologian and a Catholic believer, who recognizes the call of the church to be faithful in a creative way to the word and work of Jesus and who gratefully and loyally accepts the papal and episcopal functions in the church.

This paper will now focus on what in my judgment are the primary issues involved in my case. In the process I will state briefly my own position on these issues. Five issues will be considered: the role of the theologian, the possibility of public theological dissent from some noninfallible, hierarchical church teachings, the possibility and right of dissent by the Christian faithful, the justice and fairness of the process, and academic freedom for theology and Catholic institutions of higher learning. The September 17 letter from Cardinal Ratzinger calls upon me to retract my positions in the following specific areas: contraception and sterilization; abortion and euthanasia; masturbation, premarital intercourse, and homosexual acts; the indissolubility of marriage. However, as Richard McCormick perceptively points out, these issues and agreement with my positions on these issues do not constitute the major points of contention in the dispute between the Congregation and myself.[4] These are important topics, but they are primarily illustrative of the more fundamental issues involved. However, it is necessary to point out that in all these issues my position is quite nuanced.

II. The Role of the Theologian

There has been much written on the role of the theologian and the relationship between the function of bishops and theologians in the church. It is impossible to add to this discussion in this short space, but rather the purpose is to raise up the underlying issues involved in the present controversy. Many and probably the majority of Catholic theologians writing today see the role of the Catholic theologian as somewhat independent and cooperative in relationship to the hierarchical office and not delegated or derivative from the role of pope and bishops. The theologian is a scholar who studies critically, thematically, and systematically Christian faith and action. Such a scholar must theologize within the Catholic faith context and must give due importance to all the loci theologici including the teaching of the hierarchical magisterium. The Catholic theologian to be such must give the required assent to official church teaching, but the theologian does not derive his or her theological office from delegation by the hierarchical office holders. The pastoral teaching function of pope and bishops is connected with their offices in the church and differs from the teaching role of theologians. Note that I have described this understanding of the Catholic theologian as somewhat independent and cooperative with regard to the hierarchical role in the church. That independence is modified by the call of the theologian and all believers to give due assent to the pastoral teaching role of bishops and pope.

However, there is a very different understanding of the role of the theologian found in more recent church legislation. The new Code of Canon Law, which came into effect in the fall of 1983, and the Apostolic Constitution for ecclesiastical faculties and universities, Sapientia Christiana, understand the role of the theologian as primarily derived from the hierarchical teaching office and functioning by reason of delegation given by the hierarchical teaching office. A good illustration of this understanding of the theologian as delegate and representative of the hierarchical teaching office is found in canon 812 of the new Code of Canon Law: "Those who teach theological subjects in any institute of higher studies must have a mandate from the competent ecclesiastical authority." According to the Code, this mandate is required for all those who teach theology in any Catholic institution of higher learning. Earlier versions of the Code spoke of a "canonical mission" instead of a mandate. *Sapientia Christiana*, the Apostolic Constitution governing ecclesiastical faculties, requires a canonical mission from the chancellor for those teaching disciplines concerning faith or morals.[5] The final version of the Code uses the word mandate and not canonical mission because canonical mission appears to imply the assignment of a person to an ecclesiastical office.[6] The implication of this new canon and of other recent legislation is that the Catholic theologian in a Catholic institution officially exercises the function of teaching in that school through a delegation from the bishop. The role of the Catholic theologian is thus derived from the hierarchical teaching function and juridically depends upon it.

It seems there has been an interesting, even contradictory, development in Catholic documents within the last few years. The more theoretical documents seem to indicate a recognition for a somewhat independent and cooperative role for theologians, whereas the legislative documents understand the theological role as derivative and delegated from the hierarchical teaching office. There is no doubt that from the nineteenth century until recent times the role of the theologian was seen as subordinate to and derivative from the hierarchical teaching office. However, Vatican Council II in its general ecclesiology and in its understanding of theologians can be interpreted to adopt a more cooperative and somewhat independent understanding of the role of theologians vis-a-vis the hierarchical magisterium.[7] The cooperative model does not deny the official role of the hierarchical office in protecting and proclaiming the faith, but theology is a scholarly discipline distinct from but related to the proclamation of the faith by the hierarchical teaching office. However, canonists recognize that recent canonical legislation including the new Code of Canon Law understands the theological function as derivative from the hierarchical teaching function. In the older Code of Canon Law there was no requirement for theologians in Catholic institutions to have a canonical mandate or mission to teach theology. The older Code saw the role of the ordinary or diocesan bishop in terms of negative vigilance with regard to individual teachers of theology and not one of positive deputation.[8]

There can be no doubt that present church legislation tends to see the theological function as derivative from the hierarchical teaching function. However, very many Catholic theologians today appeal to more recent developments in Catholic understanding to substantiate a somewhat cooperative and independent understanding of the theological role vis-a-vis the hierarchical role. The correspondence between the Congregation for the Doctrine of the Faith and myself never explicitly goes into this question as such, but the Congregation is operating out of a derivative understanding of the role of the theologian while I adopt the somewhat independent and cooperative understanding.

In my understanding the teaching function is committed to the whole Church. In addition, there is a special pastoral teaching office given to pope and bishops in the church. As important as this hierarchical teaching function is, it is not identical with the total teaching function of the entire church. There are many teaching roles in the church. The teaching role of theologians does not depend on an office in the church but finds its authority in the faithful expertise of the scholar. This understanding of teaching authority in the Catholic Church which is proposed by many contemporary Catholic theologians has been called a pluralistic approach as distinguished from the hierocratic approach which reduces the teaching authority in the church to the teaching offices of pope and bishops.[9]

III. Public Theological Dissent from Some Noninfallible Hierarchical Church Teachings

The correspondence from the Congregation indicates that the problem is public dissent from some hierarchical noninfallible teaching and not just private dissent. However, the meaning of public is never developed. The entire investigation centers on my theological writings so the only logical conclusion is that public here refers to theological writings. Private dissent apparently means something that is not written and is not spoken publicly.

From the very beginning the position of the Congregation surprised me because the Congregation was denying the legitimate possibility of public theological dissent from the noninfallible teachings under discussion. My surprise stems from the fact that Catholic bishops and very many theologians have recognized the possibility of such public theological dissent.

In 1979 after receiving the first set of Observations from the Congregation, I had the feeling that the investigation would soon focus clearly on the manner and mode of public dissent. Past experience was the basis for this judgment. In 1968 I acted as the spokesperson for a group ultimately numbering over 600 theologians and issued a public statement at a press conference which concluded that Catholic spouses may responsibly decide according to their conscience that artificial contraception in some circumstances is permissible and even necessary to preserve and foster the values and sacredness of marriage. In response to this statement, the trustees of the Catholic University of America on September 5, 1969, mandated an inquiry in accord with academic due process to determine if the Catholic University professors involved in this dissent had violated by their declarations and actions their responsibilities to the university.[10]

A few months later the object of the inquiry had definitely changed. "Hence the focus of the present inquiry is on the style and method whereby some faculty members expressed personal dissent from papal teaching, and apparently helped organize additional public dissent to such teaching."[11] The Board of Trustees did not question the right of a scholar to have or hold private dissent from noninfallible church teaching. In the context of the inquiry it became clear that public and organized dissent referred primarily to holding a press conference and to actively soliciting other theologians to sign the original statement. The primary question of public dissent thus was not regular theological publication but the use of the more popular media. In response to this new focus of the inquiry, the subject professors at Catholic University through their counsel pointed out the changed focus but went on to show that such public and organized dissent in the popular media was a responsible action by Catholic theologians. The shift in the focus of the inquiry seemed to come from the fact that the trustees, including the bishops on the Board of Trustees, were willing to recognize the possibility of even public dissent in theological journals as being legitimate but objected to the use of the popular media. The faculty inquiry committee fully agreed with the thrust of the argument proposed by the professors, and the professors were exonerated in this hearing.

However, to my surprise the investigation from the Congregation never moved explicitly into the direction of the manner and mode of dissent and even at times the use of popular media. The conclusion logically follows from the position taken by the Congregation that the only acceptable form of dissent on these issues is that which is neither written nor spoken publicly.

The controversy explicitly deals with dissent on the specific questions under dispute. However, the correspondence seems to imply that the theologian cannot legitimately dissent from any noninfallible, hierarchical teaching. I have always pointed out in the correspondence that I have been dealing with the noninfallible hierarchical teaching office. This position was explicitly accepted by the Congregation in all of the correspondence prior to the September 17, 1985, letter to me from Cardinal Ratzinger. A very few Catholic theologians have maintained that the teaching on artificial contraception is infallible from the ordinary teaching of pope and bishops throughout the world.[12] However, this position is not held by the vast majority of theologians and has not been proposed or defended by the Congregation. One could also maintain that the Catholic teaching on divorce is infallible by reason of the teaching of the Council of Trent. However, the phrasing of the canons with regard to the indissolubility of marriage, the attempt not to condemn the practice of *economia* of the Greek church, and the somewhat broad understanding of *anathema sit* at that time of Trent argue against the infallible nature of the Catholic Church's teaching on the indissolubility of marriage. Accepted standard textbooks, such as that of Adnes, recognize that the teaching on absolute intrinsic indissolubility is not infallible.[13] Thus, my position all along has been that I have never denied an infallible teaching of the church.

However, in the September 17 letter Cardinal Ratzinger seems to claim that the assent of faith is somehow involved in my case. I have strenuously maintained that the assent of faith is not involved, and we are dealing with the *obsequium religiosum* which is due in cases of noninfallible teaching. I hope as a result of my meeting with Cardinal Ratzinger in Rome on March 8th that we agree that the assent of faith is not involved. However, it is very clear that the Congregation definitely maintains that the *obsequium religiosum* due to noninfallible teaching does not allow the theologian to dissent publicly in these cases.

Cardinal Ratzinger himself has called the distinction between infallible and noninfallible teaching "legalistic." Only in this century have theologians made this distinction in such a sharp way. "When one affirms that noninfallible doctrines, even though they make up part of the teaching of the church, can be legitimately contested, one ends up by destroying the practice of the Christian life and reduces the faith to a collection of doctrines." Abortion, divorce, and homosexuality, even with a thousand distinctions that can be made, are acts that go against Christian Faith.[14] Ratzinger deemphasizes the distinction between infallible and noninfallible teaching to help support his position that a theologian cannot dissent publicly from these noninfallible church teachings. What is to be said about Ratzinger's understanding?

It is true that the sharp distinction between infallible and noninfallible teaching is recent, for it became prevalent only at the time of the first Vatican Council (1870) which defended the infallibility of the pope. After that time, theologians quite rightly distinguished the two levels of teaching and the two different assents which are due to such teachings. All the faithful owe the assent of faith to infallible teaching and the *obsequium religiosum* of intellect and will to authoritative or authentic, noninfallible teaching. The distinction became well entrenched in the theology manuals of the twentieth century before Vatican II.[15] Such a distinction helped to explain that official teaching on some issues had been wrong and had subsequently been corrected (e.g., the condemnation of interest taking, the need for the intention of procreation to justify conjugal relations). At the time of the Vatican Council I and later it was also pointed out that Popes Liberius (+366), Vigilius, (+555) and Honorius (+ 638) all proposed erroneous teachings which were subsequently rejected through theological dissent. Vatican Council II changed many earlier teachings such as those on religious freedom and the relationship of the Roman Catholic Church to other Christian churches and to the true church of Jesus Christ. Scripture scholars for the last generation or so have publicly disagreed with the teachings that were proposed by the Biblical Commission in the first two decades of this century. The theologians thus recognized the distinction between infallible and noninfallible teaching and used it among other purposes to explain why certain earlier errors in church teaching did not refute the Vatican I teaching on papal infallibility. These theologians likewise recognized the possibility of dissent from such noninfallible teaching at times, but did not explicitly justify public dissent.[16]

The theologians are not the only ones to use this distinction. *Lumen Gentium*, the Constitution on the Church of the Second Vatican Council, recognizes this distinction between infallible and noninfallible teaching and the two different types of assent which are due (par. 25). The new Code of Canon Law clearly distinguishes between the assent of faith and the *obsequium religiosum* of intellect and will which is due to the authoritative teaching of the pope and college of bishops even when they do not intend to proclaim that doctrine by a definitive act (canon 752). This distinction is thus not only accepted by theologians but also by official documents and by the new Code of Canon Law.

Some theological manuals and many contemporary theologians understand the *obsequium religiosum* owed to authoritative, noninfallible teaching to justify at times the possibility of theological dissent, and at the present time even public dissent. Some bishops' conferences explicitly recognized the legitimacy of dissent from the papal encyclical *Humanae Vitae* issued in 1968. Also documents from bishops' conferences have acknowledged the possibility of public theological dissent from some noninfallible church teaching. The United States bishops in their 1968 pastoral letter "Human Life in Our Day" recognize that in noninfallible teaching there is always a presumption in favor of the magisterium—a position held by most theologians. However, the pastoral letter also acknowledges the legitimacy of public theological dissent from such teaching if the reasons are serious and well founded, if the manner of the dissent does not question or impugn the teaching authority of the church, and if the dissent is such as not to give scandal.[17] Since I have developed at great length in my correspondence with the Congregation both the arguments justifying the possibility of public dissent and the many theologians and others in the church who recognize such a possibility, there is no need to repeat this here.

One significant aspect of the question deserves mention here because of some recent developments—the understanding and translation of *obsequium religiosum*. *Obsequium* has often been translated as submission or obedience. Bishop Christopher Butler was to my knowledge the first to translate the word *obsequium* as due respect.[18] Francis Sullivan in his book on magisterium rejects the translation of "due respect" but still allows the possibility of legitimate public theological dissent from noninfallible church teaching.[19] (Sullivan, a Jesuit professor and former dean at the Pontifical Gregorian University in Rome, in a recent interview strongly defends the distinction between infallible and noninfallible church teaching.[20] Sullivan sees the position taken by the Vatican Congregation in its correspondence with me as threatening the critical function of the theologian with regard to the nondefinitive teaching of the magisterium. "The idea that Catholic theologians, at any level of education, can only teach the official church position, and present only those positions in their writings, is new and disturbing." Sullivan, who considers his approach "rather moderate" and "standard," has been teaching the possibility of public theological dissent from some noninfallible teaching at the Pontifical Gregorian University in Rome. Sullivan adds that "no one has ever questioned what I teach.") Sullivan claims that "submission" and not "due respect" is the proper translation of *obsequium*, but the Gregorian University professor still recognizes the possibility and legitimacy of public theological dissent from authoritative, noninfallible teaching.

The English text of the Code of Canon Law found in the commentary commissioned by the Canon Law Society of America and authorized by the executive committee of the National Conference of Catholic Bishops in the United States translates *obsequium* as respect.[21] Ladislas Orsy in a recent commentary on canon 752 recognizes difficulties in translating *obsequium* but opts for respect. Orsy also accepts the possibility of legitimate public dissent from some authoritative, noninfallible teaching.[22] The discussion over the proper understanding and translation of *obsequium* has been an occasion for many to recognize the possibility of legitimate public dissent from some noninfallible church teaching.

There can be no doubt that church documents, the Code of Canon Law, theologians in general, and canonists in general have accepted the importance of the distinction between infallible and noninfallible hierarchical teaching. Although I believe the distinction between infallible and noninfallible teaching is very important and necessary, there is a need to say more in dealing with the possibility of public dissent. I disagree with Cardinal Ratzinger's attempt to smooth over somewhat the clear distinction between infallible and noninfallible teaching, but his remarks show the need to say something in addition to the distinction between infallible and noninfallible teaching. What about the danger of reducing the Christian Faith in practice to a small, abstract core? Are abortion, divorce, and homosexuality, even with nuanced distinctions, acts which go against Christian Faith?

In my own comments about this case, I have been careful not only to use the distinction between infallible and noninfallible teaching but also to talk about what is core and central to the faith as distinguished from those things that are more removed and peripheral. Also I have consistently spoken about the right to dissent publicly from *some* noninfallible church teaching. The distinction between infallible and noninfallible church teaching is absolutely necessary, but not sufficient. The older theology tried to deal with questions of the relationship of church teaching to the core of faith through the use of theological notes. These notes and their opposites in terms of censures attempted to recognize the complexity by categorizing many different types of noninfallible teaching.[23] In a true sense there is a need today to redevelop the concept of theological notes in the light of the realities of the present time.

As important as the concept of infallible teaching is, there are some very significant limitations involved in it. Infallible teaching, especially of the extraordinary type by pope or council, has usually come in response to an attack on or a denial of something central to the faith. However, some points which have never been attacked, such as the existence of God, have never been defined by the extraordinary hierarchical teaching office. Something can be infallible by reason of the ordinary teachings of the pope and all the bishops, but the conditions required for such infallibility are often difficult to verify. On the other hand, the limits and imperfections of any infallible teaching have been rightly recognized. Infallible teaching itself is always open to development, better understanding, and even purification. Thus, one must be careful when speaking about infallible teaching both because some things might pertain to the core of faith which have at least not been infallibly taught by the extraordinary teaching function of the pope and bishops and because even infallible teaching itself is open to development and further interpretation. However, in the present discussion the distinction between infallible and noninfallible is very important. It allows me to deal with a limited area—the area of noninfallible teaching.

Within this large area of what is noninfallible, it is necessary to recognize various degrees and levels of relationship to faith. Here an updating of the older theological notes would be very useful. It is true that I have not attempted to develop all the distinctions involved in noninfallible teaching, but in the light of the purposes of the present discussion I have tried to show that the particular issues under discussion are removed from the central realities of Christian faith.

The Catholic tradition in moral theology has insisted that its moral teaching is based primarily on natural law and not primarily on faith or the Scripture. The natural law is understood to be human reason reflecting on human nature. Even those teachings which have some basis in Scripture (e.g., the indissolubility of marriage, homosexuality) were also said to be based on natural law. This insistence on the rational nature of Catholic moral teaching recognizes such teaching can and should be shared by all human beings of all faiths and of no faith. Such teachings are thus somewhat removed from the core of Catholic faith as such. The distance of these teachings from the core of faith and the central realities of faith grounds the possibility of legitimate dissent.

In addition, the issues under discussion are specific, concrete, universal moral norms existing in the midst of complex reality. Logic demands that the more specific and complex the reality, the less is the possibility of certitude. Moral norms in my judgment are not the primary, or the only, or the most important concern of moral teaching and of moral theology. Moral teaching deals with general perspectives, values, attitudes, and dispositions, as well as norms. Values, attitudes, and dispositions are much more important and far reaching for the moral life than are specific norms. These values and dispositions by their very nature are somewhat more general and can be more universally accepted as necessary for Christian and human life. Within the church all can and should agree that the disciples of Jesus are called to be loving, faithful, hopeful, caring people who strive to live out the reality of the paschal mystery. Disrespect for persons, cheating, slavery, dishonesty, and injustice are always wrong. However, the universal binding force of specific, concrete material norms cannot enjoy the same degree or level of certitude. Norms exist to protect and promote values, but in practice conflicts often arise in the midst of the complexity and specificity involved. Thus the issues under consideration in this case are quite far removed from the core of faith and exist at such a level of complexity and specificity that one has to recognize some possibility of dissent. It is also necessary to recognize the necessary distinction between the possibility of dissent and the legitimacy of dissent on particular questions. Reasons must be given which are convincing in order to justify the dissent in practice. The central issue involved in the controversy between the Congregation for the Doctrine of the Faith and myself is the possibility of public theological dissent from some noninfallible teaching which is quite remote from the core of faith, heavily dependent on support from human reason, and involved in such complexity and specificity that logically one cannot claim absolute certitude.

There is a further question which has not received much discussion from the Catholic theological community but which should at least be raised. We have generally talked about the responsibilities and rights of Catholic theologians in general. Are there any distinctions that must be made concerning theologians? Are the rights and responsibilities of Catholic theologians and the particular right to dissent in these areas the same for all Catholic theologians? Is there a difference between the theologian as teacher and as researcher and writer? Is there a difference if the theologian teaches in a seminary, a college, or a university? In the particular cases under discussion, I would develop the thesis that these differences do not affect the possibility and legitimacy of public theological dissent. All of us can agree on the need to explore this question in much greater depth. In addition, more attention must be given to the limits of legitimate dissent.

IV. The Christian Faithful and Dissent

There is a third aspect or issue which has not received the attention it needs—the possibility and legitimacy of dissent on the part of the members of the church. In a very true sense my present controversy involves more than just the role of theologians in the church. There can be no doubt that much of the friction between theologians and the hierarchical magisterium has occurred on more practical questions including moral issues touching on sexuality. The issues are not just abstract questions about which people speculate, but they involve concrete decisions about specific actions which are to be done. Problems arise in these areas precisely because they involve more than speculation. Here the position proposed by theologians might have some practical bearing on how people live. All must recognize that the distinction between the roles of bishops and theologians would be much clearer if the role of theologians were restricted to the realm of speculation with no effect on what people do in practice. However, life is not so easily compartmentalized.

Elsewhere I have defended the fact that on some issues a loyal Catholic may disagree in theory and in practice with the church's noninfallible teaching and still consider oneself a loyal and good Roman Catholic.[24] In a sense, under certain conditions, one can speak of a right of the Catholic faithful to dissent from certain noninfallible teachings. In the aftermath of Humanae Vitae in 1968 some bishops' conferences recognized that dissent in practice from the encyclical's teaching condemning artificial contraception could be legitimate and did not cut one off from the body of the faithful. The Congregation in its correspondence with me has not gone explicitly into this issue. Those who deny the legitimacy of such dissent in practice would seem to face a difficult ecclesiological problem when confronted with the fact that the vast majority of fertile Catholic spouses use artificial contraception. What is the relationship of these spouses to the Roman Catholic Church?

The possibility of legitimate dissent by the faithful stands on its own and is not directly dependent on theological dissent. However, the importance of recognizing this possibility and even right on the part of the faithful greatly affects how the theologian functions. If there is such a possibility of dissent, then the individual members of the Catholic Church have a right to know about it. I hasten to add that the individual members also have a right to know what is the official teaching of the church and should be conscious of the dangers of finitude and sin that can skew any human decision. Public dissent by a Catholic theologian would then be called for not only because

theologians must discuss with one another in the attempt to understand better God's word and to arrive at truth, but also because the
people of God need this information to make their own moral decisions. Thus, for example, in the light of the situation present at
the time of the issuance of the encyclical *Humanae Vitae* in 1968 it
was important for Roman Catholic spouses to know that they did
not have to make a choice between using artificial contraception
under some conditions and ceasing to be members of the Roman
Catholic Church. The Catholic theologian among others had an obligation to tell this to Catholic spouses.

The possibility for legitimate dissent in practice by the faithful
also affects the matter of scandal. The United States bishops in their
1968 letter proposed three conditions under which public theological dissent is in order. One of these conditions is that the dissent
be such as not to give scandal. In my correspondence with the Congregation, I repeatedly asked them for criteria which should govern
public theological dissent in the church. No developed criteria were
ever forthcoming. However, in the April 1983 "Observations" from
the Congregation, it was mentioned briefly that to dissent publicly
and to encourage dissent in others runs the risk of causing scandal.[25]
Scandal in the strict sense is an action or omission which provides
another the occasion of sinning. In the broad sense, scandal is the
wonderment and confusion which are caused by a certain action or
omission. Richard McCormick has already discussed the issue of
scandal understood in the strict sense.[26] What about scandal as the
wonderment and confusion caused among the faithful by public
theological dissent? There can be no doubt that in the past there has
been a strong tendency on the part of the hierarchical leaders of the
church to look upon the faithful as poor and ignorant sheep who
had to be protected and helped. This same vision and understanding
of the ordinary common people also lay behind an older Catholic
justification of monarchy and government from above. Catholic social teaching itself has changed in the twentieth century and accepted
the need for and importance of democratic political institutions. No
longer are the citizens the poor sheep or the "ignorant multitude,"
to use the phrase employed by Pope Leo XIII. So, too, the members
of the church can no longer be considered as poor sheep but greater
importance must be given to their increased education and rights in
all areas including religion.[27]

Perhaps at times theologians, who often associate with people who
are well educated, will fail to give enough importance to the danger
of disturbing some of the faithful with their teachings. However, in
this day and age it seems many more Catholic lay people would be

scandalized if theologians were forbidden to discuss publicly important topics of the day such as contraception, divorce, abortion, and homosexuality. These issues are being discussed at great length in all places today, and theologians must be able to enter into the discussion even to the point of dissenting from some official Catholic teaching. In addition, if the faithful can at times dissent in practice and remain loyal Roman Catholics, then they have the right to know what theologians are discussing.

In this entire discussion it would ultimately be erroneous to confine the question just to the possibility and right of theologians to dissent publicly from some noninfallible teachings. There is need for further development and nuancing, but on all the moral issues under consideration, I have carefully tried to indicate in my writings what the legitimate possibilities are for the faithful in practice. The right of the faithful in this matter definitely colors one's approach to public theological dissent and the the dangers of scandal brought about by such dissent or the lack of it.

V. *Justice and Fairness of the Process*

Catholic theology has always emphasized the incarnational principle with its emphasis on visible human structures. Catholic ecclesiology well illustrates this approach by insisting on the church as a visible human community—the people of God with a hierarchical office. The visible church strives to be a sacrament or sign of the presence of God in the world in and through this visible community. Within the community there are bound to be tensions involving the role of bishops and the role of theologians. Both strive to work for the good of the church, but there will always be tensions. To claim there is no tension would be illusionary and ultimately would deny that the church is a living, pilgrim community. The church is always striving to know and live better the word and work of Jesus in the particular historical and cultural circumstances of time and place. The role of the theologian by definition will often be that of probing, exploring, and tentatively pushing the boundaries forward. The hierarchical teaching office must promote such creative and faithful theological activity, while at the same time it must rightly wait until these newer developments emerge more clearly. The church in justice must find ways to deal with this tension in the relationship between theologians and the hierarchical teaching office. The good of the church, the credibility of its teaching office, and the need to protect the rights of all concerned call for just ways of dealing with these inevitable tensions.

The present case raises questions of justice and of the credibility of the teaching office in the church. It is recognized by all that there are many Catholic theologians who publicly dissent from some noninfallible teachings. Likewise there are many Catholic theologians who hold similar positions and even more radical positions on the moral issues involved in the present case. However, the issues of justice and credibility go much deeper.

First, it is necessary for the Congregation to state its position on public theological dissent from noninfallible teaching. Is such dissent ever allowed? If so, under what conditions or criteria? From the correspondence it would seem that the Congregation is claiming that all public theological dissent is wrong, or at least public dissent on these particular issues is wrong. Does the Congregation truly hold such a position? As mentioned earlier, the United States bishops in 1968 in the light of the controversy engendered by *Humanae Vitae* proposed three conditions for justifying public dissent from noninfallible teaching. The three conditions are: the reasons must be serious and well founded; the manner of the dissent must not question or impugn the teaching authority of the church; and it must not give scandal. I have consistently maintained that my dissent has been in accord with these norms. The Congregation was unwilling to accept these norms. Does the Congregation disagree with the United States bishops and with the vast majority of Catholic theologians?

Archbishop John Quinn, then of Oklahoma City, at the Synod of Bishops in 1974 pointed out the real need to arrive at some consensus and understanding about dissent and urged discussion between representatives of the Holy See and representatives of theologians to arrive at acceptable guidelines governing theological dissent in the church.[28] Archbishop Quinn brought up the same problem again at the Synod of Bishops in 1980.[29] For the good of the Church there continues to be a "real need" to arrive at some guidelines in this area.

In addition there is need for juridical structures which better safeguard justice and the rights of all concerned. Some of the problems with the present procedures of the Congregation have already been pointed out in the correspondence. The Congregation in a letter to me has defended its procedures because the *"Ratio Agendi"* is not a trial but rather a procedure designed to generate a careful and accurate examination of the contents of published writings by the author. However, since the process can result in severe punishment for the person involved, it seems that such a process should incorporate the contemporary standards of justice found in other juridical proceedings.

One set of problems stems from the fact that the Congregation is the prosecutor, the judge, and jury. Some people have objected strongly to the fact that the Cardinal Prefect has commented publicly on the present case and disagreed in the public media with my position while the case has been in progress. Problems have also been raised against the existing procedures from the viewpoints of the secrecy of the first part of the process, the failure to allow the one being investigated to have counsel, the failure to disclose the accusers and the total record to the accused, and the lack of any substantive appeal process.[30] There have been many suggestions made for improvements in the procedures. The German Bishops have adopted procedures for use in Germany.[31] Cardinal Ratzinger in 1984 admitted that there has been a decree of the plenary session of the Congregation in favor of a revision of the current procedures of the Congregation. The proposals made by the German Conference of Bishops have been accepted in principle. However, because of the workload and time constraints the decree has not been put into effect.[32]

In 1980 a joint committee of the Catholic Theological Society of America and the Canon Law Society of America was formed to address the question of cooperation between theologians and the hierarchical magisterium in the United States with a view toward developing norms that could be used in settling disputes. The committee prepared a detailed set of procedures in 1983, but they are still under study by the United States bishops.[33] In the meantime there has been one case involving the investigation of a theologian's writings by the doctrinal committee of the United States bishops. Little is known about the process itself, but the final statement from the committee indicates that the dialogue was fruitful and that the theologian in question, Richard McBrien, had the right to call other theologians to defend and explain his positions.[34] Perhaps the process used in this case might prove helpful in other similar cases.

A detailed discussion of proposed guidelines lies beyond the scope of this present paper. The major points made here are that justice and the credibility of the church's teaching office call for a recognition of the norms or criteria governing public dissent in the church, the equitable application of these norms, and the review of existing procedures to incorporate the safeguards of contemporary justice in the process of examining theologians. The call for these changes has been repeatedly made in the past. The need is even more urgent today.

VI. *Academic Freedom, Theology and Catholic Institutions*
of Higher Learning

Catholic higher education in the United States well illustrates the tension between being Catholic and being American which has challenged Catholic life and institutions in our country. In this particular case the pertinent question was often phrased in the following terms: Is a Catholic university a contradiction in terms? Colleges and universities in the United States have stressed the importance of institutional autonomy and academic freedom as two essential characteristics of what constitutes a college or university.

Until 1960 most Catholic institutions of higher learning emphasized their uniqueness and either implicitly or explicitly denied the need for academic freedom and institutional autonomy. However, as the sixties progressed there was a growing acceptance of the need for these characteristics. By the end of the 1960s the major Catholic institutions of the United States had expressed a strong commitment to a true autonomy and academic freedom in the face of authority of whatever kind, lay or clerical, external to the academic community itself.[35]

Many reasons help explain this change—a greater Catholic interest in higher education at that time; the influx of people from secular universities into Catholic academe; the growing recognition of the greater compatibility between Catholicism and American institutions; the realization of the meager Catholic contribution to intellectual life in this country; a theoretical and practical appreciation of the role of the laity in higher education; a greater acceptance of professionalization in all aspects and departments of Catholic institutions of higher learning including theology and religion departments.

Today the leaders of Catholic higher education in the United States strongly insist on the need for academic freedom and institutional autonomy.[36] The crux of the problem is to reconcile the existence of academic freedom and institutional autonomy with the truth claims made by the Catholic Church and its hierarchical teaching office. More specifically, the question is: can and should Catholic theology be responsibly taught and researched in the context of academic freedom and institutional autonomy? From the viewpoint of the American academy, there is a greater awareness today of the bankruptcy of an older insistence on being value free or value neutral. Values should be very important in all the human disciplines. Thus there is in general a greater openness in American academe today to accept the academic respectability of disciplines like theology.

However, the question is can Catholic theology accept the American concept of academic freedom? There has not been as much discussion in this area as there should be.

I will briefly describe how I think academic freedom and Catholic theology are compatible.[37] Academic freedom and institutional autonomy mean that any decisions affecting promotion, hiring, or dismissal of faculty members must be made by peers in the academy and not by outside persons or forces of any kind. Academic freedom respects the freedom of the scholar to pursue truth with no limits placed on scholarship other than truth, honesty, and competency. The accepted principles of academic freedom recognize that even tenured faculty members can be terminated if they are incompetent and the judgment of incompetency is made by academic peers. Competency for the Catholic theologian demands that one theologize within the pale of Roman Catholic faith. The Catholic theologian must teach Catholic theology as such; otherwise one is incompetent as a Catholic theologian. Peers in judging the competency of a Catholic theologian must give due weight to the teaching of the hierarchical magisterium. However, the ultimate decision with juridical effects must be made by peers in the academy. The hierarchical magisterium is always free if it deems it necessary to point out the errors and ambiguities in the work of a theologian, but it cannot make decisions having direct juridical effect in the academy.

There is no doubt that academic freedom gives some added protection to the rights of the Catholic theological scholar. However, in my judgment, such protection is totally compatible with the understanding of the role of the Catholic theologian as somewhat cooperative with and somewhat independent of the role of the hierarchical teaching office. Such protection is not only good for the discipline of Catholic theology but also is good for the total church as it strives for creative fidelity to the word and work of Jesus. In this way I maintain one can do justice both to the demands of the academy and to the demands of Catholic theology and the good of the Catholic Church.

The academic freedom of Catholic institutions and of Catholic theology is an important theoretical question with many practical consequences. I think that the issue has to be settled on grounds of good theory, but one cannot ignore the practical consequences. Perhaps the most significant practical consequence at the present time concerns the financial threat to the very existence of Catholic higher education in the United States. Catholic colleges and universities receive a large amount of financial help in different forms from the public monies of the state. In the past the Supreme Court has ruled such public funding is acceptable for Catholic higher education but not for Catholic elementary and high schools. The difference between higher and lower education is that in higher education there is no indoctrination and the principles of academic freedom are observed. Thus, if there were no academic freedom and institutional autonomy for Catholic higher education, it might very well be that the Court would rule that public funding for Catholic institutions of higher learning is unconstitutional.[38] There are many complex and intricate questions that need to be discussed, but the general outline of this possible outcome is clear. The leaders of Catholic higher education are quite aware of and worried by these implications.

If the Vatican Congregation or any ecclesiastical authority can declare someone no longer a Catholic theologian and unable to teach in the name of the church and thereby prevent that professor from continuing to teach Catholic theology in a Catholic institution, this seems to be a violation of academic freedom. However, in the present context, some maintain that this is the case only for a very few ecclesiastical faculties or universities such as the Catholic University of America, but it does not apply to the vast majority of American Catholic colleges and universities which are not canonically approved by the Vatican.[39]

Yes there is some difference between Vatican approved ecclesiastical faculties or institutions and the vast majority of Catholic colleges and universities in the United States. However, in the light of the new Code of Canon Law with its canon 812, the same problems about academic freedom exist for all Catholic institutions of higher learning. According to canon 812, teachers of theological disciplines need a mandate from a competent ecclesiastical authority. Thus the decisions of ecclesiastical authority can have a direct effect in the hiring, promotion, and dismissal of faculty members. The proposed Schema for Catholic colleges and universities now being circulated by the Congregation for Catholic Education enshrines and develops the same basic structural understanding. Catholic leaders of higher education in the United States have strongly disagreed with the new canon 812 and with the proposed new Schema for Catholic higher education. Such legislation and proposed legislation are seen as threats to the academic freedom and institutional autonomy of Catholic higher education in the United States.[40] I insist that the question of the academic freedom and institutional autonomy respecting Catholic higher education and Catholic theology should not ultimately be decided because of practical consequences for Catholic higher education; but, on the other hand, one cannot ignore these possible consequences.

In conclusion, this paper has examined what I think are the five most significant issues involved in my present dispute with the Congregation for the Doctrine of the Faith—the role of the Catholic theologian, the possibility of public theological dissent from some noninfallible hierarchical teaching, the possibility of dissent by the faithful in such cases, the fairness of the process, and academic freedom. In discussing all these issues, I have also indicated my approach to the questions under discussion. I welcome your reactions.

NOTES

1. Some of the pertinent documentation in my case has been published in *Origins* 15 (March 27, 1986), 665–80.

2. John P. Boyle, "The Ordinary Magisterium: Toward a History of the Concept," *The Heythrop Journal* 20 (1979), 380–98; 21 (1980), 14–29.

3. For a discussion of all sides in the contemporary debate about morality and the hierarchical teaching office, see Charles E. Curran and Richard A. McCormick, eds., *Readings in Moral Theology No. 3: The Magisterium and Morality* (New York: Paulist Press, 1982).

4. Richard A. McCormick, "L'Affaire Curran," *America* 154 (April 5, 1986), 261–67.

5. *Sapientia Christiana*, art. 27 in *Origins* 9 (June 7, 1979), 34–45.

6. John A. Alesandro, "The Rights and Responsibilities of Theologians: A Canonical Perspective," in Leo O'Donovan, ed., *Cooperation Between Theologians and the Ecclesiastical Magisterium: A Report of the Joint Committee of the Canon Law Society of America and the Catholic Theological Society of America* (Washington: Canon Law Society of America, 1982), pp. 106–09.

7. Jon Nilson, "The Rights and Responsibilities of Theologians: A Theological Perspective," in O'Donovan, pp. 53–75. Many contemporary theologians hold a similar position. This understanding of the role of the theologian also appears in some papers prepared for a discussion of the magisterium sponsored by the United States Bishops' Committee on Doctrine. See U.S. Bishops' Committee on Doctrine, "Report: An Ongoing Discussion of Magisterium," *Origins* 9 (1980), 541–51.

8. Alesandro in O'Donovan, pp. 107–09.

9. Avery Dulles, *The Resilient Church* (Garden City, New York: Doubleday, 1977), pp. 99ff.

10. John F. Hunt, Terrence R. Connelly *et al.*, *The Responsibility of Dissent: The Church and Academic Freedom* (New York: Sheed and Ward, 1970), pp. 23ff. This volume treats the academic and legal aspects of the defense made by myself and my colleagues at Catholic University. For the theological aspects, see Charles E. Curran, Robert E. Hunt, *et al.*, *Dissent In and For the Church* (New York: Sheed and Ward, 1970).

11. Hunt and Connelly, p. 39.

12. John C. Ford and Germain Grisez, "Contraception and the Infallibility of the Ordinary Magisterium," *Theological Studies* 39 (1978), 258–312.

13. Pierre Adnes, *Le Mariage* (Tournai, Belgium: Desclee, 1963), pp. 159ff.

14. Lucio Brunelli, "Interview with Cardinal Ratzinger," *National Catholic Register*, May 11, 1986, p. 5. The original interview appeared in *30 Giorno*, Maggio 1986, pp. 10, 11.

15. Francis A. Sullivan, *Magisterium: Teaching Authority in the Catholic Church* (New York: Paulist Press, 1983).

16. Curran and Hunt, pp. 66ff.

17. National Conference of Catholic Bishops, *Human Life in Our Day* (Washington: United States Catholic Conference, 1968), pp. 18, 19.

18. B. C. Butler, "Authority and the Christian Conscience," *Clergy Review* 60 (1975), 16.

19. Sullivan, pp. 159ff. Sullivan refers only to a later article by B. C. Butler, "Infallible: *Authenticum: Assensus: Obsequium*. Christian Teaching Authority and the Christian's Response," *Doctrine and Life* 31 (1981), 77–89.

20. John Thavis, "Interpretation of Dissent Could Threaten Theologians, Says Former Dean," NC News Service, Tuesday, May 6, 1986, pp. 19, 20.

21. James A. Coriden, Thomas J. Green, and Donald E. Heintschel, eds., The Code of Canon Law: A Text and Commentary (New York: Paulist Press, 1985), canon 752, p. 548.

22. Ladislas Orsy, "Reflections on the Text of a Canon," America 154 (May 17, 1986), 396–99.

23. Sixtus Cartechini, De Valore Notarum Theologicarum (Rome: Gregorian University Press, 1951).

24. E.g., Charles E. Curran, Ongoing Revision: Studies in Moral Theology (Notre Dame, IN: Fides Publishers, 1975), pp. 37–65; Transition and Tradition in Moral Theology (Notre Dame, IN: University of Notre Dame Press, 1978), pp. 43–55; Critical Concerns in Moral Theology (Notre Dame, IN: University of Notre Dame Press, 1984), pp. 233–56.

25. Origins 15 (March 27, 1986), 670.

26. McCormick, America 154 (April 5, 1986), 266, 267.

27. Cardinal Ratzinger emphasizes the faith of the simple faithful and the duties of the shepherds and teachers in the church to these simple faithful. See Cardinal Ratzinger, "The Church and the Theologians," Origins 15 (May 8, 1986), 761–70.

28. Archbishop John R. Quinn, "Norms for Church Dissent," Origins 4 (1974–75), 319–320.

29. Archbishop John R. Quinn, "New Context for Contraception Teaching," Origins 10 (1980), 263–67.

30. Patrick Granfield, "Theological Evaluation of Current Procedures," in O'Donovan, pp. 125–32.

31. "Beschluss der Deutschen Bischofskonferenz vom 21 September 1972 zur Regelung eines Lehrbeanstandsungsverfahrens," Archiv fur katholischen Kirchenrecht 141 (1972), 524–530.

32. National Catholic Register, August 12, 1984, p. 6.

33. Joint Committee of the Canon Law Society of America and the Catholic Theological Society of America, "Doctrinal Responsibilities: Procedures for Promoting Cooperation and Resolving Disputes between Bishops and Theologians," Proceedings of the Catholic Theological Society of America 39 (1984), 209–34.

34. U.S. Bishops' Committee on Doctrine, "Father Richard McBrien's Catholicism," Origins 15 (1985), 129–32.

35. For the historical development of the attitude of Catholic higher education to academic freedom see the various writings of Philip Gleason including the following: "Academic Freedom and the Crisis in Catholic Universities," in Edward Manier and John W. Houck, eds., American Freedom and the Catholic University (Notre Dame, IN: University of Notre Dame Press, 1967), pp. 33–56; "Academic Freedom: Survey, Retrospect, and Prospects," National Catholic Education Association Bulletin 64 (August 1967), 67–74; "Freedom and the Catholic University," National Catholic Education Association Bulletin 65 (November 1968), 21–29.

36. "Catholic College and University Presidents Respond to Proposed Vatican Schema," Origins 15 (April 10, 1986), 697–704.

37. This view has been developed in greater detail in Hunt and Connelly.

38. "Catholic College and University Presidents. . .," Origins 15 (April 10, 1986), 699–700.

39. Quentin L. Quade, Contribution to "Curran, Dissent, and Rome: A Symposium," Catholicism in Crisis 4 (May 1986), 20–22.

40. Origins 15 (April 10, 1986), 697–704.

THE RESPONSE CATHOLICS OWE TO NONINFALLIBLE TEACHINGS

James Heft, S.M.
University of Dayton

ABSTRACT

Set in its proper context, discussion about the response Catholics owe to noninfallible teachings was treated by the manualists from the last half of the 19th century to the present, and referred to explicitly by the Theological Commission of Vatican II when interpreting the meaning of *Lumen Gentium's* call for the "religious submission of mind and will" even to noninfallible teachings (par. 25). While most theological discussion today assumes the legitimacy of dissent, there is little clarity on the ways in which this dissent should be registered. One contributing factor to this lack of clarity is the problematic character of the infallible/noninfallible distinction. While bishops need to recognize the legitimacy of dissent, theologians need to focus more on their responsibilities, including increased mutual criticism, openness to official teachings, ongoing conversion to Jesus Christ, and the courage to speak the truth in love. Both bishops and theologians can learn from the laity, especially in those areas in which they enjoy a special competence.

In this article I shall discuss the response that Catholics owe to noninfallible teachings. I will first review briefly the recent history of this question, consider the attitudes that Catholics should cultivate in themselves when they receive noninfallible teachings, explain some of the difficulties surrounding public dissent, and finally offer some personal reflections on the state of this question in the Church today.

Rev. James Heft, S.M. (Society of Mary), is currently the Chair of the Religious Studies Department of the University of Dayton, (Dayton, OH 45469) where he has been a professor of theology since 1977. He is particularly interested in historical theology as it bears upon current ecumenical questions. He has taught graduate courses in Christology, Mariology and Ecclesiology, and has published in the Journal of Ecumenical Studies, Archivum Historiae Pontificiae, One in Christ, and numerous other journals. His study of the historical origins of papal infallibility, John XXII [1316–1334] and Papal Teaching Authority, has just been published by the Edwin Mellen Press.

I. Legitimate Dissent: A Relatively New Question

The task of distinguishing essentials from nonessentials has been from the start a matter of serious concern to Christians. Sts. Peter and Paul and James and the whole Church, with the assistance of the Holy Spirit (Acts 15:22), decided at the Council of Jerusalem that circumcision was not to be required of Gentiles. Medieval canon lawyers assumed that there was a difference, though at times difficult to determine with precision, between matters of discipline and matters of doctrine, and medieval theologians thought it was important to determine the level of importance to be attributed to various theological statements.[1]

The question of whether it is legitimate to dissent from noninfallible teachings could arise only once there was a distinction between infallible and noninfallible teachings. It was only around 1840 that the term ordinary and extra-ordinary magisterium were first used in a papal document.[2] At about the same time, and for the first time, the term "magisterium," that is, the teaching authority in the Church, was exclusively identified with the hierarchy.[3] When the First Vatican Council set down the conditions necessary for an infallible papal definition, it became possible in a carefully circumscribed way to identify infallible teachings. In doing so, it became possible to distinguish in a more precise fashion between infallible and noninfallible teachings. That Council, however, said virtually nothing about the nature of an individual Catholic's responsibility to accept noninfallible teachings.

With the nearly complete collapse of Catholic theological faculties in Europe at the time of the French Revolution, the papacy, beginning particularly with the pontificate of Gregory XVI, and culminating with the pontificate of Pius XII, published a great number of encyclicals. The exercise of this form of papal teaching authority became identified with the exercise of the ordinary magisterium. Pius XII declared in Humani Generis (1950) that even though papal teachings of this sort on a matter of doctrine were not infallible, theologians were no longer free to discuss the matter; moreover, he taught that the ordinary magisterium of the pope demanded obedience: "He who hears you hears me." Finally, Pius XII stated that one of the tasks of theologians is to justify declarations of the magisterium, that is, to explain how those teachings are to be found in Scripture and Tradition.[4]

The Second Vatican Council addressed the issue of the respect that Catholics owe to noninfallible teachings in paragraph 25 of Lumen Gentium, which reads:

This religious submission of will and of mind must be shown in a special way to the authentic teaching authority of the Roman Pontiff, even when he is not speaking ex *cathedra*. That is, it must be shown in such a way that his supreme magisterium is acknowledged with reverence, the judgments made by him are sincerely adhered to, according to his manifest mind and will.[5]

On the surface, this statement would appear only to repeat the teachings of Pius XII. However, to interpret the text accurately, its background needs to be understood. First, the original *schema* proposed and rejected at the first session of the Council had included Pius XII's prohibition of free debate among theologians. In the final text, this prohibition was dropped. Moreover, the biblical text used by Pius XII to describe the ordinary magisterium ("He who hears you hears me") was also dropped. Three questions (*modi*) were posed to the doctrinal commission concerning the meaning of par. 25, one of which is of particular relevance for our topic.[6] Three bishops asked about the case of an "educated person, confronted with a teaching proposed noninfallibly, who cannot, for solid reasons, give his internal assent." The theological commission responded by directing the bishops to consult the approved authors (*auctores probati*), that is, to consult the textbooks of theology ordinarily used in seminary theology courses. Several theologians have done these studies.[7] What they have discovered is that the adherence to official, authoritative (rather than "authentic") noninfallible teachings should be both internal and religious: internal, which requires more than external conformity or a mere respectful silence; and religious, which indicates that the motive for adherence is not primarily the cogency of the reasoning for the fact that the Pope has been given authority to teach by Christ.

But this internal religious adherence is to be distinguished from the assent of divine faith which is due only to infallible teachings. Internal religious adherence is not metaphysically (or absolutely) certain but morally certain. This distinction is made because, as Francis Sullivan explains, "the non-definitive teaching on the magisterium is not infallible, it can be erroneous; if it is not irreformable, it can stand in need of correction."[8] A careful interpretation of paragraph 25 of *Lumen Gentium* shows, therefore, that in certain carefully circumscribed situations it is legitimate to dissent from noninfallible teachings.[9]

Shortly after the Council, the German bishops issued in September of 1967, almost a year before the publication of *Humanae Vitae*, a statement on the ordinary magisterium in which they wrote that "in order to maintain the true and ultimate substance of the faith it (the Church) must, even at the risk of error in points of detail, give expression to doctrinal directives which have a certain degree of binding force and yet, since they are not de fide definitions, involve a certain element of the provisional even to the point of being capable of including error." Nevertheless, they continued, the Church must teach if it is to apply the faith to new situations that arise. "In such a case the position of the individual Christian in regard to the Church is analogous to that of a man who knows that he is bound to accept the decision of a specialist even while recognizing that it is not infallible."[10]

Humanae Vitae, issued in the summer of 1968, forced the discussion from considerations of private dissent by individual Catholics to those of public dissent by Catholic theologians. In November of that same year, the United States bishops, in their pastoral letter, "Human Life in Our Day," stated that "the expression of theological dissent from the magisterium is in order only if the reasons are serious and well-founded, if the manner of the dissent does not question or impugn the teaching authority of the Church and is such as to not give scandal." They realized, however, that in saying this they had given support to something new in the Church, and given the complexity of the matter, called for a dialogue between themselves and theologians to clarify the matter further: "Since our age is characterized by popular interest in theological debate and given the realities of modern mass media, the ways in which theological dissent may be effectively expressed, in a manner consistent with pastoral solicitude, should become the object of fruitful dialogue between bishops and theologians." Since that time, the American bishops have not issued any statement that has advanced this discussion or clarified the criteria that would ensure that public theological dissent on noninfallible matters will be consistent with pastoral solicitude.

In the spring of 1986, after seven years of private correspondence initiated by the Sacred Congregation for the Doctrine of the Faith (SCDF), Fr. Charles Curran, a professor of moral theology at the Catholic University in Washington, D.C., explained at a press conference held in Washington immediately after returning from a meeting with Cardinal Ratzinger in Rome, that he had arrived at an impasse with the Cardinal concerning the legitimacy of public theological dissent on noninfallible matters. Fr. Richard McCormick, a Jesuit moral theologian at Georgetown University, has concluded that Ratzinger in essence is requiring that a professor must agree "with the ordinary magisterium on every authoritatively proposed moral formulation" or cease to be called a Catholic theologian.[11]

Between Vatican II and the present, most authors who have treated the question of dissent, private and public, have concluded that it is legitimate. At the same time, many of them have stressed that much still needs to be worked out. In 1974, Christopher Butler, for example, noted that in this area "we lack the guidance of good theology today."[12] Five years later John Boyle explained that the particular authority pastoral teachings should have in the Church has "not been adequately clarified."[13] In an address given on April 15, 1986, at St. Michael's College in Toronto, Ontario, Cardinal Ratzinger himself said concerning the work of theologians that "there is no question that it is important to find legal formulas by which we can safeguard the objective freedom of scientific thought within its limits and guaranteeing the necessary room for maneuver for scientific discussion."[14]

II. The Response Catholics Owe to Noninfallible Teachings

Two things should be clear at this point: individual Catholics may dissent from noninfallible teachings and there is a lack of agreement on how this can be done responsibly, particularly when it is a case of public dissent. In this section I will discuss how an individual Catholic should approach authoritative noninfallible teaching.[15] In particular, I want to discuss the attitudes that a Catholic should have in order to ensure the proper openness to noninfallible teachings.

We have already noted that the theological commission of Vatican II referred the bishops who asked about dissent from noninfallible teachings to the "approved authors." These authors, or manualists, all stress that at the outset the presumption should always be in favor of the teaching of the ordinary magisterium, and that one's adherence should not be suspended rashly or casually, or because of pride, "excessive love of one's own opinions" or "over-confidence in one's own genius."[16] They assume that it is very unlikely that the ordinary magisterium would be in error. The German bishops offer a similar caution:

> Anyone who believes that he is justified in holding, as a matter of his own private opinion, that he has already even now arrived at some better insight which the Church will come to in the future must ask himself in all sober self-criticism before God and his conscience whether he has the necessary breadth and depth of specialized theological knowledge to permit himself in his private theory and practice to depart from the current teaching of the official Church. Such a case is conceivable in principle, but subjective presumptuousness and an unwarranted attitude of knowing better will be called to account before the judgment seat of God.[17]

The then Monsignor Philips, one of the two secretaries of Vatican II's Theological Commission, explained in his 1967 work, *L'Eglise et Son Mystère*, that Catholics should be deeply ready ("auront à coeur") to respect ("vénérer") the authority with which the ordinary magisterium is exercised.[18] Bishop Butler explains that in "all cases, the mood of the devout believer will be not resentment at what appears to be a constraint upon his thinking, but a welcoming gratitude that goes along with a keen alertness of a critical mind and of a good will concerned to play its part both in the purification and the development of the Church's understanding of its inheritance."[19]

Several authors stress the importance of an attitude they call "docility." In his 1962 study, *L'Église est une communion*, the Dominican theologian Jerome Hamer, now the Prefect of the Congregation for Religious, explains some of the key ideas of St. Thomas on docility. It is located in the intelligence, and has to do with the acquisition of knowledge and helps a person to appropriate teaching personally. There are also degrees of docility that are "proportionate to the distance that lies between the qualifications or doctrinal authority of the teacher and the knowledge of the pupil." Hamer states that docility should not be confused with the obedience of faith, since it is a virtue of the intelligence whose object is knowledge, rather than a virtue of the will which submits to the will of the teacher.[20]

Francis Sullivan contrasts the attitudes of obstinacy and docility, and explains that obstinacy is to be renounced and docility adopted:

> Renouncing obstinacy would mean rejecting a tendency to close my mind to the official teaching, to refuse even to give it a fair hearing, to adopt the attitude: "I've already made my mind up; don't bother me." Positively, what would an attitude of docility involve? Docility is a willingness to be taught, a willingness to prefer another's judgment to one's own when it is reasonable to do so. Docility calls for an open attitude toward official teaching, giving it a fair hearing, doing one's best to appreciate the reasons in its favour, so as to convince oneself of its truth, and thus facilitate one's intellectual assent to it.[21]

Sullivan adds that since the ordinary magisterium seeks adherence that is an act of the judgment, it must appeal not just to the will but also to the mind. It must present its teachings with reasons that are clear and convincing, particularly in those matters which have to do with the natural law, since such matters are said to be discoverable by human reasoning, over which the hierarchy of the Church has no monopoly.[22] Nevertheless, this is not to say that the magisterium "has no more claim on our assent than the strength of its arguments would warrant." Were this the case, an individual would give to the pope, explains John Gallagher, "no more authority than one would give to one's bartender or hairdresser or anyone with whom one might discuss an ethical question."[23]

In an entire chapter devoted to a discussion of the magisterium and dissent on moral matters, Gallagher raises a series of questions that a devout Catholic should try to answer before dissenting from the ordinary magisterium. Since Gallagher's checklist is the most extensive I have come across, I wish to quote a major portion of it:

Am I biased? Am I rationalizing a decision I have made on selfish grounds? Am I being honest, humble and courageous in facing my own limitations? Does my life exhibit patience, kindness, and the other gifts and fruits of the Holy Spirit? Or is my thinking too much influenced by anger, or disdain, or hurt feelings, or arrogance?

Before deciding that dissent is legitimate one should look at one's own capacity for making moral judgments. Am I well qualified to judge in these matters? If I attempt to make up for my lack of qualifications by seeking expert advice, am I well qualified to choose good advisors? Do I choose advisors because they are likely to say what I want them to say? One should take counsel not only to get the views of specialists but also to gain objectivity. The advice of objective counselors in an important means for overcoming one's own bias and tendency to sub-jectivism.

On any important moral judgment one should pray, not as a pious afterthought but as an essential step. Moral decisions have conse-quences and implications beyond our ability to grasp. We must open ourselves to the Holy Spirit to guide us by a wisdom greater than our own. Prayer is especially important if one is considering dissent from a papal moral teaching.[24]

Besides examining one's attitude, there are also intellectual re-quirements for determining the degree of authority that ought to be given to noninfallible teaching. "We must know whether we are faced with a warning, advice, the settling of a controversy, a caution, or a doctrinal pronouncement in the strict sense of the word."[25] Again, Gallagher describes a number of differing degrees of authority for noninfallible papal teachings:

Other things being equal, a teaching repeated many times by several Popes over a long period of time has more authority than a teaching stated only once or twice. A papal statement on some point which has arisen recently usually will not carry as much weight as a papal teaching held consistently over a long period of time during which the subject has received frequent consideration. A papal statement on a point which has recently arisen may well be cautionary rather than definitive. It indicates that at this stage of the development of thought on the point, the new ideas cannot be accepted in the form in which they have been presented. At some later stage in the development of thought on a point, further formulations may be found which allow the acceptance of what is good in the new ideas without the acceptance of error or the denial of truths arrived at in the past. If the issue has arisen recently, the papal teaching is more likely to be cautionary and admitting of development than if the issue has been discussed for several generations.

Other things being equal, a papal teaching which has not been repeated for several decades, in spite of some Catholics disregarding it, does not have as much authority as a teaching which is repeated by Popes who try to convince dissenters to accept it.[26]

Finally, it is important to recall that the "right to dissent" can never be absolute.[27] What this means is that it takes place within a larger context of an acceptance of Jesus Christ as Lord, of the Church as the place where Christ is present and celebrated in Word and Sacrament.[28] In other words, dissent is possible not against infallible teachings, but only against noninfallible matters, some of which, however, do nonetheless have great importance in the Christian life. One need only think of matters having to do with nuclear deterrence or liberation theology to see the serious consequences and vital importance of noninfallible teachings. Nevertheless, all of the authors cited in this section of our study accept the possibility of dissent from noninfallible teachings as legitimate when the individual Catholic has been docile, that is, has done his or her best to accept the teaching.

III. The Question of Public Dissent

The question of public dissent by Catholic theologians has become most recently a critical issue for the theological community; it is, as we noted at the end of the first section of this study, the least worked out. For that reason, I will only outline a few of the issues that have become a part of this question.

If moral theologians become convinced that a noninfallible teaching is in fact one-sided, incomplete, or even in error, what should they do? Should they remain silent in order not to create confusion and cause scandal? Should they restrict their expression of reservation or dissent to personal and private letters written to the SCDF, offering better arguments or other ways of formulating the teaching or stating reasons why they find the teaching unacceptable? Or should they speak out, respectfully but clearly, against the teaching, confident that the greatest scandal is no the temporary confusion of the laity, but the perpetuation of false teaching rather than the correction of what is being taught?

We have already noted how Pius XII taught that once an issue had been treated by the ordinary magisterium, theologians were no longer free to discuss the matter. We noted also that this prohibition was dropped by Vatican II. Even though Vatican II did not state in any of its documents that a theologian could dissent publicly from such teaching, it did state in paragraph 62 of *Gaudium et spes* that all the faithful, clerical and lay, who study theology, must be assured of their "lawful freedom of inquiry and thought, and of the freedom to express their minds humbly and courageously about those matters in which they enjoy competence."

Moreover, despite any explicit endorsement of responsible forms of public dissent on noninfallible matters, some theologians, as we have noted, argue that implicitly the Council approved such dissent by the very fact that in several of its decrees it departed from previous papal teaching on a number of important questions, such as religious liberty.[29] If a theologian is to remain silent, how then, asks Rahner, "can that progress in knowledge necessary for the life of the Church and for the credibility of its preaching be achieved?"[30]

Modern media complicates genuine efforts to discover responsible ways to criticize noninfallible teachings publicly. An article published in a relatively arcane theological journal will be reported, and often in a distorted fashion, on the front page of the morning newspaper.[31] If theologians seek to set public opinion against the magisterium through manipulating the media, dialogue between theologians and the magisterium becomes impossible.

What is needed now are criteria hammered out by theologians and the magisterium that will ensure, as much as is possible, a proper respect for the truth, the teaching authority of the hierarchy, and the pastoral needs of the faithful. In the meantime, measures need to be taken by bishops and theologians that will make it more possible that criteria be developed for responsible dissent from noninfallible teachings. Avery Dulles has offered some suggestions as to how, in the absence of well-worked out criteria, the harmful effects of dissent might be alleviated:

(1) The pastoral magisterium should keep in close touch with theologians who themselves should cultivate greater sensitivity to pastoral considerations.

(2) Ordinarily pastors should not speak in a binding way unless there is a consensus, which is rarely obtainable without free discussion.

(3) Even when there is no consensus, popes and bishops and others in authority may clearly and candidly state their convictions on matters of pastoral importance.

(4) When an individual Catholic after genuine effort to adhere to a particular noninfallible teaching is unable to do so, he or she should not be made to feel disloyal or unfaithful.[32].

(5) Provided that they speak with evident loyalty and respect for authority, dissenters should not be silenced.[33]

IV. Reflections on the State of the Question

I have looked at the recent history and development of the idea of dissent from noninfallible teachings, and reviewed some of the literature on personal or private dissent on the one hand, and public dissent on the other. In conclusion, I wish now to make several observations on the current state of this question.

Theology in and for the Church. One of the most important truths of the Christian tradition is that theology will not flourish unless it is rooted in worship. Moreover, the faith of the Church provides the norm for the reflection of the theologians. This point was stressed by Cardinal Ratzinger in his April 15th presentation in Toronto, where he explained that the theologian as a believer is a theologian only in and through the Church: "if this is not true, if the theologian does not live and breathe Christ through the Church, his body, then I suggest we are not dealing with a theologian at all, but a mere sociologist, or historian or philosopher."[34] When theologians wholeheartedly enter into the living of the Christian life, when they seek to be converted to the Gospel, then their theological work will enrich the whole Christian community. To cite Ratzinger's recent address again, "a Church without theology is impoverished and blind. A theology without the Church, however, soon dissolves into arbitrary theory."[35]

To stress the ecclesial nature of theology, the need for continuing conversion to Jesus Christ, is not to imply, however, that all dissent from noninfallible teachings by theologians is rooted in a lack of faith or a departure from the true faith of the Church.[36] It is precisely this sort of conclusion that sometimes is implied when some bishops and theologians talk today about dissent in the Church. It may well be true of much of that dissent, but it should not be assumed that all dissent will disappear because of a more genuine conversion on the part of theologians. At the same time, most authors consulted rightly stress that for individuals to dissent responsibly, they must be genuinely committed to Christ, cultivate a genuine attitude of docility to the teaching authority of the Church, and remain open at all times to new evidence and insights that would make their adherence possible.

Tensions Between Theologians and the Magisterium. The Christian community has always experienced varying degrees of difference, tension over disagreements, and even harmful polarizations. One need only recall the conflicts characteristic of the Corinthian church and the confrontation between St. Peter and St. Paul on the matter of circumcision. There is today tension between many theologians and the magisterium.[37] One reason that the tension exists is that each group typically admits demands of the other group "mostly only in a quietly enunciated subordinate clause—but otherwise upholds in full voice its own maxims, as though they were the only ones which mattered in practice."[38]

It is important that ways be found to address the legitimate preoccupations of each group. Archbishop John Francis Whealon of Hartford suggested if greater trust is to be had between the groups, "bishops must understand that theologians should be able to probe sensitive areas of doctrine while remaining loyal to the Church. And theologians, while making their theological probes, must understand that the magisterium carries ultimate responsibility for defining and specifying the content of Catholic doctrine."[39] Special consideration should be given to the "Theses on the Relationship Between Ecclesiastical Magisterium and Theology" published by the International Theological Commission in 1975. Particularly valuable are theses 2, 3, and 4 which outline what the magisterium and theologians have in common in performing their respective tasks.[40]

Even though the magisterium and theologians have many common sources for their ministries, those ministries are not the same. Richard McCormick articulates well the complementary character of their distinctive roles:

> Bishops should be conservative, in the best sense of that word. They should not endorse every fad, or even every theological theory. They should "conserve," but to do so in a way that fosters faith, they must be vulnerably open and deeply involved in a process of creative and critical absorption. In some, perhaps increasingly many, instances, they must take risks, the risks of being tentative or even quite uncertain, and, above all, reliant on others in a complex world. Such a process of clarification and settling takes time, patience, and courage. Its greatest enemy is ideology, the comfort of being clear, and, above all, the posture of pure defense of received formulations.

Concerning the particular role of the theologians, McCormick writes:

Amid the variation of their modest function in the Church, they must never lose the courage to be led. "Courage" seems appropriate, because being led in our times means sharing the burdens of the leader—and that can be passingly painful. They should speak their mind knowing that there are other and certainly more significant minds. In other words, they must not lose the nerve to make and admit an honest mistake. They should trust their intuitions and their hearts, but always within a sharp remembrance that the announcement of the faith and its implications in our times must come from the melding of many hearts and minds. The Church needs a thinking arm, so to speak; but that arm is dead if it is detached.[41]

Finally, there is besides the tensions that exist between theologians and bishops those that are to be found between theologians. In recent years in the United States several groups of theologians have formed separate professional groups along, for want of better terms, liberal and conservative lines. Whatever may be the value of each grouping, it has not, in my opinion, increased the likelihood that there will be healthy mutual criticism between theologians of different persuasions. The 1985 annual proceedings of the Catholic Theological Society of America includes papers by three theologians who call their colleagues to a greater and more frequent exercise of the ministry of mutual criticism. Joseph Komonchak concludes his plenary address on "The Ecclesial and Cultural Rules of Theology" by stating that "from us (theologians) the Church should be able to expect greater care than has sometimes been shown for the methodological foundations on which we are building and especially a greater willingness to engage in the mutual conversation and criticism that have never been more necessary to our communal theological enterprise."[42] Walter Principe states that "theologians have a serious obligation for pastoral reasons to take care how they present their hypotheses and tentative conclusions. Should we not discuss them among ourselves and subject them to mutual criticism before going to the media or pulpit with declarations that can startle or upset people not able to assimilate them? And have we done enough to educate those in ministry and all our people so that they can understand what is going on in new matters in theology?"[43] Finally, John Boyle reports: "If there is any single complaint which I hear about theologians from bishops, it is that theologians are not critical of one another. There is some validity to this complaint. Is it possible that theologians too have lost sight of their obligation to be mutually critical as part of their corporate responsibility as a *schola* within the Church?"[44]

The Distinction Between Infallible and Noninfallible Teachings. Anyone who has taught ecclesiology to undergraduate students knows that a common question after a lecture on the dogma of papal infallibility is, "How many dogmas have actually been so defined?" Students often become exasperated when no definitive list is forthcoming. Others are relieved when they conclude, mistakenly, that only the Marian dogmas have actually been defined. Some are concerned to know only what has been defined, to know what the bare minimum is for inclusion in the Catholic community.[45]

Such classroom experiences point out that there is more to living the Christian life than accepting only infallible teachings. To paraphrase Scripture, the wise Christian does not live by infallibly defined propositions alone. There are many important Christian truths that have never been infallibly defined, such as the great commandment of Jesus to love God with our whole hearts and our neighbors as ourselves. Consider also the many important insights of the great spiritual writers, such as Teresa of Avila and John of the Cross and the absolutely central place the liturgy and the sacramental life should have in the Christian life, and prayer, both personal and communal. We need to recall that there are many more infallible truths than there are infallibly defined truths. In other words, all defined truths are infallible, but not all infallible truths are defined.

Archbishop John Quinn of San Francisco reminds us that we should avoid thinking that we are obligated to accept only what is formally defined and then proceed to leave everything else as though they were open questions. Such an attitude, he believes, "paves the way for the rejection of defined teaching, since often what is defined was previously taught by the ordinary magisterium for some time."[46]

In an interview yet to be released but partially reported in the May 8th issue of Origins, Cardinal Ratzinger states that Fr. Charles Curran's position that theologians can dissent from noninfallible teachings "does not seem appropriate." The Cardinal calls it a "juridical approach" which "tends inevitably to reduce the life of the Church, and its teachings, to only a few definitions." The Cardinal continues, "In the early Christian communities, however, it was clear that to be a Christian meant primarily to share in a way of life and that the most important doctrinal definitions did not have any other aim but to orient this way of life." Ratzinger proposes that we should distinguish what is essential and nonessential to the Christian faith "without recourse to the distinction between infallible and noninfallible pronouncements."[47] Ratzinger's point is well taken: any theologian who would employ the distinction in order to minimize the importance of noninfallible teachings or reduce the meaning of the Christian life to adherence to a few definitions has drastically truncated the full living of the Christian life.

While it is possible to "juridicize" the distinction, it would be wrong to minimize its value because of the way in which it may be abused. In fact, properly understood, all infallible teaching, that is, all dogma, must be salvific in import, otherwise there would be no reason to clarify, defend and stress that facet of saving truth expressed, however inadequately, through its formulation. Rightly understood, the distinction does not lead to the "juridical approach." I do believe, therefore, that some sort of distinction is necessary for theological work and for the development of doctrine.

Criteria for Public Dissent. Our review of the literature on the question of dissent shows that there is a place in the Catholic tradition for both personal dissent and public dissent, but that there is little agreement as to how public dissent, particularly by theologians, can be responsible and constructive. In a recent article written in support of Curran, Richard McCormick states that the issue between Curran and Ratzinger is "public dissent."[48] Ratzinger has stated to Curran that if a Catholic theologian expresses publicly his disagreement, there is an "inherent contradiction" because "one who is to teach in the name of the Church in fact denies her teaching," and thus "runs the risk of causing scandal." Scandal may, of course, also arise from an abuse of authority by members of the hierarchy.

I have already explained that there is an urgent need for establishing criteria for public dissent in order to reduce to a minimum the confusion and scandal that arises. I do not believe there is any way to avoid all scandal. Theologians stress that it would be impossible to have any development in doctrine without public dissent and frequently cite the example of John Courtney Murray's work which was vindicated at the Second Vatican Council. Indeed, he provides an excellent example. I think, however, that it would be wise for any theologian who dissents publicly not to assume too readily that he or she is automatically contributing to the development of doctrine or that his or her theological position will in fact be made common teaching at the next Church council. The same words of admonition proposed by the German bishops for careful consideration by any layperson about to dissent privately from a noninfallible teaching need *a fortiori* to be taken to heart by theologians about to do the same publicly. Theologians should ask themselves in all "sober self-criticism" whether they have already come to a better insight that the rest of the Church will come to only in time.

I agree with the German bishops, and others I have cited in this study, that such dissent, that is, public dissent by a theologian, is in principle possible, and even obligatory, although, as I have noted, we have only begun to elaborate ways in which this can be done constructively.[49] I expect that some of the criteria needed will help us to distinguish between various levels of authority to be attributed to different noninfallible teachings, and will have to take into consideration pastoral dimensions that may differ from country to country.

Education of the Laity. There are those who would prefer bishops either to speak with their full authority or to remain silent. The German bishops, we have already noted, state well the need the Church has to address the issues of the day, issues which because of their newness and complexity will usually not be able to be dealt with definitively. In these official but still provisional teachings, there is the possibility of error. Nevertheless, such teaching must be provided, for "otherwise it would be quite impossible for the Church to preach or interpret its faith as a decisive force in real life or to apply it to each new situation in human life as it arises."[50]

The American bishops have demonstrated in a clear way the provisional nature of their teachings on war and economics by stressing the difference between what they present as binding universal moral norms, to which they rightly expect adherence, and specific applications of these norms, on which they fully anticipate and welcome difference of opinion and even disagreements from persons of good will.[51] For members of the hierarchy to stress the various levels of authority that pertain to what they teach is, however, not the rule. More typical is the tendency in practice to obscure the difference between infallible and noninfallible teachings, particularly by treating all official papal and episcopal statements as though they were infallibly taught, such as the prohibition of the ordaining of women or the condemnation of artificial contraception. Such an approach, in the judgment of Francis Sullivan, has led many people, once they discover that such teachings are in fact not infallibly taught, to conclude that they need to pay no attention to them at all.[52]

We have already mentioned that the mass media has made it virtually impossible for theologians to keep any of their written opinions and probings from immediate, and often one-sided and incomplete, "coverage." The fact that the latest papal encyclical, episcopal statement or theologians' ideas has on the ordinary Catholic less direct religious impact than an article in the religion section of *Time* or *Newsweek*, or some discussion on the Phil Donohue Show, suggests that theologians and bishops really have no choice but to work more effectively at educating the laity.[53]

According to Richard McCormick, four things should be kept in mind about the process of education during these complex times. First, reality itself is often complex and confusing and that it takes time for the Christian community to formulate an adequate response.

Second, people need to learn that different times often require different formulations of the same truths, and that some questions that were once perceived as closed in fact are not. Third, the unity so necessary for the Christian community does not require absolute uniformity on the application of moral norms to detailed questions. And fourth, the laity needs to take theologians seriously, but not all that seriously: "If theologians are mistakenly thought to be the ultimate teachers in the Church, they risk losing, besides their freedom to probe and question, their humility."[54]

Not only theologians, but members of the hierarchy as well have reason to be humble. While both of these groups engage themselves in different but complementary ways in the education of the laity, there is a growing awareness among both groups that the laity in fact play an active role in educating theologians and the hierarchy. All official teaching and theological reflection in fact must be founded in the *sensus fidelium*, or the "sense of the faith," possessed by the entire people of God. At the International Synod of Bishops that met in 1980 to discuss the family, Cardinal George Basil Hume stressed the need to consult the laity on matters that have to do with the family. He explained that the prophetic mission of husbands and wives is based on their experience as married people "and on an understanding of the sacrament of marriage of which they can speak with their own authority." Both their experience and their understanding constitute, the Cardinal suggested, "an authentic *fons theologiae* from which we, the pastors, and indeed the whole Church can draw." It is because, the Cardinal continued, married couples are the ministers of the sacrament and "alone have experienced the effects of the sacrament" that they have special authority in matters related to marriage. But it must be remembered that what is sought is the sense of those who are faithful, that is, those who are converted to the Lord. That is why, the Cardinal added, "parents themselves must commit themselves to the action of the Holy Spirit who also teaches them anew through their children." Because of this "*a fortiori* it would seem that pastors should listen to the parents themselves."[55]

From this perspective of the centrality of the *sensus fidelium*, which in a real way along with Scripture is a norm for magisterial teaching, all of us who strive to be faithful, that is, the laity, theologians and the bishops, need to learn, to be docile, to be taught by the Lord, and to be led by the Spirit. All of us need to undergo continuing conversion and sustain effective conversation[56] so that, among other things, we may speak with confidence about those matters within our competence, even though at times we may find it necessary to disagree in a responsible way with certain teachings not infallibly taught.

NOTES

1. James Heft, *John XXII [1316–1334] and Papal Teaching Authority* (Lewiston, NY: Edwin Mellen Press, 1986), pp. 106–19, 188–201.

2. John P. Boyle, "The Ordinary Magisterium: Toward a History of the Concept," *Heythrop Journal* 30 (1979), 380–98, and 31 (1980), 14–29.

3. Yves Congar, "A Brief History of the Forms of the Magisterium," *Magisterium and Morality. Readings in Moral Theology #3*, ed. Charles Curran and Richard McCormick (New York: Paulist Press, 1983), p. 324.

4. Congar adds: "Pius XII saw the theologian teaching only by delegation from the 'magisterium' and doing so strictly in his service and under his control. Is this consonant with what nineteen centuries of the Church's life tell us about the function of '*didaskalos*' or doctor? No, not exactly" (p. 325). In asking theologians to "justify" the teachings of the magisterium, Pius XII was stressing the necessity for doctrine to be grounded in Scripture and Tradition.

5. *Magisterium*, trans. Francis Sullivan (New York: Paulist Press, 1983), p. 154. Ex cathedra definitions by a pope or doctrine *defined* by an ecumenical council constitute an exercise of the extraordinary magisterium. All other exercise of teaching authority by the pope (e.g., encyclical letters) and the bishops (e.g., pastoral letters) represents the functioning of the ordinary magisterium. It is possible, according to *Lumen Gentium*, par. 25, that under certain conditions the ordinary universal magisterium can teach infallibly, though normally it does not. Our concern in this paper is with noninfallible teachings, be they taught by the pope, a council or the bishops.

6. Joseph Komonchak, "Ordinary Papal Magisterium and Religious Dissent," *The Magisterium and Morality*, pp. 68–69.

7. See, for example, Komonchak, just cited, pp. 70–78, and Richard Gula, "The Right to Private and Public Dissent from Specific Pronouncements of the Ordinary Magisterium," *Église et théologie* 9 (1978), 319–43. The "approved authors" are usually negative on the legitimacy of public dissent.

8. Sullivan, p. 157. On the distinction between religious adherence and the assent of divine faith, see Ladislas Orsy, "Reflections on the Text of a Canon." *America* (17 May, 1986), 396–99.

9. Several theologians explain that Vatican II, through its actions (e.g., the "rehabilitation" of theologians such as Congar, Rahner and DeLubac, who were suspect by the Vatican before the Council, and its teachings on religious freedom, ecumenism and collegiality) underscored the constructive power of some dissent (see Sullivan, pp. 157–58), and Avery Dulles, "Doctrinal Authority for a Pilgrim Church, *The Magisterium and Morality*, pp. 264–65.

10. Cited by Karl Rahner, "The Dispute Concerning the Teaching Office in the Church," *The Magisterium and Morality*, p. 115.

11. Richard McCormick, "L'Affaire Curran," *America* (5 April, 1986), 264.

12. Christopher Butler, "Authority and the Christian Conscience," *The Magisterium and Morality*, p. 186.

13. John Boyle, "The Natural Law and the Magisterium," *The Magisterium and Morality*, p. 452.

14. Joseph Cardinal Ratzinger, "The Church and the Theologian," *Origins* 15 (8 May, 1986), 769. The Cardinal immediately added, however, that "the freedom of the individual instructor is not the only good under the law nor is it the highest good to be safeguarded here. As to the question of the ordering of the various goods in the community of the New Testament, there is an inflexible divine judgment from which the church may never stray: 'Whoever is a cause of scandal to one of these little ones who believes, it would be better for him to be cast out into the sea with a millstone tied around his neck' (Mk. 9:42)."

15. Concerning dissent from infallible teachings, it is important to recall that traditionally a person must *know* that what they hold is contrary to what the Church teaches and then *persist* in denying the Church's teaching if they are to become a heretic and thereby cease to be a Catholic. In 1973, the Sacred Congregation for the Doctrine of the Faith published *Mysterium Ecclesiae* in which it explained that infallible teachings, though irreformable as Vatican I taught, are open to reformulation, not in order to change their meaning, but in order to bring out more clearly the infallibly defined truth they aim to articulate. This, in principle, is always possible, due to, as the SCDF document states, (1) the limited state of human knowledge at the time of definition, (2) changeable conceptions and thought patterns that belong to a certain period in time, (3) the specific concerns that motivated that definition, and (4) the limited expressive power of the language use (see my article, "Papal Infallibility and the Marian Dogmas," *Marian Studies* 33 (1982), 58–59). It is also necessary to take into consideration that pastorally speaking the meaning and import of some dogmas are more difficult to grasp than others (important in this context is Vatican II's teaching on the "hierarchy of truths").

16. Komonchak, p. 72.

17. Rahner, p. 115.

18. Cited by B. C. Butler, "Infallible: Authenticum: Assensus: Obsequim," *Doctrine in Life* 31 (1981), 85.

19. Butler, 186. That eagerness and welcoming attitude may be contrasted with the description given by John Henry Newman of the way in which most people treat the truths of religion: "Men are too well inclined to sit at home, instead of stirring themselves to inquire whether a revelation has been given; they expect its evidences to come to them without their trouble; they act, not as supplicants, but as judges." *The Grammar of Assent* (Garden City, NY: Image Books, 1955), p. 330.

20. From the English translation of Hamer's *The Church Is a Communion* (London: Geoffrey Chapman, 1964), pp. 25–26.

21. Sullivan, p. 164.

22. Sullivan, p. 162. Cardinal Heenan is supposed to have described docility in very simple terms as "being prepared to admit that it is just possible that the pope is right and I am wrong" (Butler, 85).

23. John Gallagher, *The Basis for Christian Ethics* (New York: Paulist Press, 1985), p. 228.

24. Gallagher, pp. 228–29.

25. Hamer, p. 26.

26. Gallagher, p. 223. Perhaps included by Gallagher in the qualification "other things being equal" is the realization that it is possible that a teaching could be repeated by many popes who do so primarily because they thought that they were obligated to repeat it simply because other popes had taught it before them. This would place formal authority (*who* says something) over material authority (*what* is said). In such a situation, the teaching in question would not acquire more authority merely through repetition by popes. Some things can be repeated, in an unexamined way, for centuries.

27. McCormick admits that he has always been uncomfortable with the phrase "right to dissent," because "we are concerned, as believers, with the behavioral implications of our being in Christ, with moral truth." Since the phrase "right to dissent" tends to juridicize what ought to be a more corporately and communally grounded search for moral truth, McCormick prefers to speak of "a duty and right to exercise a truly personal reflection within the teaching-learning process of the Church, a duty and a right that belongs to all who possess proportionate competence." ("Reflections on the Literature," *The Magisterium and Morality*, p. 464).

28. Dulles, p. 262

29. See, for example, Sullivan, pp. 209–10, and Dulles, who writes (pp. 264–65) that "by its practice of revision, the Council implicitly taught the legitimacy and even the value of dissent. In effect the Council said that the ordinary magisterium of the Roman Pontiff had fallen into error and had unjustly harmed the careers of loyal and able scholars. Some of the thinkers who had resisted official teachings in the pre-conciliar period were among the principal precursors and architects of Vatican II."

30. Karl Rahner, "Theology and the Teaching Office?," *Doctrine and Life* 31 (1981), 633. Rahner asks further "if the biblical decrees of Pius X had been granted the sincere allegiance of all theologians in obedient silence, it would not be possible for the present Pope to speak so freely of Yahwists."

31. See Sullivan who writes: "The question (of how to express criticism responsibly) was fairly easy to decide when theologians could share their views with their professional colleagues through the medium of scholarly journals, with little likelihood that their ideas would reach the wider public. However, the 'information explosion' of modern times, and the tendency of popular journals to publicize any opinion that is critical of positions taken by those in authority, drastically increases the probability that what is carefully and moderately put forward in a scholarly article may subsequently be broadcast to the general public in a crude or tendentious way" (p. 211).

32. Dulles adds that in view of the deference owed to noninfallible teachings, "the dissenter will be reluctant to conclude that the official teaching is clearly erroneous; he will carefully reassess his own position in the light of that teaching, and he will behave in a manner that fosters respect and support for the pastoral magisterium, even though he continues to strive for a revision of the current official teaching" (p. 266).

33. Dulles, pp. 266–67.

34. Ratzinger, 765.

35. Ratzinger, 763.

36. Bernard Lonergan notes, however, that some disagreement among Christian theologians can be traced to a lack of conversion: ". . . Christian theologians disagree not only on the areas relevant to theological research but also on the interpretation of texts on the occurrence of events, on the significance of movements. Such differences can have quite different grounds. Some may be eliminated by further progress in research, interpretation, history, and they can be left to the healing office of time. Some may result from developmental pluralism: there exist disparate cultures and diverse differentiations of consciousness; and such differences are to be bridged by working out the suitable transposition from one culture to another or from one differentiation of consciousness to another. Others, finally, arise because intellectual or moral or religious conversion has not occurred . . ." *Method in Theology* (New York: Herder and Herder, 1972), p. 150. Lonergan's notion of 'conversion' in the theologians is not irrelevant to the issue of dissent. Besides the intellectual, moral and religious components of conversion, there should be added, in view of our topic, a "Catholic" element: a commitment to this historical community as home. Such a conversion is fundamental to the whole theological enterprise, for without it, one is simply not in touch with the realities to be explored. As Anthony Kelly, the Australian Redemptorist put it to me recently in a letter, "It is not a matter of practicing a certain virtue or having the right attitude. It envisages a rather thoroughgoing transformation of mind and heart in the theologian. A dissent coming out of this would tend to be the dissent of a prophet. The dissent of the unconverted, however, might be nothing more than attention-seeking behavior, or, as we Australians would say, the ravings of a ratbag."

37. It is important not to overstate these tensions. See Raymond Brown, "The Magisterium vs. the Theologians," *The Magisterium and Morality*, pp. 277–96.

38. Rahner, p. 623.

39. John Francis Whealon, "The Magisterium," *The Magisterium and Morality*, p. 192.

40. See Sullivan, pp. 174–218, for the text and his commentary. Among the elements in common are: both bishops and theologians are committed to ecclesial ministry for the sake of the salvation of others, both are bound by the Word of God, by the sense of the faith of the Church, by the documents of the Tradition, and to the personal and missionary care they must have towards the world.

41. McCormick, pp. 496–97.

42. Joseph Komonchak, *CTSA Proceedings* 40 (1985), 32.

43. Komonchak, *CTSA*, 125. In the Rahner article cited in note 38, theologians are invited to make the following confession to the bishops: "First of all we are not some kind of Mafia, in which each can speak in the name of theology and theologians, nor do we feel obliged as a matter of principle to lash out in the name of truth and theological freedom whenever an individual theologian comes into conflict with Rome. We have indeed the right and the duty to speak out against another theologian and for Rome, when we are convinced of the correctness of a Roman pronouncement. Clannishness among theologians is perverse. Is it necessary today to say that a theologian does not in any way betray himself by supporting a Roman decision?" (630).

44. "The Academy and Church Teaching Authority: Current Issues," *CTSA Proceedings* 40 (1985), 180.

45. One way to distinguish between the immature and the mature conscience is that the immature conscience wants to know only what must be done while the mature conscience asks what is the best thing to be done.

46. John R. Quinn, "The Magisterium and the Field of Theology," *The Magisterium and Morality*, p. 274.

47. Ratzinger, 764. Excerpts from the same interview may also be found in the *National Catholic Register* (8 May, 1986), 5.

48. McCormick, "L'Affaire," 261.

49. A first effort at elaborating the elements of responsible public dissent was made, as we have noted earlier, by the American bishops in November of 1968 in a pastoral letter they released which affirmed the teachings of *Humanae Vitae*. They also recognized the legitimacy of dissent. The relevant paragraphs follow: "There exist in the Church a lawful freedom of inquiry and of thought and also norms of licit dissent. This is particularly true in the area of legitimate theological speculation and research. When conclusions reached by such professional theological work prompt a scholar to dissent from noninfallible received teaching, the norms of licit dissent come into play. They require of him careful respect for the consciences of those who lack his special competence or opportunity for judicious investigation. These norms also require setting forth his dissent with propriety and with regard for the gravity of the matter and the deference due the authority which has pronounced on it.

"The reverence due all sacred matters, particularly questions which touch on salvation, will not necessarily require the responsible scholar to relinquish his opinion but certainly to propose it with prudence born of intellectual grace and a Christian confidence that the truth is great and will prevail.

"When there is question of theological dissent from noninfallible doctrine, we must recall that there is always a presumption in favor of the magisterium. Even noninfallible authentic doctrine, though it may admit of development or call for clarification or revision, remains binding and carries with it a moral certitude, especially when it is addressed to the universal Church, without ambiguity, in response to urgent questions bound up with faith and crucial to morals. The expression of theological dissent from the magisterium is in order only if the reasons are serious and well-founded, if the manner of the dissent does not question or impugn the teaching authority of the Church and is such as not to give scandal." Cited by Harry McSorley, "The Right of Catholics to Dissent from *Humanae Vitae*," *The Ecumenist* (Nov/Dec, 1969), 8–9.

50. Rahner, "The Dispute," *The Magisterium and Morality*, p. 115.

51. See *The Challenge of Peace*, par. 9.

52. Sullivan, p. 172.

53. See Raymond Brown's comments, 282.

54. McCormick, pp. 504–05. A salutary but sobering Gospel truth reveals that it was the learned and the religious leaders who most often had difficulty accepting the person and message of Jesus. As one moral theologian puts it, "Certain truths are best recognized not by those who are learned but by those who are good" (Gallagher, p. 197). C. S. Lewis spent his whole life in academia and described well one of the greatest dangers of the intellectual life, pride: "The intellectual life is not the only road to God, nor the safest, but we find it to be a road, and it may be the appointed road for us. Of course it will be so only so long as we keep the impulse pure and disinterested. That is the great difficulty. As the author of the *Theologia Germanica* says, we may come to love knowing—our knowing—more than the thing known: to delight not in the exercise of our talents but in the fact that they are ours, or even in the reputation they bring us. Every success in the scholar's life increases this danger. If it becomes irresistible, he must give up his scholarly work. The time for plucking out the right eye has arrived" (from an essay entitled "Learning in War Time," in a collection of his essays, *Fern-seed and Elephants* [Collins/Fountain Books, 1977]), p. 34.

55. G. B. Hume, "Development of Marriage Teaching," *Origins* 10 (16 October 1980), 276; see my article, "Papal Infallibility," 63–65.

56. David Tracy's notion of "conversation" in *The Analogical Imagination* (New York: Crossroads, 1981) offers a rather good model of "docility" (see especially pp. 446–55).

AUTHORITY:
A HOUSE OR A HOME?

John V. Apczynski
St. Bonaventure University

ABSTRACT

The aim of this essay is to explore the function of authority in theological judgments. It begins with an "archaeological" exploration of
the traditional assumptions regarding authority which is based on
the recent work of Edward Farley. Then it indicates characteristics
that seem to be necessary for theological judgments that do not rely
on such traditional assumptions. Finally some conclusions are offered for a revised understanding of the role of authority, including
those formerly deemed "inerrant" or "infallible," in theological
judgments.

The phenomenon of authority touches in some fashion and to some
degree nearly every element of religious life. A religious community's
emergence in history, its duration through time, and its ability to
command continued allegiance into the present all testify to the
power of its authority. Ultimately, of course, the basis for this authority lies in the community's presumed capacity to mediate effectively some manifestation or awareness of transcendent reality. To
the extent that the community effectively mediates such transcendent power, to that extent is the religious community's authority
tacitly upheld. Its bearers of authority—be they sacred texts, rituals,
classical interpretations, governing offices, patterns of social life,
contemporary applications, and the like—are simply presumed to
be the legitimate means of access to transcendent reality.

While challenges to the vehicles of religious authority may come
from without in the form of persecution or cultural dominance and

*John V. Apczynski, who received his doctorate in the philosophy of religion from
McGill University, teaches and works in the areas of contemporary theology and
religious thought. He serves on the Board of College Theology Society and edited its
1982 annual volume, Foundations of Religious Literacy. Currently he is a professor
in the department of theology of St. Bonaventure University (St. Bonaventure, NY
14778).*

absorption, much more serious difficulties arise from within the community itself. In these cases the very legitimacy of the community's mediating capacity is called into question—at least to some degree. I believe that the current concern over the phenomenon of authority within Roman Catholicism is a manifestation of this crucial issue of the legitimacy of certain vehicles of authority.[1]

One crucial facet of this problem concerns the role of authority in theological reflection. To what extent *must* authority function in theological reflection in order that it be legitimately theological? Must theology accept the authority of scripture, conciliar statements, or official teachings if it is to remain theological and not revert to being simply descriptive? On the other hand, what role, if any, *can* authority play in theological reflection so that it be recognized as properly reflective? Is it possible for theology to presume the truth of certain authoritative sources while still remaining a genuine inquiry? This line of questioning appears to be at the heart of the recent controversies which have emerged from the investigations initiated by the Vatican's Congregation for the Doctrine of the Faith.[2] Apparently operating here are divergent—perhaps even radically contradictory—understandings of the role of authority which have generated so much of the heat in these controversies.

In an effort to cast some light on the question, I propose to expose some of the tacitly held assumptions regarding a traditional understanding of the role of authority in theological reflection and to indicate the problems inherent in these assumptions. Then a description of characteristics necessary for theological activity to function without these assumptions will be proposed. Finally some conclusions will be drawn that will provide a coherent and defensible understanding of the role of authority for theological reflection.

This undertaking will be guided throughout by insights drawn from the recent work of Edward Farley presented in *Ecclesial Reflection*.[3] The decided advantage in this procedure is that Farley has subjected the use of authority in the classical period of theology to a radical critique and has argued that remnants of such uses still remain in contemporary theology, rendering much of it problematic. He has proposed an alternative vision of theology which, he believes, does not rely on authority for any of its judgments. Thus even though a major portion of this essay will be expository, the application of Farley's proposal to this particular setting will suggest a modification of his constructive thesis which I hope will contribute to the ongoing discussion.

The initial task of understanding the role of authority in theological activity requires more than an assessment of explicit claims made by theologians concerning authority in any of its more obvious forms such as the light of faith, revelation, scripture, and the teachings of the church. While the precise manner of handling such sources has varied among theologians over the centuries, a consensus among all the major forms of classical Christianity has emerged which acknowledges, with varying degrees of reflexive awareness, these sources as criteria for assessing theological judgments. What counts as "evidence" for theological judgments, to put it very bluntly, is an appeal to, or an interpretation of, an authority. The authority itself is a criterion whose truth is unquestioned. This operational matrix constitutes the "house of authority."

Evidently, then, the "foundations" of the house of authority lie at a deeper level than the explicit theological or ecclesiastical procedures devised to use them. In fact the legacy of the house of authority is so deeply entrenched in the Christian tradition, particularly up to the Enlightenment, and so subtly pervasive in most of contemporary theology that Farley believes nothing short of a "psychoanalytic purge of theological consciousness"[4] can expose the parameters of the question in all its radicality. What this requires, then, is an "archaeology" of the house of authority conducted in the manner of Michel Foucault.[5] The aim is to bring to reflective awareness its underlying strata including the dominant metaphors and assumptions, the founding axioms, and the locations of authority which permit the uppermost level of theology as an interpretation of the faith to operate.

This archaeological exploration assumes that theology is a form of understanding derived from a determinate community of faith.[6] Careful phenomenological analysis indicates that faith involves a cognitive dimension wherein the self is shaped by socially shared intentionalities mediating reality apprehensions. The founding stratum of meaning shaping theological reflection thus consists in the symbolic expressions of the faith of Christianity and its antecedents in Israel. Their material content, to which we shall next attend, shapes this founding stratum.

The basic intentionalities of the Christian community derive from the faith of Israel the Adamic myth with its particular insights into the human condition and the salvation history symbolism dominated by a royal metaphor for God. Certain developments of this in Judaism were maintained but in a modified form. Thus the universalism of the faith of Israel and Judaism were retained, but without the ethnic-territorial particularities. Similarly certain modes of social persistence were maintained in a transformed way. For example, missionaries, often charismatic, replace teachers, and the Jesus kerygma replaces the *Torah*. This enables a modification in the understanding of scripture and the local congregation. In effect, Christianity became a new kind of social entity, "a pan-ethnic group of local communities whose authority, memory, and tradition are the faith of Israel, certain elements of Judaism, and the apostolic kerygma about Jesus."[7]

Mediating between the strata of the material content of the faith world and of the explicitly acknowledged sources of authority are the founding axioms of salvation history and the principle of identity, together with their middle axioms. Salvation history is a teleologically interpretative framework of a people standing under and governed by a royal deity. Its middle axioms include the periodization of history, the fixing of the time of revelation, and eschatological dualism, where death establishes each individual's eternal destiny— a most important presupposition for supporting institutional authority.[8]

The second presupposition, the principle of identity, affirms that the divine intention and its human, linguistic interpretation are identical (p. 35). This identity is not one of world maintenance through ritual as is mythical religion; nor is it ontological as in certain Eastern, mystical traditions (e.g., Advaita Hinduism). Rather the understanding of identity in "religions of revelation" is epistemological. Three middle axioms characterize the principle of identity. The axiom of secondary representation moves the originating locus of identity to its perpetuation through secondary mediators. Typically this movement involves a series of transitions from a charismatic figure (who would be the original locus of identity) to a tradition, to a written deposit, to a correct commentary, to institutional structures to oversee the process. Keep in mind that the principle of identity is dependent upon the principle of salvation history for much of its vitality. Secondly, the axiom of leveling tends to shift the emphasis from the original message to the validity of the vehicle itself insofar as the very elements of the vehicle in its entirety are equally valid. Thirdly, the axiom of immutability, which is the logical extension of the first two axioms, asserts that the detailed parts of the divinely communicated contents and its bearers are valid for all time.[9] Generally the three middle axioms of the principle of identity are not reflectively addressed in theology, although they do arise under the themes of inerrancy or infallibility.

The mediating axioms of this second level are actualized next in a third stratum which historically has provided theology with its explicit and unquestioned "foundations" or "principles." Specifically these self-consciously acknowledged locations of divine identity have become scripture, dogma, and church (in the sense of a teaching authority). The radical character of Farley's program begins to become clear at this point. His thesis is that the self-conscious appropriation of the "scripture principle" (and by extension the other two locations of divine identity) was a historical contingency in Christianity.[10] This is to say that, while the historical development of Christianity in fact took form within the confines of the house of authority, it was not necessary for it to do so. Consequently, if this thesis is correct, then it is conceivable that Christianity and Christian theology can function outside the house of authority. In order to appreciate the significance of this insight, we should indicate briefly Farley's analysis of the process that led to Christianity's acceptance of the scripture principle.

Strictly speaking, the origin of a canonical scripture occurred with synagogal Judaism and not the faith of Israel.[11] The religion of Israel persisted at first through its self-understanding as a territorially bounded covenant people. The crises undergone by Israel led to replacement of the temple by the synagogue and the development of a sacred scripture as the completed deposit of revelation whose primary function is to be a source for the regulations of communal life (*Torah* and *halakah*). Christianity, of course, inherited this scripture principle from Judaism, with the obvious shift in understanding scripture as a source of *halakah* to its being a source for messianic prophecy. But as Christianity became an increasingly gentile movement and the polemic with Judaism receded, the reliance on a scripture principle seemed to become correspondingly superfluous. Marcion's rejection of the Jewish scripture in the second century is an indication of this tendency. Only by a reperiodization of salvation history and by the device of granting a provisional validity to the Jewish scriptures did Christianity begin to overcome the difficulties that allowed the assimilation of the Jewish scripture principle.[12] The extension of the scripture principle to the New Testament did not occur until the mid-second century when internal disputes within Christianity could not be resolved by appeals to Jewish scriptures. After this the Christian movement began to extend the location of the divine not only to Jesus, but to the apostolic witnesses and their writings, even though earlier they did not have this status. By the end of the second century their writings became a canon, and the scripture principle was firmly established in Christianity.[13]

Nevertheless Christianity has remained ambivalent regarding the scripture principle throughout its history. In order that Christianity assimilate the Jewish scripture principle, it became necessary to modify it by a new periodization of history, by changing its function in the community from *Torah* to doctrine about Jesus, and by universalizing its corporate reference from the nation to all peoples. Taken strictly these modifications are incompatible with the middle axioms of the principle of identity, particularly secondary representation and leveling.[14] Despite this ambiguous status, scripture continues to function as an unquestioned source for many forms of argument and exegesis in theology. Farley surmises that a major reason for this historical contingency is to be found in the royal metaphor for God which was uncovered in the first stratum of the archaeological analysis. Its logic of sovereignty implies that whatever is necessary for the completion of God's reign will come to pass, so that there must be a reliable reduction of the event of Jesus to verbal testimony.[15]

The classical criteriology in Christian theology, of course, was not limited to the single criterion of the canonical collection of the earliest Christian writings. Because of controversies and syncretistic movements in hellenistic culture, the church had to propose a hermeneutical key for understanding the meaning and unity of a scripture written for diverse situations and contexts. At first this was the regula fidei and later simply doctrina, teaching of the church. This takes on a written form whose status is equivalent to scripture when the middle axioms of the principle of identity are extended. Dogmas become another locus of divine-human identity and serve as criteria, that is, authoritative givens, for theological activity.[16]

Presupposed in the acceptance of the scripture principle and the extension of the divine-human identity to dogma are the generation-bridging structures of the church. Concurrent with these two sources of authority, then, is the emergence of the institutional structure of the church as a third locus of divine-human identity. The mere fact that bishops arose as successors to the apostles and their authoritative witness to become the authentic bearers of correct teaching provides a socio-historical account for the church's extension of the divine-human identity to itself. Beyond this, though, were inner theological reasons: the church's legacy as God's newly elected people, its guardianship of dogmas necessary for salvation, and its presiding over an individual's ultimate destiny all lead to a new extension of the middle axioms of secondary representation and immutability which is required by the logic of the monarchical God's victory in establishing his reign.[17]

So far the following strata of meaning supporting the classical method of theological procedure have been described: (1) the life-world of religious faith with its basic metaphors, (2) the founding presuppositions and their middle axioms, and (3) the locations of authority in scripture, doctrine, and church. The fourth stratum consists simply in the description of theology as it is done in that context.

Here theology is understood as the reflective interpretation of the meaning of the faith. The fundamental issue at stake involves the notions of evidence or of criteria. What counts as evidence or what serves as a criterion when theologians offer interpretative judgments regarding the faith of the Christian community? Farley's argument is that the classical criteriology was in fact a method of authority. This consists in locating the evidence for a judgment in authorities which serve as vehicles of social persistence rather than in realities directly manifest.[18] This requires, in turn, that theology operates in a manner of citation rather than open inquiry. And finally the way of authority removes the question of truth from substantive issues by restricting it to formal operations.[19]

This can be clarified by contrasting the notion of evidence as it is generally construed in science or knowledge with the appeal to authority in theology. In normal science, judgments are made on the basis of an appeal to regions of evidence or a realm of reality manifestations which are directly available and in principle open to all competent inquirers. The way of authority in theology, however, replaces any direct appeal to evidence precisely because the assumption of the divine presence in scripture, dogma, or the church constitutes something as evidence.[20] Consequently the proper mode of theological argument is not so much inquiry as it is citation. If a dogma already expresses the divine intention, the proper mode of argument is not to inquire under the presumption that the issue at hand is still open and to be settled through an as yet undetermined process of sifting the evidence. Rather the proper mode of discourse is exposition with the citation of texts functioning as the criterion. This is to say that in the house of authority theology is fundamentally hermeneutics.[21] Finally the question of truth never involves asking about the relation of given doctrines to any range of reality apprehensions. Instead the issue of truth is restricted to formal conditions exploring how doctrines may harmoniously cohere (as in systematics) or how they are required by some rational, universal understanding of being or reality (as in apologetics).[22] Such, in brief, are the characteristics of theological judgments made from within the house of authority.

At this juncture many Christians might question the significance of the qualification, "house of authority." Has not the preceding sketch of theological activity simply outlined that which is constitutive of theology as such? Can a theologian who operates out of a religious tradition which accepts the gracious self-revelation of God perform the tasks involved in theological reflection in any other way but by citation of the locations of divine identity? Would not the adoption of any other criterion be in effect a sign of a loss of faith and hence a discrediting of any judgments made through a reliance on that criterion?

There are two distinct issues raised by such questions. One asks whether the classical criteriology is essential to, or part of the foundations of, theological judgments. The other inquires into the possibility of an alternative method for theological inquiry which can remain faithful to the positivities of the Christian faith. The former, in other words, asks whether Christianity and the house of authority are coterminous. The latter, presuming the collapse of the house of authority, asks what the possible mode of perdurance for Christian faith and theology might be outside the house of authority.

The first question requires that theology be able not only to describe its presuppositional strata, but also to subject them to internal criticism. This is possible because in any field a determinacy exists regarding the given reality apprehensions and fields of evidence. This is as true in the physical or social sciences as it is in history or humanistic studies. Granting the requisite determinate intentionality, the directly manifested reality presentations and fields of evidence can lead to a reinterpretation or even a rejection of any previously held authoritative assumption. This same possibility exists for faith since even in its "predoctrinal" form it is a way of being in the world with cognitive possibilities that are subject to criticism and assessment. Hence faith, in the form of theological reflection, can direct criticism at itself.[23]

Farley offers three levels of arguments in an effort to defend his thesis that the house of authority does not constitute the necessary presuppositions of theological method. The first points to factual incompatibilities among the authoritative sources discerned by insights derived from a historically critical consciousness.[24] It could be argued that this is smuggling in an extraneous criterion into the theological task; but since a theologian necessarily thinks in a determinate setting, it appears legitimate to include this sort of consciousness as internal to theology since the time of the renaissance. The typical response by liberal theology has been not to reject the house of authority, but merely to modify it by seeking some hidden dimension or kernel in the ostensibly incompatible claims.

A second level of argument against the house of authority involves the structural incompatibility between the vehicles of authority and the ideal nature of the Christian community.[25] This presupposes that the ideal intersubjectivity of a group is always actualized in some particular way and that certain instances of such actualization could stand in contradiction to its ideal nature. Farley argues that the adop-

tion of the scripture principle in Christianity does stand in contradiction to its ideal existence. One facet of his argument points to the
ethnic particularity of the scripture principle and Christianity's acceptance of cultural pluralism. This tension is what led Christianity
to develop a post-scriptural, doctrinal tradition which at times had
only vague resemblances to the scriptural narratives.

Both of these criticisms, if valid, provide reasons why Christian
theology ought to abandon the house of authority. At the third level
of criticism, Farley carries the argument to the very foundations of
the formative elements of the community of faith. Here he offers, I
believe, his most effective challenge to the house of authority. Recall
that the scripture principle presumed the salvation history framework with its monarchical metaphor for God. Inherent in this is a
fundamental contradiction in the material content of the metaphors
of faith. The Adamic myth, which assumes the reality of human evil
and human freedom, is itself subsumed by the imagery of salvation
effected by a God of love. If these symbolic patterns are foundational
for shaping Christian existence, then the monarchical metaphor of
God cannot be.[26] Similarly once the logic of triumph is discredited,
then, too, the principle of identity collapses because it cannot accept
human freedom in the requisite sense.

One further implication of this critique for our original question
may now be brought out. If Farley is correct in his contention that
the house of authority was constructed by Christians as a response
to a particular historical situation, then we should become aware of
the idolatrous possibility present when authority is understood as a
form of divine identity.[27] Any human creation can become not only
a means for transformation, but also may metamorphose into a vehicle for sin, a particularly insidious vehicle when it is deified.

The direction of the argument so far has been that the classical
criteriology in theology has consisted in an explicit reliance on authorities and that when the assumptions of the house of authority
are thematically exposed they appear to be at least inadequate, and
perhaps even illegitimate, instantiations of the Christian faith. I believe all of us are indebted to Farley for stating the case so forcefully.
I believe, further, that once this is adverted to and clearly grasped,
then theology has no choice but to abandon the house of authority.

This brings us back then to the question regarding the form or
manner of reflection that theology ought to adopt outside the house
of authority. Since the underlying concern of this essay is the relatively restricted issue of authority in theological reflection rather
than theological methodology as such, I shall limit these observations
to note a few features of theological judgment that have been pointed

out by Farley and which appear to be constitutive of any theological program.

Any field of inquiry operates out of a pre-reflective matrix of reality apprehensions constituting a world of intersubjectively shared meanings. A physicist, as Michael Polanyi might have expressed it, dwells in the communal framework of science and by relying tacitly on its many levels of meaning integrates features of his experience to discern patterns or structures of reality which he judges to be true and which he expects to be revealed to further inquiry in ever more profound ways.[28] Without such an indwelling, in other words, the determinate sorts of integrations of reality upon which the physicist relies to support his theoretical claims would be impossible. Similarly for theology there are concrete reality apprehensions which occur at the pre-reflective level of the faith world and which serve as reference points for theological reflection.

None of this should be taken to mean that somehow hidden in the historical husks of the Christian tradition are changeless contents accessible to theological reflection.[29] Such a liberal and neoorthodox move does not fully accept the implication of historical consciousness that any determinate content is already an interpretation of reality which is not separable from the framework which discerned it.

Nor should this be taken to imply that the theologian finally must appeal to "experience."[30] By now it should be well established that experiences, even though they be "raw," or facts, even though they be "brute," cannot by themselves function in any cognitive enterprise as a field of evidence.[31] Rather a reality is always apprehended through a framework of meaning disclosing some facet of its activity or structure. This entire nexus is directly present to the inquirer and in this sense is "experienced." But the reality is experienced through a determinate set of intentional meanings. Moreover relevant dimensions of these meanings may be brought to reflective awareness so that they may function as a field of evidence. This reflectively expressed field, which is directly accessible to the inquirer and thus again is "experienced," can serve to validate judgments about reality made through them.

Theology, therefore, must always begin with the determinate mode of existence derived from Christian faith in order for its basic realities to come to light and be made accessible for reflection. At the level of faith this form of life may be described as an act toward God, which involves many levels of meaning expressed through worship, linguistic formulas, beliefs, moral decisions, social patterning, and the like. This form of existence, which Farley calls "ecclesial existence," has a normative quality insofar as it brings to expression the transformation to redemptive existence.[32] As these realities are brought to expression they constitute the elements for fields of evidence to which theology might appeal in making its reflective judgments. How might this occur?

The first phase of theological inquiry consists in "portraiture," the properly hermeneutical task which tries to bring to reflective awareness the ideal, teleological character of ecclesial existence under its historically conditioned character of being founded and continually reconstructed through diverse cultural settings.[33] Insofar as the pre-reflective level of faith manifests its realities and implies a truth-intention, these will be explicitly acknowledged in the ideal-historical task of portraiture. Theological reflection, however, is not completed by the hermeneutical task of portraiture, since this arrives only at the level of a reflective understanding of realities with a truth-intention. This might be satisfactory for a provincial, denominational world of meaning which assumes the truth of its sources, as is the case in the house of authority.

Theological reflection must include, therefore, a second moment, the formulation of an "ecclesial universal" and its acceptance (or rejection). An ecclesial universal formulates a prospective claim that describes a reality or a dimension of reality which is not an empirical universal (as might be the case in science) nor a formal universal (as in ontology), but a determinate universal.[34] This means not only that the ecclesial universal is discerned as a reality solely in the determinate context of ecclesial existence, but also that it makes a prospective claim about reality as such. What this requires then is that the theologian grasp the evidential field that permits a particular symbol (e.g., grace) to be accepted as real insofar as it is a legitimate, universal modification of some general features of the world while not being reducible to some empirical dimension of it.[35]

Karl Rahner's explication of the "supernatural existential" might serve as a helpful illustration of this moment of theological judgment.[36] This facet of his theology of grace can be understood to formulate a prospective ecclesial universal insofar as the symbol of grace is shown to disclose a specification of general ontology or anthropology (such as an anticipatory realization of a capacity or desire for infinite fulfillment) which is not discernible in philosophical anthropology as such (since it is "unexacted"), while at the same time it is not merely a psychologically empirical phenomenon (such as "unction" or "inward attraction") since it discloses a determinately universal feature of human existence. To the extent that such an analysis reveals the actual structural reality of the world and appeals to fields of evidence supporting the analysis, to that extent can it be accepted as true.

These brief explorations do not presume to constitute even the outline of a theological method, nor do they go beyond providing a glimpse at the range of Farley's own position. They have been proposed simply to indicate features that appear to be necessary for any program of theological reflection undertaken outside the house of authority, namely the explicit formulation of reality apprehensions that derive from the faith world and their assessment in terms of directly available fields of evidence for their claims to universality. If these proposals have any validity, then there are profound implications for the theological enterprise and for our understanding of the role of authority in theological reflection. Their theological significance might be highlighted by applying these insights to the theological programs recently developed by David Tracy and Gordon Kaufman.[37]

Tracy has developed a powerful and comprehensive hermeneutical theology that explores the significance of religious texts in terms of their status as classics.[38] Why we should choose to allow any given classic, such as a gospel, to illumine the meaning of our lives is not clearly and explicitly explained. Since one of the publics a theologian must address is the church, it might be that the choice of the gospel account as a classical candidate for interpretation is more of a historical accident than a methodological exigency. Furthermore, once an insightful retrieval of a religious classic is accomplished, why must it be accepted as true? Why not simply acknowledge the meanings disclosed through the hermeneutical retrieval as "fictions" rather than "facts"?[39] Does the lack of a method for assessing realities present to faith mean that Tracy's program, in spite of its revisionist aspirations, is still operating in some fashion out of the house of authority?[40]

For Gordon Kaufman, on the other hand, theology is a matter of imaginative construction of the concept of God and its correlate, the world.[41] It appears that "God" functions as a schematic device for the explanation of the unity of our experience and at this level the reconstruction of this concept is a factor in the coherence of our understanding. In addition the imaginative reconstruction of the concept of God should have evocative or humanizing power, and at this level it has a pragmatic justification. But nowhere in the proposal does there appear to be any attempt to understand "God" as true in the sense of "real." Does Kaufman's proposal, therefore, turn out to be in the public realm another proclamation of God's burial by Christian theologians so perceptively argued by Michael Harrington?[42] Or is it a provincial theology that simply assumes the reality of God on the basis of authority? Whatever the answer to these questions may be, it appears legitimate to conclude that, until theological formulations include appeals to determinate fields of evidence to support their judgments, reservations such as these will always be forthcoming.

What, finally, do these reflections allow us to conclude about the role of authority in theological judgment? As far as Farley's proposal itself is concerned, some clarifications regarding the actual operation of authority seem to be required.[43] Farley acknowledges the normative status of a community's originating events and their portraiture at the level of piety.[44] This means that they are authoritative sources for apprehending, at a prereflective level, the realities of the faith world. At the level of theological judgments, however, the depiction of the realities of faith through an ecclesial universal or a doctrinal formulation must be defended (or rejected) through appeals to fields of evidence. What Farley is trying to avoid by this distinction is any understanding of theological judgments which make them operate on basis of givens that have an *a priori*, unquestionable validity. This, in turn, appears to require the restriction of the meaning of the term "authority" to something which is *a priori* true. Farley's archaeological analysis of the house of authority makes this restriction understandable insofar as it is historically accurate. Nonetheless on the methodological level this restricted understanding of authority is confusing to the extent that the acknowledgement of the authoritative status of ecclesial existence seems then to place theology back into the confines of the house of authority.

This issue may be clarified, I believe, by considering a distinction offered by Michael Polanyi on the role of authority in cultural traditions. A "general authority" lays down guidelines but demands freedom in their exercise even to the point of altering or overturning the guidelines, whereas a "specific authority" lays down finished conclusions.[45] The example commonly used by Polanyi to illustrate this insight was, of course, the scientific community.[46] A scientist submits to the authority embodied in the scientific community precisely so that she may discern more complex realities represented through scientific theories and normal practice. As a result of her reliance on these authorities and her own creative efforts she may eventually be led to discern new dimensions of reality which she goes on to affirm with universal intent. These judgments, in turn, may confirm, modify, or even replace elements of the original authoritative structure of the scientific community.

When applied to theological activity, this requires that anything that functions as an authority be taken in the sense of a general authority. Only when authority is understood as "specific" does the problematic character of the house of authority emerge. Existence in a community of faith, then, is authoritative on the prereflective level insofar as it guides believers to certain reality apprehensions. It is authoritative for theological activity to the extent that it serves as a guide for the reflective expression of these reality apprehensions through doctrinalizations. But then theological judgment assesses these expressions in terms of their adequacy to directly manifested fields of evidence. At this level theological activity is ongoing and open; and it must be so if its fundamental aim is the ever more adequate understanding of the realities presumed to be apprehended in ecclesial existence.

Furthermore, I believe that there have been many instances in Christian practice where such an understanding of authority has been implicitly, even if unfortunately not explicitly, acknowledged. The very rise of the Christian form of existence is a most telling case. Unless one were to grant that the early Christians were implicitly responding to reality apprehensions, then the excommunication of the Jesus movement by rabbinic Judaism, which presumably was operating in this case out of a framework of specific authority, would seem to be correct. More recently, the dramatic modifications in theological attempts to understand the reality of the resurrection[47] can be understood as legitimate only in a context of general authority. Even more radical have been the recent proposals, generated out of an evidential field which now includes the Christian encounter with other major world faiths, regarding the universality of the mediating role of Jesus for all humanity.[48] If theology were required to operate in the mode of specific authority, both of these recent examples of inquiries would have to be regarded as false since they question recognized authorities. But if theology were to be guided by a general authority to discern realities and judge the adequacy of its formulations on the basis of evidential fields, then the issues appear to be still unsettled and open to further inquiry.

My proposal then is that a Christian theologian ought to operate under authorities that guide in the perception and explicit formulation of realities apprehended in faith. But this very guidance provides the theologian with both the capacity and the obligation to assess the adequacy of these formulations in terms of directly accessible fields of evidence. Consequently, authority functions legitimately in theology only in a general way, never in the manner of a specific authority.[49] Concretely this means that any locus of authority, even those deemed "inerrant" or "infallible," may be subject to revision, modification, or even rejection. Authority, in short, is a necessary condition for theological reflection, but it is never sufficient by itself for the assessment of theological truth.

Thus, while I take exception to certain limitations in Farley's metaphor, in this respect I agree: when authority functions like a "house," its very structure becomes the issue which is at stake, not the purposes it is supposed to serve. Hence, theology must abandon the house of authority. But theology needs authority as its "home," for a home provides us with our starting point, our place in life, our orientation, and even our capacity to face reality. When the authority of the faith-world is our "home," it permits us to learn, to grow, and perhaps even to move to another dwelling place.

NOTES

1. See Edward Schillebeeckx, *The Church with a Human Face: A New and Expanded Theology of Ministry*, trans. John Bowden (New York: Crossroad, 1985) and Leonardo Boff, *Church, Charism, and Power: A Radical Ecclesiology: Toward a Militant Ecclesiology*, trans. John W. Dierchsmeier (New York: Crossroad, 1984) for recent attempts to revision the phenomenon of authority on a ministerial, liturgical level and on an ecclesial level. Needless to say, these proposals have appeared to some to strike a blow at the very foundations of Catholicism.

2. See, for example, the excerpts from Charles Curran's correspondence with the CDF presented by Arthur Jones in the *National Catholic Reporter*, vol. 22, no. 24 (April 11, 1986), pp. 9–11, 14–17, especially Curran's repeated requests for the CDF to set out its understanding of the norms for dissent from noninfallible teaching.

3. *Ecclesial Reflection: An Anatomy of Theological Method* (Philadelphia: Fortress, 1982).

4. *Ibid.*, p. 5.

5. See his *The Archaeology of Knowledge*, trans. A. M. S. Smith (New York: Harper & Row, 1972).

6. Edward Farley provides a finely nuanced phenomenological exploration of the reality-apprehensions of faith in *Ecclesial Man: A Social Phenomenology of Faith and Reality* (Philadelphia: Fortress, 1975).

7. *Ibid.*, p. 25.

8. *Ibid.*, pp. 28–34.

9. *Ibid.*, pp. 41–45.

10. *Ibid.*, p. 65.

11. *Ibid.*, p. 51.

12. *Ibid.*, pp. 67–68.

13. *Ibid.*, pp. 72–73.

14. *Ibid.*, p. 79.

15. *Ibid.*, p. 81.

16. *Ibid.*, p. 96.

17. *Ibid.*, pp. 102–04.

18. Farley generally uses the expression "immediately" rather than "directly" manifest. My preference for the latter expression is based on the observation that the realities and fields of evidence given in perception (as well as those given in "apperception") are always mediated by networks of meaning.

19. *Ecclesial Reflection*, pp. 108–09.

20. *Ibid.*, p. 110.

21. *Ibid.*, p. 112.

22. *Ibid.*, p. 116.

23. *Ibid.*, p. 132.

24. *Ibid.*, pp. 135ff.

25. *Ibid.*, pp. 140ff.

26. *Ibid.*, p. 157.

27. *Ibid.*, p. 167.

28. For a brief account of Polanyi's understanding of our knowledge of reality, see *The Tacit Dimension* (Garden City, NY: Doubleday, 1967). In my estimation, Polanyi's description of the process of knowing in science bears striking similarities to Farley's phenomenological analysis of theological inquiry.

29. *Ecclesial Reflection*, p. 173.

30. *Ibid.*, pp. 175ff.

31. Recall how logical positivism foundered on the foundational shoals of "sensation" and how philosophers and historians of science came to admit that all facts are "theory laden." N. R. Hanson, *Patterns of Discovery* (Cambridge: Harvard University Press, 1958).

32. *Ecclesial Reflection*, p. 186. An intriguing question might arise at this point regarding whether or not Farley is smuggling back in the house of authority via the back door, i.e., at the prereflective level. This is especially provocative when he maintains that theology cannot "disestablish" (183) the realities of faith. To the extent that they "really are" this is correct. But is that not part of what is at issue? Nonetheless Farley does admit that even the paramount reality of God may be questioned at the intentional level of truth (185). Precisely to what degree Farley would admit the realities of faith to come under reflective scrutiny is not clear to me.

33. *Ibid.*, pp. 195–200.

34. *Ibid.*, p. 310.

35. *Ibid.*, pp. 337ff.

36. For Rahner's early explorations of this theme, see "Concerning the Relationship between Nature and Grace" and "Some Implications of the Scholastic Concept of Uncreated Grace," *Theological Investigations*, trans. Cornelius Ernst (Baltimore: Helicon, 1961), I, 297–317 and 319–46.

37. Many of these observations were inspired by the discussion among Farley, Tracy, and Kaufman of each other's positions at the December, 1982 meeting of the American Academy of Religion. Farley's presentation, "Three Revisionist Theologies: Issues Posed by a Trialogue," is available in typescript.

38. David Tracy, *The Analogical Imagination: Christian Theology and the Culture of Pluralism*. (New York: Crossroad, 1981).

39. This is precisely what Lonnie D. Kliever has proposed recently as the most appropriate way of understanding religious symbolism in our post-Enlightenment culture in his "Confessions of Unbelief: In Quest of the Vital Lie," *Journal for the Scientific Study of Religion*, 25 (March, 1986), 102–15.

40. It must be acknowledged that in *Blessed Rage for Order: The New Pluralism in Theology* (New York: Seabury, 1975), Tracy does affirm that fundamental theology has as one of its tasks the explanation of the adequacy of theological formulations to a transcendental ontology. But this might still be the formal procedure of apologetics in the mode of authority which does not raise explicitly the substantive issue of the reality apprehensions of faith.

41. *The Theological Imagination: Constructing the Concept of God* (Philadelphia: Westminster, 1981) and *An Essay on Theological Method* (Missoula, MT: Scholars Press, 1975).

42. *The Politics at God's Funeral: The Spiritual Crisis of Western Civilization* (New York: Penguin Books, 1983), pp. 150–73.

43. A similar point has been made in David Ray Griffin's review essay of *Ecclesial Reflection* in *Religious Studies Review*, 10 (July, 1984), 246.

44. *Ecclesial Reflection*, pp. 208, 216.

45. Michael Polanyi, *Science, Faith and Reality* (Chicago: University of Chicago Press, Phoenix edition, 1964), p. 59.

46. For one instance of Polanyi's analysis, see *The Tacit Dimension*, pp. 63–92.

47. See Francis Schüssler Fiorenza, *Foundational Theology* (New York: Crossroad, 1984), pp. 1–46, for a historical survey of approaches to the resurrection and an assessment of contemporary analyses. Schüssler Fiorenza's constructive proposal, particularly the analysis of "reflective equilibrium" (pp. 301–11), appears to have an intent similar to the one being proposed here. For a study that depicts the current

state of the question on the exegetical issues, see Pheme Perkins, *Resurrection: New Testament Witness and Contemporary Reflection* (Garden City, NY: Doubleday, 1984).

48. See Paul Knitter, *No Other Name?* (Maryknoll, NY: Orbis Books, 1985) for one version and defense of this thesis.

49. This claim appears to be analogous to Lonergan's contention that the power of authority is exercised legitimately only when it is authentic. See his essay, "The Dialectic of Authority," in *A Third Collection*, ed. F. E. Crowe (New York: Paulist, 1985), pp. 5–12.

Part Three
FAITH TRADITION
AS CREATIVE DIALOGUE WITH
HISTORICAL CONTEXT

REASSESSING ISRAEL'S INTELLECTUAL RELATIONSHIP TO THE ANCIENT WORLD: BIBLICAL FOUNDATIONS FOR AUTHORITY AND THEOLOGY

Robert Gnuse
Loyola University, New Orleans

ABSTRACT

Viewing the Old Testament as a holy history of divine actions in human affairs has been a popular pedagogical model. Concurrent with it has been the frequent comparison of ancient near eastern and Israelite values in stereotypical fashion. Recently the pejorative views of the ancient Near East created by this model have been criticized and Israel's continuity with the ancient world has been stressed. In the future scholars need to emphasize continuity and gradual development when discussing Israel's reconstruction of ancient near eastern social and ideological values. Thus our holy history models will reflect the data in a more nuanced and sensitive fashion.

Introduction

One of the most significant sources of authority for the Christian tradition has been the Bible, used now for two millennia with varying degrees of intensity by different segments of the Christian tradition. When asked why the Bible is authoritative Christians offer many responses.[1] One such affirmation refers to the Bible's direct testimony or witness to the primal events of salvation, the Exodus and the Resurrection of Christ.

Robert Gnuse is an associate professor in Old Testament at Loyola University in New Orleans (New Orleans, LA 70118). His graduate work was completed at Concordia Seminary in Exile (St. Louis) (M.Div. 1974, S.T.M. 1975) and Vanderbilt University (M.A. 1978, Ph.D. 1980). His books include Jewish Roots of Christian Faith (Loyola, 1983), The Dream Theophany of Samuel (University Press of America, 1984), You Shall Not Steal (Orbis, 1985), and The Authority of the Bible (Paulist, 1985). In addition, he has published several articles and numerous book reviews. Currently he is regional president of the New Orleans College Theology Society (1985–1987).

One of the great breakthroughs of the modern intellectual quest is the perception of human development. We have realized that thought and social norms are not static but ever evolving values. As a result, in the theological endeavor the Bible came to be regarded in a new light. Material in the biblical text was perceived in the greater context of the ancient near eastern culture. Hence, our understanding of its authority changed. It remained authoritative, but no longer as a static repository of divine truth, but as a record of the organic process of religious growth in response to the divine encounter. The Bible was foundational to our theology because we have "grown" forth from this primordial divine-human encounter.

The question which remained, however, was how to perceive the relationship of this biblical tradition to the intellectual and social environment from which it arose. History of Religions scholars at the turn of the century emphasized continuity and simple unilinear evolution. Later biblical theologians influenced by Neoorthodoxy stressed the radical dialectical break which caused ancient Israel to part ways with its environment. The resultant implications for contemporary theologians were implied either to be in accommodation with the modern world or to stand over against it with critical proclamation. The understanding of how the Bible relates to its intellectual and social milieu may still carry authoritative implications for doing theology today.

Biblical theologians for the last generation have viewed the Bible as a narrative account of divine actions. Two primal events, Exodus and Resurrection, were divine irruptions into human affairs to alter the course of human existence. Other biblical events were seen in the same paradigm so that the entire Bible was a coherent testimony to a gracious God who acted in the sphere of human history.[2] The term holy history or *Heilsgeschichte* was used to describe this perception. *Heilsgeschichte* was distinguished from *Weltgeschichte*, the former referred to events apprehended by faith while the latter was empirical history, though some theologians extended the category to all history, so that history and revelation were equated.[3] Throughout the movement a great contrast was drawn between biblical thought and that of the surrounding world, whether it be Israel versus the ancient Near East or the New Testament versus the contemporary hellenistic or Greek world.

In recent years this intellectual construct has been criticized in many ways. James Barr has offered the most significant theological as well as biblical criticism, and Brevard Childs has even spoken of the death of the greater biblical theology movement which supported this construct.[4] The following criticisms include some of the objec-

tions raised by critics: 1) History and historical events were not defined in clear philosophical terms. How can the Exodus and
Resurrection be concrete historical actions and events apprehended
only by faith at the same time?[5] 2) The relationship of an event and
the text which narrates it was blurred. We spoke of historical revelation when what we had was a text originating from oral tradition,
or word revelation.[6] 3) The historiography of Israel was pre-modern,
but too often that understanding was overlooked or treated too lightly.[7]
4) Not only did the biblical tradition not use a word for history, much
of the biblical material was nonhistorical, such as Wisdom Literature,
Psalms, other cultic material, and Law.[8] 5) The contrast between the
Bible's linear or historical perspective of reality and the so-called
cyclic or mythic perspective was criticized for being too stereotyped
and unfair to the contemporary cultures.[9]

This last critique shall be the focus of our paper, particularly the
debate concerning the contrast between Israel and the ancient Near
East. We have gone through two stages of evaluation since World
War II: first, the radical differences were highlighted; more recently,
continuity between the cultures has been stressed. This paper will
seek to appraise those stages of research and then offer suggestions
for future direction of the discussion. Our thesis is that Israel's values
are different but not unique in relation to the ancient Near East; Israel
received latent values from predecessor cultures and reconstructed
them in a new construal which brought previously unemphasized
perspectives to the fore.

Our format shall be to trace the progression of scholarship in understanding the notion of holy history and its uniqueness in ancient
Israel.

I. Holy History Advocates

Biblical theologians often compared the ancient Near Eastern world
view with its emphasis upon nature, cult, myth, and a cyclic view
of reality with the emphasis upon history, morality, law, epics, and
a linear view of reality in Israel. Their ideas were expressed best by
George Ernest Wright in his books, The Old Testament Against Its
Environment and God Who Acts: Biblical Theology as Recital.[10]
Similar comparisons were voiced by Martin Noth, Georg Fohrer,
Sigmund Mowinckel, Theodore Vriezen, Oscar Cullmann, Millar
Burrows, and others.[11]

Dichotomies were established by these scholars on a number of
issues:

• Ancient near eastern people experienced the divine in the forces of nature as a cosmic interplay into which they had to be integrated, and because the patterns of nature flowed in an ever-repetitious pattern, so all reality must be a predetermined cycle of regular activity.[12] Israelites, however, viewed nature as inanimate because the one God, Yahweh, transcended nature. Therefore, they superseded cyclic modes of thought and perceived reality in linear or historical categories.[13]

• Cyclic patterns in nature translated into literary categories of myth which recounted archetypal patterns in the divine realm. The resultant mythopoetic accounts described the creation of unchanging natural and social structures. Myths provided the understanding for human integration into the cosmic pattern. Israel, however, spoke in epics wherein the human realm was described in its relationship to the divine. Events did not repeat endlessly, and the greatest emphasis lay on human freedom and responsibility.[14]

• Integration into the cosmic flow for the ancient world was accomplished by rites, sacrifice, and ritual performed in a way called sympathetic magic by biblical theologians. The cosmic flow and the deities could be manipulated in cult and sacrifice. Israel deemphasized the importance of cult and sacrifice by subordinating it to the Law. Sympathetic magic and divination were condemned, for the universe was open-ended; God and people were free to change. The festivals were historicized to commemorate past saving events not to reenact timeless cosmic themes or myths.[15]

• The ancient world's quest for security and the timeless myths of creation legitimated a static social, economic, and political order. Social reform or social justice was not tolerated. Israel, however, encouraged reform and justice. The rise of monotheism created equality, for if there was one god, everyone related to him equally. Yahweh was dynamic and promoted change.[16] This was manifested in a new notion of kingship: while ancient near eastern kings were aristocrats claiming divine status or sanction and absolute obedience from their people, Israel's kings were meant to be subordinate to law and the prophetic voice, and their human finitude was quite obvious in the biblical traditions.[17]

• The morality of the ancient Near East was limited and confined primarily to cultic matters. Their sense of predestination stripped them of ethical-moral responsibility. In Israel the notions of covenant, law, equality, and justice arose as people sensed their freedom and corresponding responsibility.[18]

Biblical scholars presented their paradigm to communicate the unique contributions of Israel's beliefs and to make a significant statement concerning the relevance and implications for modern theology and religious-social values. Israel's experience was described as a breakthrough, a radical revolution, and an epigenesis, as opposed to simple evolution. One sensed the radical newness of Israel's world view implied indirect evidence for the action of God in their experience. As a pedagogical model this was excellent for classroom use and popular writing. This author must admit also to using the model for such purposes.[19]

II. Critical Response

These stereotypes of Israel and the ancient Near East received strong criticism in the past twenty years, and an energetic debate has resulted. In addition to a number of articles, four lengthy works have been produced: Bertil Albrektson, *History and the Gods*, 1967; Morton Smith, *Palestinian Parties and Politics That Shaped the Old Testament*, 1971; H. W. F. Saggs, *The Encounter with the Divine in Mesopotamia and Israel*, 1978; and John Van Seters, *In Search of History*, 1983. In general biblical theologians have been accused of not applying the same criteria to Israel and the ancient Near East. Ancient near eastern texts are assessed phenomenologically, while the Bible is seen theologically. Ancient near eastern texts were drawn from all periods of development while the Old Testament material under consideration had been edited by very moral post-exilic monotheists. Material in the biblical text which appeared to be primitive was dismissed as mere superstition or a holdover from an earlier primitive period or the result of syncretism, while the same beliefs and practices were regarded as very representative when discovered in ancient near eastern texts.[20] Often the comparison was established between early ancient near eastern material and the Old Testament rather than contemporary first millennium B.C. texts, which were more ethically advanced.[21]

Overall the biblical theologians painted their contrasts in order to find Israel advanced and unique among the nations so as to apply insights to contemporary social and religious issues.

Defense of Ancient Near Eastern Values

Ancient near eastern historians responded to biblical theologians defending the character of ancient thought. Their observations might be summed up by the following:

• The Near East developed historiography in its annalistic tradition, particularly in the military reports of the Egyptians, Hittites, and Assyrians.[22] Biblical theologians had moved beyond a simple definition of historiography to a philosophical category which entailed human freedom and eschatology. Of course the ancient Near East lacked this, but so does modern secular or humanistic historiography.[23]

• The ancient near eastern deities were perceived as acting in human affairs in a way which we would call intervention in history. Their arena of activity included nature and history in an indistinguishable fashion.[24]

• Not only did the deities intervene in human affairs, they had a plan for the direction of history. (This is the particular thesis of Bertil Albrektson.) Deities frequently affirmed and directed the affairs of royal dynasties, and they would punish kings and cities for past cultic offenses.[25]

• Historical events may be perceived as a mode of divine revelation from the gods. Deities made their will manifest in acts of judgment against kings and cities, and thus these historical acts might be seen as revelation in history. (This, too, is a thesis peculiar to Albrektson.)[26]

• As in Israel so also the ancient Near East had a concept of the divine word as an active agent in determining human actions both in the natural and the historical arena. Several phrases may be highlighted as meaning the "word of a god" comparable to Israel's notion of the dabar-Yahweh. (Albrektson's thesis here probably would be rejected by most other ancient historians.)[27]

• Any contrast which characterizes the ancient near eastern cult as magical and manipulative while maintaining Israel's to be ethical and oriented toward affirming human freedom is incorrect. Ancient cults did not seek to manipulate the gods any more than did Israel. Both sought good blessings from the divine realm for this life and forgiveness for a right relationship.[28]

• Idealistic visions of justice for all people and attempts at social reform can be found already in the third millennium B.C. in Mesopotamia and Egypt. The notion that the king defended the poor and the weak, brought justice to the land, and led the people in gentleness and humility was an ideal that permeated the ancient world. They fell short of the ideal, of course, but so did kings in Judah and Israel.[29]

• Contrawise, Israel should not be viewed as historical, linear, ethical, or moral as biblical theologians portray. Many ideas found throughout the ancient Near East existed in Israel's normal beliefs and practices, and these ought not be regarded as merely primitive superstitions which endured or the result of syncretism.[30]

The Ongoing Debate

Evidence produced by ancient near eastern historians and philogists did not go unchallenged, however. Critical response to Albrektson and others engendered a lively debate.

W. G. Lambert criticized Albrektson's work, though admitting its value. Albrektson legitimately demonstrated that the gods intervened in human affairs and human history with criteria for judging kings and nations, but Lambert responded that this control was far more limited than for Israel's god and was based on a cultic rationale. Furthermore, said Lambert, Albrektson confused the notion of predetermined destiny in Mesopotamia with the more developed concept of history in Israel. Finally, Albrektson's critique and attempt to limit Israel's notion of holy history was "labored" and "inadequate."[31]

Paul Hanson discussed prophetic and apocalyptic historiography to reaffirm a holy history model and critiqued Albrektson and others. Mesopotamian material reflected only "timeless episodes" and lacked "historical sequence spanning centuries in an unbroken development," whereas Israel's epic and prophetic material showed the idea of a divine plan.[32]

J. J. M. Roberts defended Albrektson, criticized George Ernest Wright, and responded to the critiques of Lambert and Hanson in a number of articles. He criticized the way in which biblical theologians stereotyped Mesopotamian historiography by appealing primarily to earlier materials. He also saw little difference between later ancient near eastern historiography and the Deuteronomistic Historian, for both arranged preexisting blocks of material together in somewhat disparate fashion. He did admit the existence of differences between Israel and the ancient world, but called for a more sensitive analysis of these differences.[33]

H. W. F. Saggs compared ideas of history, good and evil, personal piety, cult, universalism, and the idea of God in Mesopotamia and Israel. His discovery of essential similarities led him to criticize those who forced comparisons to affirm Israel's uniqueness.[34]

John Van Seters evaluated historiography in Israel and the ancient world. His findings supported the critique of Albrektson and Roberts, and he portrayed Israel's historiography as contemporaneous with

Greek historians and built upon the ancient near eastern annalistic tradition.[35]

Only Joseph Licht has defended the uniqueness of Israel's historiography recently. Mesopotamian materials are labeled as merely annals, recording only recent events or those occurring over a short period of time. Israel's deity, however, had a deliberate long-term policy over successive generations for future events. With Lambert he accused Albrektson and Saggs of confusing Mesopotamian notions of destiny with Israelite history.[36]

On the whole the debate thus far favors the critics of holy history models; however, the final word may not have been said. The debate does tell us that if we are to speak meaningfully of holy history and Israel's unique perspective, we must be more guarded and sensitive. Pejorative evaluations of the ancient Near East ought to be avoided. Most of the critics of the model would concur with that agenda.

III. Reconstruction of a Holy History Model

Ways of Approach

Modern ways of describing holy history might move in one of three directions: affirmation of simple continuity, affirmation of similarity with a degree of difference, or affirmation of similarity with a particular point of divergence, the last being the most popular among scholars.

Continuity

One might say that the notion of Yahweh acting in history was no different than that of neighboring cultures. The Israelites merely had more literature on this subject, or it was of higher quality.[37]

Degree of Difference

Many critics of holy history models would prefer to speak of a degree of difference between ancient near eastern and Israelite understandings. Israelites may have emphasized human freedom and responsibility and the non-cultic perspective of divine action in human affairs more than their contemporaries, but they were not unique in this regard, Roberts noted how they emphasized the historical dimension to a greater degree with the modification of agricultural festivals into commemorative events and the recollection of great events of the past in the cultic setting.[38]

Particular Points of Divergence

A number of ideas have been mentioned as ways of describing Israel's uniqueness which are more precise and avoid the broad sweeping generalizations of earlier holy history models: 1) Some might emphasize Israel's total freedom from nature imagery in the portrayal of Yahweh, an approach which old established polytheistic religions were not capable of doing.[39] 2) Similar to this is the idea that Israel totally affirmed the historical dimension as the arena of divine activity. For Israel history was a primary category, for others it remained secondary.[40] 3) Some scholars argue that Israel perceived divine actions in history to have moral purpose, while among ancient near-easterners the gods merely punished nations and kings for cultic offenses. Ancient near eastern deities preserved the status quo, while Israel's god moved people toward a goal.[41] 4) Related to this is the notion that Israel's deity had a long range purpose or plan in history, a promise-fulfillment pattern which arched over successive generations and the history of the nation.[42] The gods of the nations acted on particular issues for a shorter period of time with a less defined goal. Ancient near-eastern deities acted for kings and dynasties, while Yahweh acted for a whole people. 5) A different approach stresses the increased ethical or moral level of awareness found in Israelite material. While the gods punished kings for cultic offenses, Israel's god was motivated by deeper ethical norms, the Mosaic legal tradition.[43] 6) Finally, one scholar (Lambert) advocates that Israelite monotheism and the subsequent hypostatization of the divine word set Israelites apart from their contemporaries. The more developed notion of Word of God as agent of the divine will in human history made Israel unique.[44]

Any contemporary discussion of holy history might begin with any of these observations or synthesize several of them. But the model should reflect the sensitive awareness of Israel's greater continuity with their contemporaries.

Causes of Change

A further aspect worthy of consideration is the mechanics or causes by which Israel came to differ from surrounding cultures with this new world view. Two different approaches are suggested by scholarship in the past two generations. Some attribute Israel's attitudes to ideational or religious causes, such as the faith experience in the Exodus, a new awareness of God, monotheism, the covenant process, or apprehension of election for all the people not just leaders. Other scholars seek to discern concrete explanations in social, political,

economic, or geographic terms. The former might appear more religious, the latter more secular, but the social scientist may not necessarily deny divine presence with a social historical explanation.
The rift between George Mendenhall's affirmation of the covenant
value system and Norman Gottwald's affirmation of class struggle as
the motivation behind the conquest experience typifies such division
of ideational and social historical approaches within one school of
interpretation.[45]

Several significant evaluations have proceeded from ideational
categories. Walter Eichrodt used covenant as the unifying notion and
the precipitating factor for Israel's ethos.[46] William Foxwell Albright
highlighted the Mosaic experience and radical monotheism as the
integrating factor.[47] Many other scholars have used the notion of
election in a general sense.

Concrete explanations have been advocated by significant social
historians. Max Weber implied that since Israel was not a river valley
culture, it was not burdened with complex social and economic
systems necessary for irrigation and agriculture. Hence, as a "peripheral culture" they had access to the great intellectual heritage
and freedom to reconstruct older values.[48] Weippert stressed that
Israel differed from the ancient Near East in social-economic terms
and the experiences of settlement and exile crystalized these values
into a new world view.[49] Gottwald offered an extensive social-scientific evaluation which defines class struggle as the precipitating
factor in the rise of Israel's values.[50]

The debate may never be resolved, and the distinction may promote a false dichotomy. When describing the mechanism by which
Israel set forth a new ethos, one ought to combine both ideational
and social categories, for in this way alone may the complex experience of many human beings over several centuries be understood.
Ideational and social factors arise together and cross-fertilize each
other.

Thus the paths lie open for discussion of holy history models. The
results should be more nuanced, more cautious in regard to the
description of Israel's values, more sensitive to the values of the
ancient Near East, and more reflective concerning the ideational and
social-historical causes.

IV. Conclusion

The author offers the following general observations for future
discussion of holy history models:

• Whereas a previous generation may have made excessive claims concerning Israel's uniqueness, we must not now move to the opposite extreme by denying the importance of Israel's reconstruction of ancient near eastern values (as does Albrektson at times). The critique of most scholars in the past generation was not only sober, objective, and balanced; it provided the basis for a more accurate and sensitive portrayal of Israel's contributions to the understanding of divine action in history.

• Israel's perspective on reality was not historical as we understand the notion, or even as the ancient Greeks understood historiography, but rather it was protohistorical. Perhaps linear is a better word to use than historical. The continental nuance between *Geschichte* and *Historie* has simply not made an impact in the English speaking world. We cautiously and unconsciously regard Israel's historical narrative to be factual because we wish to avoid the subjective views of Von Rad and Bultmann, who permit the possibility that there may be little or no factual event behind the text. We need to avoid this fear and speak more tentatively of Israel's concept of history, for it is developmentally speaking quite prior to historiography as we know it.

• Israel did not invent this linear perspective but adopted it from the ancient Near East and gave it greater emphasis. We must not place Israel in diametric opposition to her contemporaries but perceive Israel's role as contributing significantly to a developmental process.

• Israel's contribution might be described best as reconstruction or reconstrual of previous ideas rather than an epigenesis or breakthrough. We should not search for the new and the unique but for how old ideas were placed into a new construct and how different ideas were brought to the fore in a fresh fashion.

• This reconstruction was made possible because Israel was a fresh new society relatively speaking, a "peripheral people" on the edge of great civilizations. They inherited ancient near eastern values but were not bound to the old social-political-economic structures. As pastoralists entering the land or as Canaanites withdrawing from old social structures, they were in position to reconstruct a new matrix of the old ideas.

• Israel did not discard instantly all of the old, primitive, magical elements of ancient thought. The prophetic-priestly Yahwistic tradition remained a minority movement until the exile. It would be better to describe Israel's arrival at this new ethos as one of gradual transformation or evolution, a form of evolution comparable to what is called macro-evolution in biology. (Herein individual mutations occur slowly and remain as recessive or latent in the genetic pool of an animal population, until they arise together in a newly construed matrix which enables them to become dominant factors.) This model enables us to perceive how Israel moved beyond contemporary cultures without pejoratively portraying the values of those cultures in comparison with Israel.

In sum we postulate that Israel did not invent a world view in contrast to neighboring societies but drew upon existing ideas and reconstructed them in a fresh fashion. Dominant emphasis was given to ideas previously subordinated for social, political, economic, and religious reasons in the established cultures of the ancient world. Because Israel was not bounded by old established social structures reconstruction was possible. Parallels with Greece might be drawn, for here, too, was another society on the periphery of great old civilizations which drew upon cultural accomplishments and advanced them in a bold, fresh, new way. Thus we advocate that Israel was part of a spectrum, where one might observe gradual but significant advance along the path of human development.

Implications for Theological Endeavor

Religious development never occurs in a vacuum. The process by which the Christian Church has inherited its theological traditions is a long historical development where interaction with the social and intellectual environment has produced significant religious articulations by theologians. As Israel grew out of its milieu, so also the Christian tradition has grown out of its environment. Just as it is inappropriate to place Israel in opposition to its world and declare it "unique," so it would be hybris on our part to separate the Christian tradition from its greater cultural setting and call it unique or superior. As with Israel, so with the Church, the intellectual material came from the surrounding world.

Likewise, as the reconstruction of a new matrix out of the common theology of the ancient world was Israel's accomplishment, so also the task of the modern Church is to draw forth from its intellectual and social environment a new theological construal to proclaim anew in every generation the hope of divine love. The theology of the Church is a process of tradition formation, and the ever current task of theologians is to continue that process.

If our study of ancient Israel has made us consciously alert to how theology arises as a reconstruction of older values, then we shall be able to commit ourselves to the task of doing theology as we consciously draw upon the humanities, social sciences, other "raw materials" of our intellectual heritage. Not to do this consciously in our task of theology means that presuppositions will creep into our theology subliminally. Such unacknowledged agenda produces a poor and dogmatic theology. A good theology knows well its presuppositions and methods and has arranged them effectively. A Buddhist monk once said, "Enlightenment means to be fully aware of what you are doing at all times, no matter how great or small the task."

NOTES

1. David Kelsey, *The Uses of Scripture in Recent Theology* (Philadelphia: Fortress, 1975), pp. 14–119; and Robert Gnuse, *The Authority of the Bible: Theories of Inspiration, Revelation and the Canon of Scripture* (New York: Paulist, 1985), pp. 14–101, both offer evaluations of the different models by which biblical authority is perceived.

2. George Ernest Wright, *God Who Acts: Biblical Theology as Recital*, Studies in Biblical Theology, vol. 8 (London: SCM, 1952), pp. 12–32, and "From the Bible to the Modern World," *Biblical Authority for Today: A World Council of Churches Symposium on the Biblical Authority for the Churches' Social and Political Message Today*, eds. Alan Richardson and Wolfgang Schweitzer (London: SCM, 1951), pp. 219–39; Wright and Reginald Fuller, *The Book of the Acts of God*, Christian Faith Series, ed. Reinhold Niebuhr, (Garden City: Doubleday, 1957), pp. 27–33; Norman Snaith, *The Inspiration and Authority of the Bible* (London: Epworth, 1956), pp. 9–46; Charles Harold Dodd, *The Authority of the Bible*, rev. ed. (London: Fontana, 1960), pp. 216–19, 257–63; and Richardson, *The Bible in the Age of Science* (Philadelphia: Westminster, 1961), pp. 122–41, provides a good summary of Wright, Dodd, and Oscar Cullmann.

3. Jürgen Moltmann, *Theology of Hope*, trans. James Leith (New York: Harper and Row, 1975), pp. 15–338; and various essays in *History and Hermeneutic*, ed. Wolfhart Pannenberg, *Journal for Theology and the Church*, vol. 4, ed. Robert Funk (New York: Harper and Row, 1967), pp. 14–152, and *Revelation as History*, ed. Pannenberg, trans. David Granskou (New York: Macmillan, 1968), pp. 1–181.

4. James Barr, *Biblical Words for Time*, Studies in Biblical Theology, vol. 33 (Naperville, IL: Allenson, 1962), pp. 11–162, and *Old and New in Interpretation: A Study of the Two Testaments* (London: SCM, 1982), pp. 36–64, has criticized the simplistic distinctions between Hebraic and Greek thought as well as the notions of holy history so frequently used in the biblical theology movement; Brevard Childs, *Biblical Theology in Crisis* (Philadelphia: Westminster, 1970), pp. 13–87; and Henning Graf Reventlow, *Problems of Old Testament Theology in the Twentieth Century* (Philadelphia: Fortress, 1985), pp. 59–124, has provided the best bibliography and a terse summary of the debate.

5. Barr, "The Interpretation of Scripture: II. Revelation Through History in the Old Testament and in Modern Theology," *Interpretation* 17 (1963), 193–205, and *Old and New*, pp. 66–69.

6. Barr, "Revelation," p. 197, and *Old and New*, pp. 15–33, 77–82; and Bertil Albrektson, *History and the Gods: An Essay on the Idea of Historical Events as Divine Manifestations in the Ancient Near East and in Israel* (Lund: Gleerup, 1967), pp. 119–22.

7. Barr, "Revelation," p. 199; and J. J. M. Roberts, "Myth Versus History: Relaying the Comparative Foundations," *Catholic Biblical Quarterly* 38 (1976), 3–4.

8. Barr, "Revelation," pp. 196–97, and *Old and New*, pp. 15–23, 72–76; and Gnuse, *Authority*, pp. 68–69.

9. This is the essential thrust of works by Albrektson, *History*, pp. 11–122; Roberts, "Divine Freedom and Cultic Manipulation in Israel and Mesopotamia," *Unity and Diversity: Essays in the History, Literature, and Religion of the Ancient Near East*, eds. Hans Goedicke and Roberts (Baltimore: Johns Hopkins, 1975), pp. 181–90, and "Myth Versus History," pp. 1–13; H. W. F. Saggs, *The Encounter with the Divine in Mesopotamia and Israel*, Jordan Lectures in Comparative Religion, vol. 12 (London: Athlone, 1978), pp. 1–188; and John Van Seters, *In Search of History: Historiography*

in the Ancient World and the Origins of Biblical History (New Haven: Yale, 1983), pp. 1–362.

10. Wright, The Old Testament Against Its Environment, Studies in Biblical Theology, vol. 2 (Chicago: Regnery, 1950), pp. 7–112, God Who Acts, pp. 11–128, and Acts of God, pp. 15–38; and comparable work in the New Testament was provided by Oscar Cullmann, Christ and Time: The Primitive Christian Conception of Time and History, trans. Floyd Filson (Philadelphia: Westminster, 1950), pp. 11–242.

11. Martin Noth, "The Understanding of History in Old Testament Apocalyptic," The Laws in the Pentateuch and Other Studies, trans. D. R. Ap-Thomas (Philadelphia: Fortress, 1967), p. 195; Georg Fohrer, History of Israelite Religion, trans. David Green (Nashville: Abingdon, 1972), p. 182; Sigmund Mowinckel, He That Cometh, trans. G. W. Anderson (Nashville: Abingdon, 1956), p. 151, and "Israelite Historiography," Annual of the Swedish Theological Institute 2 (1963), 4ff; Theodore Vriezen, An Outline of Old Testament Theology (Oxford: Blackwell, 1958), p. 187; Cullmann, Christ and Time, p. 51; and Millar Burrows, "Ancient Israel," The Idea of History in the Ancient Near East, ed. Robert Dentan, American Oriental Series, vol. 38 (New Haven: American Oriental Society, 1955), pp. 127 and 101–30 in general.

12. Wright, Old Testament, p. 17, and Acts of God, p. 30. Biblical theologians often used the ideas of Mircea Eliade, The Myth of the Eternal Return or Cosmos and History, trans. Willard Trask, Bollingen Series, vol. 46 (Princeton: University Press, 1954), pp. 3–162. Thorkild Jacobson, The Treasures of Darkness: A History of Mesopotamian Religion (New Haven: Yale, 1976), pp. 23–73, described fourth millennium B.C. Mesopotamian religion in this fashion, but his discussion of subsequent development in Mesopotamia contradicts this simplistic stereotype.

13. Wright, Old Testament, p. 23.

14. Ibid., p. 19, and God Who Acts, p. 39.

15. Wright, Old Testament, pp. 78–90, and God Who Acts, p. 28.

16. Wright, Old Testament, pp. 44–45, and God Who Acts, pp. 19–29.

17. Henri Frankfort, Kingship and the Gods: A Study of Ancient Near Eastern Religion as the Integration of Society and Nature (Chicago: University Press, 1948), pp. 339–44.

18. Wright, Old Testament, p. 106, and God Who Acts, p. 20; and Frankfort, Kingship, p. 278.

19. Gnuse, You Shall Not Steal: Community and Property in the Biblical Tradition (Maryknoll: Orbis, 1985), pp. 53–58, 61–63, 67–78.

20. Saggs, Encounter, pp. 1–29.

21. Jacobsen, "Religious Drama in Ancient Mesopotamia," Unity and Diversity, pp. 65–77; and Roberts, "Cultic Manipulation," pp. 182–83.

22. Herbert Butterfield, The Origins of History (New York: Basic Books, 1981), pp. 44–79; Van Seters, History, pp. 18–31; and Hayim Tadmor, "Observations on Assyrian Historiography," Essays on the Ancient Near East in Memory of Jacob Joel Finkelstein, ed. Maria de Jong Ellis, Memoirs of the Connecticut Academy of Arts and Sciences, vol. 19 (Hamden, CT: Archon, 1977), pp. 209–13.

23. Roberts, "Myth Versus History," pp. 3–4.

24. Jacobsen, "Ancient Mesopotamian Religion: The Central Concerns," Proceedings of the American Philosophical Society 107 (1963): 473–84; Albrektson, History, pp. 17–49; and Saggs, Encounter, pp. 81–85.

25. Albrektson, History, pp. 68–111; and Saggs, Encounter, p. 83. However, W. G. Lambert, "History and the Gods: A Review Article," Orientalia 39 (1970), 170–77, has criticized Albrektson expressly for overstatement on this point.

26. Albrektson, *History*, pp. 100–08.

27. *Ibid.*, pp. 53–67.

28. Roberts, "Cultic Manipulation," pp. 181–87, and "Myth Versus History," pp. 7–8; and Saggs, *Encounter*, pp. 70–76, 153–82.

29. James Henry Breasted, *Development of Religion and Thought in Ancient Egypt* (New York: Scribners, 1912), pp. 165–256, and *The Dawn of Conscience* (New York: Scribners, 1933), pp. 182–222; and Charles Fensham, "Widow, Orphan, and the Poor in Ancient Near Eastern Legal Literature," *Journal of Near Eastern Studies* 21 (1962), 129–39.

30. Morton Smith, "The Common Theology of the Ancient Near East," *Journal of Biblical Literature* 71 (1952), 135–47, and "Religious Parties among the Israelites before 587," *Palestinian Parties and Politics That Shaped the Old Testament* (New York: Columbia, 1971), pp. 15–56; Saggs, *Encounter*, pp. 21–26, 65–66; and Van Seters, *History*, pp. 249–362, pointed out that Israel's historiography was not so early nor so advanced over its ancient near eastern counterparts.

31. Lambert, "A Review," pp. 170–77, and "Destiny and divine intervention in Babylon and Israel," *Old Testament Studies* 17 (1972), 65–72.

32. Paul Hanson, "Jewish Apocalyptic Against Its Near Eastern Environment," *Revue biblique* 78 (1971), 31–58.

33. Roberts, "Cultic Manipulation," pp. 181–90, "Myth Versus History," pp. 1–13, and "Nebuchadnezzar I's Elamite Crisis in Theological Perspective," *Essays on the Ancient Near East*, pp. 183–87.

34. Saggs, *Encounter* pp. 1–188.

35. Van Seters, *History*, pp. 1–362.

36. Joseph Licht, "Biblical Historicism," *History, Historiography and Interpretation: Studies in biblical and cuneiform literatures*, eds. Hayim Tadmor and Moshe Weinfeld (Jerusalem: Magnes, 1984), pp. 109–11.

37. Smith, "Common Theology," pp. 135–47, and "Religious Parties," pp. 15–56; and Albrektson, *History*, p. 110.

38. Roberts, "Myth Versus History," pp. 7–8, 12; Saggs, *Encounter*, p. 4; and Albrektson, *History*, pp. 115–17, admitted that Israel did historicize the festivals more than contemporary cultures.

39. Wright, *Old Testament*, p. 22, and *God Who Acts*, pp. 48–49; Lambert, "A Review," pp. 171–72; and Saggs, *Encounter*, p. 92.

40. Barr, "Revelation," p. 201; Hanson, "Apocalyptic," pp. 31–58; and Butterfield, *History*, pp. 86, 116, 159.

41. Lambert, "A Review," pp. 173–75.

42. Johannes Lindblom, *Prophecy in Ancient Israel* (London: Blackwell, 1962), p. 325; Butterfield, *History*, pp. 89, 98, 159; and Licht, "Biblical Historicism," pp. 109–11.

43. Butterfield, *History*, pp. 64–69.

44. Lambert, "A Review," p. 172.

45. Bernhard Anderson, "Mendenhall Disavows Paternity: Says He Didn't Father Gottwald's Marxist Theory," *Bible Review* 2, No. 2 (1986), 46–49.

46. Walther Eichrodt, *Theology of the Old Testament*, 2 vols., trans. James Baker (Philadelphia: Westminster, 1961–1967), I:25–520, II:15–529.

47. William Foxwell Albright, *From the Stone Age to Christianity: Monotheism and the Historical Process*, 2nd ed. (Garden City: Doubleday, 1951), pp. 1–403.

48. Max Weber, *Ancient Judaism*, trans. and eds. Hans Gerth and Don Martindale (Glencoe: Free Press, 1952), pp. xviii–xix, 7–8, 252–63. Karl Wittfogel, *Oriental Despotism: A Comparative Study of Total Power* (New Haven: Yale, 1957), pp. 1–449,

would concur with this analysis, for in his work he analyzed many societies, including ancient near-eastern models, as expressions of "hydraulic economies," where authoritarian government develops to maintain control over water resources; William Davisson and James Harper, *European Economic History*, vol. 1: *The Ancient World* (New York: Appleton-Century-Crofts, 1972), pp. 30–85, described the ancient near-eastern economic system as a "status-redistributive" or "storehouse" economy, and pointed out that Israel was the first to deviate; and Gnuse, *Steal*, pp. 55–56.

49. Manfred Weippert, "Fragen des israelitischen Geschichtsbewusstseins," *Vetus Testamentum* 23 (1973), 415–442.

50. Norman Gottwald, *The Tribes of Yahweh: A Sociology of Liberated Israel 1250– 1050 B.C.E.* (Maryknoll: Orbis, 1979), pp. xxi–v, 3–709.

FREE AND VOLUNTARY:
THE AMERICAN EXPERIENCE OF THE
ROMAN CATHOLIC CHURCH

Robert Kress
University of San Diego

ABSTRACT

The contrast between measurable religious faith and practice in
Europe and the United States has been widely remarked. That they
should be so high in the United States is also surprising since the
classical critique of religion maintains that religion is rooted in un-
freedom, misery, and oppression. Although the United States is enormously prosperous and free, religion has not withered away. Indeed,
it flourishes. Why is this? I locate the roots in the American religious
experience in general—the unique religious orientation of the American revolution, the Millennialist expectations of the earliest settlers,
the absence of an established national state church and the predom-
inance of the free church mode of Christianity. All these Roman
Catholicism made its own according to its own nature and thus
developed a Catholic Voluntarism and became a Catholic Free Church.

In these last days some attention is finally being paid to the Roman
Catholic Church and its special history in the United States of America, its past achievement, its present performance, and its future
promise.

That this has not always been the case is readily confirmed by
even the most cursory glance at standard histories of Catholicism.
For them, the American Catholic Church is at best a phthisic ap-
pendage of European Catholicism. Indeed, only in 1908 was the
American Church removed from the tutelage of the *Congregatio de
Propaganda Fide*, a move whose repeal some seemingly wish now
to secure. The same cursory glance at standard histories of American

*Robert Kress is Associate Professor in the Department of Religious Studies at the
University of San Diego (San Diego, CA   92110). He is the author of six books and
many articles, both scholarly and academic, on a wide range of theological subjects.
His most recent book is* The Church: Communion Sacrament Communication. *In final
preparation is an introduction to sacramental theology entitled* Touching the Divine.

religion readily yields the same impression—American Catholicism is neither interesting nor significant.[1] A recent letter from a prominent German theologian admits that "Here in Germany we know little, indeed nothing, about the [Roman Catholic] Church in the United States."[2] Often enough, those who, for whatever reason, do take an interest in the American Catholic Church do so in a Spenglerian spirit of crisis, decline, and fall.[3] From all sides of the ideological spectrum, it has become a popular pastime to berate the American society for its materialistic securalism and hedonist consumerism. Western, especially American prosperity, so proclaim these prophets of parsimony, themselves, of course, all propped up in their own hardly frugal life-styles by American prosperity, is pagan and perverse, corruptive of Christian ideals and virtues.[4]

On the other hand, some do find the American Church among the most impressive of all contemporary Catholic Churches.[5] Certainly, all statistical evidence indicates that Christianity in general and Catholicism in particular are flourishing significantly better in the United States than in other Western countries with customarily Christian populations.

> A recent study indicates that 95 percent of Americans believe in God, 71 percent in life after death, 84 in heaven, 67 in hell. In regard to the Ten Commandments, 93 percent agreed that the prohibitions against murder and theft still applied, 87 percent those against adultery. Whether they go or not, 81 percent consider themselves religious; 48 percent of all Americans said that God was most important in their lives. All these percentages are higher, often considerably, than those of Western European countries. Also noteworthy is the finding of another study that although two of every five Roman Catholics discontinue church practice, usually between the ages of 16 and 25, most do return to the church later on.[6]

This statistical evidence can be buttressed by anecdotal evidence. In the summer of 1985, I gave several lectures in Germany and Austria on the history and current state of the American Catholic Church. As indications of the current interest in the Church, I mentioned that at the University of Illinois in Champaign-Urbana, of the estimated 12,000 Catholic students (out of a total of about 35,000), about 6,000 were weekly participants in the Sunday liturgy. I also described other activities such as Bible study, theology classes, fraternal and sororal groups, retreats, liturgy preparation, choir, convert classes, etc. I also noted similar statistics for other, certainly not all, but nonetheless many, campuses. My audiences were nonplussed. They were too polite to suspect and accuse me of mendacity, but such participation, especially by university youth, is simply not part of their contemporary Church.

When I narrated this experience to my Illinois students, one of them told me of her experience as a tourist in Europe. Although she is likely to attract attention any place, she said that she and her girlfriend were the center of attraction when they went to Mass on Sundays. They were in striking contrast to the small and senior synaxis which had collected to celebrate the Sunday liturgy. By this state of affairs my students were as amazed as the congregation was at their presence.

Finally, I shall mention the favorable impression American Catholic practice made on Cardinal Jean-Marie Lustiger of Paris during his April 26-May 10 tour in 1986: "Today of all Western societies, it seems to me that the United States is the 'most religious' . . . I say the 'most religious.' I do not say 'the most faithful to the demands of Christianity.' "[7] Of course, the last comment must, de rigeur, be added. How difficult for the European to acknowledge that America, even the Catholic Church, could ever have really faithfully responded to the challenge of Christianity. However, in general his remarks indicate a reliable grasp of the religious role and dimension of American society and of the American Catholic Church, an amazing contrast to the customary envy[8] of European, including Catholic, intellectuals, which prompts them toward pure negativity toward anything American.

I spend some time detailing this situation because on all counts it is an amazing account. First of all, according to the classical critique of religion (F. Nietzsche, L. Feuerbach, K. Marx, S. Freud), religion is rooted in the misery of the masses.[9] Religion is an opium for the oppressed. Remove the oppression and you remove the fertile soil in which religion must necessarily take root. Once human beings are free, their religion will also automatically wither and die, the religious analgesic having become otiose. Accordingly, the United States should be among the least religious of all nations. However, here the emancipation of the people from economic, social, political, and cultural oppression, even from the tutelage of the state-church and church-state, has not been accompanied by their emancipation from religion and church. At least not until now.

The flourishing of American Catholicism is even more surprising. Not only has it survived economic and cultural prosperity, it has also survived religious and cultural persecution. Even early on, when the American Catholic population was substantially Anglo-Saxon, it was subject to the discrimination and disenfranchisement of the English anti-Irish and anti-Catholic penal laws. Indeed, Arthur S.

Schlesinger, Sr., has felt compelled to tell John Tracy Ellis, "I regard the prejudice against your Church as the deepest bias in the history of the American people."[10] Should anyone think that anti-Catholicism began and ceased with anti-immigrant Nativism and that its robes and hoods are only of the Ku Klux Klan, Andrew Greeley's handy little compendium on this topic can serve as a ready antidote.[11]

In spite of American and Catholic freedom and prosperity, and in spite of undeniable sectarian religious intolerance, both the Christian religion in general (as well as other religions) and Catholicism have flourished in the United States. Perhaps, as we shall see, we should not say "in spite of," but "because of."

How could and can this be? Our answer will focus on the American Catholic Church.

The answer I shall suggest is composed of four elements. Chief among them is the voluntary nature of the American Church. In America, the Roman Catholic Church, previously a prototypically and paradigmatically established Church, has become not only juridically a non- or dis-established Church; it has also become existentially[12] a free and voluntary Church.

Among the various titles I had considered for this paper were "The Free-Churching of Catholicism in the United States" and "Ecclesial Voluntarism: The Transformation of Roman Catholicism in the United States." Admittedly, "Free Church"[13] is a term which has overtones that, as colleagues not only noted but manifested, grate on Catholic ears. Indeed, Cardinal Joseph Ratzinger has noted, with alarm, what he discerns to be a "Free Church" tendency in contemporary Roman Catholic ecclesiology and ecclesial practice.[14] Furthermore, some Free Church adepts themselves judge the customary Free Churches to have betrayed their heritage and to have become, in their own way, established churches.[15] If the original Free Churches have failed, why should another Church even consider assuming the term.

In spite of the polyvalence of the term, in spite of the alleged failure of the Free Churches themselves, I still find the term appealing. For, of all the elements in the concept of Free Church, one stands above all others, namely the free will choice, the free will decision to be a member of the Church:[16]

> There is a geological fault line between the state-church Reformers who continued the medieval territorial parish definition of the corpus christianorum, and the radicals who espoused not reformatio but restitutio, who envisioned the True Church (die rechte Kirche) as a covenant people united in voluntary membership. The conceptualization of the voluntary covenant took various forms.

I think that it is possible to argue that a new form of this "voluntary covenant," considerably transformed and enhanced, is the American Roman Catholic Church.

As for "Voluntarism," I am myself not enamored of the term. It has customarily designated a theological attitude and position which I find distinctly and deathly un-Catholic. Together with its twin, Nominalism, it assures that finite and contingent created being is evacuated of both being and light. As Hans Urs von Balthasar has remarked, when Voluntarism and Nominalism assume the ascendancy, "the entire creation is completely robbed of all divine illumination; es wird Nacht."[17] Precisely America and American Catholicism have taken this created world seriously. Voluntarism is, then, a term that has to grate on American and Catholic ears. On the other hand, even in its excess, it does semantically stress the first and key element of the nature of American Catholicism, namely its free will, voluntary character. In any case, then, in what I hope is the middle way of virtue (In medio stat virtus) and not the fence straddling of lukewarm cowardice, I have entitled this paper "Free and Voluntary," hoping to stress the valid and stifle the distressing elements of both "Free Church" and "Voluntarism." My point is that the history of the American Catholic church, its kairos if you will, has both exacted and enabled its transformation into a voluntary and free Church, whose members belong and participate by virtue of their free will, not by virtue of Caesaropapist coercion or by absence of other options.[18]

And thus we come to the second element of American Catholic history, its ability to survive and thrive in a pluralist society brimming with options. Neither religion in general nor any religion in particular is required by state or society. In a society awash with options, religion has been and is one of many options, but in America it is an option that is often chosen and exercised.[19]

The enabling context of this pluralist and optional society is the decisive hallmark of American history and civilization. However well or poorly America has actually practiced its creed, the creed itself is clearly and emphatically one of freedom.[20] We shall resume this topic shortly and in some detail. It is not awry to think of the pluralism and optionalism noted above as properties, in the Aristotelian-Scholastic sense, of this freedom. The Catholic Church has learned not only to survive, but also to thrive in this free, optional, and consequently competitive society. This ability is the third element in the history and character of American Catholicism.

The fourth element is a necessary concomitant of the first three elements, namely the importance, indeed the precedence of the people, the "common man," the average citizen/member in not only the civil, but also the ecclesial society. American Roman Catholic history has produced a Church in which neither pope nor emperor nor Caesaropapist, neither bishop nor priest nor monk/religious member is the key member. The key member is, rather, the people, the "common man," the ordinary, the average citizen.[21]

How did this new way of being the Catholic Church come about? To answer this question we shall proceed in two steps. First, we shall see how the United States came to be a religious nation. Then we shall see how the Roman Catholic Church learned to survive and thrive in this greater religious context.

I. The Nation With the Soul of a Church

G. K. Chesterton, never at a loss for a bon mot, once characterized the United States as "A nation with the soul of a Church."[22] Of course, one need not have waited for Chesterton for this insight. Years before, another European had observed that "Religion, which never intervenes directly in the government of American society, should therefore be considered as the first of their political institutions."[23] Whence came this American ecclesial soul? This religious nation? And what does it mean?

The genesis of this ecclesial soul, the birth of this religious nation is to be sought in the motives and character of the European immigrants who not only came to the North American continent, but discovered America, and created the American nation in the image and likeness of their own pluralist and polyglot selves.[24]

The religious dimensions of the discovery and settling, the founding and organization of that society and culture which came to be known nationally as the United States of America are too obvious to be denied.[25] The missionary motivation of early explorations and explorers is manifest. However intensely these religious motives may have been accompanied by economic ones, and however much economic gold diggers may have undermined evangelist missioners, the religious motivation of the European explorations remains secure. Furthermore, the settling of North America was also clearly religiously, as well as politically, motivated. America was to be not only a refuge for those dissenting Christians fleeing established churches in England and then on the continent, it was also to be a missionary expedition for the conversion of the heathen and sinners.

Since these missionaries were members of free and dissenting churches, one must recall that the heathen and sinners were not only, not even primarily, unbaptized pagans. No, free church missionary activity is first and foremost for those already baptized but leading lives not converted to the Lord. For these missionaries the American continent was a New World, uncorrupted by the villainy of pope and emperor, but, above all, of established state-churches. Dissenters date the Fall of the Church, quite comparable to the Original Sin of all humankind in Adam and Eve, to Constantine and the incorporation of the Church into the imperial government. America was the time and the place, perhaps the last such opportunity ever to be provided by Godly Providence for the erection of the just and holy city. Especially the Puritan Pilgrims were convinced that they had been divinely sent on an "Errand into the Wilderness" (Cotton Mather) where they were to establish a new and holy "City upon a Hill," a beacon for all other nations—"the eyes of all people are upon us" (John Winthrop). America was to be a "New Eden," a "New Zion." Later on, Abraham Lincoln would, in view of American failures, especially slavery, to achieve this goal, speak of the "almost chosen nation."[26] This understanding of a "national vocation" has continued unabated throughout history. Jerald Brauer thinks that the Puritan theocratic ideal led to the conviction that "God's will for America was eventually his will for the human race."[27]

Against this general religious background of the original discovery and settlement of the North American continent we can better understand the American Declaration, and war, of Independence as well as its Constitution and subsequent history.[28] What better bridge between these two phases of the formation of the American nation than Seymour Lipset's contention that "the United States is the Protestant country. By 'Protestant' I am referring to Protestant sects as opposed to State churches . . . The majority of Americans . . . from practically the beginning of the Republic down to the present have been members of churches that are not supported by the state and, in turn, do not support the State."[29] The Dissenters and Free Church members who played such an important role in settling America dissented and wanted to be free from not only Rome, from not only the established state church, whether Catholic or Protestant, but from practically everything. Thus, at the time of the Declaration and War of Independence, whatever may have been the cultural and personal attachments to the Motherland, American colonists were nevertheless in a mood, cultural and religious, in which independence and freedom were the preferred values.

It was this religious articulation of the American revolutionaries that made their revolution so different from the three classic European revolutions—French, Russian, and Enlightenment. Those three were clearly and distinctly not only un-, but anti-religious. They were anti-church, anti-clerical, anti-God. One need recall only the French Enlightenment's war cry, *"Ecrasez l'infame."* In contrast, the American Revolution precisely invoked the deity, the divine will and plan for mankind in its favor. Although not all individual Christians and local churches in America were in favor of that liberation movement known as the War of Independence, most were. Consequently, in contrast to the European experience, where Church and state were often allies, and even united, and where revolution against the emperor meant revolution against the Church, in the United States the freedom fighters found the church(es) on their side. Indeed, it is possible to argue that popular participation in the actual fighting for independence was chiefly religiously motivated.[30] The calls for independence and freedom came "most commonly from pulpits in New England . . . the conjunction of freedom and religion, twin ideals which America was to preserve, perfect, and propagate through the world."[31] Of the French Revolution's triad "Liberty, Equality, Fraternity," in contrast to Europe, America has clearly and decisively chosen freedom.[32] And in this choice, organized religion, the churches, were clearly prime participants and motivators. There had been a liberation theology, practical and effective, long before 1971.[33]

In the American experience, however, revolution and liberation were not against and from religion, but out of and for religion. This is the clear intention of the founding generation. In their view, only religion could provide the moral and philosophical foundation and support for the continuance of a free society. As Thomas Hanley has noted, the founders of America "were content that they had disestablished a Church of England without disestablishing Christianity." He then expressly notes the "State's patronage of religion in the interest of fostering public morality."[34] A free and pluralist society does not ensure the pure practice of religion, but it does require the practice of religion—precisely in order to be free.

Religion in the United States has always been pluralist. Even when the original colonies were overwhelmingly Protestantly Christian, there was no mere and pure homogeneity. Not only diversity but also division obtained among the Puritans of New England, the Quakers of Pennsylvania, the Anglicans of Virginia. Then there were also the Lutherans who did not fit into any of these three ecclesial and theological categories. Even in the earliest history of America, New York was its own unique polyglot and polyreligious self. The Catholic presence, its admittedly brief hegemony in Maryland and its even briefer one in New York, added to the pluralism. Not to be omitted are the Jews, whose smallness made them less influential, and the native American, whose largeness did not, on that account, make them more influential in the religious pluralism of early America.[35]

Although the freedom and religious pluralism of the American population made the European *cuius regio eius religio* impossible, they did make possible, and indeed, necessary, what can be called a religious free market, in which all the churches and religions were able, indeed were forced, to compete for members, presence, and influence in the larger society. This situation was neither ideal nor egalitarian. For various reasons various churches were in privileged positions. Some were even established in the colonies, a situation which perdured into nationhood. Massachusetts, for example, did not dis-establish until 1833; New York did not fully repeal its anti-Catholic penal laws until 1806. Nevertheless, at the national level there was never an established church or religion.

We can only briefly note that this is what the Constitution of the United States provides—non-establishment of a national church or religion. It does not provide for separation of church and state, however much this phrase is trumpeted about. The phrase itself is a *hapax legomenon*, appearing only in a private letter of Thomas Jefferson.[36] It has been widely wielded as an ideological and political talisman and bludgeon by various groups for their own purposes, originally chiefly by Protestants against Catholics, now by secular humanists against both Catholics and the formerly dominant Protestant churches.[37] Unfortunately, it is also used carelessly by Catholics, who should know better, and who, by such semantic, historical, and philosophical carelessness compromise not only their own cause, but that of all the traditional religions and churches.[38] One may legitimately speak of the non-establishment of a single religion or church; one might even speak, although one would be better not to, of the separation of the civil government and a church or a religion; one may not and should not speak of the separation of church and state. For the American experience has been precisely of the communion, not the separation, of state and church (better, the churches and the religions) in the achievement of a society securing for its citizens "life, liberty, and the pursuit of happiness."[39]

It must be emphatically stressed that American Christianity has always stressed the pursuit of happiness in *this* life, on the part of all the people, as Alexis de Tocqueville already and clearly noted:[40]

> Another observation can be made which applies to the clergy of every communion. American priests do not try to divert and concentrate all of people's attention on the future life; they freely allow them to give

some of their hearts' care to the needs of the present, apparently considering the good things of this world as objects of some, albeit secondary, importance. While they themselves do no productive work, they take an interest in the progress of industry and praise its achievements; while they are ever pointing to the other world as the great object of the hopes and fears of the faithful, they do not forbid the honest pursuit of prosperity in this. Far from trying to show that these two worlds are distinct and opposed to each other, they seek to discover the points of connection and alliance.

Wanton luxury need not, of course, be God's will, but neither are prosperity and the good life against it. And the good life, its pursuit at least, is, according to the American Declaration of Independence and Constitution, not reserved to the aristocracy, whether this elite be ecclesial or civil. In this respect, once again the churches, organized religion, were again on the side of the people, of the "common man," the average citizen.

Here we can see the serendipitous or providential (it depends on the depth and agility of one's faith) circumincession of religious Puritan Millennialism and philosophical (natural law) political Classical Republicanism. Puritan Millennialism, which saw in America the last God-given chance for the advent of the just and holy society in accord with the divine will and ordinances, was always much tamer than its continental counterpart. The latter was essentially apocalyptic, mystical, ecstatic,[41] while the former was Puritanly pragmatic, moral, and utilitarian. The just society would be called into existence not by a celestially conducted cataclysmic upheaval of the society (Umsturz und Umwertung aller Werte) under the charismatic control of a DUX, but by the humanly virtuous and moral conduct of a pious free citizenry, free of all monarchical and totalitarian tutelage. This Puritan religious understanding of society coincided with the philosophical-political understanding which held that the twin evils of totalitarian monarchy and the equally totalitarian anarchy could be avoided only by a limited government, in scope and tenure, whose officers would be responsible to evaluation and continuation or dismissal by the citizenship who, themselves, would be capable of this calling only if they themselves were schooled in virtue and virtuous living. For this reason, whatever may have been the Deist influence (and we must, in any case, understand that it was Deism and not militantly missionary atheistic secular humanism) in the formation of the new nation, the new nation's birth was undeniably religiously (and Christianly) motivated and configured.

This is most strikingly evident in the emphatic voluntary nature of the American national character. Strangely enough, this voluntary-ness is sourced in Calvinist theology, not customarily noted for its enthusiasm about *human* freedom, and Voluntarism.

To the Puritans, Calvinism presented questions of will, and of voluntary and involuntary association, in the most pointed and psychologically acute fashion. To be elect, to be a member of the invisible body of Christ, is to suffer involuntary association at the very core of existence. As a compensation, virtually every other conscious part of Puritan life was given to the remaking of the moral world by disciplined will and through voluntary association.[42]

There is, first of all, the covenant between God and man. According to John Winthrop, easily applying the principles of Israel's divinely established nationhood to the Massachusetts Bay Company:[43]

Thus stands the cause between God and us. We are entered into Cov-enant with him for his worke. . . . [If God] bring us in peace to the place wee desire, then hath hee ratified his Covenant and sealed our com-missions . . . will expect a strict performance of the Articles contained in it. . . . Beloved there is now sett before us life, and good, deathe and evill in that wee are Commaunded in this day to love the Lord our God, and to love one another to walke in his wayes and to keepe his Com-maundements and his Ordinances, and his lawes, and the Articles of our Covenant with him that we may live and be multiplyed . . . or perishe out of the good Land. . . .

This primary theological religious covenant calls into existence, in its own image and likeness, a human political covenant. In the words of the Preamble of the Massachusetts Bill of Rights:[44]

The body politic is formed by a voluntary association of individuals; it is a social compact by which the whole people covenants with the each citizen and each citizen with the whole people that all shall be governed by certain laws for the common good.

Thus, neither the arrogated divine right of the monarch nor the Caesaropapist presumption of the established state-church is the principle of civil and ecclesial social organization. In America, the mode of participation in Church and State was, is, and remains voluntary, free will participation by the people. As the Constitution of the United States emphasizes, "We, the People . . . do . . . ordain and establish this Constitution. . . ."

The absence of state and/or church-state coercion and tutelage, as well as the heightened voluntary sense and self-concept of the people (it is, after all, they of whom the nation's officials are representative! It is from and by their consent that the officials govern!), clearly put the churches themselves in a new situation. In non-established churches the ordained officials, whether preacher or pastor, priest or pope, must clearly pay more attention and respect to the people, their abilities and interests, as well as their needs. This does not mean that the religious ministers need cravenly capitulate to the whims and fancies of their congregations—only that they must pay attention to them. Alexis de Tocqueville already noticed this, and related it to two special features of the American democratic society in contrast to the European aristocratic society.[45] Equality eliminates the cohesive rule supplied by royalty and nobility in the stratified aristocratic society. In the equalitarian (**NOT** egalitarian![46]) society of a democracy, this cohesive element is supplied by free and voluntary associations and institutions. Tocqueville also noted the role played by prosperity in the enthusiastic and voluntary participation by American citizens in both church and state. Here is most strikingly manifested the attention the clergy must pay to their members in an equalitarian, prosperous society:[47]

All the clergy of America are aware of the intellectual domination of the majority, and they treat it with respect. They never struggle against it unless the struggle is necessary. They keep aloof from party squabbles, but they freely adopt the general views of their time and country and let themselves go unresistingly with the tide of feeling and opinion which carries everything around them along with it. They try to improve their contemporaries but do not quit fellowship with them. Public opinion is therefore never hostile to them but rather supports and protects them. Faith thus derives its authority partly from its inherent strength and partly from the borrowed support of public opinion.

Thus, by respecting all democratic instincts which are not against it and making use of many favorable ones, religion succeeds in struggling successfully with that spirit of individual independence which is its most dangerous enemy.

We can now sum up the general American religious situation in which the tiny and infant American Church found itself. From its inception and throughout its history, America has been and has claimed to be a religious nation. This religion has been predominantly Christian, and originally Dissenting, Anabaptist, Free Church Protestant Christian. Nevertheless, America has also always been religiously free, pluralist, and disestablished, sometimes more so, sometimes less so, often reluctantly.[48] But pluralist it has been and remains, and consequently it has been a nation of many options and unbounded opportunities.[49] Not only commerce and economics, but also religion is conducted in a free market where competition for presence and prestige, members and influence is the normal state of affairs. As the dominant religion was dissenting Protestant, so was the dominant culture Anglo-Saxon. Finally, in this general context, two important shifts took place in both the civil and the ecclesial society. Equality and the absence of an established church created a social climate in which voluntary participation by the citizens became necessary as the glue of society. The role of the aristocrat, civil or ecclesial, in the orderly conduct of the society diminished considerably. Likewise, in both societies there was not only tolerance but even enthusiasm for the development of a materially prosperous society and citizenry.

This world, sacred and secular, in which Roman Catholics found themselves, is aptly described by Martin Marty:[50]

> Along with the fresh accent on personal experience, the voluntary spirit, and the freedom of choice that followed itineracy, the new movements left a legacy of competition for souls. . . . Ever after, the need to win converts and support institutions led to competition: free enterprise had come to the world of religion.

II. The Roman Catholic Church in the Nation With the Soul of a Church

In Part I we have seen what Catholics found when they came to America—a free, open, religiously and otherwise pluralist, and an option-oriented society in which the absence of a dominant central government and also of an established state church produced a free market not only in commerce but also in religion. In a word, it found a voluntary society.

How did the Roman Catholic Church, customarily a prototypical established Church, fare in these strange conditions, in this alien land and culture? It not only survived, it thrived. In Boorstin's word, it "discovered" both the external situation and the internal resources to create a new way of being the Catholic Church. We could use John Tracy Ellis' felicitous phrase and say that the American Catholic Church found a new and congenial homeland (Patria, Fatherland), whose features were panis et libertas cultus—bread and freedom of worship or religion.[51]

Since these two elements are so closely intertwined in American

religious history in general, and in American Catholic history in
particular, what better place to begin our reflection on the American
Catholic Experience than Maryland, where the Catholic "Errand in
the Wilderness" had its own proper beginning. The Maryland experience illustrates how Catholics from Europe used and built upon
their previous experience, but also how they were able to transform
this past experience into a new way of being both human and Catholic. The fate of Catholics in England and Ireland at this time was
not a happy one, although some times were not as bad as others.
These Catholics had already learned that one could be Catholic without belonging to and without the support of the established Catholic
Church, for they had been disenfranchised politically and generally
discriminated against.[52] But they had also learned, and would continue to learn, that it was not and would not be easy. Not only
endurance was necessary, but also creativity. We have already addressed persecution and endurance. We shall now turn to the creativity.

Catholic creativity in Colonial Maryland already illustrated a dimension of religiosity in America which has persisted to this very
day, namely, the positive correlation among religious, political, and
economic motivations, expectations and performance. In the true
Catholic spirit, this relationship was characterized by the "Catholic
And," as it has been called.[53] Not "either . . . or," but "both . . . and"
characterized the relationships between economics/commerce and
religion. Properly correlated, they produced a benevolent state of
affairs and a benevolent state and a thriving Church, as Tocqueville
already noted.[54] Jay Dolan has well noted the perichoresis of eco-
nomics/commerce and religion in the enterprise of Lord Calvert in
the New World: "Maryland was established first and foremost as a
commercial enterprise, with profit, not religion, the primary purpose." On the other hand, "Another attraction of the Maryland col-
ony was the opportunity for Roman Catholics to live in a land 'free
from persecution on account of their religion.' " On still another
hand (if tri-manualism be permitted), although "Calvert's primary
concern was profit, not religious freedom, a pragmatic realist, he
realized that to achieve success in the New World, he had to be open-
minded about religion. Considering what things were like at the time
in Virginia and New England, or for that matter in New Mexico and
Canada, this was indeed an advanced and enlightened policy."[55]

The 1649 "Act Concerning Religion" illustrates the "non-ideolog-
ical" pragmatic[56] American way of dealing with that pluralism of
religions which was so unfamiliar and problematic for all the new
immigrants, both Protestant and Catholic. In the past, the pluralism

had been dealt with basically either by suppression or separation. Even in the New World, "Religious toleration was not the purpose of founding Maryland. Religious toleration was the modus operandi of the 'Maryland Design.' "[57] William Craven is right on target when he judges the Act of 1649 to be "the product of good sense rather than of extraordinary intelligence, a call for no surrender of basic convictions. . . . [It] urged only that men of different faiths live in peace, concede to one another the free right of worship, and eschew in their daily intercourse the use of terms which merely serve to breed ill will."[58]

The Maryland experience is also valuable insofar as it illustrates that the relationship between clergy and laity would become increasingly a matter of mutual respect and cooperation rather than simple command and obedience. In Catholic Maryland, the Jesuits objected that the state failed to provide "for the church the Immunitye and priviledges which she enjoyeth every where else." Some prominent Marylanders wanted to provide the traditional and customary privileges, but Calvert did not, and his position prevailed. As Dolan notes, "If the Jesuits were going to stay on, they would have to do so without any special privileges from the government. Since the government was not going to support the church, the clergy would have to support themselves."[59] Here we certainly have a crucial event, if not the crucial one, in the "Voluntaryism" of the Roman Catholic Church in the United States. In America, Catholicism would be an equalitarian and voluntary Church, even for those who, in the aristocratic European Church, had been regarded as the nobility.[60]

What is striking is how quickly the Catholic Church developed the capacity to function and flourish in the New World, pluralist and democratic as it was. The theoretical and theological reflection and elaboration of this capacity and performance have developed with nothing of the same alacrity, both understandably and unfortunately, but they are at least beginning to appear with greater frequency. In practice, though, Roman Catholics were a "minority second to none but Roger Williams in the broad toleration granted to men of other religious beliefs. . . . The half-century, however, of Baltimore's regime in Maryland and the five years when there was a Catholic governor in New York afford us two instances by which to judge them extraordinarily tolerant for the seventeenth century."[61] In America, Catholics truly discovered that Catholicism was not bound to monarchical states and established state churches; Catholicism could also thrive in democratic societies and could reveal its own internal democratic capacities. Alexis de Tocqueville was led by observation of Roman Catholicism in America to note:[62]

Nevertheless, they [Roman Catholics] form the mot republican and democratic of all classes in the United States. . . . I think one is wrong in
regarding the Catholic religion as a natural enemy of democracy. Rather,
among the various sects of Christianity, Catholicism seems one of the
most favorable to equality of conditions. . . .
If, then, the Catholic citizens of the United States are not forcibly led
by the nature of their tenets to adopt democratic and republican principles, at least they are not necessarily opposed to them; and their social
position as well as their limited number, obliges them to adopt these
opinions.

Similarly, confronted with the familiar—and bigoted—contention
that Catholicism and republicanism were incompatible, Bishop John
England replied that, to him, republicanism meant that "no set of
men had any inherent natural right to take precedence over their
fellow men and that all power to regulate the public affairs of individuals, united in social compact, was derived from the public
will freely expressed by the voice of the majority." After this summary, John Tracy Ellis quotes the Bishop directly: "This is what we
understand by Republicanism, and we know of no doctrine of Catholicism, if we must use the expression, opposed to this. . . ."[63]
That this Catholic acceptance of the republican ideal and form of
government was not a ploy or subterfuge based on their small numbers is attested by a later historian:[64]

Whatever conclusion might be drawn from a scrutiny of Catholic doctrine, the fact was that Catholicism had flourished as a major religion
for three quarters of a century without raising serious difficulties except
in the imaginations of men and that democratic institutions seemed as
sound when the church numbered twenty-four million members as they
had been when it counted its communicants by the hundred thousand.
. . .
It might, indeed, be maintained that the Catholic Church was, during
this period, one of the most effective of all agencies for democracy and
Americanization. Representing as it did a vast cross section of the American people, it could ignore class, section, and race; peculiarly the
church of the newcomer, of those who all too often were regarded as
aliens, it could give them not only spiritual refuge but social security.

Again, we have the coinciding of the religious with the social, po-
litical, and economic.
How deeply compatible and congenial Roman Catholicism and
American democracy are is indicated by an observation of Harriet
Martineau already in 1873. It indicates that the republican, demo-
cratic spirit was not only externally acceptable to Catholics, they

had already begun to internalize it. She wrote: "The Catholic body is democratic in its politics, and made up from the more independent kind of occupations. The Catholic religion is modified by the spirit of the time in America; and its professors are not a set of men who can be priest-ridden to any fatal extent."[65] Note that she says "modified," not corrupted or undone. This may be of small consolation to those who date the decline of the Church at the Second Vatican Council or the reaction to the publication of *Humanae Vitae*. What is crucial about the democratic spirit in the Roman Catholic Church in America, then and now, is that it has led to neither a mass rejection of the Church nor to that hostile anti-clericalism, which is such a plague for the Church, in Europe certainly and perhaps Latin America, too. As the American Catholic Church becomes more and more unclerical, it has not become anti-clerical. This is certainly an American discovery, unique in the history of the Roman Catholic Church heretofore.

American Catholics have remained remarkably loyal to both their country and their Church. Is this anything but the result of that voluntary-volunteer membership, which we have stressed throughout this paper? In the context of religious and ecclesial pluralism, which produced a sort of free market in religion, the Roman Catholic Church has competed well. Certainly, the need for self-defense, individually and ecclesially, against the pervasive anti-Catholic Nativism and bigotry has played a significant role. But even here, it has had to have been a matter of voluntary participation by the faithful in the Church and churchly activities. After all, one could have simply left the Church and thus escaped the persecution. Furthermore, the experience of a new and strange land, coupled with the anti-Catholic discrimination, provided a prod for clergy and laity to be more closely united than was the case in Europe and Latin America. I have no doubt that often enough the priest was "over" and "above" the people, especially in certain regions and ethnic groups, but by and large the priest was still also "with" the people. The affection which American priests generally enjoy from the people is an unusual if not unique phenomenon in the history of the Church. In regard to what is more properly the European situation, one French author suggested that an ecumenical movement was needed within the Church, to try to bring (back?) into unity the clergy/religious and the laity.[66] Again, has not the absence of Establishment on the part of the Church in a free and pluralist society been the occasion for all the members of the Church to be more voluntarily participative and more concerned to be in practicing communion with one another?

This can be readily illustrated by two phenomena which are hall-
marks of the American Catholic Church. First of all, it was not American Catholicism which either caused or suffered the scandal of the
nineteenth century proclaimed by Pope Pius XI, namely, the loss of
the working class to the Church, although American Catholics in
American Catholic schools supported by the workers of the American
Catholic Church dutifully learned that this was the case, even though
precisely their learning situation demonstrated that it wasn't so in
the United States. This is not to say that all in the American Church
were on the side of the workingman/woman. While James Gibbons
was trying to insure the communion of the official Church with the
workers, other hierarchs clearly manifested the customary aristocratic predilections of their European counterparts.[67] Jay Dolan also
narrates an episode which illustrates the initiative of the laity in the
social policy and action of the American Catholic Church:[68]

> More telling . . . was Catholic support for socialist political candidates.
> Milwaukee was the best example of this. For a number of years in the
> twentieth century, the Socialist party ran the city of Milwaukee; they
> were able to do this because Irish, Polish, and German Catholics voted
> for the Socialist ticket despite the protestations of bishops and clergy.

This phenomenon of the union of Church and workers has been
accompanied by a second hallmark of American Catholicism, namely,
the enormous number of institutions and programs voluntarily provided, by both people and priest, for the ecclesial and civil welfare
of the Catholic population. The statistics need not be repeated in
detail here; they can be found in any standard history of American
Catholicism. One need think only of the schools and other educational programs, the hospitals and other health care programs, the
construction of churches and other buildings, the extensive charitable and welfare agencies and activities, the creation of and participation in socio-economic institutions, not only the labor unions as
such, but other programs such as credit unions, cooperatives, etc. In
all of this we see a remarkable communion of priest and people,
with considerable initiative from the people.[69] This voluntary participation has not been restricted to only "churchly" matters, although, as we shall shortly see, the American Catholic Church has
never been restricted to only "churchly" matters. What de Tocqueville had noticed in the American citizen as such also holds for the
Catholic, in both ecclesial and civil matters: "Each man takes pride
in the glory of his nation; the successes it gains seem his own work,

and he becomes elated; he rejoices in the general prosperity from which he profits."[70]

It is in view of this that we must approach the much vaunted and today much criticized patriotism of American Catholics. In spite of American anti-Catholicism, American Catholics have been more than loyal and patriotic. It has become fashionable among Catholic intellectuals, especially those of liberal bent, to attribute the readiness of Catholics to do military service, even to fight and die for their country, to their need to demonstrate their patriotism. "One way for Catholics to prove their loyalty to the nation was to serve patriotically in the nation's wars," expounds Gerald P. Fogarty.[71] The always excitable and irascible Daniel Maguire proclaims that "Insecure, immigrant Catholicism does have a sorry American record of fawning patriotism."[72] Apparently Fogarty and Maguire are unaware that in 1982 seventy-one percent of all Americans said that they would fight for their country. To whom are most of these, then, to be presumed to feel the need to demonstrate their patriotism? Has it ever occurred to Maguire and Fogarty that people might be willing to fight because they actually like living in a free country? Have they ever considered that Catholics actually are proud to be American? In 1983, eighty percent of Americans were.[73] They know that under some circumstances one might have to be willing to engage in military action, if one does not regard his/her country as the pits. Military service is not necessarily militarism, for neither individual nor group. Pacifism and non-violence are legitimate, but hardly requisite options within the Catholic spectrum. And to speak of American Catholic patriotism in the past and present as "fawning" and "counterprophetic" as Maguire does is not only ill-conceived but also ill-mannered. In any case, Maguire might consult even Sidney Mead's increasingly tragic history of American religion—the desire and certainly the self-declension of prophecy can themselves be counterprophetic.[74]

This is the fitting place to note a certain tension not only between the "common people" of the Church and the ordained clergy, but also between the people and that clerisy described above by John Nisbet as "intellectual." This tension was pointedly remarked by Margaret O'Brien Steinfels already in 1974 in her acerbic review of Mary Daly's *Beyond God the Father*: "and if the choice between religious leaders becomes a choice between a feminist theology professor from Boston College and a carpenter's son from Galilee, I say stick with the working class."[75] I shall use this remark to introduce my contention that the American Catholic Church has always been a people's Church and therefore also and inevitably a public Church.

I deem this necessary since a growing number of commentators delight in berating the American Catholic Church, past and present, as an (excessively) "private" and "privatized Church."[76] However, the chief spokesman for the so-called "Public Church,"[77] a term emanating from Martin Marty, is the Rev. J. Bryan Hehir. He built his commencement address at the Catholic University of America around this theme in 1984.[78] In 1986 at the Catholic Theological Society of America Convention (CTSA) he used it as the basic category of his address, "Religion and Politics: Theological and Political Perspectives." The only trouble with Hehir's position is that the Catholic Church in the United States has always been a public church. It had no choice in the matter. Given the conditions in which it existed, it had to be public to survive. Hehir is so caught up in bishoply matters that he unfortunately equates them with the Church, although there are fleeting protestations that this (popes and encyclicals, bishops and pastoral letters) is not all there is to the Church. But his approach to the Church can best be termed "ecclesiasticism," a clericalism that seems quite innocent of Yves Congar's demonstration that "Ecclesiology is not hierarchology." Who knows the history of the Catholic Church in the United States knows simply and clearly that it has always been a Church in the public arena, chiefly in its "simple" members, but also in its priests, and even it its bishops. What Hehir represents as a public Church is really the old clerical, hierarchical private Church (one is even tempted to say Eigenkirche!). Only now its hierarchy, ritual, and rhetoric are of the left and the liberals instead of the customary conservatives and the right. At the CTSA and elsewhere, Hehir has even presumed to describe the preparation of the pastoral letters on nuclear strategy and economics as a "democratic" process.[79] A strange democracy, since none of the people preparing the documents was accountable to an elected official, and none of the officials appointing the committees is accountable to any electorate or any electoral process. Democratic is hardly the word. Better would be aristocratic, oligarchical, or, as I have contended elsewhere in regard to Church governance in general, cronyist.[80]

Ultimately the reason the American Catholic Church has been a Public Church is that it has been both a people's and a voluntary Church. And it had to be these because it was not an established Church. What the nobles did for the Church and nation in an aristocracy has to be done by voluntary associations and institutions in a democracy, by the people. That is the constant contention of de Tocqueville.[81] And his contention has been successfully demonstrated, his principle incarnated by the people of the American Catholic Church. And it still is.

It is, of course, the common people, the average citizen, the "common man"—in ecclesial terminology, the "simple faithful"—who have accomplished this, and again I rush to emphasize, not in opposition to and separation from the ordained leaders and administrators, but in communion with them. With this emphasis I also wish in no wise to belittle the role and achievement of priests, bishops, and religious in the American Catholic Church. Their achievement has been prodigious. But, in a free society and in a free, voluntary, non-established Church, the key is the "little people." Sidney Mead has emphasized their key role and significance in American history, both civil and ecclesial: "the people shall be judge of what they want, and deserve what they get. For the whole system rests on public consensus."[82] Indeed, "the voice of the people is the voice of God." For Mead, the "big people" are not the key factor in humanity or Church; it is, rather, the "great amorphous body [of] little people."[83]

In his appraisal of American history and civilization, Jacques Maritain has noticed a similar dimension and emphasis:[84]

> There is indeed one thing that Europe knows only too well; that is the tragic significance of life. . . .
> There is one thing that America knows well, and that she teaches as a great and precious lesson to those who come in contact with her astounding adventure: it is the value and dignity of the people . . . America knows that the common man has a right to the pursuit of the elementary conditions and possessions which are the prerequisites of a free life. . . .
> The great and admirable strength of America consists in this, that America is truly the American people.

This "great and admirable strength of America" obtains not only in general, but in particular, and especially, in the American Catholic Church. From its diminutive and often disadvantaged beginnings, the Catholic population has grown into a large and prosperous people and Church. Among empirically discernible religious bodies, it ranks second in measurable categories such as education, profession, career level, income.[85] Perhaps the most striking manifestation that the American Church is truly a people's Church is the startling fact that only recently the pastor/priest may well have been the only educated and professional person in the parish. Today it is quite possible that he may be among the least. Also striking about the American Catholic achievement is that prosperity has neither emancipated Catholics from the Church, as the classical critique would have it,[86] nor hardened them to the poor, as the self-styled centers of concern, lovers of the poor, professional ascetics and prophets of parsimony and relinquishment would have it.[87]

In spite of this neo-clericalist pessimism about prosperity and religion in general, about prosperity and the American Catholic Church in particular—even better, precisely because of it—I shall make bold to suggest that the American Catholic Church of the "common man" who has succeeded in a free, pluralist, option-filled, prosperous society, may well be the Church of and for the future.[88] For the present and future world, short of the cataclysm, is and will be the world of the "common man." As Goetz Briefs has pointed out, in regard to Walter Webb's theory about the American Frontier, the modern era is not the age of God or the devil or the state, but of "the ordinary man." This ordinary or common man has stood at the center of modern Western thought. In America the frontier enabled him to rule himself, to achieve prosperity, and to save his soul on his own terms and account, at his own risk.[89] The American Catholic Church has shown that the modern era can be the age of the successful common man *and* God.

But will the American Catholic Church, now become prosperous, continue to prosper? Martin Marty has wondered, suggesting that "after Vatican II . . . true voluntarism hit Roman Catholicism."[90] I'm not so sure. As I have shown, true Voluntarism hit Roman Catholicism as soon as it hit the American coast. What did hit American Catholicism in the mid and late 1960's was an extraordinary advance in education, professional status, income. But along with this upward mobility came no lessening of the affection and loyalty American Roman Catholics have for *their* Catholic Church.[91] Of course, they will no longer be members of the Church in precisely the same way as were their immigrant forebears. But they will be Catholics. As Andrew Greeley gleefully remarks:[92]

> Those Church leaders who might in some of their darker moments wish that they could get rid of the contentious, opinionated, independent professional-class Catholics who are now becoming typical are wasting their time. The well-educated Catholic professional is here, he/she is here to stay and is not about to leave the church. But not about to participate in the Church on any other terms but his or her own.

III. Conclusion

What has the American Catholic Experience revealed? A new way of being Catholic and the Catholic Church—free, voluntary, competitive in a pluralist society and religious free market, successful both civilly and ecclesially, for it and its members have to an amazing extent accomplished the American Promise, namely, life, liberty, and the pursuit of happiness, all the while remaining loyal and practicing Catholics.[93] Such a "New Catholic" would be in keeping with the general American experience and history, which already in 1782 prompted the question, "What then is the American, this new man?" and the answer:[94]

> He is either an European or the descendant of an European . . . who leaving behind him all his ancient prejudices and manners, receives new ones from the new mode of life he has embraced, the new government he obeys, and the new rank he holds.

Much later the religious provenance of this new man was emphasized by Sydney Ahlstrom who claims that "Puritanism almost created a new kind of 'civic person.' "[95] This new citizen is highly moral, with his voluntary and personal observance of the law and conscience being his distinguishing characteristics.

Against this general background we can readily understand the contention that a "New Catholic" has also been given birth in America. As of now, this "born again American Catholic" remains without a baptismal name. One suggestion, "Communal Catholic," well describes the reality.

Andrew Greeley has spoken of the "emerging, in America, communal Catholic, that is, a Catholic who is loyal to his tradition and heritage—even proud of it—but who does not take the clergy or hierarchy seriously as intellectual, political, moral, or social leaders. You will not be able to understand American Catholicism unless you realize how powerful this tendency is."[96] More recently Greeley has spoken of "selective Catholicism" and the "do it yourself Catholic" to describe the same situation.[97] With typical Greeleyian rhetoric, he notes: "As humiliating as it may be to church leadership, it would seem that they have influence on their people only when their people decide to permit them to have such influence. The authority of the government apparently rests on the consent of the governed, not only in civil matters of the United States but also in Catholic ecclesiastical matters."[98]

I find "Selective Catholicism" an intriguing selection of words, if and insofar as it is allowed to signify selecting or choosing not only from or from among a variety of options, but also and primarily of selecting and choosing at all. The word carries with it the necessary connotation of voluntary. Furthermore, American Catholics would have been prepared all along for this "Selective Catholicism," for they have always lived in a free and pluralist society where Catholicism was only one of many readily available options. Hence they would have been able and required to develop the skill of partial but true identification with and membership in the Church.[99] In a pluralist, option-filled society, the unbothered one hundred percent identification/membership possible in a homogeneous monolithic society is simply not to be expected. Thus, "Selective Catholicism" would not designate capricious, diminished, vacillating Catholicism, but voluntary, freely-chosen and persevered-in Catholicism. American Catholicism is truly voluntary, and in this sense is truly a Free Church.

However, in conclusion, I shall suggest yet another baptismal name for the "New American Catholic," one true to both the Roman Catholic and American Christian traditions. Certainly, contemporary American Roman Catholics, loyal as they may be, are more "casual"[100] than those Christians who first came on the "Errand in the Wilderness," but their Catholicism is quite consonant with the original emphasis, so well-illustrated by the 1629 Covenant of Salem:[101]

> We Covenant with the Lord and one with an other; and doe bynd our selves in the presence of God, to walke together in all waies, according as he is pleased to reveale himself unto us in his Blessed word of Truth.

May we not then baptize this New American Catholic the

"Covenantal Catholic"?

NOTES

1. Thus Mary Schneider emphasizes: "One of the recently published landmarks in the field of American religious history is Sydney Ahlstrom's monumental work, *A Religious History of the American People*. Notwithstanding its excellence, however, the book follows the basic pattern of most Protestant histories of religion in America. . . . The Structure of the book reveals the basic and implicit assumption that when it comes to the formation of a normative American culture, the primary input has been the Protestant influence . . . it is clear that Catholicism, despite its numerical advantages, is not regarded as either the formative or the normative influence in the development of an American self-image," Mary Schneider, "A Catholic Perspective on American Civil Religion," in Thomas McFadden, ed., *America in Theological Perspective* (New York: Seabury 1976), pp. 123–24. See also David O'Brien, "American Catholicism and American Religion," *JAAR*, XL (1972), 36–53.

2. Since this is a private letter, I prefer not to name the theologian. In support of his admission, see, for example, Raymund Schwager, "Kritische Bemerkungen," *Korrespondenzblatt des Canisianums* 119:1 (1986), and Norbert Greinacher, *Konflikt um die Theologie der Befreiung* (Zurich: Benziger, 1985), pp. 11–23. In this so-called "Dikussion und Dokumentation," not one North American author is included, although, in keeping with the penchant of Latin American Liberation theologians, the United States of North America (Greinacher's strange entitlement of the United States of America) serves as the whipping boy for all troubles south of the Rio Grande. This is confirmation of another statement in the private letter (see also *Newsweek*, December 9, 1985, p. 70), namely that, in German speaking theological circles, the only interest is for matters Latin American, certainly a strange phenomenon since the characteristics of Latin America and Germany could hardly be different. I mention this here to illustrate both the ignorance of and disdain for the United States and the American Catholic Church on the part of European and Latin American theologians and intellectuals, and also the basic source and identity of Latin American liberation theology, which is not the poverty of the people of Latin America but the professors of the classrooms and libraries of Europe, especially Germany.

3. See George A. Kelly, "The Uncertain Future of the American Church," *Thought*, XLVII, 187 (Winter 1972), 485–506, who begins, "The Catholic Church in the United States is in trouble." It is legitimate to summarize Kelly's perception of the sources of the trouble as prosperity (p. 499) and a sort of Free Church transformation of American Roman Catholicism, although he, of course, did not use this term. But he is alarmed by excessive or false emphasis on freedom (or on a false freedom) and what he perceives to be "a new latitudinarian definition of the Catholic Church commonly called 'plural Catholicism' . . . (pp. 502–04). From another direction, Thomas O'Dea, *The Catholic Crisis* (Boston: Beacon, 1968).

4. Joseph Cardinal Ratzinger with Vittorio Messori, *The Ratzinger Report* (San Francisco: Ignatius Press, 1985), pp. 45–47. How poorly Ratzinger understands the modern world, and the specific nature of American Catholicism is indicated by his ceaseless Jeremiad about the hostility of contemporary Western culture and society, especially insofar as it is materialist, consumerist, and prosperous. In the *Report* I have counted such complaints on at least thirty-three pages, with prosperity and its cognates singled out on at least six—for example (p. 188): "Stefan Cardinal Wyszinski warned of the dangers of Western hedonism and permissiveness no less than of Marxist oppression. Alfred Cardinal Bengsch of Berlin once said to me that he saw a greater danger in Western consumerism and a theology infected by it than in Marxist ideology." Similar sentiments resound regularly from quarters as diverse as Pope John

Paul II [see "John Paul's Challenge to Us," *National Catholic Reporter* (Oct. 19, 1979), 12], and, of course, from countless Centers for Concern, Liberation Theologians, Episcopal Conferences.

5. On the perichoresis of Church in all its articulations and actualizations—domestic, local (parish, diocese), regional, universal—see Robert Kress, *The Church: Communion, Sacrament, Communication* (New York: Paulist, 1985), pp. 30–107.

6. Already in 1961, see Joseph Folliet, *World Catholicism Today* (Westminster: Newman, 1961) pp. 25, 94. He attributed it to the Irish-Anglo-Saxon nature of the population, certainly a misapprehension of the nationally and ethnically pluralist American Church. The data are from a study conducted by the Center for Applied Research in Apostolate, Washington, D.C., in 1982. These data were highlighted by the NC News Service, June 4, 1982. Furthermore, the 1982 Gallup Poll, *Patterns of Charitable Giving by Individuals: A Research Report* (Washington, D.C.: Independent Sector, 1982), reports that 71 percent of Americans gave to churches and religious organizations, but only 32 percent to educational programs and 24 percent to hospitals. Furthermore, in 1982, $313.00 out of the average contribution of $475.00 was given to churches and religious organizations. Most recently, George Cornell, "Gallup Poll: Americans Respect Religion More than Nation's Other Institutions," *The Champaign Urbana News Gazette* (4 May 1985), p. A-8, reports: "Americans have more respect for organized religion than for any of the country's other major institutions, and the impression is growing that religion is having a greater impact on society ... the proportion of Americans who think religion is increasing its influence on American life has risen almost steadily from a low of 14 percent in 1970 to a current 42 percent. The importance of faith to individuals has remained relatively steady over the past five years, with 86 percent saying it is 'very important' or 'fairly important'—the same as in 1980." For the study on the return of Catholics who had temporarily dropped out, see Dean Hoge, *Converts, Dropouts, and Returnees* (Washington: Catholic Evangelization Center, 1982).

7. See the NC report, "U.S. Religious Practice Called Impressive," *The Message* (Evansville, IN, 29 August 1986), p. 12.

8. Envy has customarily been explained in terms of an individual's sadness in regard to the good, especially the honor and glory enjoyed by another (S.T. II-II, q. 36, a.1). This is perceived to diminish one's own glory. However, this notion should be expanded to include not only individuals, but also collectivities, so that one class or nation may be seen to envy another. Furthermore, and more to the point being made here, there is what Heinz Schuster calls an *invidia clericalis* (clerical envy) in regard to a perceived inadequate distribution of authority and publicity or public presence. In the current situation of Church and world, where the realm of the hierarchy and clergy steadily shrinks, there will be ample manifestations of this *invidia clericalis*, which is not, of course, restricted to the professional religious hierarchy and state. H. Schuster, "Neid," *Lexikon für Theologie und Kirche*, 7 (Freiburg: Herder, 1962), pp. 869–70.

9. See Bernhard Casper, *Wesen und Grenzen der Religionskritik* (Würzburg: Echter, 1974). Unfortunately, the attitudes and evaluations pointed out in footnotes 4 and 87 put prominent concerned Catholic hierarchs and theologians in the strange position of being on the side of this classical critique.

10. John Tracy Ellis, *American Catholicism*, 2nd rev. ed. (Chicago: University of Chicago Press, 1969), p. 151.

11. See Andrew Greeley, *An Ugly Little Secret: Anti-Catholicism in North America* (Mission, KS: Sheed, Andrews, and McMeel, 1977).

12. Whether one would ever want to say "essentially" (I doubt it, since "essence" is often taken ahistorically as an abstract, perfect, absolute from which all change is excluded), one certainly would not want to today.

13. For accessible descriptions of Free Church theology and ecclesiology, see Franklin H. Littell, *The Anabaptist View of the Church* (Boston: Starr King Press, 1958), and Donald Durnbaugh, *The Believers' Church* (New York: MacMillan, 1968).

14. *Report*, pp. 46, 155–57.

15. Franklin H. Littell, "The Radical Reformation and the American Experience," in *America in Theological Perspective*, pp. 81–85.

16. Ibid., p. 72.

17. Hans Urs von Balthasar, *Rechenschaft 1965* (Einsiedeln: Johannes, 1965), p. 31.

18. The plethora of options in the United States was brought home to me by a student from Finland, hardly a lesser developed, deprived country, who told me of her amazement/wonder (the "admiratio" of Aristotelian metaphysics), not only upon her arrival, but during her extended sojourn in her adopted country.

19. In contrast to Lustiger's remark that "Among us [French], Christianity takes its place among optional matters"—obviously an option that is not exercised. See note 7 above.

20. In a study conducted by the Center for Applied Research in the Apostolate in 1982 (Note 4 above), 72 percent of Americans chose personal freedom over equality, which was chosen by only 20 percent. In Europe overall, 49 percent chose freedom. The same point is made explicitly by German H. C. Schröder, *Die Amerikanische Revolution* (Munich: Beck, 1982). Another German notes that "In Amerika ist nichts eindeutig" and relates this to America's faith in the goodness of the human being and its commitment to the striving for personal satisfaction. See Heinrich von Borch, *Amerika—Dekadenz und Grosse* (Munich: Piper, 1981). A Canadian notices the same emphasis on freedom in America in contrast to Europe. See D. J. Hall, "America: Living Up to the Image," *The Christian Century*, 99 (19 May 1982), p. 589. Perhaps the greatest tribute of all to the American love of freedom and the attraction this love of freedom has for a good part of the world comes from an elderly, 83-year-old woman who became a citizen in Detroit on July 4, 1983. She said, "I'm going to die American. I got me my freedom now. Thank you God." NBC, "The Today Show," 4 July 1983. According to James F. Maclear, "The Republic and the Millennium," in *The Religion of the Republic*, ed. Elwyn Smith (Philadelphia: Fortress, 1971), p. 184, one disgruntled guardian of orthodoxy complained about the interest of the "common man" in freedom and his devotion to it: "Liberty is a cant word with them." The quotation is from Walter Harris, *Characteristics of a False Teacher* (Concord, NH: Geo. Hough, 1811), p. 5.

21. See Sidney Mead, "The People," *C. T. S. Register*, 39 (Jan. 1949), pp. 22–23. "The voice of the people is the voice of God. . . ."

22. G. K. Chesterton, "What I Saw in America," in *The Man Who Was Chesterton*, ed. Raymond Bond (New York: Dodd, Mead, 1937), pp. 183–245; here p. 188. On this, see Sidney Mead, *The Nation With the Soul of a Church* (New York: Harper & Row, 1975).

23. Alexis de Tocqueville, *Democracy in America*, p. 269; I, 2, 9. Alexis de Tocqueville, *De las democratie en Amérique, Oeuvres Completes I*, ed. J.-P. Mayer (Paris: Gallimard, 1961). It should be noted that Tome I consists of two volumes. There are various American translations. Page references here are to *Democracy in America*, ed. J.-P. Mayer and Max Lerner, tr. George Lawrence (New York: Harper & Row, 1966).

To facilitate consultation, I have also included references to the original division of the text after the pagination. Thus, I, 1, 1 means volume I, part 1, chapter 1; II, 2, 2 means volume II, part 2, chapter 2. Volume I has two parts with many chapters each; Volume II has four parts with many chapters each.

24. Daniel Boorstin makes this distinction in regard to the northern and southern European "discovery" of America. For them, the Vikings did not discover America; they simply touched down here. One might say that they were at America, but never in America, for "what they did in America did not change their own or anybody else's view of the world. . . . Their America was no new encounter. . . . What is most remarkable is not that the Vikings actually reached America, but that they reached America and even settled there for a while, without *discovering* America." What we want to do in this paper is describe the encounter of the Roman Catholic Church with America and what was discovered in this encounter. Daniel Boorstin, *The Discoverers* (New York: Random House, 1983), p. 215.

25. See Mark Noll, Nathan Hatch, George Marsden, *The Search for Christian America* (Westchester, IL: Crossway Books, 1983).

26. See Paul Johnson, *The Almost-Chosen People: Why America is Different* (New York: The Rockford Institute, 1985).

27. Jerald Brauer, "The Rule of the Saints in American Politics," *Church History* 27 (1958), pp. 240–55. See also Paul Nagel, *This Sacred Trust: American Nationality, 1798–1898* (New York: Greenwood, 1971). Of course, this "national vocation" can be misinterpreted variously, especially in a jingoistic, nationalistic, imperialistic sense. However, how the misinterpretation of the misinterpretation is even worse is amply demonstrated by Daniel Maguire, *The Moral Choice* (Minneapolis: Winston, 1978), pp. 424–32. The misunderstanding continues and worsens in his later *A New American Justice* (Minneapolis: Winston, 1980), pp. 9–25.

28. An interesting point is made by de Tocqueville about the nature of the American liberation movement. What really is the proper term to describe this movement—war, movement, revolution, independence, freedom? "The Revolution in the United States was caused by a mature and thoughtful taste for freedom, not by some vague, undefined instinct for independence" (p. 64; I, 1, 5). "No such necessity has ever faced the Americans, for never having had a revolution and being from the beginning accustomed to govern themselves . . ." (p. 651; II, 4, 4). ". . . in America, there exist democratic ideas and passions; in Europe we still have the revolutionary ones" (p. 614; II, 3, 21). "It [the great social revolution of democracy/equality] took place in a simple, easy fashion, or rather one might say that that country [America] sees the results of the democratic revolution taking place among us, without experiencing the revolution itself" (p. 11; Introduction). Is this perhaps the key to the neglect and disdain lavished on the "American Revolution" by the intellectuals of Europe and Latin America: it simply wasn't revolutionary—real, cataclysmic—enough.

29. Seymour Lipset, "Religion in American Politics," in Michael Novak, ed., *Capitalism and Socialism* (Washington: AEI, 1979), p. 61. See also his *The First New Nation: The United States in Historical and Comparative Perspective* (New York: Basic Books, 1963), pp. 140–69.

30. As Perry Miller has noted, "it was neither [William] Smith's genial Anglicanism nor the urbane rationalism of these statesmen [Thomas Jefferson, Benjamin Franklin] which brought the rank and file of American Protestants into the War. What aroused a Christian patriotism that needed staying power was a realization of the vengeance God denounced against the wicked . . . what kept them going was an assurance that by exerting themselves they were fighting for a victory thus providentially predestined." Perry Miller, "From the Covenant to the Revival," in James Ward Smith and

A. Leland Jamison, eds., *The Shaping of American Religion* (Princeton: Princeton University Press, 1961), p. 341.

31. James F. Maclear, "The Republic and the Millennium," in Elwyn Smith, ed., *The Religion of the Republic* (Philadelphia: Fortress, 1971), p. 184.

32. See note 20 above.

33. As has been pointed out by Russell Barta, "Liberation: U.S.A. Style," *America*, 152, 14 (13 April 1985), 297–300.

34. Thomas O. Hanley, "Church/State Relations in the American Revolutionary Era," in *America in Theological Perspective*, pp. 90, 91. This has been constant in the speeches (sermons) of American Presidents from Washington through Lincoln and Eisenhower to Reagan. Let these samples from the first and the current suffice. From George Washington's "Farewell Address": "Of all the dispositions which lead to political prosperity, religion and morality are indispensable supports." Not only does Ronald Reagan delight in quoting this passage, he also develops it on his own: "How can we hope to retain our freedom through the generations if we fail to teach our young that our liberty springs from an abiding faith in our Creator. . . . I have never believed that non-establishment of a state church, or, as so many inadequately say, separation of church and state, was supposed to protect us from religion. It was to protect religion from government tyranny." President Reagan is deeply rooted in the Presidential tradition, at least in this respect, and to the distress of many. The quotation from George Washington is in Ronald Reagan, "Address to the K of C," *Origins*, 12 (1982), 172. The quotation from President Reagan himself is in James Lackey, "Reagan Endorses School Prayer Amendment," *The Message* (Evansville, IN), 14 May 1982, p. 2.

35. See Martin Marty, *Pilgrims in Their Own Land* (New York: Penguin, 1984), pp. 53–89; Daniel Boorstin, *The Americans: The Colonial Experience* (New York: Vintage, 1958), pp. 1–144.

36. Saul Padover, ed., *The Complete Jefferson* (New York: Ovell, Sloan & Pearce, 1943), p. 519. See Gerard Bradley, "Cracks in the Wall," *Illini Review*, I, 6 (May, 1985), 9–11.

37. An egregious example of the ideological misuse of the phrase is Leo Pfeffer, "The Case for Separation," in John Cogley, ed., *Religion in America* (New York: Meridian, 1958), pp. 52–94.

38. For a prime example of the careless use of the term, which usage necessarily and automatically puts one at a disadvantage, for one has practically ceded to one's opponent the outcome of the argument, see Joseph Cardinal Bernardin, "Church Impact on Public Policy," *Origins* 13, No. 33 (1983), pp. 566–69. A fine exposé of the ideological straits, if not downright caprice of the hardnosed "separationists," is offered by Milton Himmelfarb in a debate with Lionel Shapiro, "Church and State— How High the Wall?" in Fred Krinsky, ed., *The Politics of Religion in America* (Beverly Hills: Glencoe, 1968), pp. 79–117. Most recently, Harry J. Byrne, "Tragic Paranoia: The Supreme Court and Parochial Schools," *America*, Vol. 153, No. 8 (October 5, 1985), 185–89.

39. That Secular Humanism itself functions as a competing religion in the American religious free market can be doubted by no serious student of American civilization and law. The Supreme Court and Appeals Courts have declared that that phenomenon readily identified as Secular Humanism or Ethical Culture plays the same role in some people's lives as do the traditional religions in other people's. The following cases are pertinent: *Torcaso v. Watkins*, 397 U.S. 488 (1961) at 495, n 11; *United States v. Seeger*, 380 U.S. 193 (1965); *Peter v. United States*, 324F.2d173 (9th Cir. 1963); *MacMurray v. United States*, 330F.2d928 (9th Cir. 1964). Self-confessed Secular

Humanists are not always averse to admitting their religiosity. See *The Humanist Manifesto* of 1933, and the comments thereon, by Edwin H. Wilson, "The Humanist Manifesto," *The Humanist*, XXII, No. 6 (Nov-Dec, 1962), pp. 173–74. See also Herbert Wallace Schneider, *Religion in 20th Century America* (New York: Atheneum, 1964), pp. 151–56. John Courtney Murray counts the secularist, along with the Protestant, Catholic, and Jew, among "America's Four Conspiracies," *Religion in America*, pp. 36–38. An able account of contemporary American Secular Humanism's concrete religious tenets and programs is provided by James Hitchcock, *What is Secular Humanism?* (Ann Arbor, MI: Servant, 1982). Should anyone still doubt that Secular Humanism is a religion—and a hostile, aggressive one at that—all doubts may be allayed by perusing a "textbook" sponsored by People for the American Way (a total misnomer, if there ever was one!), written by David Bollier, *Liberty and Justice for Some: Defending a Free Society from the Radical Right's Holy War on Democracy* (New York: Ungar, 1982).

40. *Democracy*, p. 414, II, 1, 5.

41. See Norman Cohn, *The Pursuit of the Millennium: Revolutionary Millenarians and Mystical Anarchists of the Middle Ages*, rev. ed. (New York: Oxford University Press, 1972).

42. S. K. Johannesen, "Christianity, Millennialism and Civic Life: The Origins of the American Republic," in Joseph Bettis and S. K. Johannesen, eds., *The Return of the Millennium* (Barrytown, NY: IRF, 1984), p. 217. On this, see Wade Clark Roof, "America's Voluntary Establishment: Mainline Religion in Transition," in Mary Douglas and Steven M. Tipton, eds., *Religion and America: Spirituality in a Secular Age* (Boston: Beacon, 1983), pp. 130–33. On the positive correlationships between the millennial imagination of the First Awakening and republicanism, see Nathan Hatch, *The Sacred Cause of Liberty* (New Haven: Yale University Press, 1977). That Puritan Millennialism was thoroughly moralistic is also indicated by the dire threats preached about Puritan failure in regard to their "Errand in the Wilderness" and their vocation to be a "City on the Hill . . . a Beacon to all Nations." See Sacvan Bercovitch, *The American Jeremiad* (Madison, WI: University of Wisconsin Press, 1978). Also Richard T. Hughes, "From Primitive Church to Civil Religion: The Millennial Odyssey of Alexander Campbell," *Journal of the American Academy of Religion*, XLIV, No. 1 (1976), pp. 87–104. Among the various chapters in M. Darrol Bryant and Donald W. Dayton, eds., *The Coming Kingdom: Essays in American Millennialism & Eschatology* (Barrytown, NY: IRF, 1983), see especially M. Darrol Bryant, "From Edwards to Hopkins: A Millennialist Critique of Political Culture," pp. 45–70; Donald W. Dayton, "Millennial Views and Social Reform in Nineteenth Century America," pp. 131–48; and Richard L. Rubenstein, "Religion, Modernization, and Millenarianism," pp. 223–46.

43. John Winthrop, "A Model of Christian Charity," in Edmund Morgan, ed., *The Founding of Massachusetts: Historians and Sources* (Indianapolis: Bobbs-Merrill, 1964), p. 191.

44. Henry Steele Commager, ed., *Documents of American History* (New York: Appleton-Century-Crofts, 1963, seventh ed.), pp. 97–98. Much later, Yves Congar [*The Word and the Spirit* (San Francisco: Harper and Row, 1986), p. 50] will speak of "the United States of America, which is above all the country of personal initiatives."

45. See de Tocqueville, pp. 3–14, 408–20; Introduction; II, 1, 5–6.

46. Pertinent are these strictures about the Western states' "clerisy of power . . . the long succession of philosophers and intellectuals . . . [who, in the modern state,] 'attempt to level, but never equalize' [Edmund Burke] . . . extinguishing normal diversity of strength and talent . . . equality of result . . . the kind of equality that goes

with uniformity and homogeneity." Robert Nisbet, *Twilight of Authority* (New York: Oxford, 1975), pp. 199, 207.

47. de Tocqueville, *Democracy*, p. 414; II, 1, 5.

48. On the not recurring, but constant temptation, of the originally Free, Dissenting, and Dis-established churches to establish themselves, see Martin Marty, *Righteous Empire: The Protestant Experience in America* (New York: Dial, 1970). Also, Sidney Mead, "From Coercion to Persuasion: Another Look at the Rise of Religious Liberty and the Emergence of Denominationalism," *Church History*, 25 (December 1956), 317–37.

49. According to the Tettnanger Onkel Rudolf Aich, "Amerika ist das Land der unbegrenzten Möglichkeiten." See also notes 18, 20, and 32 above.

50. Martin Marty, *Pilgrims*, p. 121.

51. Modifying Crèvecoeur's original "Ubi panis ibi patria" to "Ubi libertas cultus et panis, ibi patria," *American Catholicism*, p. 50.

52. I am indebted to Prof. Patrick Carey of Marquette University for making this explicit. At no time do I wish to assert only a *tabula rasa* Roman Catholic Church came to the shores of the New World and here made some kind of absolute new beginning, a sort of *creatio ex nihil sui et subjecti*. Rather, my point is that especially Catholics were able, in the very different context of the New World, to discover and create a new way of being the Roman Catholics they always had been. In this regard Thomas Sowell also makes a compelling point. In regard to the capacity of various immigrant groups to compete in the general free market of American society—in this instance, in politics—he notes the contrast between the Irish and the Eastern European Jews in New York City: "The Irish were well ahead of them in all of these qualities (as a result of *their* history in Ireland. . . . " Thomas Sowell, *Ethnic America* (New York: Basic Books, 1981), p. 92. In view of later American Catholic hierarchical history, an accompanying sentence of Sowell's is worth noting: " . . . whereas the Irish were preoccupied with getting into power, which they did very successfully." We should not omit German Catholics, who, because of the Prussian(!)-induced *Kulturkampf*, also knew what it was to be the Church without benefit of Establishment and the support of "*Vater Staat*." See Colman J. Barry, *The Catholic Church and German Americans* (Milwaukee: Bruce, 1953), p. 5. On page seven, Barry emphasizes that not only "many priests and nuns were forced to flee. . . . Many of the common people among German Catholics . . . also turned their eyes toward foreign lands." I cite this to emphasize that the American Church is not the Church of the cleric, the monk, the hierarch. It is the Church of the "Common Man," of the "Common People."

53. This precisely Catholic theological insight and principle is thus seen to be not merely speculative-theoretical, but also practical-ministerial. Catholicism is not only dogmatically but also pastorally inclusive. See Karl Rahner, *Herausforderung des Christen* (Freiburg: Herder, 1975), p. 84; Hans Urs von Balthasar, *Katholisch* (Einsiedeln: Johannes, 1975), pp. 18, 22, 167; Hermann Volk, *Gott Alles in Allem* (Mainz: Grünewald, 1958), pp. 149–51.

54. "America is the most democratic country in the world, and it is at the same time (according to reliable reports) the country in which the Roman Catholic religion is making the most progress." *Democracy*, p. 415; II, 1, 6.

55. Jay P. Dolan, *The American Catholic Experience* (Garden City, NY: Doubleday, 1985), pp. 72–74.

56. References to at least early American experience in general, and religion in particular, as being practical, pragmatic, not anti- but simply un- or non-theoretical abound in Daniel Boorstin, *The Americans: The Colonial Experience* (New York: Random House, 1958), for example, pp. 122, 175, 180, 213, 232, 235–241, 299, and

304. On page 124, he emphasizes the presence and role of "practical godliness" in the American churches and religion.

57. John D. Krugler, "Lord Baltimore, Roman Catholics, and Toleration: Religious Policy in Maryland During the Early Catholic Years," *Catholic Historical Review*, 65, No. 1, (1979), p. 60.

58. William Craven, *The Southern Colonies in the Seventeenth Century, 1607–1689* (Baton Rouge, LA: Louisiana State University Press, 1949), p. 235.

59. Jay P. Dolan, *The American Catholic Experience*, pp. 78–79.

60. Even as recently as 1887, so enlightened a theologian as Matthias Scheeben could write, "In virtue of its higher 'order,' the priesthood constitutes, so to speak, the nobility in the Church, a nobility whose higher dignity and control of the society's supernatural goods . . . set it apart from the other members." *The Mysteries of Christianity* (St. Louis: Herder, 1946), p. 551.

61. John Tracy Ellis, *American Catholicism*, 2nd rev. ed. (Chicago: University of Chicago Press, 1969), p. 31.

62. Alexis de Tocqueville, *Democracy in America*, p. 265–66; I, 2, 9. I have modified the translation here, in accord with the original French text.

63. Ellis, *American Catholicism*, p. 59.

64. Henry Steele Commager, *The American Mind: An Interpretation of American Thought and Character Since the 1880's* (New Haven: Yale University Press, 1950), p. 193. As I have emphasized, this was *lived* Catholicism. Reflection and conceptual elaboration, although not entirely absent, came later. Otherwise, John Courtney Murray's theological reflection would not have encountered such reluctance in the mid-twentieth century.

65. Harriet Martineau, *Society in America*, III (London: 1837), p. 237.

66. J. P, Audet, "Priester und Laie in der christlichen Gemeinde," in *Der priesterliche Dienst*, with A. Deissler and H. Schlier (Freiburg: Herder, 1970), pp. 149–75.

67. On this, see Aaron I. Abell, "The Catholic Factor in the Social Justice Movement," in Thomas McAvoy, ed., *Roman Catholicism and the American Way of Life* (Notre Dame, IL: University of Notre Dame Press, 1960), pp. 70–98. Dolan, *The American Catholic Experience*, pp. 321–46.

68. Dolan, *The American Catholic Experience*, p. 337.

69. This has not been at all sufficiently investigated. For a small beginning, see Timothy Smith, "Lay Initiative in the Religious Life of Immigrants, 1880–1950," in Tamara Haven, ed., *Anonymous Americans: Explorations in Nineteenth-Century Social History* (Englewood Cliffs, NJ: Prentice-Hall, 1971), pp. 214–49. A move in this direction is also seen in James Hennesey, *American Catholics* (New York: Oxford University Press, 1981). Of great interest here are the data, assembled by Andrew Greeley and his associates, which indicate continued widespread support for Catholic schools among the Catholic population at large. The hesitation and reluctance are on the part of those termed "leaders," especially the clergy, of all levels, and the religious. Andrew Greeley, *The American Catholic: A Social Portrait* (New York: Basic, 1977), pp. 164–86, esp. pp. 167–71. There, he also summarizes the results of two earlier studies done in 1966 and 1976.

70. *Democracy*, p. 85; I, 1, 5.

71. Gerald P. Fogarty, "Why the Pastoral is Shocking," *Commonweal*, CX, No. 11 (3 June 1983), 336.

72. Maguire, "Catholic Ethics with an American Accent," in *America in Theological Perspective*, pp. 18–20. This trendy elitism—the intellectual clerisy "in-the-know" versus the unwashed, common citizen-patriot—reaches its expected climax in Thomas J. Reese, "The Third Draft of the Peace Proposal," *America*, Vol. 148, No.

16 (23 April 1983), pp. 320–21, and the enthusiastic letter of Lucy L. Bridges lauding it and drawing the appropriate conclusion: Reese has said "what finally needs to be said: Better Red than Dead" (America, Letters, 28 May 1983), 428).

73. The data are from a report by Marjorie Hyer, "Americans Willing to Fight, Proud of U.S.," Washington Post (19 May 1982), A-15.

74. Above all, Sidney Mead, "The Theology of the Republic and the Orthodox Mind," JAAR, Vol. XIV, No. 1 (March, 1976), 111–12: "Even learned academic organization men have defined 'authentic faith' as 'prophetic,' meaning that it sets one over against his society." One might call this, with apologies to Dietrich Bonhoeffer, "cheap prophecy." See, also, The Lively Experiment (New York: Harper & Row, 1963); The Nation with the Soul of a Church (New York: Harper & Row, 1975); and, finally, "American History as Tragic Drama," The Journal of Religion, 52 (1972), 337–59.

75. Commonweal, XCIX (1 February 1974), 443.

76. For example, Gerald Fogarty, "Why the Pastoral is Shocking," pp. 335–38, passim. Daniel Maguire in the two works in footnote 27 above.

77. Martin Marty, who distinguished between "private" evangelicalism and revivalism (and fundamentalism) on the one hand, and "public" Protestantism on the other (Righteous Empire), has been called to task for this. See George M. Marsden, "Preachers of Paradox: The Religious New Right in Historical Perspective," in Mary Douglas and Steven Tipton, eds., Religion in America (Boston: Beacon, 1983), p. 161. Marty's attempt to distinguish fundamentalist activities as "political' but not "public" is certainly an exercise in exotic etymology [Martin Marty, "Fundamentalism as a Social Phenomenon," Review and Expositor, 79, 1 (Winter, 1982), pp. 24–25]. What is at play here is also what is at play in Hehir, Fogarty, and Maguire—since their own public agenda is not the preferred and privileged public policy and presence of the Church membership at large, the Church is judged and condemned as private and privatized, code words for selfish and unconcerned.

78. J. Bryan Hehir, The Discipline and Dynamic of a Public Church (Washington, D.C.: Catholic University of America, 1984; Xeroxed).

79. J. Bryan Hehir, "Justice: A Pastoral Perspective," The Priest, September, 1985, p. 35.

80. See Robert Kress, The Church, pp. 161–212.

81. Democracy, p. 8, Intro; 560–65, II, 3, 8; 655–64; II, 4, 5 and passim.

82. Sidney Mead, The Nation with the Soul of a Church, p. 60.

83. Sidney Mead, "The People," C.T.S. Register, 39 (January 1949), 22–23. Furthermore, Daniel Boorstin, The Americans: The Colonial Experience (New York: Random House, 1958), p. 188, writes thus: "A wholesome fear of the exotic and hieratic, of the power of the mind to raise any man above men, inspired American faith in the 'divine average,' a faith which would not have grown without American opportunity."

84. Jacques Maritain, Reflections on America (New York: Scribners, 1958), pp. 194–96. Similar sentiments in Raymond Bruckberger, Image of America (New York: Viking, 1959).

85. Andrew Greeley, The American Catholic. These data are summarized in his American Catholics Since the Council: An Unauthorized Report (Chicago: Thomas More, 1986). Even if all Catholics of all national origins have not shared equally in this Catholic prosperity, the achievement of Catholics in general is still enormous. Furthermore, the condition of precisely Hispanic Catholics may be other than that represented as "typical" in this paper. As Greeley has emphasized, the research on Hispanic Catholics is at best spare (American Catholics Since the Council, p. 79). One should also consult the reports (there are now eight of them, from December 1984 through July 1986) edited by David C. Leege and others, entitled the Notre Dame

Study of Catholic Parish Life (Notre Dame, IN: University of Notre Dame Press, 1201 Memorial Library).

86. See Footnote 9 above.

87. One can hardly not agree with Ratzinger (*Report*, pp. 130–32; 186–88) when he claims to discern a modern, romantic, utopian, revolutionary, triumphalist neo-clericalism of the intellectuals, which claims to represent the poor, but which really needs them as the raw material of their ideologies and object of their "care" and "concern." Previous clericalism has asserted its superiority to the people at large in the realm of sexuality. Abstinence was better, celibacy a higher state. This strategy is obviously no longer effective. According to Andrew Greeley, "Almost four-fifths of the weekly church attenders (and at least as large a portion of the weekly communion receivers) do not accept the Church's official sexual teaching" (*American Catholics Since the Council*, p. 209; reference is primarily to contraception, but see also pp. 80–100).

If sexuality will no longer serve, what better replacement than economics, an equally unavoidable dimension of human being. Advocates of the current economic clericalism have also hit upon a remarkable strategy, that of institutional or institutionalized sin. From liberation theologians to centers of concern to Episcopal pastoral pronouncements, this term is so widespread that it can be spared documentation. One should note that after we finally became somewhat cautious in our speech about sin as original, personal, habitual, mortal, grave and venial, because of the at least analogical if not polyvalent nature of sin, some have rushed into the fray to unleash a new broadside of sin, this time even more inescapable than the old sexual. From institutionalized social, economic sin, there is no escape, no exit. If one is a citizen of a prosperous country, one must be and is *ipso facto* automatically sinful, for it has been discerned that the prosperity of one can only be at the expense of the other. All of economics and commerce is reduced to a sort of exhortatory moralism about the evils of consumerism and property, extolling the virtues of relinquishment and pauperism. See, for example, Marie Augusta Neal, *A Socio-theology of Letting Go: The Role of a First World Church Facing Third World Peoples* (New York: Paulist, 1977), p. 103. This attitude is personified by Raymund Schwager (footnote 2 above). He contrasts the "American Faith" (whatever that might be, although he so totally misunderstands the term "civil religion" that one can be fairly sure of what "American Faith" means for him) with the "Christian Faith," and continues: "If social conditions acquire normative value, then the Christian Faith is always threatened by distortions. This danger is especially great when glee about one's own riches rather than an understanding of poverty in the manner of Latin American liberation theology is elevated to the norm." So little does Schwager understand about the American and American Catholic experience! There is some gleeful self-satisfaction by the rich, doubtlessly; but most Americans and American Catholics rejoice not in riches, but in being freed from the pauperism so dear to Schwager's theological heart, and from the clericalist concern so necessary to his occupational ideology. What Schwager shares with all these prophets of poverty and parsimony, whether from the traditionalist right or the revolutionist left, is, first of all, a heightened sense of the sin of *others* as the cause of economic distress, and second, an economic and social security, provided by those whose prosperity they so delight in castigating, which enables Schwager and his kind to be relieved of the economic cares with which most people have to deal. In contrast to and rebuttal of all this clericalist concern about the evils of prosperity and consumerism stands the conclusion reached by the surveys conducted by Andrew Greeley and his colleagues:

In summary, then, the American Catholic in the last quarter century has become more educated and more affluent . . . if under forty, part of the best educated and most affluent gentile group in America. . . . Those who suggest that the 'embourgeoisement' of American Catholics means less concern about the poor or the oppressed are, according to the evidence, simply wrong. . . . There is not the slightest bit of evidence that economic and occupational success and religious change in the last quarter of the century have diminished these concerns (*American Catholics Since the Council*, p. 48).

This long note is justified, it seems to me, by the crucial consequences the pauperist ideology advocated by so many clerics and religious could have. The consequence will not, of course, be the conversion of the prosperous Catholics to this abstinential, penitential economy of pauperism [They have to work for a living.], nor their forced exit from the Church [They have always been in the Church voluntarily; they can be forced neither in nor out.]; but the reduction of the effectiveness of the leadership of the clerical-religious cadre in the Church, and the needless obfuscation about the nature and role the American Catholic Church does in fact, and should in theory, play in the universal Church. [To add support to the above statement, one is tempted here to borrow and modify Lionel Rothkrug's insight and speak of this as a "penitential economy," in which purification from fleshly appetites reigns as the chief feature. Lionel Rothkrug, "Religious Practices and Collective Perceptions: Hidden Homologies in the Renaissance and Reformation," *Historical Reflections/Reflections Historiques* (1980); and also "The Order of Sanctity and the Hebrew," *Origins of Christian Relic Venerations*, 8 (1981).]

88. There is a striking parallel between the American Catholic experience and the Indian experience. See Thomas Gannon, "The Catholic Church in India," *America*, Vol. 154, No. 6 (15 February 1986), 112–17. In support of my contention that the American Church has become a Church of the People, see Alois Parg, "Der Gott der Welt: Zur Spiritualität der Laien in den USA," *Geist und Leben*, Vol. 59, No. 5 (1986), 372–79. He notes the contrast between the two hundred or so programs for education and formation for lay people in the United States and the situation in West Germany, which he evaluates in terms of "eine dunkle Wolke von Hoffnungslosigkeit" (p. 379).

89. Geotz Briefs, "Die 'Frontier,' ein Problem der Beziehungen zwischen Religion und Wirtschaft," in Franz Greiss and Fritz Meyer, eds., *Wirtschaft, Gesellschaft und Kultur* (Berlin: Duncker & Humblot, 1961), p. 519. There are some who like to explain the unique development of the United States solely in terms of the open spaces, small population, and the frontier. However, as Briefs notes here, the same attributes were available in Central and South America, but the development there was quite different and distinctly not democratic, republican, or in terms and favor of the "common man." He attributes the different development there to the dominating influence of Spanish Reconquista Catholicism. Alexis de Tocqueville had already noted the same contrast (*Democracy in America*, pp. 257–59, 280–84, I, 2, 9; 366–73, I, 2, 10).

90. Martin Marty, "Religion in America Since Mid-century," in Mary Douglass and Steven Tipton, eds., *Religion and America* (Boston: Beacon, 1983), 274.

91. "Loyal" runs refrain-like throughout Greeley's *American Catholics Since the Council*, pp. 22, 23, 60, 71, 76–78, 98, 174–76, and 210.

92. *American Catholics*, pp. 33–34.

93. According to Greeley, the precipitate decline in active Catholic membership and participation in the Church in 1969–1975 was "a single shot" (p. 72) and tightly correlated with the encyclical, *Humanae Vitae* (*American Catholics*, pp. 50–79).

94. J. Hector St. John de Crèvecoeur, *Letters from an American Farmer* (New York: Penguin, 1981), p. 83.

95. Sydney Ahlstrom, "Thomas Hooker—Puritanism and Democratic Citizenship: A Preliminary Inquirey into some Relationships of Religion and American Civic Responsibility," *Church History* 32 (Dec. 1963), 423. This is in keeping with Mead's observation that "Religiously, then, what was unique about this American—this 'new man' after 1787—was his practice of religious freedom" (*The Lively Experiment*, p. 3). And we would add emphatically his free practice of religion, because in America freedom has been for, not from, religion.

96. Andrew Greeley, *An Ugly Little Secret*, p. 90; more detailed in *The American Catholic*, pp. 270–74.

97. Andrew Greeley, *American Catholics Since the Council*, pp. 60, 71.

98. Andrew Greeley, *American Catholics*, pp. 98.

99. On "Teilidentifikation," see Wilhelm Riess, *Glaube als Konsens* (Munich: Kösel, 1979). To those who might deem my approach too optimistic, I reply: 1) that the Jeremiad is a proper American religious literary form and provides ample exhortation to humility and repentance; 2) that other cautions may be found in my paper, "The People's Church" (Notre Dame, IN: University of Notre Dame Cushwa Center, 1986), where there is expanded discussion of topics such as Civil Religion, the Religion of the Republic, and the inadequate response of all Americans to their "Errand in the Wilderness"; and 3) that, according to Karl Rahner, "It is blasphemous to assert that it is easier to do evil than good" [*Schriften zur Theologie*, V (Einsiedeln: Benziger, 1962), p. 402] (American translation, V, 358).

100. Andrew Greeley, *American Catholics Since the Council*, p. 75.

101. In Williston Walker, *Creeds and Platforms of Congregationalism* (Boston: Pilgrim Press, 1960), p. 116.

Part Four

RECONSTRUCTING VALUES AND SYMBOLS FOR OUR TIME

THE "PREFERENTIAL OPTION FOR THE POOR" IN *ECONOMIC JUSTICE FOR ALL:* THEOLOGY OR IDEOLOGY?

William E. Murnion
Ramapo College of New Jersey

ABSTRACT

In the "preferential option for the poor" the American Catholic bishops have adapted a principle of social analysis from liberation theology to a critique of the U.S. economy. But their failure to avoid ideology in the form of the pastoral is reflected in an ambivalence in its substance. The bishops recognize that the Bible says faith in God is a sufficient condition for a preferential option for the poor, but not that it also reveals this option to be a necessary condition for faith in God. In following the recent shift in Catholic social theology to this new principle of social analysis, they ignore its equivalence to a socialist principle of justice. And in applying it to the U.S. economy, they do not specify the force of the economic rights they say it implies, nor have they attempted to organize the poor to vindicate these rights. Thus the inspiration for the preferential option for the poor may have been theological, but in the pastoral its function is largely ideological.

The bone of contention in *Economic Justice for All: Catholic Social Teaching and the U.S. Economy*[1] is the "preferential option for the poor." This was not evident in the initial reactions to the first draft, nor is it patent from the criticisms of the final draft. The policy proposals were what originally seem to have prompted the Lay Commission on Catholic Social Teaching and the U.S. Economy to produce its counterpastoral[2] and what, in the end, bore the brunt of the commission's unmollified critique.[3] They were also what aroused the concern of business publications[4] and, in general, drew the at-

William E. Murnion, S.T.L. (Gregorian University, 1958), Ph.D. (Gregorian University, 1970), Associate Professor of Philosophy and Religious Studies in the School of American and International Studies at Ramapo College of New Jersey (505 Ramapo Valley Road, Mahwah, NJ 07430). Recent publications include articles on the American bishops' peace pastoral, the logic of learning, the foundations of ethics, and the morality of nuclear power.

tention of the secular press.[5] On matters of principle, both William Simon and Michael Novak, the co-chairmen of the Lay Commission, professed to be in accord with the bishops—in Simon's case, even to the extent of an explicit endorsement of the preferential option for the poor,[6] and in their critique of the final draft they could not applaud the bishops enough for focusing upon the needs of the poor.[7] But, as Peter Steinfels argued, the basic reason for criticism of the pastoral was not the policy proposals themselves, "relatively modest and open-minded" as they are, but the bishops' premises, which "sharply challenge the deeply rooted assumptions of the present moment."[8] "The problem lies," according to E. Bruce Douglass (in an otherwise laudatory analysis of the letter), "with the notion that justice means, *tout court*, a concern for the well-being of the least advantaged."[9] This preoccupation with the poor, say more conservative critics, has led the bishops to abuse their authority as teachers of moral theology in making an ignorant and ideological attack upon the United States, "the most productive, the most democratic, the most generous-spirited, and yes, the most egalitarian nation on earth."[10] As critics have had time to digest the full meaning of the letter, the charge has become that the preferential option for the poor implies a repudiation of the foundation of Catholic social theology upon human dignity and the common good for a partisan, indeed a socialist, and, worse still, perhaps a Marxist ideology of class struggle.[11]

In revising the first draft of the pastoral, the bishops were sensitive to this kind of criticism. Some of them had second thoughts about resting the entire pastoral upon a relatively novel and obviously controversial principle.[12] But with majority approval, the committee for the pastoral strengthened the position of the preferential option for the poor in the second and again in the third drafts, until now it remains, in the final draft, the key to the entire letter and the index to its acceptability. The bishops assert it is the epitome of the biblical conception of justice (4:52), the primary economic moral obligation of the American people (4:86; see also 85–89, 335, 355), the guideline for policies to meet the problems of the U.S. economy (4:137 [implicitly], 171, 186, 216 [implicitly], 229–30, 252, 258, 260, 263, 267, 274), and the motive for a "new American experiment" to guarantee economic rights (4:295 [implicitly], 319). To reject the preferential option for the poor, therefore, is to repudiate the entire pastoral.

In this case, it becomes important to determine whether the preferential option for the poor has a theological or an ideological function in the pastoral. But before answering this question, it will be necessary to analyze the degree to which the letter as whole has a theological or an ideological character. Simon and Novak have charged, in fact, that "the reasoning in the final draft is in place unmistakably ideological . . . far more so, apparently, than the bishops intended to be." It will be my contention that the bishops have made a deliberate, but ultimately deficient, effort to purge every trace of ideology from the pastoral, with the result that their conception of the preferential option for the poor is theological in intent but ideological in effect. Hence, *Economic Justice for All*, while it advocates extensive reform of the U.S. economy, serves as an apology for the capitalist system.

In making this assessment I shall mean by "theology" "the rationalization of experience in the light of faith" and by "ideology" "the rationalization of experience in the light of self-interest." "Rationalization" will mean in either case "interpretation" or "explanation," without regard to whether it is supposed to be authentic, objective, and true or rather specious, tendentious, or false.[13] I do not presume, therefore, that theology and ideology are mutually exclusive, nor do I make a value judgment about either of them. In the course of the argument I shall introduce further stipulations about the meanings of terms as the complexity of the issues makes them necessary.

I. *The Effort to Avoid Ideology in Economic Justice for All*

The bishops took three steps, with partial success, to eliminate ideology from the pastoral. They shifted from a strictly deductive to a more dialectical methodology. They revised the structure and the content of the pastoral to reflect this change. And they explicitly refused to align their teaching with any ideology.

The shift in methodology reflects a change even from the approach they took in *The Challenge of Peace*. In the peace pastoral the bishops made a logical distinction between universal moral principles or formal church teaching and the policy applications or prudential judgments deducible from them.[14] This distinction they also quoted in the first draft of the economics pastoral (1:155), but in the second draft this reference was abbreviated and reduced in importance (2:32), and in the third draft it was deleted altogether. To the end, though, the bishops retained from the first draft a complementary statement—albeit in successively briefer and more perfunctory forms in the second and the third drafts of the letter—about a rhetorical difference between moral principles and policy recommendations (1:156–57, 2:133–34, 4:135).

The significance of this shift in methodology is that it eliminated any explicit commitment of the bishops to ethical rationalism. No longer did they suppose moral teaching had to be divided logically between universal principles, binding in conscience for everyone always and everywhere, and specific policies, of dubious force and only local or historical import. Nor did they retain the complementary supposition that the principles could be combined with historical facts in a deductive argument to yield the appropriate policies.

This had been the method employed in official church documents from Leo XIII's *Rerum Novarum* (1891) until John XXIII's *Mater et Magistra* (1961) to lend authority to the particular provisions of the "social doctrine" of the church.[15] In alleging a God-given and immutable foundation in human nature for the church's endorsement of private property and the free market, this doctrine had had the effect, and some would argue the intent, of defending liberal capitalism from the threat of a socialist revolution.[16] In *Pacem in Terris* (1963), however, John XXIII initiated a more inductive and dialectical approach to social theology, basing his policy proposals as much upon an analysis of the "signs of the times" as upon deductions from the natural law.[17] Vatican II made this analysis of the "signs of the times" the primary basis in *Gaudium et Spes* for its analysis of the relationship of the church to the world (The Pastoral Constitution on the Church in the Modern World).[18] And in *Octogesima Adveniens* (1971) Paul VI gave a mandate to national episcopal conferences (which the bishops quote in *Economic Justice for All*, 4:26) "to analyze with objectivity the situation which is proper to their own country" before attempting to apply to their communities the generic prescriptions in the social teaching of the church.[19]

So the decision of the American bishops to adopt this more inductive and dialectical approach in *Economic Justice for All* is a somewhat belated accommodation to what has become the prevalent methodology in Catholic social theology. Yet the accommodation is incomplete. The bishops do admit the necessity for tempering principles by circumstances to devise appropriate policies but not the complementary necessity for scrutinizing circumstances for clues to the relevant principles. Thus they recognize that the interaction of moral principles "with empirical data, with historical, social, and political realities, and with competing demands on limited resources" in "the movement from principle to policy" prevents moral values from dictating specific solutions to problems (4:134). But they say nothing of the fact that the movement from problems to principles is equally complex and difficult since historical conditions must interact with moral values to suggest principles relevant to the issues. What they do not explicitly acknowledge is that the interaction between the mind and reality entails an inductive movement from experience to principle to anticipate and balance the deductive movement from principle to judgment.

What the bishops do not acknowledge in theory, however, they go a long way toward recognizing in practice. This is the second step they have taken to avoid ideology in the pastoral letter. It was evident in the remarkable transformation from the first to the second draft in the structure of the pastoral. The first draft still reflected a simplistic methodological distinction between moral principles and policy proposals in being divided into two major parts, "Biblical and Theological Foundations" and "Policy Applications," sandwiched between a brief introduction and an equally brief conclusion. But the division of the second draft into five chapters reflected the introduction of a more inductive and dialectical methodology to the letter. The first chapter expanded the perfunctory introduction of the first draft into a detailed analysis of how the "signs of the times" in the U.S. economy called for the kind of new moral vision represented by a preferential option for the poor. The second and the third chapters retained the division from the first draft between moral principles and policy recommendations, but now both factors were interpreted in a new way. The moral principles were interpreted more concretely in light of the preferential option for the poor. And the policy recommendations (with the addition of a section on the farm crisis not ready for the first draft) were now formulated in the light of the implications of this option for the U.S. economy. In addition, a section called "The New American Experiment" was lifted from the third chapter of the first draft and expanded into a chapter of its own, to suggest the radical transformation a recognition of economic rights would entail for American economic life. Finally, the vague "call to holiness and wholeness" in the conclusion of the first draft was revamped into a chapter on the specific measures for the American church and for individual Catholics to take in rectifying the deficiencies noted in the first chapter in the U.S. economy.

This methodological shift continued into the third draft. The analysis of the "signs of the times" in the first chapter was made tighter but more detailed. In the third chapter the pertinence of the preferential option for poor to policy issues became more explicit. And an explanation of the complementarity between "conversion of heart" and "transformation of structures" was introduced into the specifications in the fifth chapter for carrying out the policies of the pastoral. While the final draft added nothing more on this issue, the pastoral had come to represent, as the bishops said, "an ethical framework that can guide economic life today in ways that are both faithful to the Gospel and shaped by human experience and reason" (4:61).

By no coincidence, the genesis of theology from a dialectic between experience and revelation is the distinctive method of liberation theology.[20] The charter for this approach to theology was the ag-

giornamento John XXIII inaugurated between the Church and the world and that Vatican II turned into a policy. But liberation theology was in turn the inspiration for Paul VI's recommendation in *Octogesima Adveniens* for local churches to develop their own interpretations of Christian social theology. Since liberation theology was the source from which the American bishops borrowed "the preferential option for the poor," it was only natural for them also to appropriate something of the method by which liberation theology had conceived of this option.

Yet the bishops' recognition in *Economic Justice for All* of the importance of experience for the formation of theology remains inchoate. Although they place their analysis of poverty as a "sign of the times" before their derivation of the preferential option for the poor from the Bible, they fail to acknowledge that their experience of poverty in the United States today was what prompted them to make such an exegesis of the Bible. Likewise, though they follow their explanation of the social justice implications of the option for the poor with a critique of the injustices in the U.S. economy, they fail to admit that they analyzed the option for the poor in anticipation of making such a critique. Without any personal experience of poverty or participation in poor peoples' movements—despite their claims to "firsthand knowledge" of poverty (4:143, 172, 217, 231, 311)—they lack the solidarity with the poor from which liberation theologians have gained an intuitive appreciation of the significance of the Gospel for economic issues.[21] Indeed, the bishops have to admit they "would be insincere were they to deny a need for renewal in the economic life of the church itself and a renewed zeal on the part of the church in . . . reinforcing . . . values that support economic justice" (4:349). Therefore, although the pastoral begins with an analysis of poverty, hinges upon the preferential option for the poor, and concludes with policies to eliminate poverty, it is not a gospel from the poor to the poor, nor a manifesto from the poor to the rich, but a plea for the poor from the rich.

Yet there is a third step the bishops have taken to free this pastoral from ideology. In keeping with what they say is Catholic social teaching, they profess to reject "all ideologies that claim to have the final answer to humanity's problems" (4:125). By this they seem to mean, not that they might accept an ideology which did not make such a claim, but that they reject the claim of any ideology to have such an answer. The reason? It would be "likely to produce results contrary to human dignity and economic justice" (4:129). Two examples they describe without naming, in terms of basic principles and typical policies (4:128). One is based upon the principle "that an unfettered free-market economy, where owners, workers, and consumers pursue their enlightened self-interest, provides the greatest liberty, material welfare, and equity" and follows the policy of intervening "in the economy as little as possible because it is such a delicate mechanism that attempts to improve it are likely to have the opposite effect." For the other, the basic principle is "that the capitalist system is inherently inequitable and therefore contrary to the demands of Christian morality, for it is based on acquisitiveness, competition, and self-centered individualism," and the consequent policy is to replace this "fatally flawed" capitalism "with a radically different system that abolishes private property, the profit motive, and the free market." This coy refusal to name names does little to disguise the bishops' evenhanded rejection of both capitalism and socialism.

To what they call "these ideological extremes" the bishops oppose what they believe is their own pragmatic and critical approach (4:129). From traditional Catholic social teaching they adopt the principle "that the economy has been created by human beings and can be changed by them." And the policy they believe is in accord with this principle is "not to create or promote a specific new economic system," but to "work for improvement in a variety of economic and political contexts." The intent of such a policy would be to encourage "all reforms that hold out hope of transforming our economic arrangements into a fuller systemic realization of the Christian moral vision" and to challenge "practices and institutions that impede or carry us farther away from realizing this vision." Not being "bound to any particular economic, political, or social system," the church can then evaluate each ideology "according to moral and ethical principles: What is the impact of the system upon people? Does it support or threaten human dignity?" (4:130).

This explicit rejection of ideology in the name of a critical theology can be understood, however, from either a theological or an ideological viewpoint. From a theological viewpoint it represents progress. For it is an implicit rejection of the official position from Leo XIII to Pius XII that Catholic "social doctrine" provided a third way, a rival ideology to capitalism and socialism, in favor of John XXIII's position that the church did not have a distinctive social doctrine but rather a mandate from Christ to evaluate every ideology in terms of its conformity to Christian moral standards. The "social doctrine" approach was essentially reactionary. It was directly inspired by the "social Catholicism" of the middle-class European Catholic social movements which arose in the late nineteenth and the early twentieth century to combat the threat to the liberal capitalist social order from the appeal of socialism to the working classes. This "social doctrine" advocated a restoration of the medieval social order, with the church once again the arbiter of morals, with managers and workers united in industry councils like the guilds of yore, and with a corporatist state endowed with the formerly royal prerogative of set economic as well as political policy.[22] It also implied the promotion of separate Catholic trade unions, Catholic Action for the laity (under the supervision of the hierarchy, of course), and Christian Democratic parties.[23] While this "social doctrine" was manifestly an ideology in the service of the church, it was also latently an ideology of liberal capitalism—supporting it in principle, while it sought to rectify its abuses, in order to avert what the papacy believed to be the far greater danger of socialism.[24]

But in *Mater and Magistra* (1961) John XXIII began to remove ideology in substance as well as form from Catholic social theology.[25] Abandoning the pretense to a distinctive Catholic "social doctrine," he committed social theology to the task of evaluating the morality of both capitalism and socialism. This was also the tack Vatican II took in *The Church in the Modern World*. Much to the dismay of some Catholics, Paul VI made the shift explicit and programmatic in *Populorum Progressio*.[26] And this is also John Paul II's position. He has insisted on the distinctiveness of Catholic social teaching; at Puebla (1978) he even resuscitated the usage of "social doctrine."[27] But he has not attempted to develop a Catholic ideology to rival capitalism and socialism, and he has, at the same time been as severe in denouncing the evils of capitalism as those of socialism.

Hence, in renouncing ideology and criticizing capitalism as well as socialism, the American bishops are in tune with the latter-day transformation of Catholic social theology from social doctrine to social criticism. Yet the bishops' action can also be understood within the American context as implying an acceptance of the neoconservative ideology from the fifties of an "end of ideology." When the bishops say they want "to continue the search for a more just economy . . . in the spirit of the American pragmatic tradition of reform" (4:131), when they add that they intend "to focus primarily on some aspects of the economy where we think reforms are realistically possible" (4:132), this sounds very much like the neoconservative claim that economic disputes have become, apart from purely political conflicts about the equitable distribution of wealth, essentially value-free technical issues—questions about the most effective way to assure economic stability; that is, growth without inflation.[28]

Now the bishops certainly do not assume that economics is value-free or that economic choices are simply technical issues (See 4:5, 292, 321). And in the fourth chapter, "A New American Experiment," they raise the possibility of radical reforms to the American system. But in their policy proposals they have renounced the task of treating "larger questions concerning the economic system itself" (4:132), and they assume debate about the pastoral will be confined to "specific policy recommendations" rather than expanding to include underlying principles and values (4:94, 135). Hence, while purporting to take a pragmatic approach to the problems of the U.S. economy, the American bishops have adopted, in effect, the neoconservative ideology of defending capitalism by stigmatizing any fundamental critique of the system as ideological.[29]

In forswearing a Catholic ideology and denouncing both capitalism and socialism, the bishops apparently thought they could avoid any ideology at all: they could rise above ideological conflict and settle the problems of the U.S. economy pragmatically. But this was to adopt the neoconservative ideology that there is nothing basically wrong with the U.S. economy, nor with capitalism. The result is to restrict the possibilities of social change to piecemeal reform rather than to allow for the possibility of revolution.

In general, therefore, the bishops' deliberate efforts to avoid ideology in *Economic Justice for All* have been dogged by an inadvertent adherence to ideology. Although they have dropped any allusion to a logical distinction between moral principles and prudential judgments—acknowledging the need for principles themselves to be tempered by circumstances—they have not recognized that circumstances can also be the matrix from which principles are derived. Although they have transformed the structure of the pastoral from a deductive to a dialectical framework—acknowledging in practice, as they could not in theory, the bearing of experience upon ethical analysis—they have not appreciated how their own inexperience of poverty or of social activism deprives them of any right to speak for the poor. Although they criticize the ideologies of both capitalism and socialism—preferring a pragmatic to an ideological method of social analysis—they have, in effect, adopted the neoconservative ideology of piecemeal reform. This contradiction between intention and performance has infected their interpretation of the preferential option for the poor.

II. *The Derivation of the Preferential Option for the Poor from the Biblical Notion of Justice*

The bishops say that the basis for "what is today called the 'preferential option for the poor' " is the biblical notion of justice, epitomized in how Jesus took the side of "those most in need, physically and spiritually." This example of Jesus, they say, challenges the church today to do likewise:

• It imposes a prophetic mandate to speak for those who have no one to speak for them, to be a defender of the defenseless, who in biblical terms are the poor.

• It also demands a compassionate vision that enables the Church to see things from the side of the poor and powerless, and to assess life-style, policies, and social institutions in terms of their impact upon the poor.

• It summons the Church also to be an instrument in assisting people to experience the liberating power of God in their own lives, so that they may respond to the Gospel in freedom and dignity.

• Finally, and most radically, it calls for an emptying of self, both individually and corporately, that allows the Church to experience the power of God in the midst of poverty and powerlessness (4:52; paragraphing added).

In other words, as the bishops say in the Pastoral Message (no. 17) accompanying the letter, for Christians to make "fundamental 'option for the poor' " means to "speak for the voiceless, to defend the defenseless, to assess lifestyles, policies and social institutions in terms of their impact upon the poor."

The question is, though, whether this interpretation of the Bible is historical or ideological. To settle that question, there must first be some understanding of what "history" means. "History" has both a subjective and an objective meaning: it refers to the writing and to the making of history. Each of these aspects has two facets. Writing history comprises both the process of research, interpretation, and narration necessary to understand the past—what can be called "historiography"— and the motive behind this process of understanding the past—what can be called "historicity." Likewise, making history includes both the process of human development—what can be called the "historical"—and the sedimentation of this process in the environment, in customs and institutions, and in memory—what can be called the "historic." Historiography and the historic are, by necessity, identical in the concrete, for historiography is limited to recovering from the past what can be detected from its remains, while the historic becomes whatever historiography can make into and make out of the remains of the past. But this identity of historiography with the historic does not necessarily produce a synthesis of historicity with the historical. For one thing, the historicity behind the historiography must be a genuine concern for understanding what really happened—what can be called "historical consciousness"—and not just a propensity to exploit the past for the sake of present interests—what can be called "presentness." Presentness can take the form either of anachronism (attributing present conditions to the past) or of archaism (appropriating past conditions for the present). On the other side of the equation, historical events remain "prehistoric" to the extent the people involved in them do not record what they meant and leave only relics of their own activities; they become "historic" even prior to any subsequent historiography, however, to the extent people record what they mean by their actions and how they interpret the consequences. The development of historical consciousness—in the sense of a concern for the historical as such, of an interest in relics as well as in records, of an intent to interpret what records reveal in addition to what they say—is itself a modern achievement, of which the relics are academic historiography and the records are the history and philosophy of history.

Thus the question of whether the bishops' interpretation of the biblical basis for a preferential option for the poor is ideological or historical comes down to whether the interpretation is a product of presentness or of historical consciousness. And that question can be settled, for all practical purposes, by determining whether the interpretation conforms to the standards of modern historiography. If it does not, it is a product of presentness, either the anachronism of attributing modern conditions to the biblical era (what, in theology, is called liberalism or modernism) or the archaism of supposing biblical conditions apply to modern culture (what, in theology, is called fundamentalism). In either case, the interpretation would be ideological. From a faith perspective, however, a historical interpretation would also be a theological one, neither modernist nor fundamentalist, but simply a contemporary understanding of what the Bible, together with other records and relics of the biblical era, reveals as well as says about what really happened at the time.

The evidence from the pastoral letter is ambivalent. Evidence that the preferential option for the poor is a product of presentness, and of a modernist rather than a fundamentalist persuasion, appears from the fact that the bishops seem to have made a preferential option for the poor, in all but the use of the term itself, before they ever looked to the Bible for any legitimation of the idea. This is clear from the single viewpoint from which they have chosen to analyze the U.S. economy, to interpret a commitment to human dignity, and to address policy issues.

This viewpoint is the one they adopted from Vatican II's *The Church in the Modern World:* "*The joys and hopes, the griefs and anxieties of the people of this age, especially those who are poor or in any*

*way afflicted, these too are the joys and hopes, the griefs and anx-
ieties of the followers of Christ"* (4:2). *It leads them to add a specific
difference to their generic standard for judging the morality of an
economy.* First the say: "Every perspective on economic life that is
human, moral, and Christian must be shaped by three questions:
What does the economy do for people? What does it do to people?
And how do people *participate* in it?" (§1). But then they modify
this to say: "Decisions must be judged in light of what they do *for*
the poor, what they do *to* the poor, and what they enable the poor
to do *for* themselves. The fundamental moral criterion for all economic decisions, policies, and institutions is this: They must be at
the service of *all people, especially the poor"* (§24). Thus the bishops
presume that care for the poor is the index of the morality of an
economy.

The "signs of the times" this principle leads the bishops to high-
light in the U.S. economy are, it is true, partly signs of hope (4:2,
added only in the third draft), but mostly they are signs of trouble:
the persistent and growing problems of unemployment, poverty, op-
pressive working conditions, hunger, malnutrition, and starvation
(4:3–4, 15–19); the conflict and suffering engendered by the "American experiment" in political and economic freedom (4:7); the gap
between the "American dream" of freedom and abundance for all
and the reality of need and poverty for many (4:14–19); the disparity
between the wealth and power of the United States and the poverty
and dependency of the less developed countries (4:6, 12, 13); and
the enormous "investment of human creativity and material resources" in the arms race (4:20). The viewpoint of identifying with
the poor leads the bishops, therefore, to emphasize the poverty and
not the wealth, the failures and not the successes, of the U.S. economy.

Likewise, this viewpoint shapes the moral vision the bishops urge
upon the American public. *"The dignity of the human person, realized in community with others, is,"* they say, *"the criterion against
which all aspects of economic life must be measured"* (4:28; see 25).
But they argue that the division of labor brought by the industrial
revolution, while it has produced job satisfaction for some, has also
resulted in "social fragmentation, a decline in seeing how one's work
serves the whole community and an increased emphasis on personal
goals and private interests" (4:22). The "common ground," "the public moral vision" necessary for getting the American people to renew
their commitment to human dignity is, they claim, for them to take
as "the fundamental moral criterion for all economic decisions, policies and institutions . . . the service of *all people, especially the
poor"* (4:24).

The same viewpoint of identification with the poor predetermines the economic policy issues the bishops have chosen to address. Unemployment, poverty, the farm crisis, and Third World dependency: these are the issues they found most relevant "to both the economic 'signs of the times' and the ethical norms of our tradition" (4:133). From the beginning to the end of the letter, therefore, the viewpoint of identification with the poor has shaped the bishops' outlook on the U.S. economy.

Doubtless, this viewpoint also shaped their interpretation of the Bible. But before assuming the attribution of the preferential option for the poor to the Bible is simply a product of presentness—something the bishops read into the Bible because of their concern about poverty in America—it is necessary to ask whether, instead, the bishops' concern about poverty in America was what sensitized them to the historical basis in the Bible for a preferential option for the poor. Certainly, the notes to the section on the Bible are replete with references to biblical scholars whose commitment to historical exegesis is impeccable.

Yet the bishops' use of modern biblical scholarship has been only partially successful. The literary-historical hermeneutic they have chosen to adopt has, indeed, enabled them to appreciate the distinctive significance of various books and sections of the Bible for gaining an understanding of the biblical sense of justice. They have treated the Bible as a record and asked what it has to say about poverty. Thus there is no denying the authenticity of their interpretation of the biblical basis for a preferential option for the poor. It is neither a modernist nor a fundamentalist ideology, but a biblical theology, couched in biblical categories and reflecting the biblical authors' own interpretations of current events. It shows that according to the Bible faith in God is a sufficient condition for a preferential option for the poor.

The framework of the biblical categories of creation, covenant, community, and discipleship is what the bishops have adopted to impart their interpretation of the biblical sense of justice (4:31–55). This comprises, as they interpret it, both righteousness and good judgment. In either sense, justice was, the prophets said, the practical expression of faith in God, the author of creation and covenant, just as injustice was tantamount to idolatry. The acid test of the justice of an action was whether it manifested a concern for the poor and the powerless. This was the concern Jesus made the burden of his mission. To the poor he preached the good news that "at hand" was the reign of God, in which the Son of Man would judge people by their treatment of the poor, the outcast, and the oppressed. The church is, the bishops say, the community of those who heard this news and, as disciples of Christ, have ever since dedicated themselves to serving others, particularly the poor, even to the point of being willing, like Christ, to sacrifice their lives. The history of Christianity shows, they add, that this is the ideal the Christian community has tried to live up to "in very different historical and cultural contexts" (4:56-59). They conclude, therefore, that a concern for social justice— more specifically a preferential option for the poor—is "not at all peripheral to the central mystery at the heart of the Church," but "integral to the proclamation of the Gospel and part of the vocation of every Christian today" (4:60).

But what the bishops have not done is also to treat the Bible as a relic of its time and ask what it reveals about the meaning of poverty in the biblical era. That is, they have failed to employ the kind of social-historical hermeneutic that some biblical scholars—including many of those they cite—have appropriated from modern historiography to reach an understanding of what the Bible reveals about the context in which it was written.[30] Hence, they have not fully appreciated the theological significance of the biblical notion of justice, for, as Wayne Meeks has remarked, "The force of a belief-statement is determined by the whole matrix of social patterns within which it is uttered."[31] They were able to understand that the Bible *says* faith in God is a *sufficient* condition for a preferential option for the poor, but they were unable to appreciate how it also *reveals* that a preferential option for the poor is a *necessary* condition for faith in God.[32]

Faith in Yahweh as the one true god emerged as a covenantal bond to unite the peasant farmers and transhumant nomads of the tribes of Israel into an intertribal confederacy capable of maintaining itself as a free and egalitarian society against the onslaughts of surrounding empires[33] This belief in God as the guarantor of a free and egalitarian society became the motif for the biblical interpretation of the patriarchal period and the Exodus as steps leading toward the liberation of Israel and for the subsequent legitimation of the monarchy as the divinely anointed (messianic) means for preserving Israel's independence in a new social context.[34] When the monarchy betrayed Israel into subjugation and exile by combining oppression with idolatry, the prophets recalled Israel, once again poor and powerless, to the faith of its covenant with Yahweh, the sole guarantor of freedom and justice.[35] This time, however, the covenant was to be heartfelt and universal; Israel, as the servant of Yahweh, would bear its poverty as a sacrifice for the salvation of the world; and an ideal Messiah, rather than a military leader, would be the one to bring freedom and justice.[36] Yet messianic pretenders nevertheless led abortive military revolts against the Ptolemies and the Romans in vain efforts to re-establish Israel as a Davidic kingdom. Their defeats induced both the Temple priesthood and the wealthy Sadducees to collaborate with the conquerors in imposing ruinous taxes upon the rest of the population.[37] At this point, the destitute peasantry from the same hill country of Galilee where the Mosaic covenant had originated began in desperation to hope Yahweh would keep faith with by sending a Son of Man finally to restore the world to the peace and justice in which they believed he had created it.[38]

This social-historical interpretation of the Hebrew Bible is complemented by the social-historical interpretation of the New Testament.[39] It is interpreted as the good news that Jesus of Nazareth had fulfilled the hopes of the poor of Israel by inaugurating the reign of God.[40] Born among the destitute peasants of Galilee, Jesus proclaimed that he was the one whom Yahweh, like a Father, had sent to lead his children, the poor, into a reign of freedom and justice.[41] If at first Jesus was, like David, a bandit who promised the people a military victory over their oppressors, at least by the time of his baptism he had repented of such folly and turned to God for help. But the threat his leadership posed to the authorities, Jewish as well as Roman, led them—after Jesus had carried his campaign into the Temple precincts in Jerusalem—to capture him, try him, and crucify him as a would-be revolutionary.[42] Still, the Jesus movement, destitute and persecuted though it was, continued to believe Jesus had instituted the reign of God upon earth and, true to his Spirit, held everything in common, spreading the word of his wonders and waiting anxiously for his second coming in glory.[43] This communitarian and egalitarian ethic did not survive the demise of the primitive Christian community in Jerusalem and the concomitant disillusionment over the indefinite postponement of the eschaton.[44] Throughout the empire, the Christian sect spread among urban, upwardly mobil artisans and freedmen, Gentiles as well as Jews, who believed the reign of God would bring them the status to which they felt their power entitled them.[45] Sharing their possessions with poor Christians did remain a mandate for such people, but they did not take it to require either voluntary poverty or communal property.[46] Paul's attempt to get this movement of petty bourgeoisie to support the "poor among the saints in Jerusalem" was futile.[47] The Christian church developed as a stratified rather than an egalitarian society; almsgiving instead of communal property became the normal way to share wealth with the poor; and, short of the millennium, poverty became something to be mitigated rather than eliminated. Yet to Jesus of Nazareth the church attributed the titles Son of Man, Messiah/

Christ, Lord, and Son of God, to signify its faith in him as the agent of the unprecedented social transformation implied in even such an attenuated egalitarianism.

Just as the bishops ignore the social history of the Biblical era, so do they gild the history of the church's impact on society. The history of the Church is the sad tale of how it perpetuated the kind of society it was founded to supplant. Before Constantine initiated the process which eventually led to the establishment of Christianity as the official religion of the empire, apostles of the church demonstrated the power of God, not by trying to change the social structure, but by working miracles, mainly healings, in God's name.[48] Afterwards, the church took every advantage of its privileged position, first to get landowners to convert their households en masse, then to have the state build Christian basilicas on the ruins of temples destroyed by Christian mobs, force conversion upon the peasants of the countryside, and persecute any heretics as also traitors.[49] The apostolic tradition of communal ownership remained alive in the social teaching of the early fathers of the church, who inveighed against the violent usurpation of property by theft and conquest.[50] And the vita apostolica of "evangelical poverty" became the peculiar pursuit of those who entered "religion" as hermits or monks, nuns or sisters, only too often to find themselves indicted as heretics unless they conformed to the church hierarchy. The church as a whole, though, became the legitimating force of an empire still as stratified and authoritarian as when it had first persecuted it.[51]

The subsequent history of Christianity has shown no significant change in the church's conception of its social role until modern times.[52] Even in the Reformation, otherwise cataclysmic, the mainline churches persecuted poor people's movements. True, Puritanism had a revolutionary role in the transition from the medieval to the modern world, but it is a matter of historical controversy how much it produced or was produced by social change. At any rate, the political and social revolutions of the modern era were all directed against the church as the bastion of old regime. Only in reaction to these revolutions did the church, either Catholic or Protestant, finally recall its social mission, and even then "Christian socialism" in the Protestant churches served as often as "social Catholicism" in the Catholic church to forestall more radical change as to promote social justice.

What this means is that the bishops' assertion of a biblical basis for a preferential option of the poor is ideological as well as historical. But the ideology of this interpretation does not come from their use of the Bible to legitimate a critique of poverty in the United States.

That is, on the contrary, what enabled them to be sensitive to the contemporary meaning of the biblical sense of justice. It made their interpretation neither a modernist nor a fundamentalist ideology, but a historical understanding of biblical theology. No, what makes their interpretation ideological is, first, their failure to go beyond what the Bible has to say, to find out what it reveals, about justice. While the Bible says, in effect, that faith in God was a sufficient condition for a preferential option for the poor, it reveals, in effect, that this preferential option for the poor was a necessary condition for faith in God. The bishops also omit to confess that it was because the church failed to act upon this option, becoming rich and condoning poverty, that many of its members finally lost their faith in God and, revolting against the church, chose the kernel of social justice rather than the husk of empty ritual. And the bishops show no recognition of the fact that only this forcible impoverishment led the Catholic church to recover—initially and partially in papal "social doctrine," latterly and more completely in the "preferential option for the poor"—the grounds of its faith. Therefore, the bishops' interpretation of the preferential option for the poor is ideological rather than historical insofar as it fails to recognize the significance of this option for faith in God and implies the church has always acted upon the option.

III. *The Ethical Analysis of the Preferential Option for the Poor*

The American Catholic bishops give Jesus' mandate to the Church as the motive for their preferential option for the poor, but they also try to justify this option on a purely rational basis. For the point of the pastoral is to convince not just Catholics but the American people as a whole that "*the obligation to provide justice for all means that the poor have the single most urgent claim on the conscience of the nation*" (4:86; see 61). The reason? Human rights, the bishops contend, include not only the civil and political rights—to freedom of speech, worship, and assembly—already guaranteed in the Constitution; they also comprise social and economic rights—recognized, for example, in the United Nations Universal Declaration of Human Rights—to basic material needs, to earning a living, to social security, and to active participation, through decent employment or property ownership, in the economic life of the community (4:79–88, 95, 290, 295–96). And these economic rights require positive action, by the nation as well as by individuals, since they are forms of empowerment, not, like civil rights, simply immunities from interference (4:81–82). Hence, the highest moral priority for America and Americans is, in the bishops' opinion, to enable the poor to enjoy the economic rights of which they have hitherto been deprived (4:89–94). "As individuals and as a nation, therefore, we are called to make a fundamental 'option for the poor' " (4:87).[53]

This option implies, as the bishops interpret it, an obligation and an opportunity. For the "more fortunate" it implies, in Paul VI's words, that they " 'should renounce some of their rights so as to place their goods more generously at the service of others' " (4:87; see also 70, 75, 106, 115, 119, 291–92). For the poor, that they should be empowered "to become active participants in the life of society," able like everyone else "to share in and contribute to the common good" (4:88; see 71–72, 80, 91, 96–97, 119). Thus the option the bishops say should be made for the poor would require the more fortunate to sacrifice some of their economic rights so that the poor could vindicate theirs.

This is the appeal that has prompted the charge of ideological bias in the social ethics of *Economic Justice for All*. Despite the bishops' contention that "the 'option for the poor' . . . is not an adversarial slogan that pits one group or class against another" (4:88), it certainly represents a departure form the traditional foundation of Catholic social theology upon human dignity and the common good.[54] But in making this shift, the American bishops were simply following the lead of Rome. What obscures the significance of this shift, though, is that they have not admitted that the preferential option for the poor amounts to the adoption of a socialist principle of social justice and attempted nevertheless to justify this as the best way to protect human dignity and assure the common good.

First, then, the bishops' adoption of the preferential option for the poor is simply an acceptance of a recent shift in Catholic social theology. No doubt about it, the "preferential option for the poor" is a departure from the Catholic social theology of the "social doctrine" period, from Leo XIII to John XXIII. "At this stage," Donal Dorr has written, "Catholic social teaching had come to represent in practice almost the exact opposite of what is now meant by an 'option for the poor.' "[55] In vain does one look in the scholarly summaries of the Catholic social teaching of this period for any hint of such an option; on the contrary, there is a clear recognition of the aim of Catholic "social doctrine" to avert class conflict.[56] But this was the period, we must remember, when Catholic social theology was, in fact, ideological. Rationalist in form, reactionary in substance, self-serving in intent, the "social doctrine" of this period was an attempt to avert the threat of a socialist revolution by mitigating the evils of capitalism, all in the hope of somehow restoring in the process the

Church's medieval hegemony (*potestas indirecta*) over the social order. "While theoretically offering a 'third way' that was neither capitalist nor socialist, in practice it gave solid religious legitimation to the 'free enterprise' model of society."[57] This bias was not overcome until first John XXIII and then Paul VI, forswearing a distinctively Catholic ideology, inaugurated a more evenhanded evaluation of socialism and capitalism alike.[58]

The "preferential option for the poor" did not enter Catholic social teaching until the Latin American bishops introduced it at their conference in Medellín (1968).[59] But Paul VI, who had attended the conference, sanctioned the idea by using the term "preferential respect for the poor" in *Octogesima Adveniens* (1971), the *locus* to which the American bishops refer in *Economic Justice for All* for their adoption of the term (4:87). Since then, the option for the poor has become the *leitmotif* of the Catholic social teaching.[60] At Puebla (1979), the Latin American bishops, in the face of some internal opposition, explicitly reaffirmed their stand at Medellín: "We affirm the need for conversion on the part of the whole Church to a preferential option for the poor, an option aimed at their integral liberation."[61] John Paul II, in attendance at the conference, added his endorsement of Medellín's "option for the Latin American human being seen whole, its preferential but not exclusive love for the poor, and its encouragement of full, integral liberation for human beings and peoples."[62] The following year, in Brazil, he himself used the term "option for the poor" to speak of the necessity for the Church to link a commitment to social justice to its mission of evangelization.[63] To this papal endorsement of the term was added the sanction of the extraordinary Roman synod (1985) convened to "celebrate, verify, and promote" the Second Vatican Council: "This preferential option [i.e., the church's mission "in the service of the poor, the oppressed and the outcast"] means that the church must prophetically denounce every form of poverty and oppression and everywhere defend and promote the fundamental and inalienable rights of the human person."[64]

Nor did the two instructions on liberation theology from the Congregation for the Doctrine of the Faith do anything to reduce this refoundation of Catholic social theology upon a preferential option for the poor. In the first instruction, a warning against Marxist tendencies in "certain forms of liberation theology," Cardinal Ratzinger emphasized, "This warning should in no way be interpreted as a disavowal of all those who want to respond generously and with an authentic evangelical spirit to the 'preferential option for the poor.' "[65] And though he condemned Marxist-inspired interpretation of the

New Testament, he said, nevertheless, that Jesus' teaching required the Church to aid the poor throughout the world in their struggle for a radical reform of structural poverty and violence.[66] In the second instruction, devoted to "the main elements of the Christian doctrine on freedom and liberation," Ratzinger deliberately substituted for "the preferential option for the poor" the alternative formula of "a love of preference for the poor."[67] Yet the lengthy section under this new title is similar in biblical references and much of its substance to the parallel section on "the preferential option for the poor" in the Puebla statement, and the "love of preference," like the "preferential option," impels the Church to help the poor not only by works of charity but by support of structural social reform. Despite a preference for personal conversion over the "myth" of revolution, the instruction asserts a biblical mandate for the Church to commit itself to the liberation of the poor and oppressed.[68]

There can be little doubt, therefore, that in advocating a preferential option for the poor, the American bishops are simply accommodating to the shift that has taken place in Catholic social theology in the last fifteen to twenty years. Yet the critics are still correct to say that, in doing so, the bishops are urging the American people to adopt a socialist principle of justice. To appreciate why, it is necessary to understand that each of the alternative conceptions in the modern debate about social justice is the product of a specific ideology (table 1).[69]

Table 1
Ideological Principles of Justice

Basis of Contribution	Basis of Distribution	
	Merit	Need
Choice	Libertarianism	Anarchism
Ability	Liberalism	Socialism

* *

Ideology	Principle of Justice
Libertarianism	"From each according to choice, to each according to merit."
Liberalism	"From each according to ability, to each according to merit."
Anarchism	"From each according to choice, to each according to need."
Socialism	"From each according to ability, to each according to need."

Each ideology presumes that the principle of social justice comprises a duty to contribute to the common good and a correlative right to share in the distribution of it.[70] Where they differ is in the particular combination of bases they recognize as constitutive of this principle. Libertarianism and liberalism both assume justice is served if people get what they deserve. But for libertarianism, this is accomplished if people profit or lose from the return what they choose to invest of their fortune (that is, whatever they are fortunate enough to possess). "Merit" is interpreted as "value" (in the economic sense), and social justice is reduced to commutative justice. For liberalism, though, just desserts are the rewards or punishments people get from adding to or subtracting from the common good in accordance with their ability to contribute to it. Equal opportunity becomes, therefore, a condition of justice, and justice acquires a specifically political as well an economic dimension. By contrast to these two ideologies, anarchism and socialism both suppose that social justice requires people to get from society whatever they need. Anarchism believes this can best be accomplished by allowing everyone freely to choose the kind of contribution one wants to make to the community. The assumption is that freedom is the condition for equality, and consensus the medium of democracy. But socialism rests upon the contrary assumption that it is up to society to judge what each person should contribute to the common good. For socialists, equality is the condition for freedom, and ability the criterion of social responsibility. Each ideology—moderate or radical, individualist or collectivist—assumes that the basis of distribution provides the motivation for people to contribute to society what society must have to distribute enough to them in return.

Of these four ideologies, it is clearly socialism that is implicit in the American bishops' interpretation of the preferential option for the poor. The combination of bases they incorporate in the contributive and distributive clauses of the principle of social justice with which they interpret the preferential option for the poor is "From each according to one's ability, to each according to one's need."

Contributive justice, they say, implies that each should give according to one's ability. For it entails "that persons have the obligation to be active and productive participants in the life of society and that society has a duty to enable them to participate in this way" (4:71). This means, they specify, that those who can contribute to the common good—whether as owners, managers, or workers—must do so, and must do it in proportion to their ability to contribute (see 4:84, 96–117). "For example," they say, "a system of taxation based on assessment according to ability to pay is a prime necessity for the fulfillment of these social obligations" (4:76; see 202). And those who *cannot* contribute to the common good—the poor—*must* be empowered to do so, and must be empowered in proportion to the demands of human dignity and communal solidarity (4:80–84, 88, 91, 188, 292). The primary means the bishops advise for doing this under present circumstances is "work with adequate pay for all who seek it," but they also advocate the possibility of a widespread ownership of productive property (4:73; see 80, 91, 103, 114, 137, 300). The goal, negatively stated, would be to eliminate what they call the "social sin" of marginalization and powerlessness; positively it would be to guarantee everyone "the ability to participate actively in the economic, political, and cultural life of society" (4:77–78). The obligation of reaching it falls, in a balance between the principles of solidarity and subsidiarity, upon both the private and the public sectors (4:119–24; see 99–101, 189). It binds the powerful and the affluent to "empower the poor to become self-sufficient," just as it binds the poor themselves to "work together as individuals and families to build up their communities by acts of social solidarity and justice" (4:119, 198–99). And it requires, the bishops say, the reform of economic and social institutions as well as "positive steps to overcome the legacy of injustice" inherent in patterns of discrimination (4:72–73, 76).

Correlatively, distributive justice implies, the bishops say, the right of each to receive according to one's needs. This right, too, implies both an individual and a social, both a private and a public, obligation. It requires individuals "to come to the relief of the poor . . . not merely out of [their] superfluous goods," but even to the sacrifice of otherwise justifiable rights to certain conditions of employment or to the use of their own property (4:70, 87, 90, 106, 115). It obliges a society like the United States, where there is no absolute scarcity of resources, to fulfill the basic economic rights of every member of the community (4:70). As the bishops explain it, there is no excuse, in theory or in practice, for American society not to meet the needs of the poor.

From the viewpoint of both contributive and distributive justice, therefore, the bishops advocate a socialist principle of justice.[71] They also treat work, in the socialist mode, as both an obligation in contributive justice and a need in distributive justice (4:72–73, 80, 91, 97, 103, 136, 151).[72] They interpret capital as a product of labor (4:8, 96, 113, 303). They subordinate the right of private property to the demands of the common good, which, in the words of John Paul II, may even entail "the socialization, under suitable conditions, of certain means of production" (4:115). The kind of widespread ownership of productive property they advocate would be incompatible only with the subspecies of socialism found in communism, or state capitalism. Although they deny that "a flat, arithmetical equality of income and wealth is a demand of justice," they criticize the injustice and the danger latent in the "extreme inequalities of income and consumption" in the United States today, and they demand enough equality for everyone to be able to participate actively in economic, political, and social life (4:74, 78). The radical reforms they adumbrate for the "new American experiment" in economic rights—worker ownership, community development, national economic planning, and world government—are all socialist goals (4:295—325). In spirit as in letter, therefore, the bishops' conception of justice is socialist.

Yet this ideological conception of justice does not impugn the theological character of the preferential option for the poor. The transcendence of theology to class interests does not require of it a neutrality before conflicts of interest but an unmasking of any injustice hidden in social conflict, a task which makes theology functionally equivalent in the concrete to an ideology, but an ideology of the oppressed rather than of any dominant class.[73] What is more, in a modern society like the United States, with a coherent social structure but competing social classes, any conception of justice, whether theological or secular, is bound to be ideological.[74] The only question is whether, in Karl Mannheim's terminology, it will function as an ideology in the strict sense—that is, as a rationalization of a dominant class's monopoly of power—or, rather, as a utopia— that is, as a rationalization of an oppressed class's quest for power. There is neither the possibility nor the necessity for its advocates to be neutral about the concrete implications of their prescription for protecting human dignity and achieving the common good. By supporting the rights of the poor to social justice, therefore, the preferential option for the poor in *Economic Justice for All* is at the same time both ideological—in Mannheim's terms, though, utopian, rather than an ideological—and theological. The only question is why the bishops have declined to be overt about the character of the principle they have chosen to articulate their conception of social justice.

IV. The Policy Proposals Based on the Preferential Option for the Poor

The practical question about the preferential option for the poor in *Economic Justice for All* is whether it is as challenging in policy as it is in principle. The pastoral is, after all, a political document, not an ethical treatise. But if the option can be interpreted as revolutionary in theory, the bishops have explained it as reformist in effect.

We have already seen how they declined to analyze the American economic system and opted, instead, to examine "some aspects of the economy where . . . reforms are realistically possible" (4:132). This precluded any direct confrontation between the preferential option and the U.S. economy. To the extent the bishops have confined their use of the option to the justification of reforms within the system, they have made it into a support of the system itself. It thereby functions as an ideology in the invidious (that is, Mannheim's) sense of the term.

What is more, the connection the bishops have made between the preferential option and economic problems is sometimes obscure and superficial. They do not even mention the option in dealing with unemployment or the farm crisis. In analyzing poverty, they refer to it only in passing (4:170, 186). Only in examining the relationship between the U.S. economy and the developing nations (and, then, beginning with the third draft) do the bishops use the preferential option as a principle of analysis and an inspiration for policy directives (4:252, 258–60, 263, 269, 274–76, 283, 291). Perhaps because they did not conceive of the option themselves, they did not appreciate its full ramifications for the American context.

But it is in the nature of the policy proposals themselves that the reformist character of the pastoral becomes most evident. True, the issues the bishops have chosen to address are all concerned with poverty—poverty itself, of course; but also unemployment, the farm crisis, and Third World debt—and the policies they propose for dealing with these issues are obviously meant to attach the underlying problem of which they are only the symptoms. And it is also true that the policies the bishops propose—full employment, the eradication of poverty, support for the family farm, and global interdependence—are more radical than the majority of Americans, including the Catholic laity, are now likely to accept. What is more, the long-term possibilities they broach as means to institute a "new American experiment" in economic rights—worker ownership, community development, national economic planning, and world government—are truly revolutionary in their implications. The problem is, though, how seriously the bishops mean their proposals to be taken.[75] They say they are proposing things to which people have rights—but what kind of rights? That question can, perhaps, best be answered within a matrix of distinctions Ronald Dworkin has devised for denoting kinds of rights (table 2):[76]

The denotation of rights requires a specification of both the basis of justification and the form of definition. Justification is by insti-

Table 2
The Nature of Rights

Basis of Justification	Form of Definition	
	Concrete	Abstract
Institution	Legal Right: Entitlement	Constitutional Right: Warrant
Background	Social Right: Claim	Ethical Right: Need

tution if a society or a social unit formally acknowledges the legitimacy of a particular course of action; it is only in the background, however, if there is but an arguable basis for the right in cultural conditions or ethical theory. Yet a basis in the background does have the compensatory advantage of being able to justify institutional change—new legislation or constitutional amendment—to enable the exercise of a right. Correlative to the basis of justification is the form of definition. The form is concrete if it specifies the conditions for the exercise of a right and its relationship to other rights, whereas it remains abstract if it denotes only the *prima facie* validity and the generic practicability of the right. Here again, though, abstractly defined rights do have the countervailing value of being necessary for adjudicating conflicts between existing concrete rights or for articulating new ones. At one extreme, therefore, are the concrete institutional rights to which law provides an *entitlement* and, at the other, the abstract background rights for which ethical theory indicates a human *need*. In between are, on the one hand, the concrete background rights to which there is a *claim* on the basis of social conditions and, on the other, the abstract institutional rights for which a constitution supplies the *warrant*.

Now the American bishops clearly believe that in the preferential option for the poor they have established a basis in the ethical theory for a human *need* to certain economic rights (4:80, 95). This basis, they assert, is not just theological, but—as is evident from the United Nations Declaration of Human Rights—rational as well. It establishes rights to the minimum conditions for "human dignity, social solidarity, and justice," which include basic material needs, the earning of a living, social security, and decent conditions of employment or property ownership. The obligation to make sure the poor enjoy these rights constitutes "the single most urgent claim on the conscience of the nation" (4:86). It sets certain moral priorities for the nation: the fulfillment of the basic needs of the poor, the empowerment of the poor to participate in economic life, the investment of wealth and energy for the benefit of the poor, and the organization of work and welfare for the support of the family (4:89–93). These priorities are not just policy proposals; they are fundamental norms (4:94). From them the bishops derive, first, the guidelines they recommend for action against unemployment, poverty, the farm crisis, and Third World indebtedness, and, then, the economic policies they advocate for guaranteeing full employment, for reducing (perhaps eradicating) poverty, for restoring the family farm, and for creating global economic interdependence. By the linkage they forge from the preferential option for the poor, through human dignity and social solidarity, through the foundation in justice of certain economic rights, to moral priorities for the nation, and thence to guidelines for action, the bishops clearly show that they believe the poor have a right—in the sense of a basic human *need*—to the implementation of the policies the bishops recommend for solving the problems of the U.S. economy.

Just as clearly, though, the bishops admit the poor have no right—in the sense of a constitutional *warrant*—to the institution of these policies. The Constitution of the United States, they acknowledge, recognizes civil and political, but not social and economic, rights. The first step to be taken, therefore, in gaining an acceptance of their program is, they say, to develop "a new cultural consensus that the basic economic conditions of human welfare are essential to human dignity and due persons by right" (4:83). Such a consensus is necessary if the United States is now to undertake an experiment in economic democracy comparable to the experiment it began two hundred years ago in political democracy (4:95). Just as "the nation's founders took daring steps to create structures of participation, mutual accountability, and widely distributed power," the American people, they argue, must now take steps "to expand economic participation, broaden the sharing of economic power, and make economic decisions more accountable to the common good" (4:297). But for the American people to do this they must understand and accept as basic norms the counterbalancing principles of solidarity and subsidiarity (4:64–67, 99–101), for which the precedent is clear in Catholic social teaching, but not in the American political tradition. Thus the measures the bishops think are necessary for creating a new "partnership for the common good"—worker ownership, community development, national economic planning, world governmen (4:298–325)—are not conditions to which they believe the poor have a right, in the sense of a constitutional *warrant*. And in the absence of such a *warrant* it would be difficult to secure the institution of policies for which they nevertheless believe ethical theory demonstrates a basic human *need*.

But do the bishops think, however, that social conditions in the United States give the poor a *claim* to the institution of these policies—with or without a constitutional amendment? They do seem to believe conditions are ripe for the government to make full employment a genuine possibility, contrary to those economists who contend such a policy would unleash inflation (4:151–57). But they do not seem to have decided whether the extremes of wealth and poverty and the vicious stereotyping of the poor in the United States mean that poverty in this country cannot be eradicated but just reduced (4:188 vs. 190). They profess to believe, however, that economic trends and government policies can be reversed to make the family farm once again the linchpin of agricultural development and from now on a center of resource conservation and justice to farm workers (4:231–49). No such nostalgia affects their view of international economic policy, though: for the United States to devote a significantly larger proportion of its GNP to development assistance or to take the lead in establishing a more equitable economic order would represent, they acknowledge, a "fundamental reform," a "systemic change" in American economic policy (4:259, 261–63, 277). What the bishops seem to hope for—in the absence, it must be said, of any persuasive evidence—is that economic possibilities will prevail over cultural trends to give the poor, in the Third World as well as in the United States, a right—in the sense of a *claim*—to a fairer share of the wealth of the U.S. economy.

The bishops' diffidence about asserting a basis in right for the policies they advocate increases when it comes to the question of what *entitlements* the poor may appeal to. Though there is a "nominal endorsement of the full employment ideal," there is, they admit, "no firm commitment to bringing it about" in fiscal or monetary policy (4:151; see 156). The relative success of Social Security, Medicare, and Medicaid in mitigating poverty is counterbalanced, they recognize, by the failure of other social welfare programs, which were "ill-designed, ineffective, and wasteful" (4:191–92). But in contrast to the more recent federal policy of supporting the largest farmers (4:222–23, 243), the bishops can point to a more traditional policy, embodied in the Preemption Acts and the Homestead Act, of encouraging a widespread and decentralized ownership of farmland (4:219) for their contention that farm families—and, for that matter, consumers—are entitled to government support of moderate-sized farms (4:231–33, 244–45). And to substantiate an *entitlement* to help for the poor of the Third World, they argue that the Marshall Plan is a precedent for the United States now to extend to the less developed countries the economic assistance it once gave Western Europe, while the Bretton Woods agreement is a precedent for the

United States to initiate a restructuring of the economic system, now to forestall revolution as previously to prevent war (4:259–63, 277). Yet, in the absence of a world government, the bishops concede, there is no legal authority to which the less developed countries can appeal for a strict *entitlement* to new economic rights (4:322–25). Hence, the bishops can allege only nominal ideals, ambivalent histories, antiquated policies, and remote precedents for any *entitlements* the poor may have to the policies they advocate on their behalf.

To summarize, when the bishops get to the policies to which they suppose the preferential option for the poor gives the poor a right, they are more radical in theory than in practice. They make a sound case in ethical theory for a *need* in human dignity and social solidarity to economic as well as civil rights. But they acknowledge the Constitution does not provide for economic rights the same *warrant* it contains for civil rights. And they admit American culture is biased against any *claim* from the wealth of the economy to a program for the eradication of poverty, either at home or abroad. Thus the bishops conclude, in effect, that in the United States the poor now have but a remote or a debatable *entitlement* to the benefits implied by a preferential option for the poor.

In a sense, this conclusion is not remarkable. After all, the Catholic bishops would have seen no need for a pastoral on the injustices of the U.S. economy if the American people had already acknowledged the poor were entitled to what the bishops believe they deserve. In that case, there would presumably have been no unemployment, no poverty, and no farm crisis in the United States and, in the Third World, no underdevelopment. There would have been no poor for whom the bishops had to urge a preferential option if everyone were enjoying everything to which one had a right.

Yet the bishops do not seem to have recognized that the "conversion of heart" they claim is necessary for bringing about a "transformation of social structures" (4:328) also requires the adoption of means radical enough to achieve this goal. Perhaps they are right to believe that for the American people to become convinced of the moral exigency of the preferential option for the poor nothing more will be necessary than for the Church as an institution and individual Catholics to exemplify the urgency of this option in their lives (See 4:328–60). But, surely, it is futile for them to recognize that the Constitution gives no warrant for economic rights and yet not to advocate an amendment of the Constitution. And it is naive of them to expect the American people, simply at their urging, to convert the goal of the U.S. economy from the creation for wealth for some to the elimination of poverty for all: to redirect macroeconomic policy from equilibrium (growth without inflation) to full employment; to sacrifice hard-won economic prerogatives to empower the poor; to reverse agricultural support from agribusinesses to family farms; or to renounce the residual hegemony of the United States in the global economy for the sake of Third World development. Unless the poor, abroad as well as at home, can organize to secure the institution of policies to which the bishops believe they have a right, they will never gain them. Therefore, if the bishops wish to make an effective preferential option for the poor, they will have to help the poor to organize.

Without such a commitment, the policy portion of *Economic Justice for All* may be theological in inspiration, but they are ideological in function. Unexceptionable in themselves, the policies the bishops propose lack a corresponding means of implementation. Though the pastoral has provoked resentment for the wealthy, it is likely to foster only resignation in the poor, legitimizing rather than unmasking the injustice of American economic policy. Whatever the bishops' intentions, the letter serves the interests of their predominantly upwardly mobile, middle-class flock.

Summary

In the "preferential option for the poor," the American Catholic bishops have adapted a principle from liberation theology to the analysis of the U.S. economy. The question we have asked is whether conservative critics are right to claim that this has perverted the message of *Economic Justice for All*, deforming traditional Catholic social theology into a covert socialist ideology. Our answer has been that the pastoral is ideological, all right, but that the ideology has come not from taking the "preferential option for the poor" too far, but from not taking it far enough. Hence, the bishops have failed to appreciate the full theological import of the option.

In the form of the letter, the American bishops have sought to take an approach much like one the Latin American bishops took in conceiving of the preferential option for the poor. They have jettisoned a logical distinction between principle and policy; they have adopted a dialectical rather than a deductive mode of argumentation; they have renounced any attachment to ideology. Yet they have also failed to recognize that circumstances of origin as well as circumstances of application can temper the rigor of principles; they have ignored the significance of their own inexperience of poverty for the task of representing the interests of the poor; they have implicitly accepted the legitimacy of the neoconservative ideology of piecemeal reform. Without the same openness to experience of the Latin American bishops, the American bishops have, inevitably, given the preferential option for the poor an interpretation as much ideological as theological.

The American bishops have recognized that the Bible says faith in God is a sufficient condition for a preferential option for the poor, but they have failed to see that it also reveals the preferential option for the poor to be a necessary condition for faith in God. They have accepted the shift in Catholic social theology from a defense of liberal capitalism to a preferential option for the poor, but they do not seem to have realized that this shift implies the acceptance of a socialist ideology of justice. They have educed from the preferential option for the poor policy proposals that might well eliminate the injustice of the U.S. economy, but they have not adopted effective means for getting the American people to embrace them. Therefore the theology of the preferential option for the poor becomes in *Economic Justice for All* largely an ideology in support of the convergent interests of the majority of the Catholic laity, of the American system, and of liberal capitalism.[77]

NOTES

My thanks to Ramapo College, particularly Robert Christopher and Stephen Arianias, and to the Ramapo College Foundation for release time and travel grants to aid in the writing of this article.

1. *Economic Justice for All: Pastoral Letter on Catholic Social Teaching and the U.S. Economy* (Washington, D.C.: National Conference of Catholic Bishops, 1986). References to any of the four drafts of this document will be by draft number and paragraph number, within parentheses in the text. Emphases in quotations will be from the document itself.

2. *Toward the Future: Catholic Social Thought and the U.S. Economy* (Tarrytown, NY: Lay Commission on Catholic Social Teaching and the U.S. Economy, 1984).

3. William E. Simon and Michael Novak, "Liberty and Justice for All" (New York: Lay Commission on Catholic Social Teaching and the U.S. Economy, November 1986), pp. 5–23.

4. See, for example, "The Church and Capitalism," *Business Week* (November 12, 1984), pp. 104–12.

5. For a summation of reactions, left and right, see Robert McClory, "Allergic Reaction to Bishops' Letter," *In These Times* (December 15, 1984), pp. 7–8.

6. William E. Simon, "The Bishops' Folly," *National Review* (April 5, 1985), pp. 28, 31; Michael Novak, "U.S. Catholics, U.S. Economy," *National Review* (November 30, 1984), p. 38. See also *Toward the Future*, pp. x, 4–8.

7. Simon and Novak, pp. 2, 4, 6.

8. Peter Steinfels, "The Bishops and Their Critics," *Dissent* (Spring, 1985), p. 182.

9. E. Bruce Douglass, "At the Heart of the Letter," *Commonweal* (June 21, 1985), p. 361.

10. Tom Bethell, "Prophecy at the Hilton," *National Review* (December 14, 1984), p. 23; see also, in the same issue, William F. Buckley, "Vapid Thought from Bishops," p. 54.

11. Simon and Novak, p. 4: "In bridging general principles with specific applications, the reasoning of the final draft is in places unmistakably ideological. . . . This is, of course, most obvious to those who do not share that ideology." See also Peter Berger, *The Capitalist Revolution: Fifty Propositions about Prosperity, Equality, and Liberty* (New York: Basic Books, 1986).

12. Vincent F. A. Golphin, "U.S. Bishops Move Economic Letter Ahead," *National Catholic Reporter* (July 5, 1985), p. 7.

13. I believe these stipulations are in accord with the ordinary meanings of both terms. For 'theology,' see G. F. Ackeren, "Theology," *New Catholic Encyclopedia* (New York: McGraw-Hill, 1967), 14:39–49). For 'ideology,' see the articles on the term by Edward Shils and Harry M. Johnson in *International Encyclopedia of the Social Sciences*, ed. David Sills (New York: Macmillan and Free Press, 1968), 7:66–85; by Mostafa Rejai in *Dictionary of the History of Ideas*, ed. Philip P. Wiener (New York: Scribner's, 1973), 2:552–59; and by David Braybrooke in *Encyclopedia of Philosophy*, ed. Paul Edwards (New York: Macmillan; London: Collier Macmillan, 1967), 4:124–27.

14. For a criticism of this approach, see William E. Murnion, "The American Catholic Bishops' Peace Pastoral: A Critique of Its Logic," *Horizons*, 13/1 (1986), 67–89.

15. Jean-Yves Calvez and Jacques Perrin, *The Church and Social Justice: The Social Teaching of the Popes from Leo XII to Pius XII (1878–1958)* (Chicago: Henry Regnery, 1961), pp. 58–74. This was the methodology of the 1919 "Bishop's Program of Social Reconstruction"; see Aaron I. Abell, ed., *American Catholic Thought on Social Questions* (Indianapolis and New York: Bobbs–Merrill, 1968), p. 327.

16. Marie-Dominique Chenu, La "doctrine sociale" de l'Eglise comme idéologie (Paris: Les Editions du Cerf, 1977), pp. 63, 90; see also Christine Gudorf, Catholic Social Teaching on Liberation Themes (Lanham, MD: University Press of America, 1980), pp. 55–59.

17. Pope John XIII, Pacem in Terris., in Joseph Gremillion, ed., The Gospel of Peace and Justice: Catholic Social Teaching Since Pope John XXIII (Maryknoll, NY: Orbis, 1976), nos. 39–45, 75–79, 126–129.

18. "Pastoral Constitution on the Church in the Modern World (Gaudium et Spes)," in Walter M. Abbott, ed., The Documents of Vatican II, intro. Lawrence Cardinal Shehan and trans. Joseph Gallagher (New York: Herder and Herder and Association Press, 1966), nos. 4–10.

19. Pope Paul VI, Octogesima Adveniens, in Gremillion, no. 4.

20. Gustavo Guttièrrez, A Theology of Liberation: History, Politics and Salvation, trans. and ed. Sister Caridad and John Eagleson (Maryknoll, NY: Orbis, 1973), pp. 6–13.

21. Simon and Novak, p. 18, note that the "bishops . . . maintain a standard of living suitable to their station, which certainly places them in the 80%–95% range of all incomes (for 1984, between $45,300 and $73,230), if not in the top 5% (above $73,230)."

22. See the reflection of this approach in the 1919 "Bishops' Program of Social Reconstruction," otherwise quite progressive for its time, in Abell, pp. 347–48.

23. Chenu, pp. 15–38; Joseph N. Moody, ed., Church and Society: Catholic Social and Political Thought and Movements, 1789–1950 (New York: Arts Inc., 1953); A. R. Vidler, A Century of Social Catholicism: 1820–1920 (London: SPCK, 1964), especially pp. x–xii, 100–09, 125–29; Richard L. Camp, The Papal Ideology of Social Reform: A Study of Historical Development, 1878–1967 (Leiden: E. J. Brill, 1969), pp. 111–37, 163–64.

24. Chenu, pp. 87–96; Donal Dorr, Option for the Poor: A Hundred Years of Vatican Social Teaching (Dublin: Gill and Macmillan; Maryknoll, NY: Orbis, 1983), p. 255.

25. See Bishop James S. Rausch's introduction to Gremillion, pp. ix–xi.

26. Quentin Quade, ed., The Pope and Revolution: John Paul II Confronts Liberation Theology, foreword Richard John Neuhaus (Washington, DC: Ethics and Public Policy Center, 1982), pp. 6–7, 13, 17.

27. Pope John Paul II, "Opening Address at Puebla," Puebla and Beyond: Documentation and Commentary, ed. John Eagleson and Philip Scharper (Maryknoll, NY: Orbis, 1979), p. 69.

28. Daniel Bell, The End of Ideology (New York: Free Press, 1960); Chaim I. Waxman, ed., The End of Ideology Debate (New York: Funk & Wagnalls, 1968); M. Rejai, ed., Decline of Ideology? (Chicago-New York: Aldine-Atherton, 1971).

29. Although the burden of Simon and Novak's criticism of the pastoral is that, in relying upon government intervention to eliminate poverty, it ignores the efficacy of the free market, they nevertheless assert "it is, clearly, a procapitalist document" (p. 8).

30. For the difference between a literary-historical and a social-historical hermeneutic, see Norman K. Gottwald, The Hebrew Bible: A Socio-Literary Introduction (Philadelphia: Fortress, 1985), pp. 5–34; see also Howard Clark Kee, Miracle in the Early Christian World: A Study in Sociohistorical Method (New Haven and London: Yale University Press, 1983), pp. 1–77; Wayne A. Meeks, The First Urban Christians: The Social World of the Apostle Paul (New Haven and London: Yale University Press, 1983), pp. 1–8.

31. Meeks, p. 164.

32. See Norman K. Gottwald, *The Bible and Liberation: Political and Social Hermeneutics*, rev. ed. (Maryknoll, NY: Orbis, 1981); Willy Schottrof and Wolfgang Stegemann, eds., *God of the Lowly: Sociohistorical Interpretations of the Bible*, trans. Matthew J. O'Connell (Maryknoll, NY: Orbis, 1984).

33. Norman K. Gottwald, *The Tribes of Yahweh: A Sociology of the Religion of Liberated Israel, 1250–1050 B.C.E.* (Maryknoll, NY: Orbis Books, 1979), pp. 34–46, 65–66, 489–590, 642–49, 700–09. See Stephen Charles Mott, *Biblical Ethics and Social Change* (New York and Oxford: Oxford University Press, 1982), pp. 65–70.

34. Gottwald, *Tribes of Yahweh*, pp. 32–44; idem, *Hebrew Bible*, pp. 223–27, 325–36.

35. Gottwald, *Hebrew Bible*, pp. 348–64, 374–404.

36. Gottwald, *Hebrew Bible*, pp. 482–502.

37. Gottwald, *Hebrew Bible*, pp. 443–56.

38. Richard A. Horsley, "The Sicarii: Ancient Jewish Terrorists," *Journal of Religion*, 59 (1979), 435–58; idem, "Ancient Jewish Banditry and the Revolt against Rome, A.D. 66–70," *Catholic Biblical Quarterly*, 43 (1981), 422–24; idem, "Popular Messianic Movements around the Time of Jesus," *Catholic Biblical Quarterly*, 46 (1984), 471–95; Richard A. Horsley and John S. Hanson, *Bandits, Prophets, and Messiahs: Popular Movements at the Time of Jesus* (New York: Seabury, 1985).

39. See John H. Elliott, ed., *Social-Scientific Criticism of the New Testament and Its Social World*, Semeia 35 (Decatur, GA: Scholars Press, 1986).

40. Walter E. Pilgrim, *Good News to the Poor: Wealth and Poverty in Luke-Acts* (Minneapolis: Augsburg, 1981), pp. 57–84; Richard Batey, *Jesus and the Poor* (New York: Harper & Row, 1972).

41. David L. Mealand, *Poverty and Expectation in the Gospel* (London: SPCK, 1980), pp. 4–9, 61–87; Pilgrim, pp. 39–47; Wolfgang Stegemann, *The Gospel and the Poor*, trans. Dietlinde Elliott (Philadelphia: Fortress, 1984), pp. 23–24.

42. Stegemann, pp. 25–30.

43. Martin Hengel, *Property and Riches in the Early Church: Aspects of a Social History of Early Christianity*, trans. John Bowden (Philadelphia: Fortress, 1974), pp. 31–34; Pilgrim pp. 148–59; Mealand, pp. 39–60; Stegemann, p. 22.

44. Hengel, pp. 35–36; Mealand, pp. 39–41.

45. Abraham J. Malherbe, *Social Aspects of Early Christianity* (Baton Rouge and London: Louisiana State University Press, 1977), pp. 29–31, 60–70; Hengel, pp. 36–41; Meeks, pp. 51–73, 190–92; Stegemann, pp. 31–40.

46. Luke T. Johnson, *Sharing Possessions: Mandate and Symbol of Faith* (Philadelphia: Fortress, 1981), p. 108; Hengel, pp. 45–46; Pilgrim, pp. 85–146, 160–68.

47. Hengel, pp. 57–58; Meeks, p. 110.

48. Kee, pp. 174–289; Ramsey MacMullen, *Christianizing the Roman Empire (A.D. 100–400)* (New Haven and London: Yale University Press, 1984), pp. 17–42.

49. MacMullen, pp. 43–119.

50. See, most recently, Charles Avila, *Ownership: Early Christian Teaching* (Maryknoll, NY: Orbis, 1984).

51. W.H.C. Frend, *The Rise of Christianity* (Philadelphia: Fortress, 1984), pp. 417–21; 553–92.

52. See Michel Mollat, *The Poor in the Middle Ages: An Essay in Social History*, trans. Arthur Goldhammer (New Haven: Yale University Press, 1986). For a synthesis of sociohistorical work on Christianity, see Geoffrey Barraclough, ed., *The Christian World: A Social and Cultural History* (New York: Harry N. Abrams, 1981).

53. In taking this stand, the bishops directly oppose the neomalthusian policy, advocated, for example by Simon and Novak, pp. 10–12, of providing social welfare

only for the "deserving" poor, those who "through no fault of their own" are deprived of the means of subsistence. For the origin of this outlook, see Gertrude Himmelfarb, *The Idea of Poverty: England in the Early Industrial Age* (New York: Alfred A. Knopf, 1984), pp. 100–44.

54. See Calvez and Perrin, pp. 101–32.

55. Dorr, p. 255.

56. Calvez and Perrin, pp. 343–80; John F. Cronin, *Social Principles and Economic Life* (Milwaukee: Bruce, 1959), pp. 38–60, 81–139; P. Pavan, "Social Thought, Papal: Basic Principles," *New Catholic Encyclopedia*, 13:354a–361a.

57. Dorr, p. 255.

58. For accounts of the century-long transition in Christian social teaching, see Camp, *Papal Ideology*; Arthur F. McGovern, *Marxism: An American Christian Perspective* (Maryknoll, NY: Orbis, 1980), pp. 96–124.

59. Dorr, pp. 158–62.

60. Dorr, pp. 177–251.

61. "Evangelization in Latin America's Present and Future," Final Document of the Third General Conference of the Latin American Episcopate, *Puebla and Beyond: Documentation and Commentary*, ed. John Eagleson and Philip Scharper (Maryknoll, NY: Orbis Books, 1979), no. 1134; see nos.1135–65 (pp. 264–67). See also Gustavo Guttierrez, *The Power of the Poor in History*, trans. Robert B. Barr (Maryknoll, NY: Orbis Books, 1983), pp. 111–68.

62. Pope John Paul II, "Homily at Guadalupe," Eagleson and Scharper, p. 74.

63. Pope John Paul II, "Politics Must Serve the Common Good," *Origins* (July 17, 1980).

64. "The Church, in the Word of God, Celebrates the Mysteries of Christ for the Salvation of the World," Final Document of the Extraordinary Synod of Bishops," *National Catholic Reporter* (December 20, 1985), Section D, no. 6 (p. 16).

65. "Instruction on Certain Aspects of the Theology of Liberation," *National Catholic Reporter* (September 21, 1984), Introduction, §6 (p. 11).

66. "Theology of Liberation," VII:8, VIII:5–9; IX:2–5; X:2–3, 9–10; XI:5, 10, 13 (pp. 12–14).

67. E. J. Dionne Jr., "Vatican Backs Struggle by Poor to End Injustice," *New York Times* (April 6, 1986), p. A15.

68. "Instruction on Christian Freedom and Liberation," *National Catholic Reporter* (April 25, 1986), nos. 22, 66–70 (pp. 11, 42).

69. See, for example, Nicholas Rescher, "The Canons of Distributive Justice," *Distributive Justice*, (1968), pp. 73–83, and Edward Nell and Onora O'Neill, "Justice under Socialism," *Dissent* (1972), pp. 483–91, both of which are reprinted in James P. Sterba, ed., *Justice: Alternative Political Perspectives* (Belmont, CA: Wadsworth, 1980), pp. 33–40, 200–10.

70. By 'social justice' I mean the set of rights and duties governing the relationship between individuals and society, in contrast to the 'individual' or 'commutative' justice of private transactions. This usage differs somewhat from the equivocal usage of the term in modern Catholic social theology, in which it oscillates between what Aquinas called 'legal justice,' roughly equivalent to a political conception of virtue (See Calvez and Perrin, pp. 133–61), and what the American bishops in *Economic Justice for All* (4:71) call 'contributive justice.'

71. This should be no surprise, given the bishops' interpretation of biblical justice as entailing a preferential option for the poor. Although the bishops do not make the connection explicit themselves, biblical scholars whom they cite in support of their position argue that the best way to summarize the biblical focus of justice upon the

poor is as "From each according to one's ability, to each according to one's needs": Mott, p. 70; Mealand, pp. 41ff.; Pilgrim, pp. 150, 156, 168.

72. Nell and O'Neill, pp. 204–05.

73. Juan Luis Segundo, The Liberation of Theology (Maryknoll, NY: Orbis Books, 1976), pp. 8–9, 19, 25, 69, 150, 167.

74. Peter L. Berger and Thomas Luckman, The Social Construction of Reality: A Treatise in the Sociology of Knowledge (New York: Doubleday/Anchor, 1967), pp. 123–25.

75. This is a point to which Simon and Novak, p. 11, are right to have called attention.

76. Ronald Dworkin, Taking Rights Seriously (Cambridge: Harvard University Press, 1977), p. 93. The two sets of distinctions are from Dworkin but not the matrix of the relationships between the distinctions, nor the terminology of the resulting kinds of rights. For an application of these distinctions to an interpretation of the right to be free from hunger, see Amartya Sen, "The Right Not To Be Hungry," Contemporary Philosophy, Vol. 2: Philosophy of Science, ed. Guttorm Floistad (Dordrecht/Boston/Lancaster: Martinus Nijhoff, 1986), pp. 343–60.

77. An ironic consequence of this conflict between theology and ideology in the economics pastoral is that, though the effect of the letter is to protect the interests of the upwardly mobile, middle-class majority of active Catholic laity (See David C. Leege, "Catholic Parishes in the 1980s," Church, 1 [1985], 22–23.), its message has nevertheless provoked them into widespread opposition (See Arthur Jones, reporting on an opinion survey, in "Study Calls Lay Opposition to Bishops 'Threat to Unity,' " National Catholic Reporter [February 21, 1986], p. 18).

JUNG AND TEILHARD: THE FEMININE IN GOD AND IN THE CHURCH

Robert Faricy, S. J.
Pontifical Gregorian University

ABSTRACT

This article examines the religious thought of Carl Jung and of Pierre Teilhard de Chardin with reference to their ideas on the feminine in God. Jung concludes that the God of Roman Catholic Christianity is complete because that God contains not only the masculine components of Father, Son, and Holy Spirit, but also, through her Assumption, the feminine in the person of the Blessed Virgin Mary. Teilhard, on the other hand, writes of the Blessed Virgin as a real symbol of the feminine element in God. The feminine component in God, for Teilhard, is the world, and in particular the Church, as they enter into God in Jesus Christ risen. Mary stands for the feminine in God because she symbolizes the Church and all creation as it enters into union with the Trinity in and through the risen Christ. This view has importance for understanding the Church.

Contemporary Roman Catholic theological discussion of the feminine aspect of religion sometimes tries to show how God has, essentially and integrally, a feminine as well as a masculine component: God-as-Mother, for example, or the Holy Spirit as the feminine Person in the Holy Trinity. At the same time, much contemporary ecclesiology seems to have lost sight of the feminine aspects of the Church: the Church as the "Bride of Christ," for example, or "Holy Mother Church." The effort to find the feminine in God and the neglect of the feminine in the Church, are in my opinion two sides of the same problem, the general problem of the feminine in Christianity.

A member of the Society of Jesus, Robert Faricy teaches spiritual theology, chiefly courses on the Church in the world and on the theology of contemplation, at the graduate Institute of Spirituality of the Pontifical Gregorian University in Rome. He has written many articles and several books, especially on the spirituality of Teilhard de Chardin, on prayer, and on the theology of the religious life.

The idea of the feminine has an especially important role in the religious writings of two twentieth century thinkers: Carl Gustave Jung, the father of analytical psychology, and Pierre Teilhard de Chardin, the Jesuit priest-scientist.[1] In particular, for both Jung and Teilhard, the feminine somehow enters into God. And here, the two systems of thought show some interesting parallels and complementarities. In this paper, I want to describe briefly the place of the feminine with regard to God in the writings of Jung and of Teilhard and then to evaluate their ideas in order to draw some conclusions for a better understanding of God, of the relationship between God and the world, and of authority and structure in the churches. But first of all, I want to draw attention to some differences and, especially, similarities in the methods of Jung and Teilhard.

I. Methods

The methods of both Jung and Teilhard are phenomenological in a broadly scientific sense. Both Jung and Teilhard form hypotheses based on empirical data. They order their data so as to produce a maximum of sense, a working hypothesis. Jung's analytical psychology and Teilhard's theology are made up of ordered series of such hypotheses.

Jung finds his empirical data in two places: in his clinical experience of treating patients with psychological problems; and in myths, religions, literature, and general culture. In his religious thought, Jung works with the religious symbols that he finds in his practice of therapy and in religious phenomena in general.

Jung is a psychologist. He does not study God, nor religion. rather, he examines ideas and symbols about God and about religion. "Psychology," Jung writes, studies not God, but "our ideas of God;" and he adds that "a psychological treatment or explanation does not at all 'reduce God to nothing but' psychology."[2]

When Jung writes about God or about Christ or about Mary, he does not refer to their objective realities, although he does not deny their existence. He refers to symbolic expressions of unconscious archetypes. God, for Jung, is primarily a symbol of unity, of the unity of all reality. Christ symbolizes the archetype of the self. The Blessed Virgin Mary stands for the archetypes of the anima (the feminine side of the male psyche), the shadow (the unconscious "dark side" of the psyche), and the mother. Psychologically, our faith in God, in Jesus, in Mary, finds expression in symbols that arise from our unconscious archetypes. Jung studies these symbols.

Teilhard, too, applies a broadly scientific method to religious reality.[3] At a first level of his thought, Teilhard draws up a general theory of evolution, using the data of the science of evolution to develop an ordered set of hypotheses that views evolution as taking place not only biologically but—especially —in humanity in the form of increasing socialization. As part of his theory of evolution, Teilhard posits a focal point, a "Personal Center of universal convergence" of evolution—that is, of socialization.[4]

Then he moves to a second, theological, level where he works out a Christology within the framework of his theory of evolution. Here, he moves into the area of faith seeking understanding, and new data comes from divine revelation. Unlike Jung, Teilhard lets his personal faith into his theorizing; and so, properly speaking, he does theology. And he identifies the Personal Center of universal convergence of his evolution theory with Jesus Christ risen as the future focal center of the world's forward movement in history. Since Jesus Christ, true God, has become an integral part of the world, its center, the world and God have a certain mutuality. God, in Christ, has become part of the world; the world somehow enters into God in Christ.

On this christological foundation, Teilhard builds his spirituality of an interpreted faith in both God and the world, of involvement in the world as the way to God. This is the spiritual doctrine of his classic work, *The Divine Milieu*.[5]

Teilhard and Jung have in common a methodological interest in showing the unity of all reality, in presenting a unified vision of God and the world. This concern leads them both to find the feminine in God, although in quite different ways: Jung, in terms of what he calls "quaternity," Teilhard in terms of the relationship of mutuality, in Jesus-Christ, between the world and God.

II. Quaternity and Trinity

Jung discovers a human drive to search for a unified view of reality, to find an understanding of ourselves and the world around us that has wholeness. This drive takes the unconscious form of an archetypal mold that produces quadrate symbols at the conscious level. Jung finds these symbols in dreams, in fantasies, in myths, in art, in rituals, and in religion. We tend to see things as fourfold, as quaternity. "The quaternity" Jung writes, "is an archetype of almost universal occurrence; it forms the logical basis for any whole judgement."[6] We see reality in four's: four seasons, four winds, four elements, four corners of the earth. The mandala is a quaternity. So is the cross with its four arms. The natural symbol of unity is the sphere or circle; but its natural minimal reduction is quaternity.

So Jung finds it strange that Christianity holds as its principal doctrine the Trinity. He takes the religious symbol of the Trinity and tries to make as much sense out of it as he can within his own system. And he finds it lacking. Precisely it lacks the fourth element to make it a quaternity. Even more exactly, it lacks the feminine. Jung finds the general Christian idea of God incomplete because the fourth side of the quaternity, a necessary feminine element, has no place there.

Teilhard, too, finds missing in the contemporary Christian's understanding of God a necessary element needed to complete that understanding. Teilhard finds our concept of God lacking in wholeness. A wholeness dictated not by psychology, as for Jung, but by the Christian tradition. We might say that for Teilhard as for Jung, the modern Christian concept of God lacks a "fourth part," a "Jungian Fourth."

Teilhard wants to show the value of this world by underlining the union between God and the world, a union so close that God cannot simply do without the world. On the contrary, he has freely willed to need the world. God, through the incarnation and the cross and resurrection, stands involved in the world, mutual with it. The world comes from the Creator's hand, as "a sort of echo or symmetrical response to Trinitization. It somehow fills a gap; it fits in."[7] Teilhard wants to show how the created world makes, we can say, a "fourth to the Trinity."

Notice that Teilhard does not want to change the doctrine of the Trinity. He wants to conceptualize it in a new way so as to bring out the relationship of unity between the Trinity and the world. He does this by rethinking the act of creation as a process. Teilhard wants to understand creation, not as one act of God in the beginning, as though the Great Watchmaker made the watch-world, wound it up, and lets it run, but as a continuous process, as ongoing creation. God's creative act is now, spread out in time, and it finds its expression in the world's genesis, its history, its overall evolution into the future. And toward the ultimate future, where the risen Christ awaits it so that he can come a second time.[8]

In fact, Teilhard views the creation process not as the Creator pushing the world ahead from behind, as it were, but as the risen Christ pulling the world toward himself from his position in the future, at the world's end, as its Personal Center of convergence. Teilhard calls this creative pull of God in Jesus Christ "the universal influence of Christ."[9]

This universal creative influence takes the form of love. The love of God coming to us through Jesus Christ risen progressively creates us, and the world. We see that creation as history: as our personal histories, as the history of humanity, as the evolution of the world.

Further, Teilhard understands redemption and creation both as two aspects of one world process of God drawing all things to a unity in Christ. God's plan, revealed through his church, working out in time, is to reconcile all things in Jesus Christ risen, recapitulate all creation under one head. Looking at it one way, we see that process as creation. When we look at it as a process of struggle to achieve unity, we can see it as redemption.

"Jesus Christ structurally in himself, and for all of us, overcomes the resistance to unification."[10] He bears the burden of creation. He "bears and supports the weight of the world in evolution."[11] "He bears the whole weight of a world in progress."[12] "The cross," then, "is the symbol and the meaningful act of Christ raising up the world with all its burden of inertia."[13]

So just as Carl Jung finds quaternity in the Christian symbol of the cross, so, too, Teilhard sees the cross as a great symbol of unification, of wholeness, The cross stands for creation in the category of laborious and suffering effort. It stands for the process of the progressive unification of the world in Jesus Christ risen, for the world's union with God in Christ.

Teilhard finds that the world is a kind of Jungian fourth to God, complementary to God, mutual with him. We can say that, for Teilhard, reality is quadrate, a quaternity: the three Divine Persons and Creation. The "fourth" of this quaternity is the world-in-Christ.

Jung, too, looks for a "fourth to the Trinity. He finds it, in alchemy and in Gnostic Christianity, in the devil, "the aping shadow of God."[14] But in Roman Catholic Christianity, Jung finds the Trinity's fourth in the Blessed Virgin Mary.

III. Mary and the Feminine in God

"Mary was the instrument of God's birth," Jung writes, analyzing the religious symbol of the Trinity, "and so she became involved in the trinitarian drama as a human being. The Mother of God can therefore be regarded as a symbol of mankind's essential participation in the doctrine of the Trinity."[15]

The Trinity then, becomes a quaternity by assuming into itself a "fourth" who stands for matter, darkness, the unconscious, the opaque, the intractable, the feminine. This "fourth" is Mary. Not that Jung wants to make Mary altogether an integral part of God in the theological sense. But he writes that she is as a "fourth" in the Trinity, "ninety-nine percent divine."[16]

In medieval art and poetry, Jung finds the psychological need for quaternity answered in portrayals of the close union between Mary and the Trinity in the mysteries of the Assumption and of the Coronation of Mary as Queen of Heaven. But the protestant reformation brought about an important change. In pre-reformation Christian symbolism, Jung finds it sometimes difficult to distinguish Mary and the Church. This remained true during the reformation and is true today. Mary and the Church are associated symbolically. They are almost interchangeable symbols.

The protestant reformation rejected both Mary and the Church as mother. Jung recognizes that the Church is a mother. He writes "The Church is, in the fullest sense, a mother; we speak not only of Mother Church, but even of the womb of the Church."[17] In reacting against Mother Church, the reformation removed Mary from the realm of the Trinity. Jung considers this, psychologically, a serious error.

In 1947, Jung observed the growing contemporary psychological need for wholeness, and so for the integration of the feminine in the form of a mother into the Trinity. And he predicted the definition of the dogma of the Assumption of the Blessed Virgin Mary into heaven.[18] Sure enough, Pius XII stated the doctrine in 1950 as a dogmatic definition. Jung was delighted. He saw the definition as having immense importance for everyone, Catholics and non-Catholics alike.

Jung was, as of course we all are, strongly conditioned culturally. From a long line of German–speaking pastors of the Swiss Reformed Church, Carl Jung grew up steeped in the culture of the reformation, with its rejection of the Catholic nature-grace synthesis and with its polarity between the kingdom of God and the kingdom of the world. Perhaps as a result, Jung failed to see the possibilities of quaternity in the Catholic doctrine of the incarnation.

Teilhard de Chardin, on the other hand, brought up on the devotion to the Sacred Heart and with a love for the material side of this world, has a theology that accounts for all that Jung wanted in a quaternity. Teilhard finds a quaternity, although he never calls it that, in God by reason of the incarnation, a quaternity that includes the feminine.

For Teilhard, the feminine component of reality is found concretized in women, in the Church as Bride and as Mother, and above all in the Blessed Virgin Mary. For Teilhard, the feminine is not primarily an abstract principle. It is, rather, a universal principal that we find concretized in certain existing forms.

In his early essay "The Eternal Feminine," the Feminine speaks somewhat in the manner of Wisdom in the Old Testament. "When the world was born, I came into being . . . In me is seen that side of beings by which they are joined as one along their road to unity . . . I am the essential Feminine."[19]

Finally, "I am the Church, the Bride of Christ," says the Eternal Feminine. And, "I am Mary, the virgin, the mother of all humankind."[20] Not, as Henri de Lubac has noted, that the Feminine is an abstract principle that is concretized in Mary. No, Mary, an existing person, finds herself universalized in the principle.[21] At the end of the essay, the reader understands that all along the speaker has been the Blessed Virgin Mary. Not a personalization, certainly not an allegorical figure, the Eternal Feminine is the Mother of God. Mary, for Teilhard, is a concrete universal, what Karl Rahner has often called "a real symbol." A real symbol, Mary stands for all women and all femininity, for the material and for the creative forces— especially love—that organize matter and move it toward unity.

Not an archetype, she nonetheless represents the archetypes of the mother and of the anima. And so Mary can be, stand for, the Church, Mother Nature, and every kind of mother.

Unlike Jung, Teilhard, of course, did not believe that Mary's Assumption made her ninety-nine percent divine. And, of course, he believed in the dogma of the Assumption and supported the Holy See's definition of it. But he felt real sorrow at the way the definition presented the dogma. He wrote to a friend that perhaps a psychoanalyst could find traces in the defining encyclical of "sado-masochism of orthodoxy—pleasure in swallowing or in making others swallow the truth in its most gross and bestial forms."[22]

He regarded the definition as an act of "blind conservatism" and "a challenge to physics and biology."[23] Even later, in spite of his great personal devotion to Mary, Teilhard felt a lack of empathy with most theological and pious statements about Mary and "with nine-tenths of her representatives."[24]

Still, he well understood, better than Jung, the importance of the definition of dogma of the Assumption of Mary into heaven. He was too conscious of the "necessity of the Marian (to counterbalance the 'masculinity' of Yahweh) not to feel the profound need for this gesture."[25]

IV. Conclusions

We can evaluate positively the psychology of Carl Jung without attaching theological importance to his more extreme conclusions. In my opinion, the observation that we tend to understand reality as fourfold, in terms of quaternities, has value. Quite clearly, however, his assessment even of the psychological significance of the place of the Blessed Virgin Mary in Catholic doctrine cannot be accepted. Catholics simply do not at all hold Mary divine or in any way a member of the Trinity. Nevertheless, that Mary in some way represents a Jungian fourth to the Trinity is not only acceptable, but seems to me to make sense and to suggest further reflection.

Such reflection could take place within the framework of Teilhard de Chardin's theology of the relationship between God and the world in Christ, and in the light of his theology of Mary. For Teilhard, Mary stands as the real symbol of the feminine in reality. It seems to me that this can be accepted at the levels of popular piety, of theology, and of psychological perception. If we accept it, then it follows that Mary represents the world itself as complementary to God, as entering into God in Christ.

In particular, as Jesus' mother, Mary represents the humanity of Christ, his body, into which we are incorporated through baptism. The humanity of Jesus, in my opinion, is exactly the "fourth" that Jung was looking for: the feminine side of God, and even—as we see from the Lord's passion and death—the dark and material and opaque side of the Trinity.

Insofar as we partake of Jesus' humanity by being incorporated into his body, the Church, we share in his divinity, find ourselves somehow divinized, partakers of the divine nature, raised up and caught up into the Trinity. The Church is a feminine fourth to the divine Trinity, loved by Christ as his body.[26]

The feminine principle in God, then, is not the Blessed Virgin Mary, nor the Holy Spirit, nor in some way "God-as-mother." *The feminine principle of God is Jesus Christ risen insofar as he is the whole Christ that includes especially his body, the Church, and also the whole world and all in it as it enters, in Christ, into the triune God.* This is the Jungian fourth that makes the Trinity a quaternity.

Jung, however, wants to put the fourth into God in such a way as to make that fourth God, divine in the strict sense. And so God becomes a (quadrate, that is: complete) unity. Further, Jung wants the feminine to be part of God in the strict sense so that God, in himself, holds both masculine and feminine elements.

Teilhard, on the other hand, sees clearly that his feminine fourth cannot really be integral, as such, to the divine nature in itself. The feminine fourth must be creation, all creatures. Otherwise, the Trinitarian God stands complete, not needing his creation, his extension, his "other self," us. God has freely willed to need his creation, to need us. If we understand God as aloof or as not needing his creation, that is not God as he has revealed himself to us in Jesus Christ.

Contemporary North American culture has a strong tendency to want to see the feminine in God as he-is-in-himself, to say, "We are not the feminine in God, he has the feminine in him apart from us." We should expect this kind of cultural bias and rejection of the feminine in ourselves in a society that to a great extent rejects the feminine, puts it down, demeans it in many ways.

The problem here is not what some call "macho-ism," from the Spanish "macho," meaning a cultural overemphasis on the masculine side of reality. The Latin languages divide all reality into masculine and feminine, so that they become modes of existence and not simply of sexual differentiation. But in American language, in English, only people and animals are masculine or feminine. A mammal is masculine if it has a penis; if not, it is feminine.

So in our North American society, male domination results not in "macho-ism," but in an overemphasis on the phallus, in a "phallicism" that exalts the values of male brute force, conquest, violence. Don Juan is Latin, but Rambo is American.

In a phallic culture, theologians inevitably tend to neglect the spousal imagery of the Old and New Testaments where Israel is God's spouse, and where the Church is the Bride of Christ. They easily overlook the spousal imagery of the Christian mystical tradition in which Saint John of the Cross, for example, shows no shame in understanding the Christian's union with God in terms of the Christian as feminine and God as masculine.

We are the feminine fourth, we and all humanity, we and the Church we make up as members of Christ's body, we and the world around us. And Mary stands for this Jungian fourth, for the Church and the world entering in Christ into God. She represents the feminine element, all of creation, that complements and even, in a mysterious way, completes God.

I find this whole side of Christianity sometimes, often, missing in English-speaking countries with a predominantly reformation protestant religious culture, like the United States. What I often find lacking to some or even a great extent is a whole complex of religious symbols and the attitudes that go with them. For example: recognition of Mary's role, love of the Church as the body of Christ, true appreciation of women and their rights and their gifts. I find missing an appreciation of the feminine that is real, an appreciation that takes shape in love and therefore in actions.

Where do I find this lack? Not in popular religiosity, but rather in two other echelons: the clergy and the intellectual community. Perhaps we (I belong to both groups) have received so much intellectual formation that we fail to appreciate the dark, opaque, feminine side of our religious reality. And perhaps we have felt inferior to protestant intellectuals for so long that we tend to emulate them even in their reformation faith presuppositions.[27]

When the feminine goes, when Mary stands overlooked, then, inevitably the whole question of authority and structure in the Catholic Church and in the other Christian churches takes on a heavily intellectual cast. We take a *primarily juridical approach* to church authority and structure. We then tend to address church problems in an almost exclusively "masculine," rational, strongly conceptualized way.[28] Without love.

The authority-structure aspects of any church involve that church as the body of Christ; and so as a concretization of the feminine in reality, and in God. Church authority and structure must be considered not merely in cold rational philosophical concepts, but in symbols and in love. Without love there is no real theology, and no living truth.

NOTES

1. Jung and Teilhard, although contemporaries, apparently never met. Teilhard, however, was familiar with Jung's ideas, read at least Jung's *Modern Man in Search of a Soul*, and drew up a plan for a psychoanalytical study of Christianity (*Cahier XVII*, p. 48, unpublished papers). See Ursula King, *Towards a New Mysticism* (New York: Seabury, 1980), pp. 97 and 270; and Claude Cuénot, *Teilhard de Chardin*, (Baltimore: Helicon, 1968), p. 312.

2. *Brother Klaus*, in *Collected Works of C. G. Jung* (hereafter referred to as *CW*), Bollinger Series XX, tr. R. F. C. Hull (New York: Pantheon Books) vol. 11 (1958) p. 317. See Clifford A. Brown, *Jung's Hermeneutic of Doctrine: Its Theological Significance* (Chico, CA: Scholar's Press, 1981).

3. Teilhard describes his method in "Some Reflections on the Conversion of the World," *Science and Christ*, tr. R. Hague (London: Collins, 1969), pp. 122–23; "La pensée du Père Teilhard de Chardin," *Les Etude philosophiques* 10 (1955) pp. 580–81; "Un sommaire de ma perspective phénoménologique du monde," *ibid.*, pp. 569–71.

4. "Some Reflections on the Conversion of the World," *op. cit.*, p. 122.

5. Tr. R. Hague (London: Collins, 1960).

6. "A Psychological Approach to the Dogma of the Trinity" *CW* 18, p. 167. See "Jung and Religious Belief," *CW* 18, pp. 713–17.

7. "My Fundamental Vision," *Toward the Future*, tr. R. Hague (London: Collins, 1975), p. 195.

8. Teilhard's theology of creation can be found especially in "My Universe," *Science and Christ*, tr. R. Hague (Collins: 1968), pp. 37–85.

9. See especially "Note on the Universal Christ," and "Some Reflections on the Conversion of the World," *ibid.*, pp. 14–20 and pp. 122–23.

10. "Christology and Evolution," *Christianity and Evolution*, tr. R. Hague (London: Collins, 1971), p. 85.

11. "Introduction to the Christian Life," *ibid.*, p. 163.

12. "Christianity and Evolution," *ibid.*, p. 171.

13. "Some General Views on the Essence of Christianity," *ibid.*, p. 135.

14. "A Psychological Approach to the Dogma of the Trinity," *CW* 11, p. 177.

15. *Op. cit.*, p. 161.

16. "Jung and Religious Belief," *CW* 18, p. 712.

17. "Two Essays on Analytical Psychology," *CW* 7, p. 103.

18. "A Psychological Approach to the Dogma of the Trinity," published in German in 1948, *CW* 11, p. 170.

19. "The Eternal Feminine," *Writings in Time of War*, tr. R. Hague (London: Collins, 1967), p. 192.

20. *Ibid.*, pp. 200–01.

21. H. de Lubac, *The Eternal Feminine*, tr. R. Hague (London: Collins, 1970), p. 119.

22. Letter to Pierre Leroy, August 29, 1950, in P. Leroy, *Lettres familiéres de Pierre Teilhard de Chardin mon ami* (Paris: Centurion, 1976), p. 74.

23. Letter of August 17, 1950, in *Letters to Two Friends*, tr. R. Hague (New York: New American Library, 1968), p. 213.

24. Unpublished retreat notes, sixth day of Teilhard's 1944 retreat.

25. To P. Leroy, August 8, 1950, quoted in H. de Lubac, *The Eternal Feminine, op. cit.*, p. 125.

26. Ephesians, chapter 5.

27. It might be significant that the only two references I have found among American Catholic theologians or philosophers to Jung's idea of a fourth in the Trinity both refer chiefly to Jung's idea of the devil as a fourth. But Jung finds the devil as a fourth only in deviations of Christianity like alchemy, gnosticism, manicheism. Neither author refers as extensively to the feminine or to the Blessed Virgin Mary as a fourth, a symbol that Jung finds precisely in Roman Catholicism. See David B. Burrell, C.S.C. *Exercises in Religious Understanding* (Notre Dame, IN: University of Notre Dame Press, 1974), pp. 224–25; Joseph A. Bracken, S.J. *What Are They Saying About The Trinity?* New York: Paulist, 1979), pp. 71–76.

28. See, however, the *caveats* of Elizabeth A. Johnson, "The Symbolic Character of Theological Statements About Mary," *Journal of Ecumenical Studies,* 22 (1985), 335; *ibid.*, "The Marian Tradition and The Reality of Women," *Horizons*, 12/1 (1985), 116–35; and *ibid.*, "The Incomprehensibility of God and The Image of God Male and Female," *Theological Studies*, 45 (1984), pp. 441–65.

Part Five

THE DREAMS AND VISION OF LEADERSHIP

THE BISHOP AS PASTORAL TEACHER; IMPLICATIONS FOR THEOLOGIANS

Most Rev. Daniel E. Pilarczyk
Archbishop of Cincinnati

ABSTRACT

In this address to the College Theology Society, during its convention in Cincinnati, Archbishop Pilarczyk reflects on the role of college teachers from his perspective as diocesan bishop. He confronts some very fundamental questions. What should be taught to Catholic college undergraduates so they may achieve a basic theological maturity? How can students be taught to love the Church? How should a teacher carefully distinguish the levels of acceptance called for by Church teaching? How can baptized Catholics learn their responsibility of service or ministry? Teachers of theology have an opportunity to teach the basic purpose of existence: knowing, loving, and serving.

Introduction

When I was rector of our college seminary from 1968 to 1974, one of my major responsibilities, it seemed, was having to listen to everybody's theories about what the seminary should be doing. I received all kinds of suggestions about what we should be teaching our candidates for the priesthood, ranging from larger doses of metaphysics to home economics for celibates, from voice projection to boiler repair. I became a bit annoyed at times, and I often thought that if all these people know so much about seminary education, they should be volunteering for my job, which, of course, they were not. As I began to prepare my thoughts for this presentation to the College Theology Society, I realized that I really wanted to do the

Archbishop Daniel E. Pilarczyk received a Licentiate in Philosophy and a Doctorate in Sacred Theology from the Pontifical Urban University, Rome. He also holds a Ph.D. in classics from the University of Cincinnati. A member of the board of Trustees of Catholic University, he has also served as Vice-President of the Athenaeum of Ohio and rector of St. Gregory Seminary, Cincinnati. Most recently he was elected Vice-President of the National Conference of Catholic Bishops.

same thing to you that people used to do to me, namely, tell you
how to do your job as theology teachers. It became clear to me that
such an approach was neither fair nor pleasant nor, for that matter,
healthy for the speaker. So I decided to modify the approach and
invite you to join me in an afternoon reverie, to fantasize with me
about what could be. The title of my presentation is "The Bishop as
Pastoral Teacher: Implications for Theologians." As subtitle, I offer
Perry Como's old theme song, "Dream Along With Me."

Presumptions

When I was seminary rector, the students accused me of being a
crypto-Cartesian, inclined to force all reality into categories that were
clear and distinct. To a certain extent they were correct, so now I
would like to define the concepts in which I invite you to dream
with me.

First of all, I point out that I dream with you as diocesan bishop,
as one who bears pastoral leadership responsibility. My leadership
responsibility calls for me to see that the Church's means of sanctification are made readily accessible to its members, that the unity
of the Church is maintained and promoted, and that the Church's
teaching is correctly and widely preached and taught. It is a pastoral
responsibility. That is to say, it has to do not with theory but practice;
not with abstract universals but with real people, all the real people
of the diocese in all their diversity. Etymologically, "pastoral" means
having to do with feeding a flock; and he who feeds the flock has to
be concerned with grass roots. Obviously, no diocesan bishop can
carry out his pastoral leadership responsibilities alone. He requires
collaborators in every field of his endeavor; and these collaborators
include priests, deacons, lay ministers, catechists, administrators,
and, yes, theologians. But the overall responsibility is his.

Secondly, I invite you to dream with me in your capacity as teachers. I acknowledge that there is a highly specific role for theologians
in the Church, a role which has been called the research and development component of Church doctrine. You are called to explore
the implications of Church teaching, to investigate it, to refine it, to
probe it, to push back its horizons. It is an important responsibility,
because it helps keep Church teaching alive and growing. In practice,
however, most of your professional time is spent in classroom teaching and in the preparation required for that teaching. However much
you may research and publish, your basic day to day public is composed of the students you encounter in the classroom and in that
context you share the pastoral teaching responsibility of the diocesan
bishop.

Thirdly, as we dream together I suggest that we agree to dream about the theological education of college undergraduates. You belong to this association, I presume, because you are all college teachers. And when we talk about teaching college undergraduates, we are talking about those who will, by and large, spend their lives as lay persons in the world, that is, those who bear the responsibility for bringing the presence and the vision of the Church to family, factory, office, store, school, neighborhood. These persons make up the basic fabric of the Church. The Church exists, in large part, to enable these persons to carry out their vocations as laity. They are important people for the Church, important people for the world.

Finally, and only for the sake of clarity, I observe that the teaching of Catholics is not *ipso facto* the teaching of the Church; and when I speak of Church teaching, I intend the official magisterial doctrine, that which is taught by those who bear the prime responsibility for the Church's teaching mission.

Now lets launch into our reverie.

Wouldn't it be nice if all Catholic college graduates were to know what the Church teaches in some depth and some detail? In my pastoral ministry I often hear that "kids don't *know* anything about their faith any more." I believe that this is inexact because I happen to visit a couple dozen elementary Catholic school classrooms every month, and I know that kids are learning the basic content of their faith. But the fact remains that over the past few decades of relative disarray in religious education, we have moved away from a catechetical approach in primary and secondary education which stressed "knowing the answers" to an approach that now includes a much larger component of personal faith commitment. This is an improvement, in my judgment. But one result of it is that we can no longer simply presume that every student in our college theology classes has had a systematic exposure to all the Church's teaching. I suspect that many college level students could benefit from a remedial catechetics course at the beginning of their college career.

But there is more than that. Even if every student could be presumed to know all the answers in the Baltimore Catechism, they would still need to bring that knowledge up to the level of their growing maturity in other branches of study. This means not only knowing what the Church teaches, but why the Church teaches it, how Church teaching came to be this way, how it all fits together into one consistent whole. This is not simply catechetical learning, but study *per causas* and therefore scientific theology.

Wouldn't it be nice if teachers of undergraduate Catholic theology could put together a syllabus for Catholic lay persons, a syllabus that would include a scientific overview of systematics, of moral theology, of scripture, of liturgy? Wouldn't it be nice if we could even have some kind of certification of basic theological maturity for all Catholic college graduates, something on the model of the certification of public accountants and registered nurses? (I remind you that we are in dreamland!)

I acknowledge, of course, that the acquisition of theological knowledge is never really complete, even at the end of graduate school. I am sure that you have had the same experience that I had, looking at the doctoral diploma and saying, "Now I may be ready to begin to learn in this field." But there ought to be some general, basic level of theological maturity which we can expect even undergraduates to achieve. It would be nice.

Wouldn't it also be nice if every Catholic college graduate left college deeply in love with the Church and its teaching? Avery Dulles recently said something that I found very disturbing, but which none the less has the ring of truth about it. "In our time," he says, "Christians, and perhaps Catholics more than others, are haunted by the fear of loving the church too much. They find it hard to share Christ's own love for the church (Eph. 5:25) and to accept the maxim of St. Augustine, . . . 'one possesses the Holy Spirit in the measure that one loves the Church of Christ' (*In Ioann. Tract.* 32:8 . . .). They fear that love might blind them to the faults of the church and to their own need of self-reform."[1]

I do not believe that it is inappropriate to invite theology teachers to help bring their students to a love for the Church and its teaching. For one thing, every teacher has an implicit desire to get the student to love and appreciate the subject that is offered, whether it be Sacred Scripture or subatomic physics. If the teacher is not enthusiastic about his or her subject and is not anxious to share that enthusiasm with the students, the teacher has no place in a classroom.

Moreover, if the Church is the people of God and the Body of Christ, it is inherently lovable, and the teacher of theology ought to be able to make that plain to the students. The theology teacher does not have to be a cheerleader. The theology teacher does, however, have to propose the Church's teaching cogently, clearly, fairly, and lovingly, in the expectation that the students' response will be one of understanding and acceptance, even of enthusiasm and dedication.

In this context of love for the Church, I suppose I have to say something about disputed questions and, of course, about dissent from Church teaching. It is irresponsible for any teacher of theology to give the impression that all Church teaching is of equal authority, that all Church teaching calls for the same level of acceptance. It is also irresponsible for any teacher of theology to give the impression that those who disagree with some item of non-infallible Church teaching are bad people or are outside the Church. It is also irresponsible not to teach the students what the difficult questions are. At the same time there are dangers. If the areas of dispute are not taught carefully, the student can come away with the impression that anything goes in the Church, and that cafeteria Christianity is the only thing that makes sense. The student can get angry with the Church for teaching the "wrong" stuff. The student can begin to wonder what the Church is actually right about. It is hard to love that which one has come to regard with scepticism. This is a pastoral concern that I am sure you share with me.

Another aspect of love for the Church that is of concern to me and others is an apparent decline in the sense of the Church's sacramentality. This decline manifests itself in the slack-off in Mass attendance, in the reduced use of the sacrament of reconciliation, in facile answers to an imminent shortage of priests, in the rise of fundamentalism, and in the growth of some spiritualities which seem to posit personal religious experience as the sole criterion of truth. If the Church is the basic sacrament of Christ, if the Church is the fundamental means of our contact with the Father through Christ, if the Church is somehow the continuation of the incarnation, then these phenomena which discount the need for participation in the visible Catholic church community are troubling indeed. There is no easy answer to these realities, but I am convinced that part of the answer is an increased awareness of the nature and necessity of the Church, in an increased encouragement to love the Church.

Let's dream on.

Wouldn't it be nice if every Catholic College graduate were prepared to offer conscious and generous service to the Lord and the Church in the world? I am thinking now of a cadre of educated laymen and women who are so imbued with Catholic Christian truth that they are not only aware of the ethical demands of their chosen profession—law, business, medicine, or whatever—but who are also prepared to give witness to the life of Christ in every aspect of their lives in secular society. As I remarked earlier, the Church exists to bring salvation to the world; and that salvation comes to the world largely through the life and the work of those who are called to be in the world—lay people. Professional church people by and large are not in the corporate board rooms, or in leadership positions in labor unions, or among the joint chiefs of staff, or in legislative bodies. Lay people are. And we must either have lay people who are prepared to translate the teaching of the Church into those contexts, or we must settle for a privatized Church that limits itself to devotional activity and occasional relief of the poor. I am not talking now about professional Catholics who are in the forefront of every Catholic cause, though they are important, too. Rather, here I am talking about those men and women who have assimilated Church teaching about human destiny and human dignity, about honesty and compassion, about the need to change unjust social systems whether local or national or international, and have assimilated these teachings to the point that they carry them with themselves as naturally as they carry their briefcases to work in the morning. Much of this is a matter of personal faith commitment, but much of it is also a matter of conscious learning.

One of the greatest of the Lord's gifts to the contemporary Church is the rise of lay ministry. Whereas in the past almost all ministry was exercised by priests or religious, we now have a majority of lay teachers in our schools. We have lay pastoral ministers in our parishes. There are lay business managers and lay catechists. And all this is blessing. It is a reminder to us that concern for the interior life and strength of the Church is not entrusted only to ordained or vowed persons. But there is a danger here, too. The danger is that we begin to think that only those lay persons are really committed Catholics who work for the Church. If we extend this attitude just a bit we find ourselves saying that if you are not a parish council member or a lector or an extraordinary minister of the Eucharist, you are not really faithful to your responsibilities as a Catholic. I believe there is a great danger in clericalizing the laity, and that danger lies in suggesting that the only really important part of lay persons' lives is that part which takes place in church. This is simply not true, and it is an implicit denial of the basic Christian principles of sacramentality and incarnation.

The lay person's basic responsibility as lay person is in the world. We have to be sure that somewhere along the line they have learned that.

Conclusion

This brings me to the end of my reverie with you. I think it is worth pointing out in passing that dreams are not composed of what is totally unreal, but of pieces of what already exists, heightened and intensified by our fantasy. Every "wouldn't it be nice if . . ." implies "isn't it great that . . ." Isn't it great that we have college theology to fantasize about?

As we look back over the three phases of our reverie, you will already have noticed that it is based on the old Baltimore Catechism question about the meaning of human life. "Why did God make you? To know Him, to love Him, to serve Him . . ." In my reflections I have expanded that answer a bit to suggest that we are called to know God through the Church, to love God in the Church, and to serve God as Christian believers in the world. I have suggested that in your capacity as college theology teachers you have an opportunity to assist your students to prepare themselves to carry out that basic purpose of their existence. Others share the responsibility, of course: family, pastors, campus ministers, friends and associates, as well as the students themselves, obviously. But you have your own particular contribution to make to the lives of your students. And if their life and their development are important to the life of the Church, so is your part in that development. As diocesan bishop I thank you for sharing my pastoral concern, my responsibilities as pastoral teacher. And thanks also for taking this time to dream along with me.

NOTES

1. "Vatican II and the Church's Purpose," *Theology Digest* 32 (1985), pp. 351f.

THEOLOGIANS AND THEIR CATHOLIC AUTHORITIES: REMINISCENCE AND RECONNOITER

William M. Shea
University of South Florida

ABSTRACT

In his presidential address to the College Theology Society the author begins by probing what he learned about the Catholic Church through his own life experiences. Images and memories are crucial mediators of a Church that has always been embodied in persons, places, and things. Acknowledging reasons why one can be critical of the Church one loves, Shea confronts the need for a baptized modernity in the Church: a critical intellectual understanding suffused by love of God and neighbor which does not succumb to being an unhistorical orthodoxy. Reflecting on the limited authority of theologians in the Church, Shea concludes by calling for the formation of a national committee on the ecclesial rights and responsibilities of exegetes and theologians.

It is difficult to speak calmly and quietly about what one loves passionately, and next to my wife and my children I love the Catholic church more than any other thing. The passion for it has perdured all the years, and grows stronger the longer I live in it even though it must be said that my years with it have been far from easy. I do not love the church because I examined it and found it lovable; I loved it long before I could have examined it, and no examination has lessened my love for it. I cannot go back far enough in time or dig deeply enough in my psychic archaeology to find the root of that love. I think the root is the grace of God, yet I do have memories of important places and persons.

William M. Shea, Professor of Religious Studies at the University of South Florida (Tampa, FL 33620) is a specialist in American religious thought and theological method. He is the author of The Naturalists and the Supernatural: Studies in Horizon and an American Philosophy of Religion *(1984). He is currently a fellow at the Woodrow Wilson International Center for Scholars, and is working on a book on higher education, culture, and theology.*

I remember my father kneeling in the pew in St. Raymond's Church in the Bronx, head bowed, rosary in hand, this mighty man humble, calling on his God for strength to live what I later learned was a tough life. And I recall with particular emotion the stations of the cross walked every Friday in Lent with the other children in the parish church. We all know how little attention children pay to public religious events and I paid the usual amount—except my heart was opened by the images and the music and the awful seriousness of the death of that man and the terrible suffering of his mother. I knew, because the church told me, that his death was for me and in fact is my own, and that his mother and my mother and the church itself were all in some strange way the same and would weep for me when I suffer and die. "At the cross her station keeping stood the mournful mother weeping, close to Jesus till the last." I can see it as sharply, hear it as clearly, feel it as deeply now as I did then. The church made it possible for me to face and accept death, and to hope that death does not destroy life. The church has made it possible for me to believe that God's love is stronger than death.

I remember well that, in my teenage years, reeling from the onslaught of male sexuality and an uncertain future, I took up attending early morning mass at St. Raymond's. It is a fine, big church of Romanesque architectural background, and at that time it was dark and drear with the peculiar brooding quality that the Irish love so much in their churches. The light was focused entirely on the huge marble altar so that one was not distracted from what really counts, the Mass. A fresco of Jesus enthroned loomed above the baldachino. The rest of the church was shadow-shrouded with barely enough light to read a missal. Morning after morning after morning, in winter and summer, for four years, trying to come to grips with my future, I watched the great cross above the altar and the sacrifice being offered for me on the altar and realized gradually what had been in my heart from my childhood, that I loved God and that was why I was there and not only because I was worried about my future.

I found out that I loved God and I learned what God is like there in that church, that particular church, that leaf on the branch of the Great Church. I learned there all that I ever needed to know about God. Refinements had to be made, to be sure, but they are just that, refinements. I have never gotten over or gotten away from those times in that church. For it I am profoundly grateful, and I know now in my fiftieth year that I love the church, the branch as well as the leaf, as much now as then, and I am more grateful to it as each year passes. I found the center of the world, the great tree that reaches the heavens, the navel of the earth on the corner of Castle Hill Avenue and Tremont Avenue in the Bronx. I never go to the Bronx now without a visit to it when I tell again how grateful I am for that building and all that the church accomplished within its walls.

But that is not all I learned from the Great Church. I have other memories and other moments. After two tedious years in the seminary wondering just what sense the neo-scholastic philosophy and theology could possibly make and wondering whether even the study of the law might be more interesting, I walked into a classroom at Dunwoodie and with utter fascination watched Myles Bourke interpret the scriptures. What struck me was the intelligence and utter honesty of his approach to a text which in the late fifties was still under intellectual lock and key for us Catholics. While most of what I was forced to learn in the seminary put me to sleep, Myles Bourke woke me to the role that intelligence, free and dedicated, could play in the religious life. I went to work with happiness for the first time in my seminary career. It was not until I read *Insight* ten years later that I began to understand what I had experienced watching Myles Bourke, and what I had by then placed at the center of my life, the demand to understand. I owe all this to the church, of course, for the church had given me Myles Bourke and Bernard Lonergan, and the church, God knows, is the guiding motif of their lives. I remember all this with special joy and sadness during this week, the twenty-fifth anniversary of my ordination to the priesthood.

One loves before one knows it and grasps its demand; and one understands before one grasps the nature of understanding and the demand it places upon one. Once one realizes that one needs to love and to understand, one cannot end the quest without ending oneself. It is the power of love and understanding that leads us to be better than we are, if I may use so peculiar a term, that drives us to whatever constructive good we can contribute to our fellows. Because of that love and the quest for understanding St. Paul died, Luther stood, and John XXIII was a great pope. And, it is their love and drive to understand that attracts me and binds me to my theologian friends. What I admire about them all—people like Myles Bourke and Bernard Lonergan and Gerard Sloyan and the Carmodys and Charles Curran and many others in this room and elsewhere—is that their lives are driven by those two motors, the love of God and the need to understand.

Catholicism refuses to be airy, to divorce the truth discovered and the grace received from its embodiments and occurrences. The church never quite lost itself in the salvation of individual souls; always it has been at bottom a sacramental communion with a power to preserve and touch mythic imagination and to remain rooted in archaic religious life, to bless the fields in Spring and to kneel before bread and wine. The sacred place, the sacred person, the navel of the world, the smells and bells, the Pope and the poor, the saint, the ordinary life and its extraordinary center, the here and there, the this and that of actual experience are never far from Catholic consciousness. We carry the sacred in memories, in images like the ones I have tried to communicate to you. Being a Catholic is like making love, always particular, something found and never lost, a person loved and never forgotten even when one moved on and loved again. Images root us not only in the present love but in all the loving one has ever done. I could no more turn my back on the church which has given me God and the meaning in which I live and the images in which I carry it than I could on any love I have ever had, not without sin, that is.

But there are other images and other meanings that disturb the idyll of my mythic imagination, images that will lead me directly to the subject I wish to address tonight. Two archbishops of the Catholic church this last year refused to celebrate Mass for the leaders of the congregations of women religious in the United States. In my fifty years I have never heard of a Catholic priest refusing to celebrate Mass for nuns. Do we appreciate what that refusal means to Catholic sensibility? It means excommunication. And several years ago, on the tarmac of the Managua airport, a sixty year old Jesuit priest knelt in reverence before a sixty year old bishop of Rome and found himself rebuked, with finger wagging, before a billion people for his disobedience. He was not lifted up from his knees, not embraced. This is another of the many sides of Catholicism, its hierarchy and its structure breeding the demand for obedience and the willingness to humiliate others when one's wishes and directives are not followed. What is going on, after all, when Christians behave disrespectfully? When Christians cannot meet as equals? When some Christians think it their power and right and duty to reprimand brothers and sisters in public, and to tell them what to do and think and believe even though the people are adults who have searched their minds and hearts, who act on conscience, and who have lived all their days for the church and its work?

It is always difficult to speak objectively and critically of a church one loves passionately. Nonetheless, it must be said that our church has had a bloody history, a history replete with cowardice and with manipulation of religious convictions for self-serving ends. The leaders and members of our church stood by while six million Jews and five million gypsies, homosexuals, and communists were murdered. Well-intentioned, prayerful men and women stood by. This lesson must not be lost, and it is only the worst of many. We are too often cowards who prefer to hide our lack of principle in piety. We are all capable of talking of the good of the church in order to preserve our own skin and the skin of the church when neither we nor the church need our skins in order to be what we are called to be.

There is only one thing required, Jesus tells the rich young man (Lk 18:22), and we did not keep it clearly in mind between 1931 and 1945. In fact, we have all too rarely kept it in mind. The church has not been slow in history to destroy life in the name of pure doctrine, or to let the life of individuals slip into the many dark pools that surround us in this world, all in the name of survival of the community and its traditions. The present leadership of the church is admirable in many ways, but so too were the leaders under Pius XII who chewed their fingernails while the beast devoured millions, and the leaders under St. Pius X who shackled Catholic intellectual life for half a century. Their good intentions are not at issue, of course. But we should not forget that we Catholics canonized and still honor a man to whom freedom of expression and communication seem to have meant nothing at all, and who had little else to say about the men whose lives he crushed than to call them arrogant for not obeying him. He even made out their virtues to be part of their plot. He is not a model worthy of imitation by his successors.

The Reformation left us terrible wounds, wounds from which we have barely begun to recover. It was in that century that the church ceased to be catholic. The Roman church tried to be catholic on the basis of its structures and obedience to its office holders, and by doing so, despite its ideals, it ceased to be catholic. It made itself one western Christian church among many, perhaps the one which best remembers the time of its catholicity. And it will not become universal now by insisting on obedience again, or by denying the rights of critical intelligence. To insist on obedience again is to do exactly what broke east from west, protestant from Roman. It cannot become catholic again while ignoring in its own life the virtues which our culture justly prizes: freedom of thought, freedom of communication, freely given cooperation, respect for legal process and for the intrinsic dignity of the human person. In a word, the church is up against a demand which its leaders are sore pressed to deny, the demand for equality. It is very difficult for a hierarchical structure to respect the virtues we all prize; it is near impossible for hierarchs to behave democratically. For while they may be men of grace, they are most certainly men of power and we remember what Lord Acton said about power.

I have another image or two for you. I remember sitting in a balcony in an auditorium in Yale University in 1962 listening transfixed as a young Swiss theologian by the name of Hans Küng spoke of the "liberty of the children of God," of conscience, and of reform. It was surely one of the great moments of my spiritual and intellectual life, the one in which I realized that in order to be a decent Catholic one had to be a Protestant. Years later, in a dispute fueled, I fear, by too much yuletide scotch, I returned to that memory. An uncle by marriage and a lovable Chestertonian Catholic told me that Father Küng ought to get out of the church if he could not play by the rules— meaning, obey the Pope. I had an insight which on reflection I found to be worth something even though it was used for rhetorical effect at the time. Can a Catholic talk like a Protestant and thrive in the Catholic Church? No. Can a Protestant become a Catholic while remaining a Protestant? No. If a Protestant may not be a Catholic, then is the Roman Catholic church catholic? No. It is still the fragment left behind by Luther, the church that Luther could no longer live in and that would not live with protest against itself. Luther is being heard from again—some would consider this a curse, others a blessing. But, is the answer once again to be"obey"? Are we doomed once again to drive people out or shut them up? I doubt it and I have hope, and that for two reasons: first, many of the leaders of the church have learned enormously in the past quarter century and they may check the others who have learned little; and, second, Luther will not leave this time even if he is put out. On these two graces lies the hope of revival of the church's catholicity of spirit.

But how did we, how did the church, ever miss the point of modernity? Possibly because the point was poised as a dagger at our throat. For many of us English–speaking Catholics it was Bernard Lonergan who thoroughly baptized modernity, and it took even this extraordinary thinker two distinct stages to accomplish it for himself: the first stage was embodied in the composition of *Insight* when he spelled out the procedures and exigencies of intelligence, and the second the period of the composition of *Method in Theology* when he clawed his way through the thicket of historicity and the relativity of doctrine. He taught a large number of us what thinking means in the contemporary world, and then recouped for us our old conviction that thinking that is not driven by love and faith is hardly thinking at all.

One of the advantages of reading the American naturalists like John Dewey is that they have a firm grasp on what the responsibilities of intelligence are; but there is the other point, and one must read people like Lonergan to get that straight: critical intelligence untouched by the love of God and one's neighbor is likely to turn out cramped and even destructive. Dewey is clearly correct about the first point: thinking is moral, it has moral meaning, implications, and contexts. Lonergan is correct about the second: orthodoxies of all sorts, Dewey's as well as Roman, are perverse and dark unless transformed by the love of God and by the practice of self-criticism. Orthodoxy may mean two things: the conviction that some truth has been delivered or found and should be prized and clung to and stood for; or it may mean an emotional and psychic fusion with that truth, the collapse of belief into knowledge justified ideologically, and the consequent effort to destroy opposing convictions and to end questions. It is not the first but the second orthodoxy which now threatens Catholic theologians, an orthodoxy which has lost its grip on its own historicity.

This quest for certitude, this love of the definitive, this desire for the unquestionable which powers so much of our modern Catholic history must end. The old assumption, sharply etched in my memories of childhood and seminary, is that the teaching which has had the field in every area is not merely worthy of respect but is true to one degree or another and so beyond question, critical review, and reformation. This turns the lively terms "tradition" and "magisterium" into deadly talismans. After all, Jesus modified Moses, a move pitted against the tradition and the magisterium. Matthew and Paul modified Jesus' bare and spare saying on divorce once they found themselves in circumstances quite different from those of Jesus. Are Matthew and Paul to be accused of middle-class Christianity—of which Cardinal Ratzinger recently accused Father Curran? Is Father Curran to be excluded from the circle of Catholic theology because he, in a new situation, puts questions to the text of Matthew and Paul? If the last word on marriage was not spoken by Jesus, shall we take it that Pope John Paul II has spoken it? We still suffer deeply, I fear, from the syndrome of Roman integralism.

The theologians' guild has never had much power in the church; it has had no authority in the sense that the bishops and the Roman Curia have, with the exception of the influence wielded by the medieval theologians through their institutionalized position in the universities. They have some fragment of that influence left in the present situation when and if the administrators of the universities will support them. Otherwise, theologians have had influence only when they have been invited to speak by patrons and protected by them. I have nothing against the exercise of authority by invitation since I think that is the mode by which authority ought to be established and exercise itself. But unless authority is institutionalized, unless the invitation becomes a structure of service as it did in the case of the episcopacy, we should not be surprised to see the signatures of a thousand theologians ignored.

We theologians have not dealt corporately with Rome, with our local hierarchies, with our local bishop. Except for a gasp or two such as the birth control controversy when several hundred clerical theologians surrendered their episcopal hopes, or the Küng protest, we have not spoken together. We are in fact a politically marginal group in the church—utterly essential to the Catholic way of life and just as utterly powerless. We meet and talk and pass an occasional resolution and return to our classes. The canon lawyers have understood what we have not, that it takes a strategy and relentless pressure to move the ecclesiastical mountain. The theologians must learn to act politically in the church if the mountain is to be moved. To some extent we were handed our freedom by popes and bishops, and did not achieve it ourselves. We were promoted to public responsibility by the second Vatican council, and we have our freedom on borrowed time. Our predecessors paid a terrible price over a century and more for their inability to take a stand for the church, to find a public voice, a voice of service which would not be silenced. By and large the theological community has used its newly bestowed freedom well and to the great advantage of the church for the past quarter of a century, and it is now time to look for that concentrated public voice, an institution to express and focus our service to the church in the United States.

Let me rehearse what I have been saying somewhat chattily. I think, in line with our most ancient tradition, that thinking is loving God when in fact it is so motivated. I take theology to be *fides quaerens intellectum*. That is the old thing. A new thing is this: thinking is necessarily critical. This I take to be the gift of the Enlightenment whose correction and implementation is an important aspect of the current service of theology in the church. I think that there is authority in thinking, namely the intrinsic demands of a disciplined intelligence; that belief is an authority in thinking in that it tells us where to begin and provides us with a context and an object for reflection. People invariably think in and about their traditions, and Catholic theologians think in and about theirs.

But is there authority over thinking? Yes, but only in carefully qualified senses. Communities have offices and officers who may exercise supportive and dialogic authority over thinking. After all, thinking is a communal enterprise, resting on and working for the community, and this is the great fact that keeps thinking *pragmatische*. There is no theologian, just as there is no Pope, who does not need criticism. But no one, no officer, no group, even if that group happens to be theologians, should tell anyone, order anyone, what to think or believe. The community can and at certain points must define itself, but it must not attempt to control believing or thinking about believing or use threats to enforce its will. Both critical reflection and public teaching have rights and duties in the church, and these remain to be brought into clearer and more cooperative political relationship.

Theology is autonomous not because it is secular or secularist but because it is a discipline, because it is thinking. It does not proclaim itself autonomous in order to exist in public and nondenominational institutions—although this is a consummation devoutly to be wished in my opinion—but it proclaims itself autonomous in order to exist at all, in any university and even in any church. The days when theologians might be told what to think, or what to think about, or what not to think or say or write are at an end for the good of the church. In order to be thinking at all, in order that intelligence may be put fully at the service of the church, theology must be free of external constraint whether by law or by the will of leaders. If that simple lesson has not been learned or cannot be learned, then the church, its leaders and its theologians are in serious trouble. If the church and its institutions of higher learning cannot abide the most vigorous argument and dissent, responsibly conducted, then it is not from the theologians that the term catholic ought to be stripped, but from the church itself and its institutions of higher learning. Thinking is Catholic (if indeed we need to classify it at all) by virtue of its ecclesial context, its ecclesial intention, and its subject matter, not by its conformity to any standard or to the beliefs of any office holder.

Surely there is place for the theologians to put in a theoretic context the problem of evil, to worry it through, even if they must leave it again as it always has been, a great mystery. Surely theologians may wonder aloud and publicly whether and in what sense God is— which any sane person in our world wonders about even when he or she prays. Surely it is our task to ask whether what we have been taught is true, and on what grounds we can trust its truth, and whether we have understood it correctly and lived by it authentically. Surely then we can wonder and argue the host of questions which beset us about our beliefs and, at that very same time and by that very act of wondering and worrying, be acting in the service of the church. Surely a theologian can serve the time honored role of lightning rod, spur, burr, mediator of questions and criticisms, without the leaders of the church taking us to be enemies and adopting the time honored stratagem of exile, now the spiritual exile, of lifting our title "catholic theologian," thereby meaning to rob us of our public voice. Is doubt, is wonder, is questioning, is criticizing to have no public place in the church's life? Rabbi Gamaliel has much to teach Cardinal Ratzinger (Acts 5:38–39).

We theologians have inherited the ideal by which we are to live. We find the ideal articulated and refined in our own history. Our reflection, in the first place, is existential and pluralist, as the variety of New Testament witnesses signals us and the enormous malleability of the Christian tradition displays. The fact is confirmed in the recent work of Raymond Brown and Elisabeth Schüssler Fiorenza on Christians of the first and second generations. Secondly, our reflection is to be doctrinal, for Christianity has a content which it cannot leave behind: Catholic and Protestant Christianity is not Arian and is not Unitarian, as it long ago decided not to be and, in my mind, for good reason. Doctrine can be taught nondogmatically, however, and used as an invitation rather than a club. Thirdly, our reflection is to be systematic as was that of our medieval predecessors who did not ignore their culture and its treasures and virtues in casting a homiletic and neoplatonic past into Aristotelian metaphysical terms, as we are now casting our integralist and anti-Protestant past into new terms for our new culture. Fourthly, our reflection must be prophetic, for no Catholic may go back on the Reformation. We should not allow Hans Küng to be a lone and lonely proponent of the achievement of the reformers, that is, of the unrelenting criticism of institutionalized practice and the recognition of the ubiquitous danger of bureaucratic hubris. Fifthly, our reflection must be critical: we must absorb the lessons of the Enlightenment, by embracing both philosophical criticism of every teaching and political criticism of every institution. Our revisionist and liberation theologians constantly give us good example of this. Finally, our reflection must be economical and dialogic, informed by the data and meanings of other Christian churches and other religions. We must see the hard questions raised in this regard, the question of the truth found in east and west, as put to us recently by Paul Knitter, and the question of the relation between Christianity and Judaism much in the line taken for two decades by Gerard Sloyan and more recently by Darrell Fasching.

I regard this simply as a declaration of an ideal by which we work most of the time. I have seen the ideal in operation at every meeting of our Society. The values implied in this theological ideal are human values: democracy, freedom, equality, patience, respect, dialogue. The terms are trite, to be sure, but the ideal is utterly profound and deeply religious and worth a life. These values and ideals mediate

God to contemporary consciousnness. No doubt they bring us to wonder about and reject other ideals—monarchy, and unconditioned and unresponsive and solitary exercise of authority among them. We do not, I think, oppose office or hierarchy; we are not antinomians, levelers, or even congregationalists. We do oppose ownership; no one except God owns the church, and most especially not those who hold it by canonical and civil title.

The virtues and ideals I enunciate are not strictly speaking theological; they are human ideals, religious ideals, Christian ideals which must inhere in the work of theologians. They are in fact our ideals even when we are too tired or too frightened to live by them. From these ideals it is too late to separate us. We have bit the apple. If this is to be marked as another version of modernism's fatal pride, then I am indeed doomed and so be it.

But my belief is that my ideal is not arrogant. My hope is that we live by the ideal of respectful inquiry as well as freedom; by virtue of responsibility which excludes shooting from the theological hip and disdains the practice of guerrilla warfare in the church; by the virtue of support for one's brothers and sisters in the discipline; by the ideal of frank and democratic communication with the leaders of the church, teaching both them and ourselves that Catholicism can survive egalitarianism; by the conviction that in a church that belongs to us all and which needs the ministry of each, there is no one voice, there is in fact a chorus, a chorus in need of a director rather than a censor or a product labeler.

Structures and authorities come into being to serve communities. The episcopacy was a solution to the problems of the second century church. In the wake of the second Vatican Council episcopal conferences and councils emerged and have come to serve new purposes. They have in the course of their work put a slight but real check on papal exercise of direct authority. We need this development, for no church as complex and culturally pluralist as our own can survive the exercise of unmediated and unchecked absolute monarchy. We have further needs—we need the *sensus fidelium* expressed and bishops who can listen to it; we need improved communication between bishops and Catholic higher educational institutions; and we need a display of the corporate nature of theological reflection and theological life.

While the meeting of these many needs exceeds our reach as theologians, the last does not. It is within our reach to establish and support an ecclesiastically independent national theological commission whose burden it shall be to express our service to the church, to promote responsible dialogue between bishops and theologians and among theologians themselves on especially difficult issues, and to speak for both the academic rights and ecclesial responsibilities of theologians. It should be answerable to the national societies of professionals with theological interests. It ought to be funded by the societies. And it should offer its services to individual theologians and the professors of religious studies in Catholic institutions, to administrators of Catholic colleges and universities and to bishops. It should contribute its views to the American bishops on issues and events bearing on academic freedom and theological responsibility. Indeed, its first task should be to formulate a statement of principles on freedom and responsibility for the use of bishops, university administrators, and theologians. Above all, it should function under the conviction that the church now needs not only the voices of individual theologians but a voice for theologians, and that the voice will promote the intellectual and spiritual health of the church. In this spirit the CTS board of directors this week issued the following proposal:

> The board of directors of the College Theology Society proposes to the boards of the Catholic Theological Society of America, the Canon Law Society, and the Catholic Biblical Association that representatives of the societies meet at the earliest possible date and at the invitation of the director of the Association of Catholic Colleges and Universities to consider the establishment, the structure, the goals and the composition of a national committee on the academic and ecclesial rights and responsibilities of exegetes and theologians.

You must forgive me for the circuitous route I took in order to get to the point, but I wanted to convey to you some of my personal reasons for supporting the proposal of our board and my sense of its urgency. I am deeply grateful for the opportunity you afforded me to think and speak about it, and for the honor you have done me by making me president for the past two years.

Part Six

CHARTING A NUANCED THEOLOGICAL COURSE

PLURALISM OR POLARIZATION? THE RESULTS OF A CTS SURVEY

Dennis M. Doyle,
Michael H. Barnes
University of Dayton

Byron R. Johnson
Memphis State University

ABSTRACT

In response to current debate concerning the degree of differences between the beliefs of Catholic theologians and the beliefs of Catholic parishioners, we constructed a survey designed to measure whether there is indeed a considerable gap. Although we found significant differences between the two groups on most issues of religious belief, we did not find evidence of polarization. Rather, we found much overlap, with theologians tending to understand religious beliefs in a more nuanced manner. Following our discussion of the implications of our findings is a response by William R. Shea with replies from each of the authors of the study.

In a review of Hans Küng's *Eternal Life?*, Thomas Sheehan claimed that contemporary Catholic theology is today dominated by a liberal approach that leads theologians to deny many elements of the faith thought to be essential by ordinary Catholic believers.[1] Among these

Dennis M. Doyle is an assistant professor of religious studies at the University of Dayton. He holds a doctorate from the Catholic University of America where he specialized in Catechetics, Religion and Culture, and Catholic studies. He is currently working in Ecclesiology and Pastoral Ministry. His articles have appeared in Living Light, The Thomist, and Method: Journal of Lonergan Studies.

Michael H. Barnes, associate professor of religious studies and a teacher in the CORE interdisciplinary program at the University of Dayton (Dayton, OH 45469) is the author of the introduction to religion In the Presence of Mystery (1984), of articles on religion and science, and is working on an analysis of forms of science and religion as manifestations of cognitive developmental patterns in culture and the individual.

Byron R. Johnson, Assistant Professor of Criminal Justice at Memphis State University, has written on the interrelation of religious beliefs and values for various journals, and for Crime, Values, and Religion, James Day and Wm. Laufer, eds. (1987), on statistical studies of the relation between religiousness and behavior in a correctional institution.

issues are the questions of whether Jesus thought of himself as God, whether he rose from the dead, and whether he founded a Church. Sheehan posited that the liberal consensus of theologians is moving the Catholic Church along a course that will eventually exhaust it of anything that distinguishes it from any other social or political organization. Throughout the article Sheehan implies that Catholic theologians and Catholic parishioners represent two polarized groupings, the former highly liberal and the latter highly traditional.

In response to Sheehan, critics such as Raymond Brown, Andrew Greeley, and David Tracy have argued that there is no liberal consensus among theologians and that any differences in understanding between theologians and parishioners require an analysis that goes much deeper than the simplistic charge that theologians reject what the parishioners accept.[2]

We designed a survey in the hopes of shedding some empirical light on this debate. We analyzed and compared the College Theology Society and a Catholic parish in Dayton, Ohio. We plan to make available the full socio-scientific results of this study in a future article. We will here briefly review our findings and conclusions in order to set the stage for William Shea's response to the study and for our own further reflections.

Design of the Study

Our survey covered ten religious issues: Afterlife, Church Authority, God, Exclusivity, Eucharist, Divinity of Christ, Resurrection, Founding of the Church, Jesus' Self-Identity, and Miracles. The instrument was designed to sort responses into three major categories: traditional, nuanced, and highly liberal. A "traditional" response was registered when the respondent preferred the more traditional statement on two out of two choices concerning a particular issue. A "nuanced" response was registered when the respondent preferred a somewhat liberal response on the first choice on an issue, but then preferred a more traditional statement over a highly liberal statement on the second choice. A "highly liberal" response was registered when the respondent preferred the more liberal statement on both choices.

Our rationale was that if, as implied by Sheehan (1984), there exist two radically different Catholicisms, that of the liberal consensus of theologians and that of the traditional believers in the pews, then the respondents would fall with high regularity into two different groups. Parishioners would rather consistently prefer traditional responses, and theologians would rather consistently prefer the more liberal responses. Sheehan's implications about the degree and nature of the differences between theologians and parishioners would be placed in serious question if these tendencies did not emerge.

Findings

Finding 1: Catholic theologians and Catholic parishioners differ significantly on various issues of religious belief.

Our analysis showed statistically significant differences between the responses of theologians and the responses of parishioners on nine out of ten issues. (The exception was the eucharist.) A given set of responses could predict whether the respondent were a theologian or a parishioner in 84.8% of the cases. On every issue, parishioners register more traditional than theologians.

Finding 2: Although theologians and parishioners are significantly different, they do not represent two polarized groupings.

For both parishioners and theologians the highest percentage of respondents on every issue fell into either the traditional or the nuanced category. Whereas the highest percentage of parishioners registered as traditional on eight out of ten issues, the highest percentage of theologians also registered as traditional on five out of ten issues. This finding runs counter to the assumption that theologians are highly liberal on most issues of religious belief.

Support for the finding that theologians and parishioners are not polarized is further provided by a discriminant analysis of the two groups. The findings from the discriminant analysis are summarized in figure 4. The stacked histogram reflects visually how theologians and parishioners responded in comprehensive terms to the issues of religious belief. It is clear from the histogram that theologians are different from parishioner; it is also apparent, however, that there is considerable overlap between the two groups. If theologians and parishioners were polarized, no such clustering or overlapping would exist.

In figure 1 we see that while theologians do not register as traditional so frequently as parishioners, the two groups are not polarized. Figure 2 illustrates a somewhat parallel relationship between nuanced theologians and nuanced parishioners. Theologians are more likely to prefer a nuanced interpretation of religious belief, but they do not in any way represent a group diametrically opposing the beliefs of parishioners. In figure 3 we see that there is little consistent difference between highly liberal theologians and highly liberal parishioners. In fact, overall both theologians and parishioners are more likely to be nuanced or traditional than highly liberal. In both groups the highest percentage of respondents did not register as highly liberal on any of the ten issues. For both groups, the highly liberal category was the least likely response on eight of ten issues.

Finding 3: A considerable amount of diversity does exist among theologians themselves and to a somewhat lesser extent among parishioners.

Figure 5 indicates that theologians tend most often to be nuanced; many are traditional; a notable minority are highly liberal. Theologians tend to cluster in the nuanced category on the issues of Authority and the Founding of the Church; on no other issues is there such significant clustering.

Among parishioners we do not see as wide a spread, but a considerable amount of diversity is still present. Figure 6 indicates that although parishioners do tend to cluster in the traditional category, on most issues a considerable number of parishioners registered either nuanced or highly liberal. The only exceptions to this are the issues of Miracles and Belief in God.

Conclusions

If Sheehan were correct in the way that he distinguished between the traditional believers in the pews and the liberal consensus of theologians, then (1) theologians would have clustered in the highly liberal category, (2) parishioners would have clustered in the traditional category, and (3) there would have been little, if any, overlapping between theologians and parishioners.

Our findings tend rather to support the arguments of critics such as Brown, Greeley, and Tracy. We conclude (1) that there is no such thing as a liberal consensus among Catholic theologians, (2) that while the majority of parishioners tend to be traditional a significant number also tend to be nuanced or even highly liberal, and (3) that theologians and parishioners are not polarized, but there is significant overlapping.

Our findings suggest that Sheehan has misread the current situation of the Catholic Church. We have identified a large group of Catholics who do not fall simply under the categories of traditional or liberal. This group can be easy to overlook, yet according to our study it includes the highest percentage of theologians and a significant number of parishioners. The existence of this group allows us to conclude that traditional Catholic belief is still integral to the thinking of most Catholic theologians as well as parishioners, whether or not they appear to understand such belief in a nuanced fashion.

Our study indicates that the Catholic Church is characterized by theological pluralism, but nothing like the polarization suggested by Sheehan. It is true that the Church is composed of persons some of whom are traditional, some nuanced, and others highly liberal. However, rather than a divided Church moving simultaneously in opposite directions, a picture can be drawn of a Church developing more and more nuanced positions in response to contemporary developments.

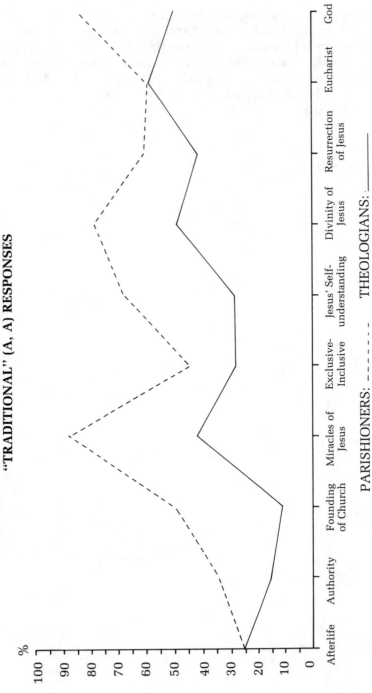

FIGURE 1

PERCENTAGES OF THEOLOGIANS AND PARISHIONERS CHOOSING
"TRADITIONAL" (A, A) RESPONSES

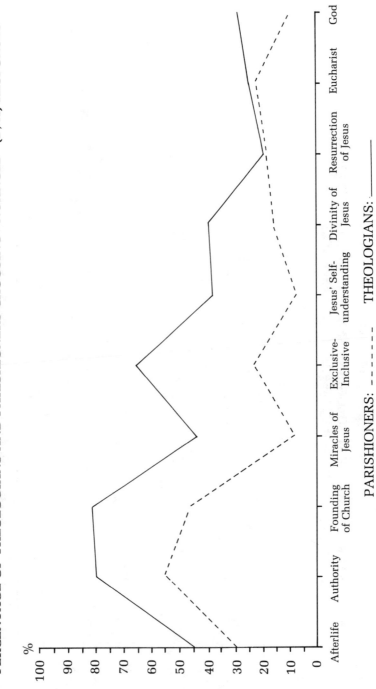

FIGURE 2

PERCENTAGE OF THEOLOGIANS AND PARISHIONERS CHOOSING "NUANCED" (B, A) RESPONSES

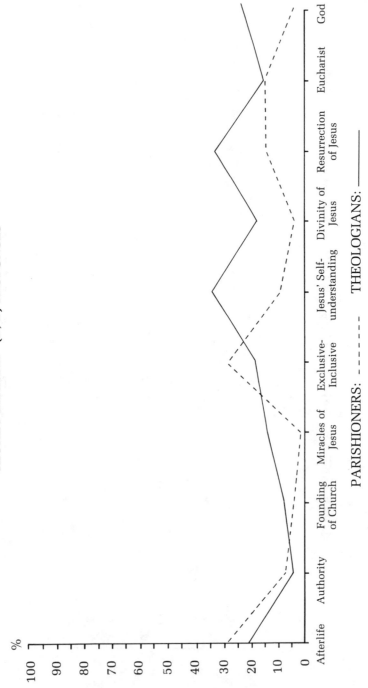

FIGURE 3

PERCENTAGE OF THEOLOGIANS AND PARISHIONERS CHOOSING "HIGHLY LIBERAL" (B, B) RESPONSES

PARISHIONERS: - - - - - -   THEOLOGIANS: ———

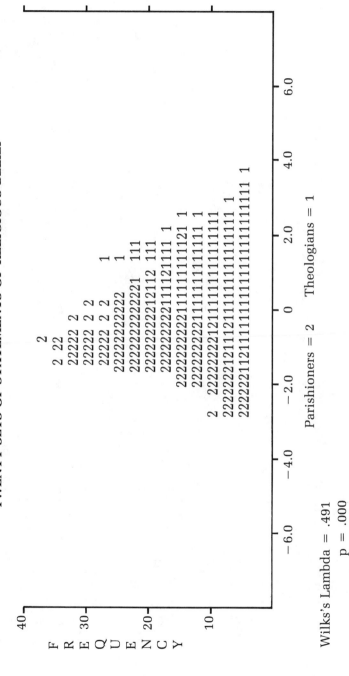

FIGURE 4
STACKED HISTOGRAM FROM DISCRIMINANT ANALYSIS
COMPARING THEOLOGIANS AND PARISHIONERS ON
TWENTY SETS OF STATEMENTS OF RELIGIOUS BELIEF

Wilks's Lambda = .491
p = .000

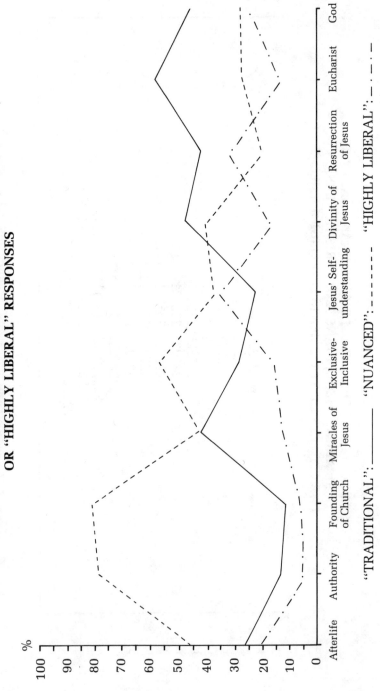

FIGURE 5

PERCENTAGES OF THEOLOGIANS CHOOSING "TRADITIONAL," "NUANCED," OR "HIGHLY LIBERAL" RESPONSES

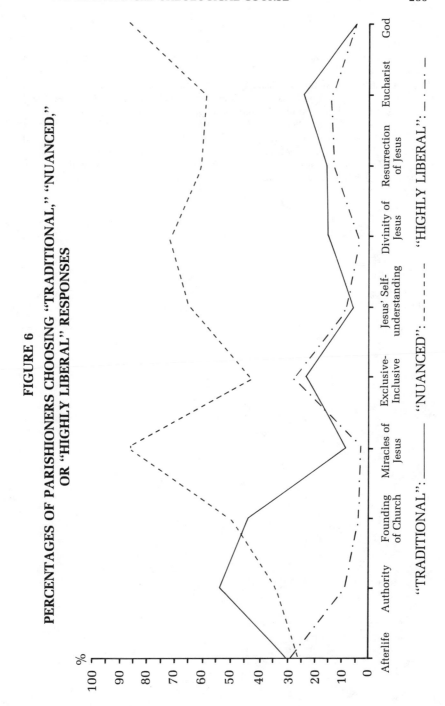

FIGURE 6

PERCENTAGES OF PARISHIONERS CHOOSING "TRADITIONAL," "NUANCED," OR "HIGHLY LIBERAL" RESPONSES

"TRADITIONAL": ——— "NUANCED": ‑ ‑ ‑ ‑ "HIGHLY LIBERAL": ‑ · ‑ · ‑

NOTES

1. "Revolution in the Church," *New York Review of Books* (June 14, 1984), pp. 35–39.

2. For criticisms of Sheehan see, Raymond E. Brown, "Liberals, Ultraconservatives, and the Misinterpretation of Catholic Biblical Exegesis," *Cross Currents* 34 (Fall 1984), 311–28; a revised version of this material appears in *Biblical Exegesis and Church Doctrine* (N.Y.: Paulist, 1985), pp. 54–85. See also Joseph A. Fitzmyer and Raymond E. Brown, "Danger Also From the Left," *The Bible Today*, 23 (March 1985), 105–10; Gerald O'Collins, *The Tablet*, (October 13, 20, 1984); Andrew Greeley and David Tracy, "The End of Catholicism?" *Commonweal* (August 10, 1984) with reply by Thomas Sheehan and brief commentaries by various authors (September 21 and October 5, 1984).

A RESPONSE

William M. Shea
University of South Florida
and
The Woodrow Wilson International Center for
Scholars
Smithsonian Institution

Andrew Greeley, in his *Commonwealth* (August, 1984) critique of
Thomas Sheehan's piece on the liberal consensus, charged that the
liberals Sheehan represents are stuck in Paul Ricoeur's "critical moment," between naivetés, and that as a result they are mired in immature agnosticism. Being thus stuck and mired, I admit, is one of
my nightmares, and I also admit that I have not solved the dilemma
of naivetés as cleanly as Greeley has. With David Tracy and Greeley,
I do not put much stock in Sheehan's claim that the distinctive
Catholic vision is slipping away. Granted, if the theologians by and
large did not believe all the doctrines that Sheehan claims that they
do not, they would hardly be Catholics or Christians at all. But the
survey appears to upend him on this, supporting my common sense
opinion that Catholic theologians remain quite fiercely Catholic
through the storms of the "critical moment."

Secondly, I think that the conclusion to the survey is correct,
namely that Sheehan is mistaken to posit a polarization between the
theologian and the person in the pew. For this bit of clarity we can
be grateful. But, does there emerge a polarity between the liberal
theologians and the nuanced and traditional theologians? How are
we to understand the ten to thirty percent of theologians who register

William M. Shea, Professor of Religious Studies at the University of South Florida
(Tampa, FL 33620) is a specialist in American religious thought and theological
method. He is the author of The Naturalists and the Supernatural: Studies in Horizon
and an American Philosophy of Religion (1984). He is currently a fellow at the Woodrow Wilson International Center for Scholars, and is working on a book on higher
education, culture, and theology.

liberal responses to the questions? And what relation might we find between those who register liberal and those who register nuanced responses, or between the nuancers and those who choose traditional language? Let us begin with the statistical pie sliced so as to join nuancers and the traditional theologians. In this reading:

> 94% of Catholic theologians take doctrinal authority seriously
> 93% of theologians think Jesus founded a church
> 85% believe that Jesus worked miracles
> 83% believe that Christianity is the superior religion
> 87% believe that Jesus is divine and
> 84% believe in the real presence.

When one reads the data in this way Catholic theologians come off a very conservative bunch indeed, and when it comes to matters of belief this reading is probably accurate.

But if one switches the meaning of "nuanced" ever so much in the direction that Sheehan (and many traditionalists!) would wish and thereby join "nuanced" to "liberal," the picture is somewhat different:

> 84% of theologians have problems with the traditional understanding of authority in the church
> 86% do not take literally Jesus' founding of a church
> 55% reject the historicity of some and even most of the miracle stories
> 70% have abandoned the salvational exclusivity of Christianity and
> 50% do no accept the strict divinity of Jesus.

The first reading would put some of the *Wanderer's* fears to rest and allow it to concentrate entirely on the small percentage of heretics, however it may miss the delicious sense of crisis and the pleasures of global denunciation. But if the second reading makes any sense at all, the *Wanderer* will be able to whoop it up for years to come. Now, is there anything to be said for this second slicing of the pie? Granted, mediators and nuancers regularly get slammed and misunderstood by the simpler folk at either end of the spectrum, is there anything to the suggestion that the nuancers are really changing things profoundly without 'fessing up, perhaps even to themselves? It seems perfectly clear that the majority of theologians choose statements of belief reasonably close to traditional language, but can we mark them off in any way from the traditionalists?

Well, there are two things that lend some likelihood to Sheehan's claim that something a bit more foundation-shaking is going forward

than the survey analysis might indicate. One is the probability established by Christian history that theologians may gnaw away at
serious issues while claiming that nothing is really changing. I offer
as an example the post-Tridentine and post-Vatican II Catholic claim
that the church is what it always was. Even the person of the most
ordinary intelligence who had no axe to grind, living on both sides
of these two great divides, would know the vast change that took
place in the transition from the medieval to the modern Roman
church and from the modern to the contemporary Roman church. It
is disingenuous to claim otherwise, and disingenuousness is the
special gift and charm of liberals and nuancers.

Secondly, what brings some of us to place even the unwilling
"nuancer" with the liberals is a decisive matter of principle, a new
principle that constitutes the "liberal consensus" that Sheehan at
once pointed out and misrepresented. That consensus, in the survey's terms, is composed of nuancers and liberals. The principle is
that answers to theological questions (a) are not already given in a
document or a tradition and (b) can not be given by any authority
outside the discipline, but (c) only through procedures and under
standards immanent to the discipline. To put it bluntly, the bishop
of Rome, a council of bishops, and the scriptures might proclaim an
answer to a theological question all day and all night and the theologian or exegete might fall silent before the proclamation, but he or
she, nuancer or liberal, would not for a moment think the proclamation an answer to a theological or exegetical question. Theological
answers to theological questions are provided by theologians, not by
the magisterium unless it wishes its claims to be assessed theologically and so throw itself into the theological arena.

Now the answers that scholars come up with to their many questions may be more or less nuanced, but the principle is not nuanced
at all. In fact, it distinguishes nuanced from traditional and joins
nuanced firmly to the liberal side of things. It represents a very
dramatic change that makes contemporary theology unlike any that
has survived within Roman Catholicism since the Reformation at
least. Tracy is correct: what is new and agreed upon by theologians
is not a new doctrine or set of doctrines. What is new and agreed
upon is the way theologians go about their public business, and it
is under the same principle whether they are nuancers or liberals.
If I were a traditionalist or, indeed, the Cardinal Prefect of the Congregation for the Doctrine of the Faith, it wouldn't take me too long
to figure out that the pieties of the nuanced and the impieties of the
liberals are flowers on the same stem. Nuancers are perhaps more
patient with a traditional mode of discourse and more devoted to it

than liberals, but in principle it would be hard to tell one from the other. In a word, while liberals are not simpleminded positivists and while the nuancers may disagree with them on matters of adequate contemporary expression, they are at one in their practice of theology, and in this are both quite distinct from the traditionals.

Finally, the change of principle for the theologians seems to be a refined and philosophically articulated version of the change among the people in downtown Dayton. They, too, in large numbers have serious reservations about what they are told is traditional Catholic doctrine. If the pew's nuancers are joined to the pew's liberals, then

64% of lay people have problems with traditional understandings of authority in the church

49% do not take literally the claim that Jesus founded the church, at least as it now stands

11% reject the historicity of some or most of the gospel miracle stories

52% have abandoned the unqualified superiority of Christianity and

20% do not accept the divinity of Jesus

Although Sheehan may have been mistaken to claim a contradiction between the desk and the pew, still there is an abyss in the church between the old and new principles for theology and for belief. My only reservation about the study under discussion, and I hope I have not treated it cavalierly, is that it may be used to avoid facing the massive change in American theology and, as the study provides a clue, in American Catholicism. In fact it seems to me to support some of the findings reported by Andrew Greeley in his illuminating *American Catholics Since the Council: An Unauthorized Report* (1985). The issue is not belief in doctrines but Catholic notions of authority.

AUTHORS' RESPONSES

I would like to thank William Shea for his careful study and analysis of the implications of our survey. He has raised for discussion many important issues.

The main thrust of Shea's response is to argue against an overly optimistic interpretation of our results. In general, I accept this qualification. Our own interpretation was directed toward suggesting that Sheehan's negative analysis of the current state of the Catholic church is wrong; our manner of presentation, therefore, stressed the positive. In contrast to Sheehan's picture of polarization we found that our data supported a picture of healthy pluralism. I agree with Shea that this cannot be taken to suggest that the Church does not face serious problems of division over particular issues and over general approaches to issues. Many such tensions exist within the Church; to minimize them or to ignore them would not be helpful, and, as Shea demonstrates, would not be supported by our data.

I feel, however, that as our presentation of our results may have been a bit optimistic because of the negativity against which it was directed, so Shea's response dwells on the dark side of things in reaction to us. I wish to reply to Shea's response in such a way as to move toward a balance.

Shea zeroes in on what he considers to be *the* underlying issue: theological method, and in particular the status of Church authority in theological method. It is here, Shea claims, that the nuancers are in agreement with the liberals, and it is here that the line of polarization within the Church may be drawn.

There are points in this analysis with which I agree. The question of the status of theological method in relation to Church authority is one of the most important issues underlying our study and the source of a significant amount of division among Church members. It is also true that the nuancers are in agreement with the liberals on many matters related to this question.

I wish, however, to make two qualifications regarding Shea's analysis. First, although the nuancers do share with the liberals many presuppositions concerning theological method and Church authority, they also have distinct differences. Shea points out that for both nuancers and liberals, the Church is not the final determiner of theological conclusions. I agree that this is so. Nuancers, however, are willing in general to grant special status to Church authority; liberals are not willing to grant any special status whatsoever. This difference has tremendous implications for theological method. Saying that Church authority is not the final determiner of theological conclusions is a far cry from suggesting that authoritative Church teaching is not to be considered by theologians with great seriousness as having some special status.

Second, as important and as divisive as the issue of theological method is, it is not the only underlying issue involved here. To focus on this issue exclusively is to miss other important matters. I will mention two: loyalty to the Church and the desire to preserve a distinctly Catholic vision. These are the underlying issues that would allow the nuancers to be connected with the traditionals. I would like to suggest, in contrast to the general thrust of Shea's response, that the issues linking the nuancers with the traditionals are at least as important as the issues linking the nuancers with the liberals.

This brings me to my final point. Shea has shown us two different ways that the statistical pie could be sliced into two pieces. As we were analyzing our data and formulating our results, we were well aware that various interpretations were possible. Of the three scholars who conducted this survey, one of us tends to be traditional, one of us tends to be nuanced, and the third tends to be highly liberal. We all had somewhat different readings of the situation, and were frequently correcting each other as to the proper view of things. One thing in the final analysis that we all agreed on, however, is that we are dealing here with three irreducible pieces of pie. It is true that liberal extremists might slice it into two pieces in one way and that traditional extremists might slice it into two pieces in the opposite way. It is true that liberal extremists might slice it into two pieces in one way and that traditional extremists might slice it into two pieces in the opposite way. To do so, however, would be to distort the findings. The differences of the nuanced from both the traditionals and the liberals are significant; to lump the nuanced in with either side is to fail to acknowledge the importance of one set of these differences. It might be legitimate to identify more than the three groups that we found, but not less than those three.

William Shea is the one who wrote in response to Blessed Rage for Order that David Tracy would do well to give more consideration to the ecclesial context within which the theologian operates.[1] I now ask the same of Shea. Is critical-mindedness necessarily inversely proportional to an attitude of loyalty to Church authority? Shea's willingness to lump the nuancers in with the liberals would imply that Shea thinks that it is, and yet I doubt that Shea himself holds such an unnuanced position.

I want to again thank Shea for making it clear that the results of our survey are in no way a panacea for current tensions and divisions within the Church. Our claim is simply that when placed against the background of the picture of polarization painted by Sheehan, our study indicates the likelihood of a much healthier picture of a pluralistic church with some members at either extreme but with much clustering somewhere between the traditional and nuanced positions.

University of Dayton   DENNIS M. DOYLE

------

[1]William M. Shea, "Revisionist Foundational Theology," *Anglican Theological Review* 58 (July 1978), pp. 263–79.

What Shea has done in his perceptive remarks is to focus on the problem of method as the major issue. The liberal consensus of which Sheehan spoke may be not so much a matter of agreement on doctrine as on a method, one that both nuanced and highly liberal theologians may share, that answers to theological questions 1) are not already in the received documents and tradition, 2) cannot be provided except by theologians, 3) using standards of theological inquiry. The implications of this would seem to be that there is a kind of theologizing going on which proceeds without due regard for the tradition and with an intellectual independence (perhaps even arrogance) that is a challenge to traditional authority. Shea does not really say that he disapproves of this new method, but only that it seems to him to represent "an abyss in the church between the old and new principles for theology and for belief;" and that there is something very troublesome occurring that should not be glossed over. There is much that is accurate in this. Something is going on that may well represent a massive change, as Shea says.

Most theologians, however, including the "nuanced," I believe, are probably not part of this massive change in a deliberate way. If they were to formulate the method of finding answers to theological questions they might say something somewhat different from Shea's three rules: that answers to theological questions 1) cannot be found in the received documents alone because further interpretation is a recurring necessity, 2) cannot be provided without doing theological reflection, and that 3) such reflection must be guided by one's life in the community of the Church.

It is the third of these three rules that is the crucial one here. It is the one that relates the theologian back to the magisterium. Even with this form of the rules there will still be arguments. The theologians will have confidence that they are doing intelligent and faithful work and will wonder why certain cardinals or bishops resist their conclusions. The magisterial authorities will have confidence they represent the authentic tradition of the Church and will wonder why certain theologians are so obstinate in flaunting their innovations. All this is normal, even in the relations between nuanced but tradition-minded theologians and representatives of the hierarchical magisterium.

Shea's version of the third rule here represents a source of tension beyond the normal differences between theologian and hierarchical magisterium. That is that the theologian is to proceed by standards immanent to the discipline of theology as a form of rational analysis and inquiry. Shea here seems to be alluding to the kind of theology that David Tracy called "revisionist," one in which the rules of the discipline become more challenging to traditional belief. Tracy expressed it strongly in his *Blessed Rage for Order* (1975):

> The modern Christian theologian cannot ethically do other than challenge the traditional self-understanding of the theologian. He no longer sees his task as a simple defense of or even as an orthodox reinterpretation of traditional belief. Rather, he finds that his ethical commitment to the morality of scientific knowledge forces him to assume a critical posture towards his own and his tradition's beliefs. He insists, to be sure, that the concept "critical" does not bear a simply negative meaning. But critical does mean a fidelity to open-ended inquiry, a loyalty to defended methodological canons, a willingness to follow the evidence wherever it may lead (p. 7).

Tracy's revisionist theology shares with other theological approaches a sense that the method of theology is not just reflection on the authoritative tradition but a somewhat equal interaction between the tradition and whatever it is that constitutes the best available methods for rational inquiry along with the best conclusions based on those methods. Correlational theologies, liberation theologies challenging tradition with the demands of praxis, existential-experiential theologies—these also are part of the massive change of which Shea speaks. They can all be called "critical" theologies, in a general way.

The question comes down to the two versions of rule #3. Is it the guidance of the life of the Church (including the role of the magisterium) that is to be predominant as the norm of theological reflection upon tradition? Or is tradition to be placed in an interaction with the canons of scientific inquiry, or with the demands of oppressed, or with the conclusions of the social sciences on matters concerning ethical issues, and so forth, in a way that places the life of the church (still including the magisterium) in a less than dominating role in theology?

Ideally a person ought not have to choose between these two versions of rule #3. If the whole ongoing life of the Church, including the magisterium, were comfortable with a critical style of theology, there could be greater unity. Or if the theologians would give up the critical style there would be easier unity. I suspect that neither will be the case. For some Catholics truth is only to be affirmed, not critically correlated. For others it is to be lived faithfully without much concern for theological niceties. For others it is to be integrated explicitly into the whole range of existential and moral concerns of humankind but with primary allegiance to a shared tradition. For yet others it is to be subjected to the kind of critical review Tracy would require. There is significant value in *each* of these approaches. They are also matters of personality and intrinsic thought style, not just of opinion or formal method. The trick for the future is to devise ways by which people who cherish different values and have such diverse personalities and thought styles can come to accept one another as part of the same believing community.

For the immediate future in the United States the risk of a great tension is there because the critical style of theology does seem to represent a massive cultural change. My guess is that many of the nuanced theologians identified in our survey have not formally adopted a critical approach in their theology. They may read Tracy and others and respect such work, but in their theologizing still follow the non-critical form rule #3, the one that gives preference to the life of the church as a guide to theology rather than to the "morality of scientific inquiry." Shea is nonetheless correct, I believe, to urge us to take seriously the change taking place. There has been a shift in consciousness at work in the West towards more critical thought, because it has much to commend it. It is a self-critical and gradually self-correcting method at work; it is a method of intellectual honesty. The critical approach has become a standard immanent to some theology today, one that is bound to create difficulties exactly as Shea says. We can hope that the more critical theologians will be consistent enough to be self-critical, as I think they generally are, and that the nuanced theologians will be willing to help hold us all together.

University of Dayton   MICHAEL H. BARNES

In Shea's response to our article he asserts, "I think the conclusion to the survey is correct, namely that Sheehan is mistaken to posit a polarization between the theologians and the person in the pew." We are all in agreement, then, on the most important point of our study, to identify whether Catholic theologians and the average Catholic parishioners were polarized in their beliefs.

Many of Shea's remaining comments are theological in nature, not within my area of social science, but there are some points that I can make concerning the interpretation of the results as part of a social science research project.

First of all, our findings indicate that the three groups we name—traditional, nuanced, and liberal—are clearly distinct from one another. Shea suggests that we could join the middle group, the nuanced, either to the traditional group, thereby creating a large number of traditional Catholics, or to the liberal group, thereby suddenly discovering a rather large group of liberal Catholics. There may be theological reasons for speculating in this fashion, but on the face of it the data does not give it support. Because of the way in which the survey was structured and the data analyzed, we feel we have identified a style of belief that is identifiable as nuanced precisely because when given the option of being simply traditional instead chooses a somewhat more liberal or symbolic mode of expression, and when given the option of being definitely liberal instead chooses the more traditional and nuanced mode of expression.

Secondly, to return to the main point of the survey, even if it were possible to lump together the nuanced with either the liberal or with the traditional, this would have no bearing on the finding that the theologians and parishioners are not polarized. The discriminant analysis procedure used in this study looked at how individuals responded to issues of religious belief. This analysis was able to predict a high percentage of the cases whether a respondent was a theologian or a parishioner, thereby indicating that they are two distinguishable groups. But they were nonetheless clustered rather closely together rather than polarized, each group having its own spread across the traditional-nuanced-liberal spectrum in a way that made them, theologians and parishioners, not too dissimilar from each other.

Memphis State University   BYRON R. JOHNSON

Part Sever

EPILOGUE: A CANDID REVIEW OF CATECHETICAL ISSUES

THE APPROVAL OF CATECHISMS AND CATECHETICAL MATERIALS

Report of a Joint Committee of the National Conference of Diocesan Directors of Religious Education, Catholic Theological Society of America, College Theology Society, and Canon Law Society of America

John P. Boyle, Ph.D., chair; Catholic Theological Society of America

Thomas P. Ivory, S.T.D.; National Conference of Diocesan Directors of Religious Education

Kathleen Gaffney, Ph.D.; College Theology Society

James H. Provost, J.C.D.; Canon Law Society of America

Introduction

The Church has traditionally been concerned about materials used for catechesis, which is the process by which "the faith of the faithful becomes living, explicit and productive through formation in doctrine and the experience of Christian living."[1] This concern has been evident in contemporary efforts to develop modern catechetical materials, to draft new catechisms designed for divers audiences, and to produce new types of audiovisual catechetical aids.

Special attention has been given in recent years to catechisms and catechetical materials. Some contemporary materials have encountered criticism from officials of the Apostolic See, even though necessary approval prior to publications had been granted by the proper diocesan authorities.[2] This has led to various questions about the

The Committee acknowledges with gratitude the technical assistance provided by Berard L. Marthaler, S.T.D., Ph.D., from the Department of Religion and Religious Education at The Catholic University of America.

approval of catechisms and catechetical materials: what are they, which of these require prior approval, who grants such approval and on the basis of what criteria?

Because of their professional interest in these matters and in continued fidelity to their commitment to service of the Church, a special joint committee to study these issues was formed by the National Conference of Diocesan Directors of Religious Education, the Catholic Theological Society of America, the College Theology Society, and the Canon Law Society of America. After initial discussions with the N.C.C.B. Bishops' Committee on Doctrine, the group was directed to work with the U.S.C.C. Committee on Education. The following report is submitted as a contribution to the ongoing study of the questions surrounding the approval of catechisms and catechetical materials, and is provided as a service to the members of the organizations constituting the special joint committee and to the U.S.C.C. Committee on Education.

This report has three major sections. The first explores the meaning of "catechisms and catechetical materials"; the second examines issues related to the approval of catechisms and catechetical materials for publication, the third explores their approval for use. The report attempts to provide a candid review of the situation as it now stands. Some evaluative comments are provided as concluding remarks.

I. Catechisms and Catechetical Materials

What are catechisms and catechetical materials? The question is not so easily answered. There are three steps in what follows: first, the context for this question in the teaching of the Magisterium at the Second Vatican Council will be explored; second, the continued relevance of the *General Catechetical Directory* on this issue will be discussed; finally, the various types of materials listed in the *Directory* will be explained.

A. Context

At the First Vatican Council the bishops debated and eventually moved toward the adoption of a proposal to draw up a *Small Catechism* modelled after that of Cardinal Bellarmine.[3] It would have been a standard catechism for the elementary instruction of children. The council was not able to take a final vote on the proposal, however, and the project languished after the interruption of Vatican I in 1870. A similar proposal did surface during the preparations for

Vatican II but it was turned down because conditions differ so greatly from country to country that a uniform catechism for the instruction of children was not considered feasible. Instead, the bishops at Vatican II voted in favor of a catechetical directory which would "deal with the fundamental principles of such instruction, its arrangements, and the composition of books" for catechetical instruction.[4]

In addition to opting for a general directory instead of a children's catechism, Vatican II called for professional training for catechists, the restoration of the catechumenate, and the recognition of the close relationship between catechesis and the celebration of the liturgy. Catechetics, as it emerged from the council, is addressed to adults and youth as well as children, and requires adaptation to the condition of the audience (cultural and linguistic conditions as well as the condition of age).

It is in this context that later developments concerning catechisms and catechetical materials need to be understood.

B. General Catechetical Directory

The Congregation for the Clergy, the office of the Roman Curia responsible for catechetics, responded to the directive of Christus Dominus 44 and, with the approval of Pope Paul VI on March 18, 1971, issued the General Catechetical Directory.[5] This directory provides "the basic principles of pastoral theology . . . by which pastoral action in the ministry of the word can be more fittingly directed and governed."[6] It contains a number of practical guidelines, and a significant summary of the doctrine to be imparted in catechesis.

The importance of the General Catechetical Directory was reiterated by Pope John Paul II in his 1979 apostolic exhortation on catechetics:

All who take on the heavy task of preparing these catechetical tools, especially catechism texts, can do so only with the approval of the pastors who have the authority to give it, and taking their inspiration as closely as possible from the General Catechetical Directory, which remains the standard of reference.[7]

The directory is a new form of canonical document, designed to implement basic church policy and law. It remains in effect under the 1983 Code of Canon Law, and would be affected by the new code only to the extent that any provisions of the directory might be contrary to a provision of the new law.[8] In effect the directory applies the law of the Church to catechetics.

C. *Types of Catechetical Materials*

The *General Catechetical Directory* provides for a variety of materials to be used in catechesis.

1. National Catechetical Directories

These are to be drawn up by the various conferences of bishops and are "concerned with promoting and coordinating catechetical action in the territory of a region or nation, or even several nations of the same sociocultural condition."[9] The *General Catechetical Directory* leaves it up to these more local documents to apply general principles to the circumstances of a particular country or region.[10]

To adopt such a directory, every local ordinary in the territory is to be consulted, and the document must be submitted to the Apostolic See for approval before it is promulgated.[11] This process was followed by the N.C.C.B. in developing and adopting the national catechetical directory for the United States, *Sharing the Light of Faith*.[12] As the then president of the N.C.C.B., Archbishop John R. Quinn of San Francisco, stated in the Foreword to *An Official Commentary on Sharing the Light of Faith*,

> This document, approved by the bishops of the United States and by the Sacred Congregation for the Clergy, sets forth official policy relating to the catechesis of all age groups in a variety of circumstances.[13]

2. Programs

Continuing Vatican II's shift toward a more comprehensive view of catechesis, the *General Catechetical Directory* next lists programs. These establish "educational goals to be attained according to ages or places or set times, the methodological criteria to be used, and the content to be taught in catechesis." In doing this, "care must be taken that the mysteries of faith to be believed by adults are already indicated in the programs for children's and adolescents' catechisms in a way adapted to their age."[14]

Programs, in effect, are to provide for an integrated, life-long catechesis, and are to be adapted to the various age groups. No special norms are given for the adoption or approval of programs.

3. Catechisms

The *General Catechetical Directory* deals with catechisms in the following terms:

> The greatest importance must be attached to catechisms published by ecclesiastical authority. Their purpose is to provide, under a form that is condensed and practical, the witness of revelation and of Christian tradition as well as the chief principles which ought to be useful for

catechetical activity, that is, for personal education in faith. The witness of tradition should be held in due esteem, and very great care must be taken to avoid presenting as doctrines of the faith special interpretations which are only private opinions or the views of some theological school. The doctrine of the Church must be presented faithfully. Here the norms set forth in Chapter I of Part Three are to be followed.

In view of the great difficulties in putting these works together and the great importance of these witnesses, it is most expedient that:
a. there be collaboration by a number of experts in catechetics and in theology;
b. there be consultation with specialists in other religious and human disciplines, and also with the other pastoral organizations;
c. individual local ordinaries be consulted and their opinions carefully considered;
d. limited experiments be tried before definitive publication; and
e. these texts be duly reviewed after a certain period of time.[15]

The 1983 code indicates catechisms may be prepared under the authority of an individual bishop and of the conference of bishops (c. 775). If the latter group sees to the publication of a catechism, the work must first be approved by the Apostolic See (c. 775, §2); if the diocesan bishop does it for his diocese, prior approval from the Apostolic See is not required.

Two points should be noted from the description of catechisms in the General Catechetical Directory and from the prescriptions of the code.

First, works are classified as catechisms not because they conform to a particular genre (e.g., questions and answers), but because they are "published by ecclesiastical authority." In the case of Pierres Vivantes, despite the disclaimers of the French hierarchy and those who prepared it, Rome argued that it is a catechism precisely because it is an official publication of the French bishops.[16]

Second, care must be taken to distinguish clearly between the doctrines of the faith and "special interpretations which are only private opinions or the views of some theological school." One of the main criticisms of Anthony Wilhelm's Christ Among us, for example, was that this distinction was not always maintained:

The Sacred Congregation for the Doctrine of the Faith "does not agree that any work, which cites individual theorists as though their views could supplant the teachings of the Church, can fairly be described as a true catechetical text, or in the author's [i.e., Wilhelm's] words, 'presentation of the Catholic faith.' It is because of this pervasive methodology that the SCDF does not consider the work to be revisable."[17]

4. Textbooks

Insisting once again that "no text can take the place of a live communication of the Christian message," the General Catechetical Directory describes textbooks as "aids offered to the Christian Community that is engaged in catechesis" and observes:

> nevertheless, the texts do have great value in that they make it possible to present a fuller exposition of the witnesses of Christian tradition and of principles that foster catechetical activity.[18]

Textbooks differ from catechisms in that they are the work of private authors and are not issued by ecclesiastical authorities themselves. Yet it is not enough that books deal with religion from an historical or merely descriptive point of view, however objective, for them to qualify as textbooks for catechetics. Catechesi tradendae states that even though books of this kind "can make a contribution here to better mutual understanding" among people of different religions and various Christian confessions, nevertheless

> such schoolbooks can obviously not be considered catechetical works: they lack both the witness of believers stating their faith to their believers, and an understanding of the Christian mysteries and of what is specific about Catholicism, as these are understood within the faith.[19]

5. Manuals for Catechists

The description of manuals for catechists in the General Catechetical Directory corresponds very closely to the major text series edited and marketed by American publishers. The directory says books of this kind should contain the following:

> a. an explanation of the message of salvation—constant reference must be made to the sources, and a clear distinction must be kept between those things which pertain to the faith and to the doctrine that must be held, and those things which are mere opinions of theologians;
> b. psychological and pedagogical advice;
> c. suggestions about methods.
> Books and other printed materials intended for study and activity by those being taught should also be provided. These printed materials can be made part of the books for the use of those being taught, or they can be published as separate booklets.
> Finally, care should be taken to publish books for the use of parents, if the question is one of giving catechesis to children.[20]

6. Audiovisual Aids, Mass Media, Programmed Instruction

The General Catechetical Directory also speaks of audiovisual aids, the mass media, and "programmed instruction."[21] Although it addresses functions, correct use, and collaborative roles in regard to these materials, the directory says nothing about their contents and subject matter.

II. Approval for Publication of Catechisms and Catechetical Materials

Catechisms and catechetical materials are subject to two types of approval. One concerns the publication of these materials; the other is relative to their use in individual dioceses. In this section the approval required for publication will be explained; the next section will deal with approval for use in a diocese.

In recent years the Church has modified its discipline concerning the censorship of books.[22] The prohibition of books has been discontinued. Although under the new norms fewer writings are subject to prior censorship or to the requirement of subsequent approval for specific uses, catechisms, catechetical materials, and textbooks do require such approval. The pertinent canons state:

> Can. 775. §2. It is within the competence of the conference of bishops, with the prior approval of the Apostolic See, to see to it that catechisms are issued for its territory if such seems useful.
> Can. 827. §1. With due regard for the prescription of can. 775, §2, catechisms and other writings dealing with catechetical formation or their translations need the approval of the local ordinary for their publication.
> §2. Books which treat questions of Sacred Scripture, theology, canon law, church history or which deal with religious or moral disciplines cannot be employed as the textbooks on which instruction is based in elementary, middle or higher schools unless they were published with the approval of the competent ecclesiastical authority or subsequently approved by it.

To understand what is involved in the approval for publication of catechisms and catechetical materials, four topics will be addressed: the notion of "approval"; the authority competent to approve various types of materials; the process for obtaining approval; and the criteria for determining to approve catechisms and catechetical materials.

A. Notion of Approval

The canons do not use the term "imprimatur"; rather, they speak of "approval" (approbatio) and "permission" (licentia). Similarly the 1917 code referred to *licentia* and *approbatio*, although in the former code the two terms appear to apply to the same objects (i.e., the same writings), and the same juridic actions. In the new code, however, the two terms seem to be applied more systematically to specific types of writings, and to particular actions by ecclesiastical authorities.[23]

Permission (*licentia*) is required to cooperate with non-Catholics in preparing and publishing translations of Scripture, to publish prayer books, to publish books which will be placed on display, sold, or distributed within a church or oratory. *Licentia* is also required to reprint collections of decrees or acts issued by an ecclesiastical authority. Clerics or religious must obtain *licentia* in order to publish in newspapers, magazines or periodicals which are accustomed to attack openly the Catholic religion or good morals, and for members of religious institutes to publish any writings which deal with questions of religion or morals.[24]

Approval (*approbatio*), however, is required for Catholics to publish original versions or translations of Sacred Scripture, outside of the ecumenical collaboration mentioned above. It is also needed before publishing catechisms and textbooks, and must be obtained for books which have already been published and are now to be used as textbooks or are going to be displayed, sold or distributed in a church or oratory.[25]

It appears that underlying the differentiations in the canons is a view that *approbatio* reflects a greater commitment by the Church to the particular publication than *licentia* does. Those writings which require an *approbatio* are more intimately involved in the Church's representation of itself to others (Catholic-sponsored Scripture texts, catechisms, textbooks, existing items now to be distributed on church premises), and hence subject to greater control by church authorities.

All the materials described in the *General Catechetical Directory* require *approbatio*.[26] This reflects the understanding of such materials as being issued by ecclesiastical authorities or at least as witnessing to the faith in keeping with the Church's own self-understanding.

B. *The Authority Competent to Approve*

The law distinguishes two different levels for approving distinct types of materials, the Apostolic See and the diocesan bishop. The conference of bishops is competent to draft various materials, but does not have a function of approving them.

1. Apostolic See

The Apostolic See itself is to provide *approbatio* for national directories and for catechisms which a conference of bishops arranges to be issued for its whole territory.[27]

The Second Office of the Congregation for the Clergy "reviews and approves catechetical directories, catechisms, and programs for preaching the word of God produced by conferences of bishops."[28] The office does not act alone, however, for in "all questions which touch upon the doctrine of faith and morals or which are connected with the faith itself" pertain to the Congregation for the Doctrine of the Faith.[29] Therefore, catechisms and catechetical materials are subject to review by the Congregation for the Doctrine of the Faith prior to their approval by the Congregation for the Clergy.[30]

2. Local Ordinary

The diocesan bishop may issue a catechism on his own authority. He does not need approval from some other authority, provided the catechism is within the prescriptions of the Apostolic See such as the *General Catechetical Directory*,[31] and the further norms adopted by the conference of bishops, such as *Sharing the Light of Faith*.[32]

If others prepare a catechism, since by definition catechisms are "published by ecclesiastical authority" the approval of an ecclesiastical authority is required. The local ordinary is competent to grant this (c. 827, §1); i.e., not only the diocesan bishop, but also vicars general and episcopal vicars acting within the scope of their responsibilities.[33]

For other catechetical materials—programs, textbooks, manuals for catechists, and audiovisual aids—approval is also required, and this approval is to come from the local ordinary (c. 827, §§1 and 2).

The ordinary may be of the locality where the author has a domicile or quasi-domicile, or of the locality where the work is published (c. 824, §1). Traditionally the latter includes the ordinary of the place where the publisher has an office, as well as the place where the actual printing is done.

C. *Process for Obtaining Approval*

The procedures for obtaining approval from the Apostolic See for publications of the conference of bishops have not been published. To obtain approval from the local ordinary, the law does provide the basic procedures to be followed.[34]

1. Submission of Materials

For catechisms and catechetical materials other than textbooks, the approval must be obtained prior to publication. Manuscripts or printed proofs can be submitted. For textbooks, approval must be obtained before the work is used as a textbook, although it may have been published already. Manuscripts or printed proofs can be submitted prior to publication, or the printed work itself may be submitted after publication.

These are normally submitted to the local ordinary from whom the approval is being sought. It is up to this ordinary to see to the next steps.

2. Review by Censor

A person other than the local ordinary is to review the submitted material. This "censor" may be selected by the local ordinary from among a list provided by the conference of bishops, but he is not limited to such a list.[35] The law does not specify any qualifications for the censor, who may be cleric or lay, woman or man. The person must obviously be able to exercise judgment and ought to have a good understanding of the Church's teaching concerning faith and morals as it is proposed by the ecclesiastical magisterium (c. 830, §2).

The censor renders an opinion about the submitted material. the opinion must be given in writing (c. 830, §3). If it is favorable, it constitutes the "nihil obstat," clearing the way for the local ordinary to decide whether to grant his approval to the work.

If the censor's opinion is not favorable, he must give his reasons for disapproving of the submitted material. The local ordinary is not free to decide whether to grant his approval, although he could entrust the work to another censor for a second opinion.[36]

3. Approval by Local Ordinary

If a censor has granted a "nihil obstat," the local ordinary must decide whether to grant the requested approval. If he decides to do so, he must issue a written document giving the approval. In addition to the name of the work and its author, the ordinary must include in the document his own name, the date and place where it was issued (cc. 830, §3), and he is to sign it.

If the ordinary decides not to grant the approval, he is to communicate his reasons for doing so to the author. The law does not require this be done in writing, although for the sake of the record it is preferable that it be in writing.

If one ordinary denies the approval, it is possible to seek approval from a different ordinary but the norms on rescripts must be followed.[37] The new ordinary must be informed of the earlier denial and is to seek the reasons for it before deciding whether to grant approval.

4. Publication

The usual practice is to include mention of the nihil obstat and approval when the work is published. Frequently for books this is done on the reverse of the title page, where copyright information is also printed. However, the law does not require this explicitly, and for works which receive approval after they have been published it is obviously not required to insert the mention of approval in the copies already published.

Since the approval is always to be given in writing, it is possible to obtain confirmation that a work has received the necessary approval by contacting the author or publisher even if the published work does not contain this information itself.

D. Criteria

General criteria are provided for all works submitted to a censor:

> In undertaking the office, the censor, laying aside any respect for persons, is to consider only the teaching of the Church concerning faith and morals as it is proposed by the ecclesiastical magisterium.[38]

In addition, specific criteria apply to approving catechisms and catechetical materials.[39]

1. Normative Criteria

Some normative criteria have been provided in the directories published for the Church universal and for the United States.

a. General Catechetical Directory

As indicated above in discussing the various types of materials, specific elements for most of them are given in the directory. The decision to approve a given work requires that it comply with those elements proper to its genre (see discussion above).

In addition, the directory provides norms governing all catechesis. "The doctrine of the Church must be presented faithfully" according to "the norms set forth in Chapter I of Part Three" (nn. 37–46).[40] These same norms are incorporated in summary form in Sharing the Light of Faith (n. 47).

Beginning with the notion of revelation, which it describes as "the manifestation of the mystery of God and of his saving action in history," these norms state that it is the task of the Church's prophetic ministry to make the content of this message intelligible so that individuals "may be converted to God through Christ, [and] that they may interpret their whole life in the light of faith."[41] Catechesis must lead to the presentation of "the entire treasure of the Christian message."[42] While emphasizing that the content of the Christian message forms a certain organic whole,[43] the Church also recognizes "a certain hierarchy of truths" in which such tenets as found in the ancient creeds are considered basic.[44]

Catechesis must necessarily be Christocentric[45] and at the same time trinitarian. To neglect the integrity of mystery latent in the phrase "through Christ, to the Father, in the Spirit," is to rob the Christian message of its proper character.[46] The directory cites Vatican I in asserting that one of the conditions required for "a fruitful understanding" of the purpose of the economy of salvation is that the diverse Christian truths be related to human beings' ultimate destiny.[47] Although the mystery of salvation "awaits its consummation in the future," catechesis should enable people to see how it is realized in the past in the incarnation, death and resurrection of Christ, and in the present through the Holy Spirit and the ministry of the Church.[48]

Despite the fact that there is a definite corpus of material that must be taught, the directory acknowledged it is not possible to dictate a particular order that must be followed; circumstances must be taken into account in selecting a pedagogical method.[49]

b. *Sharing the Light of Faith*

In the United States, any materials submitted for approval must also meet the criteria contained in the national catechetical directory adopted by the National Conference of Catholic Bishops and approved by the Apostolic See. The "Norms of Catechesis" drawn from the *General Catechetical Directory* and stated in n. 47 of *Sharing the Light of Faith* must be observed.[50] Additional norms are provided in Chapter XI, "Catechetical Resources."

2. Other Criteria

Other criteria have been suggested in official documents, or have been used in individual cases without thereby establishing a norm which must be followed in all cases.

a. *Catechesi tradendae*

An apostolic exhortation is exhortatory rather than legislative in nature; it does not establish binding norms, but rather sets forth the views of the pope on the matter under discussion and expresses encouragement for those engaged in the pastoral work of the Church. Nevertheless, the views expressed by Pope John Paul II in his apostolic exhortation on catechetics aid in clarifying the criteria mentioned in the *General Catechetical Directory* and in *Sharing the Light of Faith*.

John Paul II states several conditions which he considers essential in catechetical literature:

1) They must be linked with the real life of the generation to which they are addressed, showing close acquaintance with its anxieties and questionings, struggles and hopes;

2) They must try to speak a language comprehensible to the generation in question;

3) They must make a point of giving the whole message of Christ and his church, without neglecting or distorting anything, and in expounding it they will follow a line and structure that highlights what is essential;

4) They must really aim to give to those who use them a better knowledge of the mysteries of Christ, aimed at true conversion and a life more in conformity with God's will.[51]

b. Congregation for the Doctrine of the Faith

As noted above, the Congregation for the Clergy has the specific competence to oversee catechisms and catechetical materials. However, the Congregation for the Doctrine of the Faith is also competent in these matters insofar as questions of faith and morals may be involved.

In 1983 the Congregation for the Doctrine of the Faith responded to an inquiry from French bishops' conference. The bishops had asked if an ordinary had to grant approval to a book intended for catechetical use if the book contained nothing contrary to faith and morals, independently of any evaluation of the work's value for catechetical use. It seems some editors had been claiming a right to the approval when there was no objection to the faith and morals content. The congregation replied that when it is only a question of approval a book for publication—and not a question of whether the bishop is adopting the book officially for his diocese—then he is to consider the orthodoxy of its content and the universal ecclesiastical norms concerning catechetics.[52]

In addition to this general response there are two reported interventions of this congregation in catechetical matters which illustrate the approach officials of this office have taken.

In dealing with the book *Christ Among Us* the congregation's objections focused on methodology and content.

1) A book cannot be considered to be a presentation of the Catholic faith if it "cites individual theorists as though their views could supplant the teachings of the Church."

2) With regard to content, a number of individual points were raised which the congregation considered inconsistent with Catholic teaching, particularly if the book is to be considered a presentation of Catholic teaching.[53]

In its evaluation of *Pierres Vivantes* the congregation objected to the manner in which the work made use of contemporary biblical scholarship, preferring instead a more "traditional" approach in presenting salvation history. In the first edition, *Pierres Vivantes* traced the historical development of the people of God from Exodus, whereas the canonical scriptures begin with creation. It traced the historical development of the New Testament from the Pentecost experience in the Acts of the Apostles rather than beginning with the infancy narratives.[54]

c. Cardinal Ratzinger

Cardinal Joseph Ratzinger's position as Prefect of the Congregation for the Doctrine of the Faith has given his personal views on catechetics added attention. He has expressed these views at lectures in Lyons and Paris in 1983[55] and in various interviews.[56] The latter highlights the following concerns.

1) The catechist's own faith (p. 147): The catechist is pivotal in the process of catechesis. "Only one who believes can lead another to believe" (p. 148). In the case of catechetical materials, the author's ecclesiastical status may be an extrinsic factor in the approval or disapproval of texts (as has been surmised regarding Anthony Wilhelm).

2) Content vs. method: The relationship of these two is a major concern. "It can certainly be observed that in the last twenty years method has overshadowed content. Of course, this is not restricted to religious instruction . . ." (p. 148). Citing Aristotle, he observed that content dictates method, and in no area is this truer than in religious instruction.

3) Faith and theology: "The binding power of the Magisterium is accepted less and less. This means that the borders between theology and faith are slowly fading, that church teaching disappears and theological teaching remains the sole form of interpreting the Christian gospel" (p. 150). His concern here is that theologians seem to be taking the place of the Magisterium. Moreover, he raises an underlying question of ecclesiology: he understands the Church as the community of faith which accepts certain givens (e.g., "the Bible as lived and read in the Church") as points of departure, which is quite a different approach from what he terms a "purely congregational ecclesiology" which he says is based on consensus (or worse, "the whim of the group").

4) Story of Creation: Cardinal Ratzinger has long been concerned about the way creation is presented in catechetical materials. "The tendency no longer to open the Old Testament in catechesis with creation," he says, "has manifold and extremely significant bases" (p. 151).[57]

III. Approval of Catechisms and Catechetical Materials for Official Use

In addition to being approved prior to publication, catechisms and catechetical materials can also be adopted for official use. The new Code of Canon Law is not entirely precise in this area; the responses from the Congregation for the Doctrine of the Faith in 1983 do add some further details. For the sake of clarity this topic will be considered under headings similar to those adopted above: the notion of "approval"; the authority competent to approve various types of materials; the process for obtaining approval; and the criteria for determining to approve catechisms and catechetical materials.

A. Notion of Approval

Once approval has been given for publication, it is presumed the material can be used anywhere unless otherwise restricted. Such restrictions may be due to local requirements of certain materials for specific places or uses; they may also be due to the prohibition of certain materials from use in specific places or for specific purposes. Canon 775 states:

> §1. While observing the prescriptions of the Apostolic See it is the responsibility of the diocesan bishop to issue norms concerning catechetics and to make provision that suitable instruments for catechesis are available, even by preparing a catechism, if such seems appropriate, and by fostering and coordinating catechetical endeavors.
>
> §2. It is within the competence of the conference of bishops, with the prior approval of the Apostolic See, to see to it that catechisms are issued for its territory if such seems useful.

Contained in both these provisions are the possibility of "approval for use."

1. A distinction may be made between those materials used by parents on their own and materials used in programs conducted or at least authorized by the diocese. Parents have the primary right and responsibility to educate their children,[58] and as Christians and Catholics, to educate them in the faith.[59] They are to do this "according to the teaching handed on by the Church" (c. 226, §2), presumably using materials which the Church has approved for this purpose.

But the diocesan bishop also has a responsibility in this regard, and he may issue norms which govern catechesis in his diocese (cc. 386, §1; 775, §1). He may specify what materials are acceptable for parents to use.

The law does not say if the bishop can limit the materials parents may use, requiring them to use only those which have received special approval for use in the diocese. The July 1983 response from the Congregation for the Doctrine of the Faith does permit the use of texts published with ecclesiastical approval which have not been adopted as the official materials of the diocese, but as subsidiary means.[60]

Neither the law nor the congregation's response address a third question, namely whether the bishop can proscribe the use of such books by parents in his diocese. In light of the rights of parents and in light of the criteria for approving catechisms and catechetical materials for publication, it would seem that parents retain the right to make the final determination of what materials to use for their own catechizing of their children provided those materials were published with proper approbation.

2. For programs conducted by church authorities or with their authorization, the diocesan bishop may adopt required catechisms and materials, but is not required to do so by law.[61] The bishop has these options:

    a. He could issue a listing which is advisory; other materials may be used provided they were published with proper approval.

    b. He could issue a listing with a variety of materials, and require as a norm that only those on the list be selected; but he could permit those responsible for the individual programs to make a choice from among those on the list.

    c. He could adopt a mandatory catechism and catechetical materials which must be used in all such programs in the diocese.

Other materials not on the list but published with ecclesiastical approval could be used as auxiliary means, in keeping with the response from the Congregation for the Doctrine of the Faith.[62]

In any of these situations, could the diocesan bishop proscribe the use of other materials not on the list, but published with approbation? Although the law does not have a specific canon on this, and the congregation's response did not address the question directly, nevertheless the Church has discontinued the banning of books. The most the bishop could do is proscribe the use of certain materials in programs conducted by church authorities or with their authorization.

B. *The Competent Authority*

1. The conference of bishops is competent to see that catechisms are issued for its territory (c. 775, §2). The code is not specific on whether this is only to prepare and publish such a book, or also to mandate its use. The responses from the Congregation for the Doctrine of the Faith, however, indicate several arguments in support of a possible mandate of a national catechism.

First, the adoption of a national catechism by the conference of bishops is considered by the congregation to be an example of the exercise of legislative power by the conference.[63] If it is legislative power, then the conference could mandate as part of that legislation that this particular catechism be used throughout its territory. A local ordinary (diocesan bishop, vicar general, episcopal vicar) could, however, dispense from this requirement in a particular diocese when he judges this will contribute to the good of the faithful (c. 88).

Second, the congregation presumes that such a national catechism could be mandatory. It notes that for catechesis conducted under the authority of the pastor in parishes and schools, catechisms "approved and adopted as official texts by the bishop himself or by the conference of bishops" must be used.[64]

Therefore, a national catechism may be approved but not mandatory; or, in the wording of the response, it may have been "approved and adopted," in which case it becomes mandatory.

2. The diocesan bishop is also competent to adopt an official catechism for his diocese. Note that this is the diocesan bishop, not the "local ordinary," so vicars general and episcopal vicars are not included here, unless they have been specially delegated by the diocesan bishop.

The diocesan bishop may adopt materials prepared by others, or may himself see to the preparation of a catechism (c. 775, §1). Even if the conference of bishops has adopted an official national catechism, the diocesan bishop may still approve other catechisms and materials.[65]

The documents do not present a ready solution to the potential conflict which could arise if a conference of bishops approves a national catechism and mandates its use in the territory, yet one or another diocesan bishop approves and adopts as mandatory in the diocese a different catechism. The general principles of law side with the individual bishop. He can dispense from the particular law of the conference of bishops, and is empowered to make norms for his own diocese on catechetical matters. However, such a situation would be contrary to the underlying purpose of the law and of the

General Catechetical Directory which is looking to foster cooperation on a wider scale.[66]

C. *Process for Obtaining Approval*

Canon law does not specify a procedure to be followed in approving catechisms and catechetical materials for use in a diocese or larger territory. However, whatever procedure is adopted should at least protect the basic rights of parents, pastors, catechists, authors, publishers, and others with an interest in the matter. Special consideration might also be due potential civil law and ethical questions[67]

D. *Criteria*

The Congregation for the Doctrine of the Faith recalls that when approving catechisms destined for official use in the diocese, the bishop is to consider not only the usual questions of orthodox content and conformity to the universal norms of catechetics, but also the particular norms he himself may have issued in light of the needs of his own diocese, and those norms adopted by the conference of bishops and approved by the Holy See.[68]

Concluding Remarks

This report has attempted to set forth a clarification on various materials relating to catechetics, and on the approval for such materials. The following comments are occasioned by this study.

1. There have been significant developments in the approach official documents have taken to catechetical materials over the past twenty-five years. The emphasis in the conciliar discussion and in the *General Catechetical Directory* which drew on that discussion has moved from a child-centered catechesis and preoccupation with catechisms, to a more integrated approach to the catechesis of the whole community involving formation in doctrine and the experience of Christian living.

The norms for the evaluation of catechetical materials include considerations of doctrinal integrity, adaptability to the intended audience, and involvement in the experience of Christian living.

2. The publication of many catechetical materials requires only the approval of a local ordinary. The diocesan bishop, however, is the one competent to approve materials for use within his own diocese.

Only those materials developed under the auspices of the conference of bishops and intended for all the territory of the conference require approval by the Apostolic See before they are published or adopted for mandatory use.

3. There are evident differences of opinion among competent church authorities as to what is required in catechetical materials. The remarks of Cardinal Ratzinger and the actions of the Congregation for the Doctrine of the Faith express a particular emphasis; the directives in the *General Catechetical Directory* and *Sharing the Life of Faith* reflect other emphases.

As the 1985 Synod of Bishops noted, "the presentation of doctrine must be biblical and liturgical. It must be sound doctrine, suited to the present life of Christians."[69] How to achieve that suitable presentation depends on the conditions of life of peoples in various parts of the world, and so admits of differences in emphases. The Synod called for a catechism or compendium of all Catholic doctrine to be developed, but presented this as a point of reference for efforts at a regional or more local level.

4. As was evident at the 1969 Extraordinary Synod and again at the 1985 Extraordinary Synod, there is need for closer cooperation between officials of the Roman Curia and bishops in many areas, not the least of which is catechesis. To the extent that such cooperation is still to be developed, the approval of catechisms may remain a point of tension.

Local ordinaries by law have the right and responsibility to pass judgment on catechetical materials and to approve those they find meet the basic criteria set down in the normative documents of the Church. Local ordinaries are also accountable to higher authorities for such decisions. However, while there are clear procedures and criteria to which the local ordinaries are bound in granting approval, the procedures and criteria by which they themselves are held accountable by higher authority do not seem to be equally clear.

5. Official church documents refer to a variety of materials for catechetical use; they also encourage the development of programs for catechesis. Not all of these materials are official catechisms, nor do church authorities act alone in the catechetical enterprise. The law of the Church affirms the obligation and right of all the Christian faithful to engage in spreading the divine message of salvation (c. 211), and emphasizes the role of parents in passing on the faith to their children.[70] While the materials used in catechesis require approval of competent church authorities, members of the faithful may develop them. This diversity in the development and use of such materials also needs to be taken into consideration in the process of granting approval.

NOTES

1. This description of catechesis was given legal recognition in the 1983 Code of Canon Law; see c. 773. For a more developed concept see chapter two of the *General Catechetical Directory* (see below, note 5), and chapter two of *Sharing the Light of Faith* (below, note 12).

2. Most notable are the cases of *Pierres Vivantes* in France and of Anthony Wilhelm's *Christ Among Us* in the United States. On the former see Berard L. Marthaler, "New From France: 'Catechesis of Documents,' " *The Living Light* 18 (1981) 325–33; on the latter, see especially the December 10 letter by Archbishop Gerety to Bishop Malone; "Archbishop Explains Imprimatur Removal," *Origins* 14/28 (March 7, 1985) 619, 621–22.

3. See Michael T. Donnellan, *Rationale for a Uniform Catechism: Vatican I to Vatican II.* Ph.D. dissertation in Religion and Religious Education at The Catholic University of America, 1972.

4. See the Decree on the Bishops' Pastoral Office in the Church, *Christus Dominus,* no. 44: *AAS* 58 (1966) 696. The directive to establish a General Catechetical Directory appears along with directives for other directories—on the care of souls, and on pastoral care of special groups of the faithful.

5. Sacred Congregation for the Clergy, *Directorium catechisticum generale,* April 11, 1971: *AAS* 64 (1972) 97–176; English translation prepared and published by the United States Catholic Conference, *General Catechetical Directory* (Washington: USCC, 1971).

6. Foreword to the *General Catechetical Directory: AAS* 64 (1972) 97–98.

7. Pope John Paul II, apostolic exhortation *Catechesi tradendae,* October 16, 1979, n. 50: *AAS* 71 (1979) 1317–18. Translation from "Apostolic Exhortation on Catechetics," *Origins* 9/21 (November 8, 1979) 341; italics added.

8. See canons 6 and 33. There do not appear to be any items on which the *General Catechetical Directory* has been superseded by the new code. Moreover, the directory appears to be the chief prescriptions of the Apostolic See which are to observed in catechetical matters (c. 775, §1).

9. *General Catechetical Directory,* n. 117: *AAS* 64 (1972) 165.

10. See n. 103: *AAS* 64 (1972) 159; see also nn. 73, 77, 83: *ibid.,* pp. 143, 145–46, 149–50.

11. *General Catechetical Directory,* n. 117: *AAS* 64 (1972) 165; see n. 134: *ibid.,* pp. 172–73.

12. National Conference of Catholic Bishops, *Sharing the Light of Faith,* National Catechetical Directory for Catholics for the United States (Washington: USCC, 1979). Text approved by the N.C.C.B. at their General Meeting, November 14–17, 1977; approved by the Sacred Congregation for the Clergy, Second Office, October 30, 1978.

13. U.S.C.C. Department of Education, *Sharing the Light of Faith: An Official Commentary* (Washington: USCC, 1981), p. 1.

14. *General Catechetical Directory,* n. 118: *AAS* 64 (1972) 165–66.

15. *General Catechetical Directory,* n. 119: *AAS* 64 (1972) 166.

16. See discussion in Marthaler, "New Force From France."

17. Letter of Archbishop Gerety, p. 621. Emphasis added.

18. *General Catechetical Directory,* n. 120: *AAS* 64 (1972) 166.

19. *Catechesi tradendae,* n. 32: *AAS* 71 (1979) 1306–07.

20. *General Catechetical Directory,* n. 121: *AAS* 64 (1972) 167.

21. *Ibid.,* nn. 122–24; *AAS* 64 (1972) 167–68.

22. S. Congregation for the Doctrine of the Faith, decree *Ecclesiae pastorum,* March

19, 1975: *AAS* 67 (1975) 281–84; English translation in *Canon Law Digest* 8: 991–96. The provisions of *Ecclesiae pastorum* have been substantially retained in the 1983 Code of Canon Law, cc. 822–32. For a detailed commentary on the current canon law governing the publication of books see James A. Coriden, "The End of the Imprimatur," *The Jurist* 44 (1984) 339–56.

23. The distinction seems evident from analyzing the use of the two terms in the canons. There is no explicit statement in the law, however, claiming a technical difference between the two terms.

24. See cc. 825, §2; 826, §3; 827, §4; 828; 831, §1; 832.

25. See cc. 825, §1; 827, §§1, 2 and 4.

26. Although the 1983 code does not mention directories, the provisions of the *General Catechetical Directory* remain in force and so national directories must receive *approbatio* from Apostolic See before they are promulgated; see *General Catechetical Directory*, n. 117: *AAS* 64 (1972) 165.

27. Directories can be considered general executory decrees (c. 31); an authoritative interpretation issued by the Commission for the Authentic Interpretation of the Code in August 1985 affirmed that such decrees must be given *recognitio* by the Apostolic See—see *AAS* 77 (1985) 771. While *recognitio* is not as strong an endorsement as *approbatio*, catechetical directories require the more specific *approbatio* in virtue of the *General Catechetical Directory*.

28. *General Catechetical Directory*, n. 134: *AAS* 64 (1972) 172–73. See Paul VI, apostolic constitution *Regimini Ecclesiae universae*, August 15, 1967, n. 69, 2°: *AAS* 59 (1967) 911; English translation in *CLD* 6: 342.

29. *Regimini Ecclesiae universae*, n. 31: *AAS* 59 (1967) 897; *CLD* 6:330.

30. The Congregation for the Doctrine of the Faith, according to reports describing the revisions and final approval of *Pierres Vivantes*, exercised an important if not dominant role. See René Marlé, "La réfonte de *Pierres Vivantes*," *Etudes* 363/5 (1985) 533–40. This is also evident in the case of *Christ Among Us*, for it was this congregation which intervened directly with Archbishop Gerety; see his letter, pp. 619, 621.

31. See c. 775, §1: "While observing the prescriptions of the Apostolic See it is the responsibility of the diocesan bishop to issue norms concerning catechetics and to make provision that suitable instruments for catechesis are available, even by preparing a catechism, if such seems appropriate, and by fostering and coordinating catechetical endeavors."

32. On the authority of the national catechetical directory, see *Sharing the Light of Faith*, n. 7.

33. According to c. 134 diocesan bishops and those who are equivalent to them in law (so, also a diocesan administrator), vicars general and episcopal vicars are all "ordinaries" in law, and indeed are "local ordinaries." The powers of an episcopal vicar are the same as those of a vicar general, but only for the territory, business or persons for whom he has been appointed (c. 479, §2), and the diocesan bishop could explicitly limit the authority of the vicars (general and/or episcopal) relative to approving books (c. 479, §§1 and 2).

34. While the 1983 code does not spell this out in detail, the provisions of c. 830, §§2 and 3 provide the basis for what follows.

35. The N.C.C.B. Committee on Doctrine has discussed the possibility of preparing such a list, but nothing has been made public as of the writing of this Report.

36. That is, the ordinary freely chooses censors, and is not limited to using only one censor; he may continue to have the work examined until a censor gives his "nihil obstat." The "nihil obstat" does not result automatically in the ordinary granting approval; that is a distinct judgment entrusted to the local ordinary alone.

37. See c. 65. If the approval is denied by a diocesan bishop, it cannot be obtained from any of his vicars without his consent, and before seeking it from an ordinary in a different diocese the earlier denial should be mentioned (and the second ordinary should seek the reasons for denial from the bishop). If approval is denied by a vicar general or episcopal vicar, no other vicar of the same bishop can grant it, and the diocesan bishop cannot grant it validly unless he is informed that one of his vicars has already denied approval of the work.

38. Canon 830, §2. It is debated whether this establishes a narrower base for making the judgment of suitability. Some see in it the abrogation of the additional grounds listed in the 1917 code, c. 1393, §2: ". . . is to consider only the dogma of the Church and common Catholic doctrine which is contained in the decrees of general councils and the constitutions of prescriptions of the Apostolic See, *and the consensus of approved authors*" (emphasis added to indicate additional grounds). Others see only a rephrasing which does not exclude the possibility of accepting the diversity of views admissable within the various schools of Catholic thought. See discussion in Coriden, pp. 351–52 and note 50.

39. See the response of the Congregation for the Doctrine of the Faith of July 7, 1983, to questions posed by the French bishops' conference. "If approval is requested *only for the publication* of a catechism, without implying the adoption of the book as the official text for diocesan catechesis, this must be given according to the criteria which govern the prior censorship of books submitted to the judgment of the ordinary; that is, taking account especially of the orthodoxy of its content and the universal ecclesiastical norms concerning catechesis (new code, c. 823, §2; *General Catechetical Directory*, n. 119; preamble, §6)." *AAS* 76 (1984) 52. Emphasis in original.

40. *General Catechetical Directory*, n. 119: *AAS* 64 (1972) 166.

41. *Ibid.*, n. 37; p. 120.

42. *Ibid.*, n. 38; p. 120.

43. *Ibid.*, n. 39; p. 120.

44. *Ibid.*, n. 43; p. 123.

45. *Ibid.*, n. 40; p. 122.

46. *Ibid.*, n. 41; p. 122.

47. *Ibid.*, n. 42; p. 123.

48. *Ibid.*, nn. 44–45; pp. 123–24.

49. *Ibid.*, n. 46; pp. 124–25.

50. The obligatory force of these norms is stated in the introductory discussion on authority; see *Sharing the Light of Faith*, n. 7. On the other hand, it could be argued from the July 7, 1983 response discussed below from the Congregation for the Doctrine of the Faith (*AAS* 76 [1984] 52) that the norms of the national directory do not have to be taken into consideration in approving texts not intended as an official diocesan catechism. Yet the universal norms refer specifically to national norms, so at least in virtue of the *General Catechetical Directory* the national directory must also be taken into consideration; see nn. 103 and 117; *AAS* 64 (1972) 159, 165.

51. *Catechesi tradendae.* n. 49; *AAS* 71 (1979) 1317.

52. Congregation for the Doctrine of the Faith, Response to the French bishops' conference, July 7, 1983: *AAS* 76 (1984) 52. The congregation cites as sources for the general norms on catechetical materials canons 823, §1; 830, §2; *General Catechetical Directory*, n. 119; preamble, §6.

53. Letter of Archbishop Gerety, pp. 621–22. There are six items listed which the advisers in Newark considered problematic, but the letter indicates the congregation had "even more serious problems" which are not enumerated in detail.

54. Because of these and other similar examples, the French scholar René Marlé summarizes the differences, saying the first edition of *Pierres Vivantes* took "a historical-phenomenological approach, whereas the revised edition incorporates a resolutely dogmatic-ontological point of view." René Marlé, "Le réfonte de *Pierres Vivantes*," p. 539.

55. "Sources and Transmission of the Faith," *Communio* 10 (Spring 1983) 17–34.

56. See *Communio* 11 (Summer 1984) 145–56.

57. See discussion above on the complaints the congregation had about *Pierres Vivantes*.

58. Cc. 226, §2; 793, §1.

59. Cc. 226, §2; 774, §2; 793, §1; 798.

60. Congregation for the Doctrine of the Faith, Response to Cardinal Oddi, V, July 7, 1983: *AAS* 76 (1984) 49.

61. The canon states "make provision that suitable instruments for catechesis are available." This does not mean he must mandate specific ones, provided he sees that suitable instruments are available.

62. *Ibid.*

63. *Ibid.*, IV; p. 49.

64. *Ibid.*, V; p. 49.

65. *Ibid.*, III; p. 48.

66. *General Catechetical Directory*, n. 117: *AAS* 64 (1972) 165.

67. For example, conflict of interest if the author, publisher or other person with a financial interest in the book has a role in its selection as the mandated text for the diocese.

68. Congregation for the Doctrine of the Faith, Response to French bishops' conference, July 7, 1983: *AAS* 76 (1984) 52.

69. 1985 Extraordinary Synod of Bishops, *The Final Report*, II, B, 1, d (Washington: USCC Publications, 1986), p. 16.

70. See cc. 226, §2; 774, §2; 776; 793; 798.

APPENDIX: SIGNIFICANT DEVELOPMENTS IN CATECHETICS A CHRONOLOGY 1965–1985

The following brief chronology of significant developments in catechetics is provided as background for the report, "The Approval of Catechisms and Catechetical Materials." It is not intended as a comprehensive review of all events relating to catechisms and catechetical materials, but rather as a means of providing a context for the contemporary situation.

1965 - *De Nieuwe Katechismus*,[1] "The Dutch Catechism," was published. Commissioned by the Dutch bishops in 1962 on the eve of Vatican II, it was intended primarily for adults. The Dutch Catechism was greeted with phenomenal sales, praise from Pope Paul VI, and translated in a half-dozen or more languages. The very positive reception began to turn sour when a group of Dutch traditionalists protested to Rome "the seven deadly sins" of the catechism. Controversy erupted when their letter was leaked to the press.[2]

Because of the popularity of the translations, hierarchies from other countries were drawn into the controversy. As a result an international commission of cardinals, assisted by a panel of theologians, was appointed to pronounce on the trustworthiness of the Dutch catechism. The commission issued a statement suggesting some clarifications. They were included as an appendix in later editions.[3]

1968 - Sixth International Study Week on Catechetics met in August at Medellín, Colombia.[4] Its affirmation that pluralism in the Church is a "sign of life and energy" was important in shaping Part I of the *General Catechetical Directory*.

1968 - Hubertus Halbfas published *Fundamentalkatechetik*, a comprehensive catechetical theory.[5] Halbfas questioned not only the manner of presenting doctrine, but the linguistic and organizational structure of German Catholic education. He charged that it was a self-validating mode and self-perpetuating form of social control condemning a great number of Catholics to a partial though life-long adolescence. Piety is not substitute for competence. Halbfas criticized the language in the pastorals of the German bishops and papal encyclicals for being ineffective and uninspiring.

Even before the book appeared Halbfas was under fire for demythologizing the Scriptures in a January 1968 issue of *Katechetische Blatter*. In July 1968 the German bishops' conference issued a declaration condemning certain statements in *Fundamentalkatechetik* as inconsistent with Catholic teaching. When Halbfas refused to retract or suitably explain his position regarding the Virgin Birth, the German bishops acting in full assembly withdrew his license to teach. He lost his faculty position as professor of Catholic theology and religious education at Reutlingen College of Education.[6]

1969 - The Isolotto catechism appeared.[7] "On the Way to Jesus" is a series of short instructions to working-class catechists on how to make the gospel meaningful and relevant in the life of children. It was the result of years of experimenting in the working-class parish of l'Isolotto, a suburb of Florence.

The archbishop of Florence, Cardinal Florit, banned the use of the "catechism," stating that it presented Christ merely as a social agitator and interpreted salvation merely in the sociological sense as a liberation from oppression and exploitation. The notoriety sent sales of the text soaring, but the issue of the "catechism" was sidetracked by another episode in which people of l'Isolotto and their pastor, Don Enzo Mazzi, lent support to a group of social activists in Parma at odds with the bishop there. It was this latter incident more than the catechetical work which led to the dismissal of the pastor.[8]

1971 - Congregation for the Clergy published the *Directorium Catechisticum Generale*[9] mandated by Vatican II (*Christus Dominus* 44). An authorized English translation was published by the USCC later in the year.[10]

The *General Catechetical Directory* was accepted on the part of professional religious educators, but a controversy arose over the *Addendum*: "The First Reception of the Sacraments of Penance and Eucharist." This last section, a late insertion, had not been considered in the consultation process which produced the directory.

1971 - Congregation for the Clergy, then headed by Cardinal Wright, hosted an international catechetical congress in Rome. The principal focus of discussion was the *General Catechetical Directory*.

1971 - The last national meeting of the Confraternity of Christian Doctrine was held, in October at Miami. National meetings had been held every five years.

1971 - The USCC-NCCB called at their November meeting for a feasibility study and a plan for producing a national catechetical directory for the United States. The plan was approved at the 1972 Spring meeting in Atlanta.

1972 - Congregation for Divine Worship approved the revised Rite of Christian Initiation of Adults (RCIA).[11] Following the mandate of Vatican II (SC 64–66; AG 14; CD 14) the RCIA restored the catechumenate and emphasized the paschal character of the catechesis which prepares catechumens for baptism.

1972 - *To Teach as Jesus Did*, A Pastoral Message on Catholic Education, was adopted at the November bishops' meeting. Issued by the USCC, the document presents the educational mission of the Church as "an integrated ministry embracing three interlocking dimensions: the message revealed by God (*didache*) which the Church proclaims; fellowship in the life of the Holy Spirit (*koinonia*); service to the Christian community and the entire human community (*diakonia*)."[12]

1973 - *Basic Teaching for Catholic Religious Education*[13] was published in January by the NCCB after consultation with the Apostolic See. It generally followed Part Three, chapter two of the *General Catechetical Directory*, "The More Outstanding Elements of the Christian Message." *Basic Teachings*, however, was original in that it singled out three themes "which carry through all religious education," namely prayer, participation in the liturgy, and bible study.

1975 - Pope Paul VI issued his apostolic exhortation *Evangelii nuntiandi*[14] incorporating many points made at the 1974 Synod of Bishops. It speaks of catechesis as a means of evangelization, stressing the importance of "suitable (catechetical) texts, updated with wisdom and competence, under the authority of the bishops."[15]

1976 - NCCB adopts *To Live in Christ Jesus*, a Pastoral Reflection on the Moral Life.[16] In this pastoral letter the U.S. bishops "discuss some moral questions of our day which affect the dignity of human persons." Sections of the document were later incorporated into the national catechetical directory.

1977 - Synod of Bishops met during October in Rome on the theme "Catechetics in Our Time." The *lineamenta* circulated in preparation for the synod focused on "youth" (up to 35 years old!), but the discussion dealt with catechesis in general as well as with particular problems stemming from culture, social status, educational background, and age differences.

1979 - *Sharing the Light of Faith* published.[17] After a consultation process of almost five years which produced three drafts, the NCCB had approved the text of this national catechetical directory at their November 14–17, 1977 meeting. It had received approval of the Congregation for the Clergy on October 30, 1978.

1979 - Pope John Paul II issued an apostolic exhortation on catechetics, *Catechesi tradendae*.[18] Pope John Paul II had attended the synod as Cardinal Wojtyla. A first draft of the apostolic exhortation had been prepared by Pope Paul VI but it was left to Pope John Paul II to complete the document. It is important to note that in two places the document reiterates that the *General Catechetical Directory* remains normative for catechetical renewal.[19]

1981 - *Pierres Vivantes*, "a Catholic collection of privileged documents of the faith," was published under the direction of the French bishops' conference as part of a larger catechetical project.[20] This short work of 126 pages took its direction from the "Message to the People of God" issued by the bishops at the end of the 1977 synod on catechesis. The principal documents which transmit the faith are the Scriptures and the Creeds, but also the living witness of the Church through its history, liturgy, and saints. Marginal notes explained technical terms and gave the meaning of traditional formulas.

The first edition of *Pierres Vivantes* presented a novel approach to catechesis and was widely acclaimed by catechists. Because it was an official publication of the French hierarchy the work was reviewed by the Congregation for the Doctrine of the Faith. The congregation directed that a number of changes be made and a revised edition was published in 1985.[21]

1983 - During the discussions between the French bishops and the Congregation for the Doctrine of the Faith, the prefect of the congregation, Cardinal Joseph Ratzinger, was invited to address catechetical gatherings in Lyons and in Paris. His views were widely reported.[22]

1983 - Two responses were issued by the Congregation for the Doctrine of the Faith on the interpretation of the decree *Ecclesiae Pastorum* (concerning prior censorship of books) as it applies to catechetical matters, both dated July 7, 1983.

Responding to Cardinal Oddi of the Congregation for the Clergy,[23] the congregation addressed five questions, with the following results: a national or regional conference of bishops cannot publish national or regional catechisms or catechetical documents, to be in force on the supra-diocesan level, without prior approval of the Holy See; conferences of bishops also cannot propose and disseminate catechisms at the national level for "consultation and experimentation"; even if he has already approved a national catechism, a local ordinary can give an *imprimatur* to particular catechisms when these have a safe content and clear presentation; a bishops' commission cannot be given the permanent authority to approve or reject catechisms at the national level or for individual dioceses; in addition to an official catechism, other catechisms which have been duly approved by ecclesiastical authority may be used, but as "subsidiary means."

The congregation also provided a lengthy response to an inquiry from the French conference of bishops.[24] Their question was whether the decree *Ecclesiae pastorum*, art. 4, §1, implied the local ordinary had to take into consideration that a book is destined for catechetical use when he is asked to give his prior approval for its publication. The congregation answered in the affirmative, and then made the following distinction.[25] If the approval is only for publication, and not as an official diocesan catechism, then the local ordinary is to consider the general norms relative to orthodoxy of content and the universal ecclesiastical norms concerning catechetics (cc. 823, §1; 830, §2; *General Catechetical Directory*, n. 119; preamble §6). If, on the other hand, approval is for catechisms destined for official catechesis in the diocese, besides considering the orthodoxy of their content and the universal ecclesiastical norms concerning catechesis, the ordinary must also take into consideration the particular norms issued for the diocese (c. 775, §1) and the norms established by the conference of bishops and approved by the Holy See (*General Catechetical Directory*, n. 134).

1984 - In February, Cardinal Joseph Ratzinger, prefect of the Congregation for the Doctrine of the Faith, asked Archbishop Gerety of Newark to remove the designations *nihil obstat* and *imprimatur* from *Christ Among Us* by Anthony Wilhelm.[26] Cardinal Ratzinger's letter stated that even with "substantial corrections" the book "would not be suitable as a catechetical text."[27]

1985 - In August the German bishops published *Katholischer Erwachsenen-Katechismus*,[28] a compendium of Catholic doctrine for use by catechists. In 1976 the German bishops' conference commissioned a new catechism, but nothing was done until 1981 when Cardinal Ratzinger, then chairman of the conference's Commission for the Faith, assigned the task to theologian Walter Kasper. Kasper acknowledges that while the new German catechism is a compendium of doctrine in the tradition of the Catechism of the Council of Trent, it has more immediate precedents in the Dutch catechism, the Common Catechism, and the new Lutheran Catechism for Adults.[29]

1985 - At the Extraordinary Synod of Bishops in December the proposal for a universal catechism was discussed. In the final report the Synod stated: "Very many have expressed the desire that a catechism or compendium of all Catholic doctrine regarding both faith and morals be composed, that it might be, as it were, a point of reference for the catechisms or compendiums that are prepared in the various regions. The presentation of doctrine must be biblical and liturgical. It must be sound doctrine, suited to the present life of Christians."[30]

NOTES

1. *De Nieuwe Katechismus* (Antwerp: P. Brand, 1966); English translation, *A New Catechism: Catholic Faith for Adults* (New York: Herder & Herder, 1969).
2. An English translation of the letter appeared in *Herder Correspondence*, March 1967, p. 94.
3. Aldo Chiaruttini, ed., *Il dossier del Catechismo olandese* (Verona: Arnoldo Mondadori, 1968). Michael Donnellan says the significance of the reaction to the Dutch catechism was that for the first time since Vatican II the "conservative movement became an organized lobby opposed to catechetical reform." See "The German and Dutch Catechisms in Retrospect," *The Living Light* 12 (1975) 28.
4. Johannes Hofinger and Terrence J. Sheridan, eds., *Sixth International Study Week on Catechetics* (Manila: East Asian Pastoral Institute, 1969).
5. Hubertus Halbfas, *Fundamentalkatechetik: Sprache und Erfahrung im Religionsunterricht* (Düsseldorf: Patmos, 1968; rev. 2nd ed., 1969); English translation *Theory of Catechetics: Language and Experience in Religious Education* (New York: Herder & Herder, 1971).
6. "Freedom for Halbfas," *Herder Correspondence*, February 1969, pp. 55–59.
7. *Incontro a Gesù* (Florence: Libreria Editrice Fiorentina, 1969).
8. "The Isolotto Affair," *Herder Correspondence*, February 1969, pp. 59–62.
9. Congregation for the Clergy, *Directorium catechisticum generale*, April 11, 1971: *AAS* 64 (1972) 97–176.
10. *General Catechetical Directory* (Washington: USCC, 1971).
11. Congregation for Divine Worship, Decretum, January 6, 1972: *AAS* 64 (1972) 252.
12. USSC, *To Teach as Jesus Did* (Washington: USCC, 1973), n. 14.
13. NCCB, *Basic Teachings for Catholic Religious Education* (Washington: USCC, 1973).
14. Paul VI, apostolic exhortation *Evangelii nuntiandi*, December 8, 1975: *AAS* 68 (1976) 5–76.
15. *Ibid.*, n. 44; pp. 34–35.
16. NCCB, *To Live in Christ Jesus* (Washington: USCC, 1976).
17. NCCB, *Sharing the Light of Faith*, National Catechetical Directory for Catholics of the United States (Washington: USCC, 1979).
18. John Paul II, apostolic exhortation *Catechesi tradendae*, October 16, 1979: *AAS* 71 (1979) 1277–1340.
19. *Catechesi tradendae*, nn. 2 and 50; *AAS* 71 (1979) 1278, 1317–18.
20. *Pierres Vivantes*, Recueil catholique de documents privilegiés de la foi. Les évêques de France aux enfants du Cours Moyen, leurs catéchistes et leurs parents (Paris: "Catéchèse 80," 1981).
21. See René Marlé, "La réfonte de *Pierres Vivantes*," *Etudes* 363/5 (November 1985) 533–40.
22. English translation: "Sources and Transmission of the Faith," *Communio* 10:1 (Spring 1983) 17–34.
23. Congregation for the Doctrine of the Faith, Responses, July 7, 1983: *AAS* 76 (1984) 45–49.
24. *Ibid.*, pp. 49–52.
25. *Ibid.*, p. 52.
26. Anthony Wilhelm, *Christ Among Us* (New York: Paulist Press, 3rd rev. ed. 1981).

27. Archbishop Gerety, "Archbishop Explains Imprimatur Removal," *Origins* 14/28 (March 7, 1985) 621.

28. *Katholischer Erwachsenenkatechismus* (Kevelaer: Butzon and Bercker, 1985).

29. Walter Kasper, "The Church's Profession of Faith: On Drafting a New Catholic Catechism for Adults," *Communio* 11 (1984) 41–70.

30. Extraordinary Synod of Bishops, *The Final Report*, December 8, 1985: II, B, 1, d); English translation (Washington: USCC, 1985), p. 16.